# A History of the Egyptian Intelligence Service

This book analyzes how the Egyptian intelligence community has adapted to shifting national security threats since its inception 100 years ago.

The author argues that studying Egypt's intelligence community is integral to our understanding of that country's modern history, regime stability and human rights record. It is clear that intelligence agencies are pivotal to understanding the nature of many Arab regimes and their decision-making processes, and there is no published history of modern Egyptian intelligence in either a European language or in Arabic, though Egypt has the largest and arguably most effective intelligence community in the Arab world.

Starting in 1910, when the modern Egyptian intelligence system was created to deal with militant nationalists and Islamists, the book shows how the security services were subsequently reorganized, augmented and centralized to meet an increasingly sophisticated array of challenges, including fascism, communism, army unrest, Israel, France, the United Kingdom, conservative Arab states, the Muslim Brotherhood and others.

This book will be of much interest to students of intelligence studies, Middle Eastern politics, international security and IR in general.

**Owen L. Sirrs** is a faculty associate in the Defense Critical Language and Culture Program at the University of Montana where he specializes in the Middle East and Afghanistan. He previously served as senior intelligence officer on Iran for the US Defense Intelligence Agency.

## Studies in intelligence series
General editors: Richard J. Aldrich and Christopher Andrew
*ISSN: 1368–9916*

# A History of the Egyptian Intelligence Service

A history of the *mukhabarat*, 1910–2009

Owen L. Sirrs

Routledge
Taylor & Francis Group

LONDON AND NEW YORK

First published 2010
by Routledge
2 Park Square, Milton Park, Abingdon, Oxon, OX14 4RN

Simultaneously published in the USA and Canada
by Routledge
711 Third Avenue, New York, NY 10017

*Routledge is an imprint of the Taylor & Francis Group, an informa business*

First issued in paperback 2011

© 2010 Owen L. Sirrs

Typeset in Times by Wearset Ltd, Boldon, Tyne and Wear

*British Library Cataloguing in Publication Data*
A catalogue record for this book is available from the British Library

*Library of Congress Cataloging-in-Publication Data*
Sirrs, Owen L.
A history of the Egyptian intelligence service: a history of the *mukhabarat*,
1910–2009/Owen L. Sirrs.
p. cm.
1. Intelligence service–Egypt–History. I. Title.
JQ3829.I6S57 2010
327.62009′04–dc22

2009040883

ISBN10: 0-415-56920-6 (hbk)
ISBN10: 0-415-68175-8 (pbk)
ISBN10: 0-203-85454-3 (ebk)

ISBN13: 978-0-415-56920-0 (hbk)
ISBN13: 978-0-415-68175-9 (pbk)
ISBN13: 978-0-203-85454-9 (ebk)

# Contents

# Acknowledgments

This book is the result of several trips to Egypt, several years analyzing that country at the Defense Intelligence Agency, extensive research at British and American archives, and countless discussions with friends and colleagues. First of all, I would like to thank Ray Close and Jim Campbell for their advice and recollections. At the Mansfield Center, I thank my colleague, Mohamed El-Aasar, who not only corrected my Arabic, but also pointed out some important Egyptian sources; Dr Noureddine Jebnoun, who offered invaluable perspectives on the problem of authoritarianism and security services in the Arab world; and Jan Trickel and Dr Terry Weidner. Engineer Eshaq guided me through the intricacies of the Egyptian–Afghan intelligence relationship during the early 1990s while Nonie Darwish generously responded to questions regarding her father, Mustafa Hafez. I am also in debt to the editing crew at Routledge, including Rebecca Brennan, Andrew Humphrys and my anonymous reviewers.

In addition to my wife, Julie, I am in debt to the following individuals who accommodated my Egyptian obsessions: Brian Upton, Deena Mansour, David and Monica Paoli, Christopher Almont, Jennifer Davis, Steve Hecker, Samer Shenouda, Russ Vaughan, William Porter, Neil Moore, Martin Martinez and Robert Richardson. I also pay tribute to the staffs of the John T. Hughes Library at the Defense Intelligence Agency; the Mansfield Library at the University of Montana; the Suzzallo Library at the University of Washington; the United States National Archives and Records Administration; and the National Archives of the United Kingdom. Of course, I alone am responsible for any errors or omissions.

Finally, this book is dedicated to two wonderful daughters, Lucy and Susan, who have coped with an often absent (and absent-minded) father during the three years it took to complete this work.

# Abbreviations

| | |
|---|---|
| AID | Agency for International Development |
| ANM | Arab Nationalist Movement |
| CIA | Central Intelligence Agency |
| CIC | Counterintelligence Corps (United States) |
| CSO | Central Special Office (Egypt) |
| DIA | Defense Intelligence Agency (United States) |
| EGIS | Egyptian General Intelligence Service (*Mukhabarat al-Ama*) |
| ELINT | Electronic intelligence |
| FLN | Front de Liberation Nationale (Algeria) |
| FLOSY | Front for the Liberation of Occupied South Yemen |
| GID | General Investigations Department (Egypt) |
| GID | General Intelligence Directorate (Saudi Arabia) |
| GCHQ | Government Communications Headquarters (United Kingdom) |
| GRU | Glavnoye Razvedyvatelnoye Upravleni (Soviet Union and Russia) |
| HUMINT | Human intelligence |
| IDF | Israeli Defense Forces |
| IMINT | Imagery intelligence |
| ISI | Inter-Services Intelligence (Pakistan) |
| KGB | Komitet Gosudarstvennoy Bezopasnosti (Soviet Union) |
| MID | Military Intelligence Department (Egypt) |
| NLF | National Liberation Front (South Yemen) |
| NSA | National Security Agency (United States) |
| OLOS | Organization for the Liberation of South Yemen |
| OSINT | Open source intelligence |
| OSS | Office of Strategic Services (United States) |
| PA | Palestinian Authority |
| PLO | Palestinian Liberation Organization |
| PSO | Political Security Organization (Yemen) |
| SIGINT | Signals intelligence |
| SIS | Secret Intelligence Service (United Kingdom) (also known as MI6) |
| SSIS | State Security Investigations Service (Egypt) |
| UAR | United Arab Republic |

# End note acronyms

| | |
|---|---|
| AWST | *Aviation Week and Space Technology* |
| BNA | British National Archives |
| CIA | Central Intelligence Agency |
| DDRS | Declassified Documents Reference System |
| DOS | Department of State |
| DTG | Date time group |
| FCO | Foreign and Commonwealth Office |
| FO | Foreign Office |
| FRUS | Foreign Relations of the United States |
| IJIC | *International Journal of Intelligence and Counterintelligence* |
| INR | Bureau of Intelligence and Research (US State Department) |
| INS | *Journal of Intelligence and National Security* |
| JPRS | Joint Publications Research Service |
| MEJ | *Middle East Journal* |
| MES | Middle Eastern studies |
| NARA | National Archives and Records Administration |
| NSA | National Security Archive |
| NYT | *New York Times* |
| OSD | Office of the Secretary of Defense |
| SECSTATE | Secretary of State |
| SSU | Strategic Services Unit (United States) |
| USWD | United States War Department |

# Introduction

All Arab states rely on elaborate – often redundant – security establishments for regime security. The leaderships of states as politically diverse as Morocco, Egypt, Syria and Saudi Arabia charge their intelligence agencies with the mission of neutralizing an array of threats from ruling establishment conspiracies to terrorist groups and foreign espionage. Ultimately, Arab intelligence services are responsible for 'coup-proofing,' a mission that requires the collection and analysis of intelligence on the intentions and capabilities of real and potential adversaries.[1]

But the Arab secret services do more than collect and analyze information. In most cases, they are the 'sharp end of the spear,' symbols of a state's power to coerce its citizens and intimidate its enemies. As Saddam Hussein's Iraq most recently demonstrates, Arab regimes exploit the sinister reputations of their intelligence services to deter and dissuade; indeed, the word for intelligence service in Arabic – *al-mukhabarat* – evokes for many Arabs images of terror, torture and death. Paradoxically, by using the *mukhabarat* to project strength and fear, Arab states also reveal their 'profound weaknesses' such as a lack of popular legitimacy.[2]

Given the centrality of the security apparatus to Arab regime stability and, by extension, the importance of the Arab world to global security, it is surprising that so little has been written about the *mukhabarat* in any Arab state. Indeed, the fact remains that much more has been written about the intelligence agencies of the United States, United Kingdom, Russia, France, Israel, China and Germany than the individual Arab services.[3]

This book addresses some of these deficiencies by investigating the history of the Egyptian intelligence community. Why Egypt? First of all, the Egyptian *mukhabarat* is widely reputed to be the oldest, largest and most effective in the Arab world. Second, there are ample credible sources upon which to build a reliable assessment. The result is an intriguing portrait of an evolving intelligence community in an under-studied but nonetheless pivotal Arab state.

## Methodology

This book analyzes the historical evolution of the Egyptian intelligence community from 1910 to 2009 by answering the following questions:

1   How has Egypt's intelligence community adapted to national security threats over the last 100 years?
2   How capable has the Egyptian intelligence community been in collecting and analyzing intelligence of its adversaries' capabilities and intentions?
3   How effective has Egyptian counterintelligence been in neutralizing foreign espionage and subversive networks?
4   What role has covert action played in Egypt's national security strategy?[4]
5   What role have foreign intelligence services played in the development of the Egyptian intelligence apparatus?
6   How has the *mukhabarat* negatively influenced the development of Egyptian democracy?

The first part of this book shows how the United Kingdom helped create the modern political police apparatus in Egypt. It explores how the political police dealt with a range of threats such as the nationalist and Islamist parties, the Axis in World War II, and the new state of Israel. This part concludes by analyzing how the intelligence services failed to neutralize the army coup of July 1952.

The second part examines the Nasser period (1952–1970) through the lenses of the *mukhabarat*. It shows how the Nasser regime consolidated military intelligence and created both the General Investigations Directorate (GID) and the Egyptian General Intelligence Service (EGIS). This part analyzes how these new agencies handled internal threats posed by the Muslim Brotherhood, dissident officers, and the communists. It also explores how Cairo employed its intelligence apparatus against Israel, the United Kingdom, France, and other Arab states. The Nasser period is one of war, and this book examines the performance of the Egyptian intelligence community in the 1956 Suez Crisis, the 1962–1967 Yemen wars, the 1967 June War, and the 1970 War of Attrition.

The third part studies Egyptian intelligence under President Anwar al-Sadat (1970–1981). It shows how intelligence influenced Sadat's career and facilitated his rise to power. This part explores the role of the intelligence agencies in the 1973 war with Israel and how those services coped with the emerging Islamist threat in the mid- to late1970s. Finally, this section assesses why the security services failed to protect Sadat from assassination on 6 October 1981.

Part four deals with Egyptian intelligence during the period of Sadat's successor, Husni Mubarak (1981–present). The primary target of Egyptian intelligence during Mubarak's tenure has been Egypt's Islamist community in general and the militant Islamic Group and al-Jihad offshoots in particular. This part explores the controversial role of the *mukhabarat* in the US Central Intelligence Agency's (CIA) program to forcibly repatriate alleged terrorists to Egypt. Post-9/11, the

Egyptian intelligence services have shut down most forms of overt and even clandestine dissent to the Mubarak regime: however, Egypt remains a divided, repressed and impoverished society.

## Note on transliteration

There are numerous methods of transliteration from Arabic to English. The author's approach consists of the following:

1 The 'generally accepted' English transliteration of key names such as 'Nasser' instead of 'Nasir' and 'Farouk' instead of 'Faruq.'
2 The use of an apostrophe to delineate *hamzas* and *ains* in Arabic.
3 The use of Egyptian dialect in the case of names – i.e. 'Gamal' instead of 'Jamal.'

# Part I

# Intelligence and the monarchy

# 1   *Mamur Zapt*

If spying is the world's second oldest profession then it must have its roots in the Nile Valley – one of the cradles of civilization and foundation for some of the earliest empires in history. While Egyptians proudly trace their origins in terms of millennia, the genesis of their modern intelligence system lies not in the distant past of pharaohs and pyramids but in the more recent present – the beginning of the twentieth century to be precise when another empire created a secret police apparatus to enhance its control over the Nile Valley.

Although Egypt was never a formal part of the British Empire, London regarded its de facto occupation of Egypt in general – and the Suez Canal in particular – as integral to the health and welfare of that empire. While the French and other powers resented British control of Egypt, the British faced few serious threats to their dominance until the beginning of the twentieth century when a growing class of educated Egyptians began demanding national independence. Indeed, the story of Egypt in the first half of the twentieth century is one of frustrated demands for independence, and that frustration manifested itself in secret societies, assassinations, riots and revolution. In order to contain this rising nationalist sentiment, the British created a secret police apparatus which, as the new century progressed, grew in size, influence and capabilities. On the eve of World War II, the nascent Egyptian intelligence community was still bound by many ties to its British creator and master; however, the stage was being set for its eventual independence and further growth.

## Origins

When Great Britain formally occupied Egypt in 1882 she inherited a domestic police intelligence system in desperate need of reform. The de facto chiefs of the secret police were the Cairo and Alexandria *Mamur Zapts,* who investigated anti-regime conspiracies and monitored foreigners. The *Mamur Zapts'* sources included plainclothes policemen, informant networks known as *mukhbireen*[1] and anonymous boxes where citizens could place petitions for the release of imprisoned relatives, denounce neighbors and report on anti-regime plots.[2]

Unfortunately for the British and their Egyptian quasi-puppet known as the Khedive, the *Mamur Zapts* lacked sufficient resources and centralized management to handle the new internal threats emerging at the end of the nine-teenth century.[3] Indeed, an Ottoman official who inspected Egypt's police force in 1910 was not impressed by what he saw: 'The secret police consist of a few ignorant men in dressing gowns who have been condemned several times for theft. They are capable of nothing but watching the houses and trade of their former accomplices.'[4]

While the security apparatus languished, new political, social and economic ideas were having a major impact on Egypt's educated classes. Nationalist and Islamist ideas were emerging at this time as part of the wider Islamic world's response to European colonial domination. For nationalists, an 'Egyptian' or, later, a 'pan-Arab,' identity helped counter the humiliation of colonialism and the creeping Westernization of Egyptian society. As for the early Islamists, they sought solutions in a regenerated Islam and a rediscovery of Islamic civiliza-tion.[5] Since neither the British nor the Egyptian monarchy were receptive to these new ideas, underground groups emerged in Egypt to challenge the status quo.

The first demonstration of this underground's growing confidence was the 20 February 1910 assassination of Egypt's Coptic Prime Minister Butrus Ghali Pasha by a young nationalist named Ibrahim Nasif al-Wardani.[6] One Egyptian newspaper put the murder into perspective when it noted that 'hitherto political assassination has been unknown in Egypt... the form of crime, of which [Butrus Ghali] was the victim, is without precedent in modern Egypt.' Indeed, Ghali's murder initiated an extended era of political assassination in Egypt while mark-ing a new phase of political warfare against the British and their Egyptian allies.

## The Central Special Office

The Butrus Ghali assassination compelled the British to examine Egypt's secret police apparatus. One of the first moves was to phase out the old political police system and pension off the Cairo *Mamur Zapt*.[7] Then a triumvirate of senior British officials including High Commissioner and the Commandant of the Cairo City Police, George W. Harvey, aka 'Harvey Pasha,' agreed to establish a new intelligence organization called the Central Special Office (CSO).[8]

To direct the CSO Harvey Pasha selected an aide with experience in the Port Sa'id police named George Philippides ('Philippides Bey'), a Christian from what is now Lebanon or Syria.[9] This selection was not unusual since the so-called 'Levantines' (of which Philippides was one) and Egypt's native Copts comprised the functionaries and clerks of the Egyptian administration at this time.[10] Moreover, Philippides was not only regarded as trustworthy by his Brit-ish superiors he also had the necessary intelligence and skill for his assignment.[11] Or, as one British official put it, Philippides was 'a most subtle detective.'[12]

Official documents described the CSO as 'a thoroughly organized service for the collection of all information regarding Political Secret Societies – individuals known, or believed to be, Political Agitators.' The office was to be 'secret and confidential' and separate from other police organizations.[13] To maintain a low profile, the new office rented a residential flat and frequently moved locations in its early years for safety and security. Under Philippides each employee and informant would be identified by a letter of the alphabet; only the *Mamur Zapt* knew their real identities. Furthermore, there were few face-to-face encounters between the *Mamur Zapt* and his spies: orders were transmitted by letter and replies could only be sent in written correspondence. None of the informants was permitted to know of the CSO's existence or whereabouts.[14]

The CSO collected data from informant networks run by plainclothes Special Branch detectives. Vetting these informants was challenging, for, as one British police official pointed out, any 'pervert student' could make up a report that was 'five percent truth' for the sake of the promised financial reward.[15] And money was not the sole motive either: some spies offered information to incriminate enemies or to influence police cases involving accused relatives. Meanwhile, for their part, the secret societies discovered that, by planting false information, they could swamp the CSO system, smoke out informants, and otherwise distract the secret police.[16] Police use of torture to extract confessions was another problem, raising uncomfortable questions about ethics and the reliability of the information obtained in this manner.[17]

Data on subversive groups was maintained on CSO index cards with file folders providing supplementary information. Over time, the office developed thousands of files on Egyptian students, nationalists and foreign residents.[18] Harvey Pasha praised the CSO for its rapid ability to obtain 'accurate' information on suspects; in July 1914, that speed and reliability was tested when Philippides was able to quickly access information on a murder plot against the Egyptian monarch.[19]

The CSO cooperated with foreign security services, and it is here that we find the earliest examples of intelligence liaison between Egypt and the European powers. For example, Scotland Yard assisted the CSO in the Butrus Ghali assassination by investigating Egyptian nationalists residing in the United Kingdom.[20] While the British provided most of the training for the CSO and the city police Special Branches, one detective went to Paris before World War I to study 'police methods'[21] while two others traveled to St Petersburg for the same purpose.[22] The future head of the Cairo City Police, Salim Zaki, later claimed that he had been trained by the Russian *Okhrana* in surveillance and presumably other methods.[23]

The CSO had other missions in addition to espionage. For example, it conducted background checks on Egyptian civil servants.[24] It also produced daily intelligence summaries and periodic, comprehensive reports on subversive movements for the British and select members of the Egyptian government. But there was never any doubt about whose interests the CSO ultimately served and among those few Egyptian officials aware of its existence, the CSO was viewed with suspicion at best.[25]

Philippides enjoyed some early successes at the CSO. For example, only five months after its formal creation in January 1911, the CSO issued its first comprehensive report on secret organizations.[26] This was followed a year later by the successful monitoring and apprehension of an assassination plot against the British consul general, Lord Kitchener and the Egyptian prime minister.[27] Unfortunately for the CSO, this latter success was marred by allegations of torture and insinuations that Philippides had cooked the evidence against the defendants.[28] The Kitchener plot did lead to the extradition of an Egyptian in Constantinople linked to the dissemination of seditious pamphlets, anti-British plots, and the Kitchener assassination attempt. This might well be one of the earliest renditions of a political suspect to Egypt.[29]

## World War I

During World War I, the British relied heavily on the CSO archive for intelligence on enemy subjects in Egypt as well as Egyptians believed friendly to the Central Powers.[30] A police official later recalled that the CSO was the 'only real intelligence office with complete records of persons of interest' to the British High Commission and the British army.[31] Indeed, Philippides was regarded as such an authority on Egyptian nationalists and the Turks that one British officer called him 'the most powerful man in Egypt' during the war.[32]

In fact Philippides rode a crest of power and influence in the early war years. He often had the last word on who should be investigated and deported. Not surprisingly, given this authority, rumors circulated that the *Mamur Zapt* was using his position for extortion and revenge.[33] He certainly had a determined enemy in a British police officer named Thomas Russell who watched the *Mamur Zapt* closely. Russell especially resented Philippides' influence over the disciplining and promotion of police officers, which offered opportunities for extortion and bribery. In one description of Philippides at a reception, Russell recorded that the *Mamur Zapt*

> Walked about among them like a sleek cat, occasionally extending his finger-tips to touch the outstretched hand of some rich provincial with, at the same time, the look of a butcher at a stock show sizing up the weight and value of a fat beast.[34]

In these circumstances, a showdown was inevitable and it was a battle that Russell ultimately won.[35] Eventually, the *Mamur Zapt* was put on trial where he alarmed British officialdom with his propensity for naming undercover detectives and secret informants in open court sessions.[36] The trial also raised awkward questions about earlier *Mamur Zapt* cases: Philippides supposedly admitted to one witness that he had falsified documents in the 1912 Kitchener plot.[37] In the end, Philippides was sentenced in 1917 to five years in prison and a fine. All in all, it was not an auspicious start for the modern Egyptian security apparatus.

On 22 January 1918, Joseph McPherson, or 'Bimbashi (Major) McPherson' as he was known to contemporaries, became acting *Mamur Zapt* in Philippides' place. An employee of the Egyptian Education Ministry, McPherson was not exactly enthralled by his new assignment which he described as 'an anomaly and an anachronism,' an office of the 'chief inquisitor.'[38] Although McPherson felt he lacked qualifications, in some ways he was the right man for the job. First, he was gifted in languages and spoke Egyptian dialect fluently. Second, as he wrote in one letter home, he was 'free lance...not being in need of money...and not liable to be blackmailed by them.'[39]

McPherson discovered that his new job had several intriguing facets. First, much of his work involved that anonymous 'suggestion' box outside the city walls; he noted his surprise at how many illiterate and impoverished Egyptians would pay a scribe to write a stinging indictment of a neighbor to put in that infamous box.[40] On occasion, McPherson would disguise himself as a native (a 'Cairene Carter' a 'low-class Greek') to get a feel for what the native population thought and felt.[41] As *Mamur Zapt*, McPherson commanded the small CSO staff plus 100 or so plainclothes detectives seconded from the Cairo Special Branch. Those detectives in turn relied on armies of informants, including street kids, to serve as their 'eyes and ears' in the city.[42]

## 1919 Revolution

In his correspondence McPherson often noted the hazards of his job, including death threats. But none of these compared with the tidal wave of revolution which was about to engulf the political police, the Egyptian throne and the British in 1919. In retrospect, there were numerous signs of impending unrest. On the one hand there were those agitators whose demands for independence had not been met. Then there was the bleak rural economy marked by wartime inflation and peasant recruitment into a compulsory labor corps.[43] The result was what one author has called an 'unusual synthesis of urban and rural discontent.'[44]

The 1919 convening of the Paris Peace Conference generated hopes among many educated Egyptians that the time for national liberation had arrived. When London rejected a demand by a politician named Sa'ad Zaghlul to attend the conference and demand independence, the stage was set for an internal explosion. Zaghlul and his followers formed the Wafd Party, a coalition of the rural middle class, urban professionals, and peasant representatives which was marked by its opposition to British occupation and the Egyptian monarchy.

From the very beginning the British underestimated both the Wafd and the discontent brewing across Egypt. Some of this probably was due to erroneous intelligence reports which assured officials that all was well in much of the country despite the rejection of Wafd demands.[45] But in early March 1919, when London deported Zaghlul and three others to Malta, Egyptian discontent spilled onto the streets in the form of strikes, demonstrations and riots. More ominously still, the trouble spread to rural areas as peasants attacked railway lines and other symbols of central authority. By May 1919, the number of dead nationwide exceeded 1,000. Not even the release of Zaghlul and his associates in April was sufficient to defuse the unrest.

The police were caught flatfooted by the rapid escalation of violence. This failure was due to inadequate resources in rural areas; uprooted agent networks as a result of the unrest; the postwar drawdown in subsidies for informants; and institutional and cultural reasons which inhibited the early detection of discontent. Indeed, the picture that emerges from this period is one of a police apparatus struggling to stay abreast of events let alone trying to take control of them.

When the demonstrations began, the political police arrested activists, cordoned off cafes, and searched for bombs, weapons caches and insurgent propaganda. Officers were also dispatched to power stations and depots to prevent damage to the trams and the power grid. As for the Cairo *Mamur Zapt*, a seemingly relaxed McPherson frequently donned a disguise 'and mooned about the mosques and other centres of sedition and in the cafes and native theatres [enjoying] many amusing and exciting incidents.'[46]

But the security apparatus never caught up with events. On 3 April, an assistant *Mamur Zapt* was murdered and, by the middle of the month, Cairo was 'in the grip of mob violence.'[47] In May 1919, an exhausted McPherson resigned as *Mamur Zapt* just as the unrest began to abate.[48] Change was in the air and the Central Special Office and the plainclothes detectives were not immune from the reforming impulse.

In the aftermath of the 1919 Revolution, the authorities faced the daunting tasks of rebuilding a 'practically smashed' police apparatus[49] and restoring order. On 1 September, Gilbert Clayton was named British Adviser to the Interior Ministry and among his marching orders was the reorganization of police intelligence.[50] From the start Clayton faced an uphill battle. Even though the unrest had died down in much of Egypt, the more militant members of Wafd created a violent secret movement called the Vengeance Society. Modeled after the early secret groups, the Vengeance Society intended to liberate Egypt by intimidating and terrorizing Egyptian politicians and British officials.[51]

The Vengeance campaign began with attacks on British soldiers, but these were soon followed by assassination attempts on senior Egyptian officials.[52] In response, the Cairo Police assigned the case to a promising young political police officer named Salim Zaki whose efforts soon paid off with the recruitment of an informer within the Vengeance Society and the seizure of incriminating documents. When several Vengeance members were put on trial, the British and their Egyptian allies mistakenly assumed that the worst was over.[53]

While Zaki tackled the Vengeance Society, British Interior Ministry officials proceeded to reform the political police by trying to centralize intelligence collection and analysis at the Interior Ministry. Up until that point, the City Police chiefs were largely autonomous with sole control over the Special Branch detectives, informants and threat analysis.[54] Among the new reforms was the creation of a new ministry-level Special Section that was intended to exercise considerable power over intelligence collection and analysis.[55] Appointed to direct the new office in February 1920 was a former British army intelligence officer named Charles Frederick Ryder.[56]

At the beginning of his tenure, Ryder's efforts to assert 'coordination' authority over the political police were stymied by the City Police commanders who did not want to lose control of their detectives, informants and intelligence archives. Moreover, British officials rejected Ryder's proposal to share 'all information' with the Egyptian government.[57] Given the strength of his bureaucratic opposition, Ryder was forced to give ground and his retreat temporarily stunted the process of reforming Egyptian intelligence by centralizing collection and analysis. Despite these obstacles, the Special Section commenced operations by developing a list of 'undesirable' Egyptians and foreigners who would be denied entry into the country.[58]

Having conceded the first round to the City Police, Ryder nonetheless continued his bureaucratic struggles to give the Special Section more resources, personnel and missions. In April 1921 he pleaded for money to recruit and retain informants of his own.[59] He also lamented that Special Section reports were not disseminated to Egyptian officials, including the prime minister.[60] He appeared sensitive to Egyptian resentment of British control over the intelligence apparatus even though the Special Section was funded by the Egyptian treasury.[61]

Despite its difficult start, the Special Section survived and slowly began to assume greater control over the intelligence mission. By 1922 its Intelligence Department was collecting 'political information from official and unofficial sources' while its analytical arm provided a weekly assessment for British and, occasionally, Egyptian officials.[62] This assessment contained intercepted telegrams, summaries of Friday sermons, surveillance reports of student activists, a distillation of the Egyptian press and reporting from the provinces.[63] By the mid-1930s, the Special Section housed both a Foreigners Department, which spied on members of the large foreign communities in Egypt, and a Labor Department, which was directed against the communists.[64]

## Semi-independence

While the security organizations fought their turf wars, the political environment continued to be marked by friction over Egyptian independence. On 28 February 1922, the British unilaterally declared Egypt independent but 'reserved' their rights in certain areas such as protecting the foreign communities in Egypt and defending the country from foreign aggression. For Egyptians, the unilateral declaration was a perpetuation of British control over Egypt under the fig leaf of a truncated independence. In other words, it was unacceptable.

The unilateral declaration of independence spurred the more radical nationalists to more violence, and Special Branch officers like Salim Zaki, soon began receiving death threats.[65] In May 1922 the British deputy Cairo police chief was assassinated amid intelligence reports of other threats to British officials and their Egyptian supporters.[66] In this threatening atmosphere, some British officials pointed out that the lack of a centralized political police impeded the restoration of security. The upshot of this criticism was a further strengthening of the Special Section.[67] On 26 July 1922, Egypt's prime minister ordered the transfer of the veteran Alexandria police officer, Alexander Gordon Ingram ('Ingram Bey'), to the Special Section.[68] In addition, the government announced more money for the recruitment of informers and the consolidation of political crime investigations under the Interior Ministry.[69] Another sign of the Special Section's growing power was the 1925 closure of the Cairo Police Central Special Office and the transfer of its 8,000 files to the Interior Ministry.

While the violent nationalist movements constituted the greatest threat to internal security in the 1920s, the Special Section also investigated security challenges posed by a former Khedive, Italians, Communists, and others.[70] The ex-Khedive, Abbas Hilmi II, who was removed from his throne in World War I for pro-Ottoman sympathies, was deemed a threat until well into the mid-1920s. Although the danger posed by Hilmi never amounted to much, the political police did block several attempts by the former monarch to infiltrate Egypt with spies, bomb makers and subversive pamphlets.[71] Another source of concern was the link between the Khedive's agents and the Italian colonial authorities in neighboring Libya.[72] The political police also helped break up the first Egyptian Communist Party in August 1925; when the Soviet Union tried to revive the party a few years later, the Egyptian secretary general took Moscow's money and defected to the Egyptian government instead.[73]

Still, these were marginal threats when measured against Egypt's militant nationalists, and the government tried to tackle this greater problem with a combination of carrot and stick. While the Wafd was legalized and its leaders returned from exile, laws were passed which gave the political police new powers of censorship, arrests and imposing curfews.[74] The authorities also tried to recruit informants in such hotbeds of political dissent as the law school and the religious university of al-Azhar; however, given the tenor of the times, recruiting reliable informants was always a difficult proposition.[75]

But nothing sharpens official minds faster than a high profile assassination. On 19 November 1924, Commander of the Egyptian Army and Governor General of the Sudan, Sir Lee Stack, was gunned down on the streets of Cairo. Enraged British officials demanded an Egyptian government apology, payment of a large fine, the withdrawal of Egyptian officers from the Sudan and more irrigated land in Sudan (which meant less water for hungry Egyptian peasants). The Wafd prime minister, Sa'ad Zaghlul agreed to pay the indemnity, but he rejected the other demands and resigned in protest.

Paradoxically, while the Stack assassination highlighted political police deficiencies, the subsequent investigation demonstrated police capabilities at their best. The Special Section's lead investigator was Ingram Bey who had a reputation for efficient interrogation of suspects and an ability to don disguises.[76] Another key to the investigation was Mohamed Naguib al-Helbawi, a nationalist who had been sent to the Tura quarries for a 1915 assassination attempt on the Khedive. Amnestied in 1924, Helbawi secretly nursed certain grievances against his old nationalist compatriots and these helped the political police recruit Helbawi as an informant.[77]

At police request, Helbawi rejoined the nationalist underground to gather intelligence. Few of Helbawi's comrades questioned his motives, for the survivor of the Tura penitentiary made it clear that he sought revenge against the authorities for his imprisonment.[78] The Helbawi operation was a delicate one and the British hedged their bets by using street kids to track Helbawi's movements. According to one British official, the trackers needed little in the way of disguise, for 'our streets are so full of rubbish that no one notices an odd beggar boy asleep in the gutter!'[79] In the end, however, Helbawi proved trustworthy and his efforts helped the police arrest several Stack conspirators in late January 1925.[80] Under interrogation, one detainee broke down and it was his confessions plus some forensic evidence which sealed the case.[81]

## Political police problems

The arrest of the Stack conspirators was followed by a lull in political violence; however, the broader issues underpinning discontent, namely British limitations on Egyptian sovereignty remained unaddressed. Caught in the middle of this larger political dispute was a political police that was chronically understaffed, underfunded and lacking central management. Shortly after the Stack affair, Salim Zaki, warned his superiors that his Cairo Special Branch lacked sufficient officers and suffered from poor morale. He noted that, on one surveillance assignment, 'I had to send three of my officers to carry on the watching while they were disguised in filthy clothes, and they spent several nights in dirty and unhealthy quarters of the city. Some of them are still suffering.'[82] Staffing wasn't the only problem either. Zaki wrote that he lacked adequate funds to pay informants or reward witnesses. Therefore, he was 'not surprised… that we are having nobody to come and supply us with information as regards the bombs that are being thrown every now and then.'[83]

Zaki's boss, Cairo Police Chief, Russell Pasha, echoed these concerns in his 1926 annual report to the interior minister. For several years running Russell had complained that his Special Branch was suffering from lack of informants as well as pay and staffing deficiencies.[84] Russell also dwelt on recruiting problems, arguing that the pool of regular police officers deemed adequate for political work had been 'exhausted.'[85] According to Russell, he had to reject over 98 percent of prospective political police officers because they were persons of 'extreme poverty… living from hand to hand' or handicapped by poor eyesight or low intelligence.[86] Russell rejected hiring university graduates (the 'undersized and myopic compatriot'[87]), reflecting a colonialist's unease with young, educated, and ambitious Egyptian men who had little love for their occupier.

## Authoritarianism

Egypt's political future remained clouded as it entered the 1930s. Paralysis plagued a system consumed by a three-way struggle between the monarchy, the Wafd and the British occupier. In this depressed political environment many Egyptians gravitated to fascism, communism and the nascent Society of the Muslim Brothers.

Some Egyptians were drawn to European fascist movements and their emphasis on order, discipline, belonging and ultra-nationalism.[88] Egyptian fascism manifested itself in several forms including Ahmed Hussein's Young Egypt Society (YES) and its Green Shirt affiliate. As early as 1935, the Special Section was investigating reports of sympathy for YES among Egyptian army officers, YES ties to Italy's Benito Mussolini and donations to the group by the Egyptian monarchy.[89] When a Green Shirt tried to assassinate the prime minister in November 1937, the authorities arrested more than 30 in a nationwide crackdown; however, fascism's appeal for many Egyptians was not easy to suppress.[90]

The communists also benefitted from the political impasse that gripped Egypt in the 1930s. Although the first Egyptian Communist Party had collapsed in 1925, factions reemerged in the 1930s in response to the Great Depression, the authoritarianism of Prime Minister Siqki, the rise of fascism and growing labor unrest. To counter this new threat, the Special Section set up a Labor Office in November 1930 which focused on the communists and their allies in the small Egyptian labor movement.[91] The political police successfully penetrated the communist factions both for intelligence collection and influencing the decision-making process.[92]

During this era, the political police also began monitoring a nascent Islamist movement called the Society of the Muslim Brothers. Created in 1928 by a young school teacher named Hassan al-Banna, the Brothers believed that Islam – an 'all inclusive' and 'total system' – offered the guidance Egypt needed to emerge from its spiritual, social and political malaise.[93] From its modest beginnings, the Brotherhood quickly expanded to include civil servants, students, urban professionals, workers, peasants and army officers.[94] Still, the authorities did not regard this organization as a serious adversary until after World War II when Egypt entered a new era in her political development.

## The 1936 Treaty

In 1936, the British and Egyptian governments signed another treaty under which London agreed to relinquish its previously 'reserved' right to protect Egypt's foreign communities. One result of this deal was an agreement to accelerate 'Egyptianization' of the Interior Ministry and the political police.[95] The old British-dominated Military Intelligence Branch was to be progressively 'Egyptianized' while the new Royal Egyptian Air Force and Navy were to have intelligence offices of their own. Military intelligence was given new counterintelligence responsibilities in the civilian arena;[96] it also won the right to send military attachés abroad where they served as intelligence collectors in addition to other duties.[97]

By the end of the 1930s, Britain's once dominant position in Egypt had seriously eroded. One sign of this shift was the fact that some British officials were complaining that the Egyptians were tapping their telephones![98] Others lamented that the 'Egyptianization' of the Interior Ministry would leave the country 'open to foreign imported subversive doctrines.'[99] Nonetheless, the Egyptians were asserting their right to their own space in the intelligence world. In 1939, its Foreign Ministry sent a team to the Balkans and Turkey to study anti-espionage laws which could be copied by Egypt.[100] The Egyptian press began to pay more attention to the dangers of espionage including suspicious foreign press and tourist bureaus that had been created in the country[101] Finally there was growing cooperation between the Interior Ministry and the British in counterintelligence, counter-sabotage and the development of plans for the war-time internment of enemy aliens.[102]

All these steps were to prove beneficial only months later when the German army swept into Poland and ignited World War II. The circumstances of that war ushered in another round of changes for the Egyptian intelligence community.

# 2 Decline and fall of the old regime

When World War II broke out, Egypt was caught in an ambiguous position. Although many Egyptians were sympathetic to Germany, their government was bound by treaty to grant the British access to military bases and the Suez Canal. In the intelligence arena, the political police worked closely with the British by interning German nationals, seizing German property, intercepting mail and telegrams and tapping telephones.[1]

At war's end, Egypt had achieved a dominant position in the Arab world, and its newfound regional confidence was reflected by its creation of a small external intelligence service and its growing ties with American intelligence. But the 1948 creation of Israel followed by Arab defeats in the ensuing Arab–Israeli war left the Egyptian government unpopular, divided, weak and discredited. Finding scapegoats for the humiliation in Israel became the order of the day and a new period of political violence shook the country as the security services cracked down on the Muslim Brotherhood, the communists and a rapidly shrinking Jewish community. Ultimately, however, the real threat to the throne emerged from within the army, for on 23 July 1952 junior officers staged a coup and overthrew the monarchy. This was to be one of the biggest failures in the history of the Egyptian intelligence services.

## World War II intelligence operations in Egypt

Although Egypt did not join the Allies in declaring war on Germany in 1939, its treaties required it to grant Britain access to its bases and the Suez Canal. In the intelligence arena, the Egyptian services worked closely with their British counterparts in security, counterintelligence and monitoring and apprehending German and other belligerent nationals in Egypt.[2] A joint committee hosted by the Egyptian Interior Ministry and staffed with British and Egyptian intelligence officers handled all issues pertaining to Egyptian suspects as well as some jurisdictional disputes involving foreign communities in Egypt.[3]

From the outset the British had reservations about Egyptian loyalties. These concerns were fueled by intelligence reports detailing pro-Axis sympathies among senior Egyptian army officers like Chief of Staff, General 'Aziz al-Masri as well as contacts between al-Masri, a junior officer named Anwar al-Sadat and the Muslim Brotherhood.[4] Eventually, the British compelled Egyptian Military Intelligence to transfer Sadat out to the Western Desert where he would presumably be safe from Brotherhood inducements.[5]

The Muslim Brotherhood's growing involvement in the army was one problem, but Italian intelligence was another. Although the Egyptians didn't know it, while Rome possessed a valuable intelligence base in Libya and had made inroads in Egypt's Italian community, its actual intelligence capabilities in Egypt were poor. In fact, both Italy and Germany relied on Japanese diplomatic facilities in Cairo, Alexandria, and Port Said for military and shipping intelligence until Japan declared war on the Western allies in December 1941.[6]

The long-awaited Italian invasion of Egypt finally occurred in September 1940. Although the Italians were repulsed by the British, the invasion spurred hopes among many Egyptians that a fascist victory would give Egypt her full independence. A few, such as General al-Masri and Sadat promised Axis agents that they would spark uprisings to coincide with the anticipated German invasion of Egypt.[7] When the British counterintelligence officer Alfred Sansom learned of these contacts, he knew that any action against al-Masri would have to be made in cooperation with Egyptian Military Intelligence. But, in Sansom's view, Egyptian officials were indifferent to the Axis threat: the director of Military Intelligence (DMI) brushed off the al-Masri reports and dismissed Sansom's warnings of a junior officer conspiracy within the Egyptian army.[8] Eventually, the DMI did cooperate with Sansom in apprehending al-Masri when the latter tried to flee to German lines and create a Free Egyptian Army in Libya.[9]

But the capture of al-Masri did nothing to alter the larger fortunes of war. In the first six months of 1942, successive British military defeats brought the Germans to the outskirts of Alexandria. As the German army prepared to finish off the British in Egypt, two German spies named John Eppler and Peter Monkaster were infiltrated into Cairo to gather intelligence on the British position.[10] Although the spies reached Cairo undetected on the eve of the German offensive they were soon diverted by the city's night clubs and eventually captured by British and Egyptian security.[11] British intelligence claimed its laurels for apprehending the spies and the affair was later immortalized in the novel *The Key to Rebecca*. What is less well known is that Cairo's political police working with Egyptian Military Intelligence quietly took care of the Egyptian members of the ring, including Anwar al-Sadat. Despite British pressure to charge Sadat with espionage, the Egyptian authorities temporarily dismissed him from the army instead.[12]

Sansom warned his superiors that Sadat's involvement in the Eppler spy ring pointed to serious problems in the Egyptian army and he reiterated his fear that the Egyptian DMI was doing little to monitor pro-Axis Egyptian officers.[13] Sansom's concerns were aggravated by reports of an Egyptian 'Officers Secret Committee' that was demanding a shake-up in general headquarters and a cessation of *mukhabarat* spying on officers.[14] Spurred by anxious British security officers, Egyptian Military Intelligence stepped up its surveillance of suspect officers but still showed little inclination to move against them.[15]

## Post-war threats

With the defeat of the German army at al-Alamein in 1942, the fascist threat to Egypt slowly receded. At war's end, Egypt emerged as the de facto leader of the Arab world and a major player in the creation of the new Arab League which was headquartered in Cairo. One consequence of Egypt's new regional role was the creation of a small intelligence service focused on foreign powers and their activities in Egypt. Subordinated to the Interior Ministry this new office comprised three departments focused respectively on the United States, Great Britain, and the Soviet Union/France.[16] In addition, the Cairo Police Arab Affairs Office was created in September 1947 to monitor Arab refugees in the capital as well as diplomats assigned to the Arab League. At first, the Arab Affairs Office handled Zionist matters as well, although those responsibilities were soon transferred to the Special Section's Zionist and Jewish Affairs Department.[17]

Yet this early interest in regional affairs did not disguise the fact that domestic security remained the paramount mission of the *mukhabarat*. Indeed, a post-war wave of political violence swept over Egypt and claimed the lives of a prime minister in February 1945 and a prominent pro-British politician a year later. By virtue of its location in the Egyptian capital, the Cairo Police Special Branch spearheaded the new political police offensive against the underground through intelligence gathering, seizure of seditious materials, surveillance and interrogations. The primary target of this offensive was the communist movement which had benefitted from the Soviet victory over Germany, the decline of the Wafd, and the disappearance of fascism from the domestic scene.

King Farouk was a driving force behind the political police crackdowns on the communists.[18] For their part, London and Washington aggravated Cairo's communist paranoia by feeding the Egyptians alarmist intelligence reports about Soviet activities in the Middle East. The British also proved instrumental in planting anti-communist East European exiles like the former Yugoslav intelligence officer, Colonel Milovan Gregorovitch, in Special Section jobs. Soon Special Section counterintelligence officers began targeting the legations of the new East European communist regimes in Cairo for recruits and information.[19]

Egyptian intelligence also began committing greater resources to combating the Muslim Brotherhood which was not only growing in numbers and influence but also developing a clandestine Special Organization. The Special Organization was intended to infiltrate the government, solidify contacts with sympathetic military officers and establish the foundations for an eventual coup.[20] Yet the *mukhabarat*–Brotherhood relationship was not completely hostile, for both shared an enemy in the communist movement and the authorities were not above relying on the Brothers for intelligence on communist activities.[21]

## 1948 War

Egypt joined the other Arab states in rejecting the UN General Assembly's November 1947 decision to partition Palestine; however, in doing so, the Egyptian government had unwittingly set itself on the path to three decades of war and defeat. By May 1948, with Israel's independence looming, and under domestic pressure to do more for the Palestinians, the Egyptian government began military preparations to invade the Jewish state. The declaration of martial law on 14 May led to the mass arrests of Jews, Europeans, leftists, or virtually anyone suspected of pro-Israeli sentiment.[22] In Alexandria, home to a large Jewish population, the Alexandria Police Alien Section, headed by future Prime Minister Mamduh Salem, stepped up surveillance, detention and interrogation of suspected Zionists and communists.[23]

Egypt invaded Israel on 16 May with an army that lacked clear objectives, sufficient resources for prolonged warfare and adequate intelligence of the enemy's intentions and capabilities. A young infantry officer named Gamal 'Abd al-Nasser later complained bitterly that 'there was no concentration of forces, no accumulation of ammunition and equipment. There was no reconnaissance, no intelligence, no plans.'[24] When the war began, Egypt's ability to gather and analyze intelligence on Israel was very limited. Although the Interior Ministry's new external intelligence unit was responsible for Palestine, it lacked sources inside the new state of Israel. Similar problems afflicted Egyptian Military Intelligence where few (if any) analysts believed the Israelis could stand up to the Arab armies that were being thrown against them.[25] Unfortunately for Egypt, breezy, widespread assumptions about Israeli weaknesses were built on little or no intelligence. When it crossed its Rubicon into Israel, the Egyptian army was in for a rude shock.

Indeed, pre-war intelligence deficiencies quickly became evident as soon as Egyptian forces entered combat. Tactical intelligence was one obvious problem for Bedouin scouts and a small army reconnaissance unit could not meet the demand for intelligence on Israel's order of battle, morale and force deployments.[26] In his memoirs, Nasser recorded how poor reconnaissance and lack of maps debilitated operational capabilities:

> There was one Arab guide whose task was to lead the battalion to the site of the settlement. The guide had no information about the fortifications of the settlement or its system of defenses. Such information as he did possess was vague and unspecific.[27]

Another problem was getting existing intelligence to the front. For example, the air force had a reconnaissance squadron of Hawker Hurricanes and British-trained photo interpreters, but imagery of Israeli positions rarely reached the soldiers who needed it most.[28]

Egypt's communications security and counterintelligence capabilities were very limited. Israeli intelligence routinely intercepted and deciphered messages that passed from Egyptian headquarters to field units. In fact, Israeli SIGINT noted how Egyptian units routinely provided higher headquarters with false reports including assertions of sweeping battlefield victories.[29] On the security front, Egyptian intelligence delayed taking even basic steps to deny information to Israel, such as restricting the sale of detailed maps of Egypt.[30] Reflecting a prevailing belief that Egypt's Jews represented an Israeli fifth column, the Interior Ministry's Jewish and Zionist Department planned and managed a campaign that included surveillance, the search and seizure of Jewish properties and deportations.[31] Finally, Egyptian intelligence had no significant wartime success in penetrating and manipulating the espionage rings of its Israeli adversaries.

Anti-Jewish violence in Cairo, Alexandria and other cities increased amid Israeli air raids over Cairo and Egypt military setbacks on the front. Between June and November 1948, a series of terrorist bombings shook the Jewish quarter in Cairo, killing more than 70 and leaving hundreds more wounded. The former British intelligence officer, Alfred Sansom, recalled how he once restrained *mukhabarat* officers from coercing a Jewish man into confessing that he was an Israeli spy. Although Sansom stopped the police on this occasion, he notes that 'it was not always so easy, for usually the political police had proper warrants and did their tortures and beatings-up in private.'[32] In another case, a Jewish merchant in Port Said was arrested and charged with espionage in July 1948 after his commercial rivals planted incriminating evidence on him.[33] The result of these arrests, sequestrations, denunciations and mob violence was a marked decline in the number of Jews in Egypt. According to one estimate, half of Egypt's pre-1948 Jewish population had fled to Israel by 1950.[34]

At the same time that the Jewish community was under assault, the political police were also cracking down on the Muslim Brotherhood. In November 1948, Cairo's Special Branch captured documents which identified the existence, structure and membership of the Brotherhood's clandestine Special Organization. Those documents enabled the *mukhabarat* to crush the Special Organization at a time when the Brotherhood as a whole was reeling from the loss of many of its volunteers in the war against Israel.[35] As a result, the Brotherhood increasingly turned to violence to bring about regime change in Egypt.[36]

## Assassinations

Defeat in the Israeli war led to a search for scapegoats, and many pointed fingers at the corrupt politicians and the palace. A tide of public anger swept the country amid a new round of assassinations. One of the first to fall was the Cairo Police chief, Salim Zaki, who was killed in December 1948 during student protests.[37] Although it lacked evidence, the government blamed Zaki's death on the Brotherhood and on 8 December the movement was officially banned. This ban was followed by *mukhabarat* arrests and torture of Brotherhood cadres, the confiscation of the organization's assets and stepped up surveillance of senior Brotherhood leaders, including Hassan al-Banna.[38]

Al-Banna knew he was in the sights of the political police and he secretly met the head of the Special Section, Colonel Mohamed Ibrahim Imam, to work out a deal. But these talks foundered and, by the end of January 1949, al-Banna's contacts with the authorities had ceased.[39] On 12 February 1949 political police officers passively watched as the Supreme Guide was gunned down by assassins outside the Young Men's Muslim Association. Al-Banna died shortly after his admission to the hospital, leading to rumors that he was murdered while ostensibly receiving medical attention.[40] The story of who killed him is complicated. The government claimed he had been murdered by a disaffected Muslim Brother.[41] According to British sources, a *mukhabarat* officer accepted 1,000 Egyptian Pounds and a promotion to carry out the hit.[42] In 1955, an exiled King Farouk confessed that *he* had given the order to execute al-Banna because of the 'evil influence' of the Brotherhood.[43] In any case, al-Banna's assassination debilitated the Brothers and further radicalized them against the regime.

## Egypt's foreign intelligence relationships

After World War II, when Egypt's regional influence was waxing, foreign intelligence services established or augmented liaison relationships with Egyptian intelligence while simultaneously ramping up unilateral operations against the Egyptian government. Foremost was the British Secret Intelligence Service (SIS) which not only liaised with the Special Section but also spied on the Egyptian government, security organs and political opposition.[44] As subsequent events proved, however, the SIS station in Cairo lacked political contacts and access to military intelligence.[45] US military attachés established a liaison relationship with their Egyptian counterparts during World War II.[46] In 1942, the US Office of Strategic Services (OSS) established an office in Cairo with responsibility for intelligence collection, counterintelligence and analysis. While OSS Cairo was focused on the Axis, some of its officers like Kermit 'Kim' Roosevelt quietly cultivated useful Egyptian contacts that were to prove invaluable later on.[47]

Kim Roosevelt first came to Egypt under diplomatic cover in 1943 or 1944 and he took an immediate liking to the place.[48] He developed a network that included palace contacts and two influential journalists (and twin brothers) named Mustafa and 'Ali Amin who had been educated in the United States.[49] Roosevelt regarded the Amins as a valuable resource and, according to one account, the OSS helped fund the Amin's publication house, *Al-Akhbar*.[50] After joining the CIA, Roosevelt returned to Egypt in 1950 at a time when US intelligence was becoming an important *mukhabarat* liaison partner. The Cold War was underway and Washington hoped to stem the tide of communism in the Middle East by cultivating and supporting friendly security services in the region.

On the military level, the US air force had taken over the British mission of training the Egyptians in aerial reconnaissance.[51] Almost certainly the US Army provided intelligence training for its Egyptian counterpart as well. On the political level, a mutual fear of communism facilitated greater CIA cooperation with the Interior Ministry's Special Section. Symptomatic of the growing relationship was a March 1950 US embassy survey of communism in Egypt which was partly based on Special Section intelligence.[52] A month after this report was issued, the Special Section created an anti-communist bureau staffed by highly-qualified officers, including sociologists and economists, who liaised with similar anti-communist organizations in other countries.[53] Among these experts were those East European exiles like Colonel Milovan Gregorovich who had experience in the trenches against communism.[54]

No doubt Washington and London influenced the creation of this new anti-communist office. That March 1950 US survey of Egyptian communism reads in retrospect like a justification for pressuring the Egyptians into creating just such an office. In any case, Egypt's apparent commitment to fighting communist subversion encouraged the *mukhabarat* to seek American intelligence training and equipment. In early 1952, the Egyptian government informed the US embassy of its intent to send a 'study mission' of military officers to the US for FBI training in counterintelligence and combating communism. This request was still under discussion when the 23 July 1952 coup swept Farouk from power.[55]

## Unrest in the ranks

While the regime did not hesitate to combat the Brotherhood and the communists it downplayed unrest in the army fueled by the British occupation, the defeat in the 1948 war and leadership corruption. Some of this discontent manifested itself in secret organizations like the Free Officers which included Gamal 'Abd al-Nasser, 'Abd al-Hakim 'Amr, Anwar al-Sadat, and the future chief of intelligence, Zakaria Muhi al-Din.[56] Official lethargy aside, by the late 1940s the political police nevertheless began to close in on the Free Officers. For example, when the *mukhabarat* discovered a military manual with Nasser's name on it during a 1949 raid on a Brotherhood safe house, Nasser was warned against having any further dealings with the Muslim Brotherhood.[57]

Nasser's run-in with the authorities did not deter the Free Officers who proceeded to issue pamphlets demanding an end to martial law and censorship, the release of political prisoners and the dismantling of the political police.[58] Still, the Free Officers had not seriously dented the regime's casual sense of security. One British official recorded that senior Egyptian intelligence officers did not appear surprised or overly concerned when they were given UK intelligence on Egyptian junior officer conspiracies.[59]

But perhaps the biggest threat was the king himself. To his friends and those he wished to impress, Farouk could be 'charming, interested in their personal matters' but to his enemies and underlings, Farouk was something else again: a man 'cruel, brutal and vindictive in small matters.'[60] He also was smart enough to establish his own intelligence network that served as his 'eyes and ears' on Egyptian society and politics.[61] Regardless of what his intelligence agencies and personal networks were telling him, Farouk was complacent about the many threats to his throne. For example, the king was not particularly galvanized by the Great Cairo Fire of 26 January 1952, when a mob looted and burned a substantial portion of the city. For its part, the political police role in detecting and controlling the unrest was ambiguous at best: the Special Section chief, Colonel Mohamed Ibrahim Imam, could not be found for several crucial hours while at least one of his subordinates showed no interest in stopping the mob.[62] It was never clear who instigated the looting; however as one observer put it, the riots symbolized a regime that now 'gave off the smell of death.'[63]

After the fire, the Free Officers accelerated their conspiracy planning. The regime seemed aware of these plans but unable or unwilling to respond. One of Farouk's closest associates told a British official on 21 July 1952 that Farouk was preoccupied with creating another ruling cabinet even though he had intelligence that a group of army officers intended to seize power immediately.[64] According to another account, the CIA understood that the king was aware of the plot and planning to make arrests.[65] The Free Officers knew about the plans to apprehend them thanks to several sources, including a military intelligence officer, and, as a result, they launched their coup as a preemptive move on the night of 22–23 July.[66]

As the agency responsible for monitoring army loyalty, Military Intelligence was partly responsible for the regime's failure to move against the Free Officers in time. This may have been due to anti-Farouk sentiment among senior MI officers, some of whom provided the Free Officers with valuable intelligence on the regime's moves against them. Others joined the conspiracy as soon as the coup was underway. In this way, the organization directly responsible for investigating officer loyalty to the regime became one of the first institutions to defect to the coup plotters.[67]

The coup itself was something of an anti-climax with the relatively bloodless capture of general headquarters, the seizure of important communications nodes, the arrest of key security officials like the head of the Special Section and the isolation of the king at his summer palace in Alexandria.[68] When it became clear that his support had evaporated, Farouk left Egypt on 26 July for permanent exile in Italy.

Prior to seizing power the Free Officers had consistently called for the dismantling of the hated political police apparatus. Although this demand was reiterated after the 23 July coup, the new junta delivered a mixed message on the future of the *mukhabarat*. On 25 July, the new civilian prime minister declared that the army would 'terminate the system of political police and informers'[69] because it was 'unhealthy' and produced 'bogus information.'[70] At the same time, the prime minister told a journalist that the political police was a 'remarkable instrument of government' – an instrument apparently worth preserving.[71] It soon became clear that the junta intended to reform centralize, and substantially improve the capabilities of the *mukhabarat*.

In a portent of things to come, the Free Officers used intelligence officers to inform the British, Americans, and French about their plans and objectives. Since American support for the coup was crucial, the conspirators designated the head of Egyptian air force intelligence, 'Ali Sabri, as their emissary to the US embassy. Sabri was a logical choice: not only had he attended an air force intelligence officers' course in Colorado, he also was on excellent terms with the US assistant air attaché, Lieutenant Colonel David Evans III.[72] It was Sabri who woke Evans in the early morning hours of 23 July and informed him that the Free Officers had taken control of the government.[73] Sabri also warned the

Americans that the British would face an army-led insurgency if they intervened to prop up Farouk.[74]

In the early days of the coup, the junta used Evans as its primary American contact. On the morning of 24 July, only hours after the seizure of power, Evans was invited to Military Intelligence headquarters to discuss the new leadership's goals for Egypt. From the outset, Egyptian intelligence officers told Evans that they wanted to join a US-led joint military command and acquire new weapons and training.[75] They also promised to escalate their campaign against Egyptian communists, adding that the 'newly organized intelligence branches of army and police' would require US and British help.[76]

As Egypt entered a new phase in its political development, some observers hoped the Free Officers would restore parliamentary democracy and instill a respect for human rights. This sense of optimism did not last, however, for the junta made it clear that expanding the political police apparatus was high on its list of priorities. Although few could have predicted it at the time, Egypt was about to descend into the nightmare of a fully-fledged *mukhabarat* state.

# Part II
# Intelligence under Nasser

# 3   Creating a new intelligence community

The 23 July 1952 coup ushered in a period of rapid social, political and economic change in Egypt. In its first two years alone the military junta banned civil titles, removed its civilian politicians, abolished the monarchy, disbanded the political parties, instituted land reform, implemented progressive labor legislation, substantially increased spending on education and created a one party state. Although the shift toward non-alignment would not come until 1955, Cairo's new masters were already asserting themselves in foreign policy by negotiating a British military withdrawal from the Suez Canal and a separate deal on the Sudan. At the center of these turbulent changes was a young, dynamic army officer named Gamal 'Abd al-Nasser.

Internal security was an abiding concern. From the beginning the Free Officer regime understood that its greatest threats came from followers of the old regime, dissident military officers, communists and the Muslim Brotherhood. Consequently, one of the regime's earliest decisions was to create a new General Investigations Directorate (GID) with expanded security powers and capabilities and direct control of the intelligence collection process. The US Central Intelligence Agency (CIA) was a key GID liaison partner from the outset. Not only did the GID benefit from CIA training and funding, both services saw a common adversary in the Egyptian communist movement. By the end of 1954 the communist threat had receded as the GID found itself at war with both the Muslim Brotherhood and a ring of Israeli-backed saboteurs. At this time, Egypt was also beginning to seek opportunities overseas for the expansion of her influence and power.

## Zakaria Muhi al-Din

In the immediate aftermath of the 23 July 1952 coup, tensions were high in Cairo with many of the Free Officers fearing assassination and conspiracies by army elements, the Wafd, the Muslim Brotherhood and the former regime. Given this atmosphere it was not surprising that the new junta placed internal security and intelligence reform high on its agenda. The man it turned to for this was Lieutenant Colonel Zakaria Muhi al-Din. One of the key planners of the coup and an old Nasser associate, Muhi al-Din was quickly appointed director of Military

Intelligence (DMI) even though he had no formal intelligence background. Naturally, this appointment generated resentment among career Military Intelligence (MI) officers, but the junta understood the critical necessity of ensuring the MI's loyalty.[1] Muhi al-Din's appointment is an important one, for he is the father of the modern Egyptian intelligence community as we know it today. Not only did he overhaul and consolidate MI, Muhi al-Din also presided over the creation of a powerful internal security apparatus and a new external intelligence agency.

Zakaria Muhi al-Din left a mixed impression in his early talks with US and British military attachés. Some perceived that he was nervous, lacked intellect and was intolerant of the civilian politicians who were fronting the new regime.[2] Others regarded him as influential, very intelligent, 'a force to be reckoned with,'[3] a man who demonstrated 'moderation, modesty and pleasant reserve.'[4] His cousin and fellow Free Officer, Khaled Muhi al-Din, later wrote that Zakaria was 'balanced and calm,' gifted in organization, and the 'epitome' of an intelligence officer. He added that Zakaria was not prone to snap judgments but preferred to wait until he had assessed intelligence from multiple sources.[5]

As the new DMI, Muhi al-Din directed the senior intelligence service in the military. Moreover, given the dissolution of the civilian political police, MI was also the most powerful security agency in Egypt. Before the coup, MI investigated officer loyalty, conducted counterintelligence, regulated the foreign travel of army officers and analyzed foreign military capabilities.[6] Shortly after his appointment as DMI, Muhi al-Din told his staff that a new era was dawning for military intelligence. Not only must MI protect the 'political work of the revolution at home and abroad' it must also direct its efforts against Egypt's primary enemies which he identified as Great Britain and Israel. Apparently no mention was made of a communist threat.[7]

The junta conducted a good deal of its early foreign policy through MI channels, and the communist threat was at the center of its dialogue with the Western powers. Within weeks of the July coup, the anti-communist offices of army and air force intelligence were passing classified information on communist activities to the Western military attachés. Among these reports were allegations that Egyptian communists were contemplating a campaign of sabotage against US bases and oil pipelines in the Middle East.[8] Even on politically sensitive issues the Free Officers preferred the MI channel. For example, it was MI that first notified the US embassy of the junta's decision to sack its first civilian prime minister.[9]

## Creating the GID

But it soon became clear that MI had too many missions especially its temporary responsibility for the civilian internal security mission pending the creation of a new secret police. As we saw in the last chapter, although Egypt's new prime minister promised to abolish the political police, the military leadership had already decided to create a new civilian intelligence service that enjoyed new augmented powers and capabilities. Indeed, as early as 31 July 1952, the regime had informed Western military attachés of its intent to create a secret committee which would combat communist propaganda and arrest communist cadres. The Egyptians proposed that this committee consist of *mukhabarat* officers (presumably from MI) as well as military representatives from the United States, France and the United Kingdom.[10] While the British welcomed this proposal the US attachés were at first reluctant to participate.[11]

The British were surprised by the American rejection of the anti-communist committee. A few weeks later, the British ambassador approached his American counterpart and proposed

> To establish the kind of overt contact we had in the past with the special police. [The] latter have now been ostensibly abolished but their anti-Communist activities are being carried on by a bureau which is in the process of formation.[12]

The US ambassador agreed and recommended joint US–UK cooperation; no mention was made of the French.[13]

While these discussions were underway, the regime announced it was dismantling the political police at the governorate level (Special Branches) and the Interior Ministry (Special Section). Yet, at the same time, the US embassy was reporting that a *new* political police organization was being created under army supervision. It was understood that this new agency would absorb the personnel of its predecessor 'after ample purging.'[14]

The decision to build a new civilian security apparatus was spurred by riots that occurred on 12–13 August at a textile factory near Kafr al-Dawr. What had begun as a workers' protest for pay and better working conditions soon overwhelmed the police and the army was called in to break up the demonstrations. MI was convinced the riots were instigated by either communists or the Wafd, and Zakaria Muhi al-Din's decision to use force earned him the nickname of Stalin's infamous secret police chief, 'Beria,' from his colleagues.[15]

The new political police that emerged after the coup was called the General Investigations Directorate (GID) (*Mabahith al-'Amm*) and, later, the State Security Investigations Service (*Mabahith 'Amn al-Dawla*).[16] In its earliest days the GID was led by Zakaria Muhi al-Din and supervised by a cadre of MI officers, including 'Ali Sabri and Kamal Rif'at.[17] GID began with four departments that reflected its mission areas: Foreigners, Zionism, Communism and Internal Affairs. This last department covered the Muslim Brotherhood, the Wafd, and others.[18] There was continuity between the old political police and the GID in organizational structure, mission, and staffing; the GID also assumed control over the archives of the old Special Section.[19]

## Enter the CIA

The junta turned to the United States for advice when it decided to consolidate MI and create the GID. The Americans already had a foothold in this area having trained a generation of officers like 'Ali Sabri in military intelligence courses in the United States. Moreover, FBI was the trainer of choice when the pre-coup MI sought counterintelligence instruction in 1952. Therefore there was context for the new regime's September 1952 request that the United States train the GID in 'American methods of dealing with Communism.'[20] As a measure of the importance it attached to this, the cash-strapped Egyptians offered to pay all expenses related to the mission. Washington referred this request to London – given British sensitivities in the matter – and there it apparently languished for some time.[21]

Or perhaps it did not languish for long. We do not know the answer because at this stage the CIA took over intelligence training in Egypt and the archive on CIA activities during this period is closed. The CIA shift, which began in October 1952, may have been due in part to the work of a very well-connected 'diplomat' named William Lakeland. There is no definite evidence that Lakeland *was* a CIA case officer at this time, but there are some intriguing clues. For instance, more than a few Egyptians wondered how a man of Lakeland's junior diplomatic rank could have access to Nasser, Zakaria Muhi al-Din and others.[22] In addition, the CIA's Kermit Roosevelt showed up in Cairo in October 1952 and informed Nasser that as special counselor to the US president, he was in charge of making American foreign policy in the region.[23] Soon, Roosevelt and Nasser developed a warm relationship where they called each other by their first names.[24] With Roosevelt's arrival, a pattern emerged in the way the US embassy conducted business in Egypt. The ambassador dealt with General Mohamed Naguib who was *de jure* head of the junta and, eventually, Egypt's first president while Roosevelt handled Nasser.[25] One researcher attributes this arrangement to Nasser's preference for Roosevelt.[26] It could also be that the young army officer who relished his behind-the-scenes power regarded the CIA officer as the real locus of power at the US embassy.

Roosevelt needed help. The CIA's missions in Egypt – an outgrowth of the junta's desire for intelligence training – were growing. Soon, several new case officers showed up in Cairo to take some of the load off Kermit Roosevelt's shoulders. The first of these was the new station chief, James Eichelberger, who had previously served in the US Army Counterintelligence Corps (CIC), the OSS, and at a Chicago advertising firm before joining the CIA.[27] In July 1953, Eichelberger was joined by an old CIC and OSS buddy from Alabama named Miles Copeland, a voluble man of considerable energy. CIA veteran Wilbur Eveland wrote that Copeland's eyes 'danced with excitement,' while the Egyptian journalist Mohamed Hassanein Heikal wrote that Copeland was 'an advertising man, a nonstop talker in a permanent state of agitation.'[28] Frank Kearn rounded out the new troika of CIA officers. Another one of Eichelberger's CIC buddies whose cover in Egypt was that of a CBS journalist, Kearn's mission was to provide public relations advice to the Revolutionary Command Council (as the junta first styled itself).[29] Nasser once noted that Kearn was an 'extraordinary' man who 'seems to know more than any ambassador.'[30]

Although the CIA officers enjoyed access to Nasser and other senior leaders, their routine liaison arrangements were handled by another Free Officer named

Hassan al-Tohami. Transferred to MI after the coup, al-Tohami supervised a number of programs, including the selection of MI and GID officers for CIA training. He also was tasked by Nasser to secretly monitor the telephone conversations of junta members, government ministers and others whose behavior Nasser deemed suspicious. Although al-Tohami was later discovered tapping the telephones of Nasser himself and privately sharing intelligence with the CIA, he nonetheless managed to stay in the good graces of the leadership.[31]

One of the CIA's earliest assignments was helping build the GID. Though the State Department had left Cairo's early request for GID training in bureaucratic limbo there are indications that the CIA had in fact accepted the mission.[32] Several sources assert that Copeland was in Egypt to advise the GID, rebuild its police files and even train Nasser's bodyguard.[33]

## The Nazi connection

The Americans were not alone in advising the GID. Perhaps because Cairo feared over-reliance on Washington, West Germany's intelligence boss, Reinhard Gehlen, received an Egyptian request to 'to inject life and expertise into the Egyptian secret service'[34] with veterans of German wartime intelligence.[35] Researchers have suggested that the CIA did not facilitate Gehlen's ties to the GID.[36] Still, it is likely that the CIA knew of and condoned the Egyptian–West German intelligence liaison relationship given Langley's extensive ties to both Gehlen and the Egyptians.

In any case, the Germans were a good fit for Egypt. Pro-German sentiment had motivated Cairo to recruit former German military officers for advice on rebuilding the Egyptian army after the 1948 war.[37] Those advisers remained in Egypt after the 1952 coup, and one of them, Major Gerhard-Georg Mertins, trained a new Egyptian airborne unit and helped develop guerrilla forces for use against the British in the Suez Canal Zone.[38] To lead the GID assignment, Gehlen turned to a famous Nazi commando named Otto Skorzeny who already had some post-war dealings with the Egyptians including the proposed sale of a used German U-boat.[39] Although reluctant to leave his lucrative business in Spain, Skorzeny agreed to the GID assignment with the proviso that his contract be a short one so that he could return to Madrid and his other interests.[40]

Skorzeny arrived in Cairo in 1953 or early 1954 and he was soon assisted by some old friends in the SS and Gestapo like Franz Buensch, Joachim Deumling and Alois Anton Brunner.[41] Brunner had a particularly gruesome past: during the war, he served in the SS where his specialties included brutality toward Jewish children and 'humiliation before death.'[42] Some sources believe Brunner was serving as Gehlen's informal representative in Damascus when he was tapped to train the GID in interrogation techniques.[43] There were others too, although proof of their GID work is not as definitive. Among this latter group we find Leopold Gleim, the former head of the Gestapo in Warsaw, and SS General Oskar Dirlewanger, who helped suppress the 1943 Warsaw Ghetto uprising.[44]

From a public relations standpoint the GID could not have chosen a more disastrous cadre of advisers. But this was a secret assignment, and these were men who could help boost the GID's capabilities to a new level of brutality and intimidation. Moreover, the Egyptians exploited the war criminal status of their advisors by underpaying them and subjecting them to heavy surveillance.[45]

It is difficult to gauge the influence of the Germans on the GID and the new Egyptian Military Intelligence Department (MID). One Egyptian intelligence officer later argued that the Germans were housed in villas far from MID headquarters and tasked with writing memoirs of their wartime intelligence work. Those memoirs were then adapted to the needs of the evolving Egyptian intelligence community.[46] Miles Copeland later insisted that the Germans (and Americans) played marginal roles in creating the new Egyptian intelligence community: 'The fact is that Nasser and Zakaria ... built the intelligence and security services with remarkably little outside help ... they did a remarkably competent job.'[47]

Copeland's assertion that Egypt built its intelligence community largely on its own is borne out in the memoirs of Egyptian intelligence officer 'Abd al-Fattah Abu al-Fadl. According to Abu al-Fadl, the Free Officers emphasized self-reliance in building their intelligence apparatus; they accomplished this in part by gathering a cadre of veteran intelligence officers to collect, translate, analyze and adapt information from the German memoirs as well as books on intelligence that were available in the public domain. The cadre used this to create an intelligence training school curriculum for the armed forces, the Foreign Ministry and the GID. They also planned the reorganization of Military Intelligence (the MID) and, eventually, the creation of an external intelligence service.[48]

## CIA preeminent

Abu al-Fadl insisted that the new intelligence school was deliberately isolated from any foreign influence; however, other sources indicate the CIA provided the school with equipment, training manuals and 'managerial advice.'[49] For example, the future head of the CIA's Office of National Estimates, Charles Cremeans, helped Cairo produce a National Intelligence Estimate process as well as 'simple, factual, timely, and relevant daily assessments for Nasser.'[50]

In the end, there can be no doubt that this period was the heyday of the CIA's early involvement in Egypt. The first key to the CIA's ascendancy was its contacts. Some of these dated back to Kermit Roosevelt's OSS days in Cairo while others had been recruited since then and extended to senior levels of Egyptian politics, including Nasser. In a society where one's standing was based on who one knew, the CIA was clearly a powerful player.[51] The second key was the CIA's lavish spending and its willingness to share intelligence on Egypt's enemies. From the beginning, Kermit Roosevelt made it clear that only he could obtain the economic aid that Egypt desperately needed.[52] The CIA also provided the GID – and presumably MID – with miniature transmitters, cameras, and bugs as well as intelligence on the Soviets and Egyptian communists.[53] It also helped that the CIA could be discreet. The Free Officers preferred the intelligence channel to routine diplomacy for some of their most sensitive dialogues with the United States.[54] At the same time, Nasser not only recognized that the CIA had the ear of the White House, he also was adept at playing the CIA off against State when circumstances permitted this.[55] Finally, the CIA enjoyed a reputation for making and breaking governments and Nasser undoubtedly was aware of public reports linking Kermit Roosevelt to the ouster of Iranian premier Mohamed Mosaddeq in 1953.[56]

This combination of powerful Egyptian contacts, money, intelligence sharing, discretion and fear helped make the CIA the most powerful American player on the Egyptian chessboard throughout much of the 1950s.[57] Examples of the CIA's influence in Egypt include mediating Canal Zone talks between London and Cairo, facilitating peace feelers between the Egyptian and Israeli governments and nudging Washington toward participating in Nasser's cherished High Dam project at Aswan.[58] At the intelligence liaison level, the CIA ran joint operations against the Soviets with the Egyptian services. For instance, in 1955, a CIA case officer under non-official cover named Frank Kovaleski led a team of Americans and four Egyptian intelligence officers in an operation to tap the telephone lines of the Soviet embassy in Cairo.[59] Still, CIA's influence eventually worked against it. A victim of its own success, the CIA was suspected by Nasser of espionage, influence peddling and assassination plots against him.[60]

## Problems in the army

The Egyptian army was among the earliest targets of the new *mukhabarat*. As early as August 1952, the regime acted on a Brotherhood tip and crushed a non-commissioned officers' conspiracy.[61] The breakup of this would-be coup also led to the arrest of the Deputy Director of Military Intelligence, Brigadier General Hassan Naggar who may have known about the conspiracy but failed to warn of it.[62] Alternatively, Naggar might have been sacked because it was the Muslim Brotherhood not MID that had better spies in the army ranks. In December of that year, MID had better success in unraveling a plot among air force mechanics that was allegedly instigated by communists.[63]

But these were minor conspiracies compared to what came next. The same month that the air force plot was uncovered, MID had been probing unrest among a group of artillery officers through an informant named Sami Sharaf. On the night of 14–15 January 1953, the authorities arrested 35 officers, including a powerful colonel with Muslim Brotherhood ties and a seat on the Regency Council (Egypt was still nominally a monarchy). But the most important consequence of this would-be coup was the rise of Sami Sharaf, who was rewarded with a transfer to the MID before becoming one of Nasser's most trusted advisors.[64] The artillery officers' plot was followed by the eventual ouster of the junta's front man, General Mohamed Naguib, and his backers in the cavalry corps.[65]

The MID emerged from this period chastened by its inability to detect army conspiracies. While it was true that the artillery officers' plot (if there ever was one) was neutralized by an MID informant, the same could not be said of the later Naguib-cavalry axis where the MID had failed to warn of wavering cavalry officer loyalties.[66] Over the long term, the MID compensated for these weaknesses by improving its ability to infiltrate the ranks and identify and weed out would-be rebels. It also encouraged officers to spy on each other.[67]

## Fighting communism

Army unrest was one obvious source of concern for Nasser and his allies. As we have seen, the communists were another. In the months following the coup, MI took the lead in fighting communism – at least until the GID was ready to take over this assignment. At the same time, the MI was strengthening its counterintelligence apparatus to combat communist penetration of the ranks.[68] In February 1953, the MID created an anti-communist bureau. This was followed by proposed intelligence sharing with the Americans and the British on communism and requests for training manuals on neutralizing communist propaganda.[69] The intelligence exchange bore fruit immediately. In March, the MID and GID arrested suspected communists and shared the documents they found with the United States. The following month, an air force intelligence officer (and recent graduate of a US intelligence course) named Captain 'Issam al-Din Khalil asked the United States for assistance identifying the sponsor of communist Arabic propaganda.[70]

As the GID prepared to take over the anti-communist fight it exploited the files and informants previously controlled by the pre-coup Special Section. Led by Lieutenant Colonel Ahmed Hilmi, the GID's anti-communist office responded to American requests for information on communists and the labor movement while asking for US assistance in preparing anti-communist propaganda for distribution by GID officers.[71] During a May 1954 press conference, the GID chief, Colonel 'Abd al-Aziz Fahmi, reiterated that combating communism was the 'duty of all' Egyptians and pleaded for public assistance in combating 'subversion.'[72] Fahmi belittled the communists as 'paid agents, dismissed students or unemployed workers' who were 'instigated by elements connected with foreign countries.' He also asserted that the Zionist movement was 'closely connected' with 'every subversive movement dangerous to Egypt' including the communists.[73]

The true dimensions of the communist threat at this time are difficult to assess. Membership in the underground parties and allied labor groups had grown from 500 in 1950 to a still anemic 5,000 in 1956, but the movement was torn by schisms and lacked public support.[74] At the same time, the communists were subject to GID infiltration and propaganda.[75] While the communist threat may have been 'real' in the conspiratorial minds of Nasser and his colleagues, it also served as a basis for cooperation between the Egyptian and Western intelligence services.

Although Egyptian intelligence was strongly anti-communist – at least in meetings with its American and British partners – there is a hint that Cairo was quite pragmatic and sought an intelligence relationship with the Soviet Union in the months after the July 1952 coup. According to one source, the Egyptian ambassador in Moscow approached the Soviets with a proposal to send Egyptian intelligence officers to the USSR for training. But the Soviets rejected the proposal because they were suspicious of the Cairo junta and its ties to the West.[76]

## The Muslim Brotherhood

The regime targeted a lot of propaganda against the communists; however it knew that the powerful Muslim Brotherhood was a more formidable opponent. The Brothers not only had the numbers they also had an attractive ideology that was firmly rooted in Egyptian culture and history. More alarmingly from the Free Officers' perspective, the Brotherhood had a demonstrated capability to raise mobs and use violence to obtain its goals.[77] Even so, the new regime's relations with the Brotherhood were cordial on the surface, and it even exempted the Muslim Brothers from its January 1953 ban on political parties. Nasser and Naguib made a point of attending the annual pilgrimage to Hassan al-Banna's tomb, while the Brothers continued to share intelligence on communists and conspiracies within the military.

However, it did not take long before mutual animosities surfaced. As early as December 1953, senior officials met to discuss intelligence reports that the Brotherhood had infiltrated the army and the police.[78] In January 1954, the Brotherhood publicly criticized the government for holding talks with London over the Canal Zone. When the Naguib–Nasser feud erupted a few months later the Brothers sided with Naguib. The truce was over. The regime's first move was to ban the Brotherhood. This was followed by sequestrations of Brotherhood-run schools and hospitals. The MID and the GID sent officers into mosques to browbeat Brotherhood sympathizers and to spread pro-regime propaganda that extolled the junta's accomplishments.[79] Just as the political police did in the 1940s, Egyptian intelligence asserted that the Muslim Brotherhood was a communist ally and received money from Moscow through the Syrian communist movement.[80] At the same time, the GID and the MID purged Brotherhood sympathizers from the ranks of the police and the military: according to a US estimate, 400 out of 3,000 police officers had been dismissed since the coup for alleged pro-Brotherhood sympathies.[81]

The crescendo to the regime's escalating campaign against the Muslim Brotherhood came on 26 October 1954 after a Brother tried to assassinate Nasser in Alexandria. Nasser escaped unscathed, leading to later allegations that he had either contrived the incident or been tipped off by the CIA in advance.[82] His regime certainly took advantage of the assassination attempt to attack the Brotherhood without respite. Muhi al-Din's security apparatus arrested over 7,000 suspects for sedition and organized mobs to assault and loot the Brothers' headquarters and provincial offices.[83]

Not surprisingly, there were numerous allegations of secret police torture at this time. When US diplomats inquired about the Brothers' interrogations, they were assured by Interior Ministry sources that 'none of the confessions had been extracted by force.'[84] The regime even led correspondents and diplomats on tours of its prisons to show how well the Brotherhood detainees were being treated.[85] Nonetheless, one of the most prominent Western researchers on the Muslim Brotherhood later observed that the 'speedy collapse' of the Brotherhood defendants on trial had been 'due to torture in the prisons.'[86] By the end of November 1954, the Interior Ministry claimed that the Brotherhood was 'broken'; shortly after that it publicly executed several detainees.[87] Still, the government's confidence was premature, for Brotherhood survivors moved their operations deeper underground where cells were rebuilt, new members recruited and new leaders cultivated.[88]

By 1955 it was clear to most observers that Nasser's republic had survived the turbulent storms of its early years thanks to the new *mukhabarat*. An April 1955 US assessment noted that the Egyptian military possessed an 'effective counter-intelligence service' that could infiltrate potential army conspiracies and deter anti-regime agitation in the ranks. The same report noted that the revamped police was 'efficient and capable' in intelligence matters and worked closely with the MID to neutralize the Muslim Brotherhood and the communists.[89] That same month former Prime Minister Ali Maher echoed these conclusions in a conversation with an American contact: 'The RCC [Revolutionary Command Council] is diabolically clever: it is using Soviet intelligence methods, German police and propaganda methods, and British bribery to keep itself in office.'[90]

## Operation Susannah

Egyptian intelligence faced its first big test against a foreign power when Israel tried to subvert Egypt through a small band of young Jews resident in Cairo and Alexandria. Ironically though, given what followed, the Israeli–Palestinian conflict was not an immediate concern of the Free Officers in the early days of their regime.[91] While there was continued anti-Jewish sentiment in Egypt, the terror that had accompanied the 1948 war had largely subsided.[92] Even so, both sides waged intelligence wars against each other. Egypt's MID, for example, sent Bedouin scouts and reconnaissance patrols into Israel to monitor Israeli military deployments and the creation of new settlements. At home, MID took steps to prevent foreigners from acquiring detailed maps, particularly of the Sinai Peninsula, lest they fall into Israeli hands.[93]

Israeli intelligence engaged in similar activities. The Israeli Defense Forces (IDF) Unit 131 conducted espionage and covert action missions in Egypt, and one of these operations involved the creation of sabotage cells in Alexandria and Cairo made of up local Jews.[94] The cells were activated in summer 1954 when it became apparent that Egypt and the United Kingdom were on the verge of negotiating an agreement on the Canal Zone. For the Israelis, British military withdrawal from the Suez Canal would remove a valuable barrier between Egypt and Israel and would likely escalate regional tensions. In response, Israel launched Operation Susannah, a plan to halt the British withdrawal from Egypt by convincing London that Cairo could not ensure internal security or safeguard the Canal. The chosen means to accomplish this were those Unit 131 sabotage teams.[95]

An Israeli operative named Avri El Ad entered Egypt and ordered the sabotage cells to bomb the Alexandria central post office, United States Information Service libraries, movie theaters in Cairo and Alexandria and the Cairo Central Railway Station. But the campaign failed due to a lack of explosives, the inexperience of the young Jewish operatives and bad luck.[96] After their capture, the saboteurs were sent to Egypt's notorious military prison for interrogation and torture by MID officers. One torture method employed on Egyptian dissidents involved the use of a waist-high pool of water where prisoners were forced to stand (and defecate) until they literally collapsed (and sometimes drowned) from exhaustion. The prison was led by an army officer, a 'born sadist,' who flogged prisoners with a Sudanese whip made of rhinoceros hide.[97]

The Susannah trial began on 11 December 1954 with 13 accused of espionage and arson. Among the government witnesses was Lieutenant Colonel Mamduh Salem of the GID's Alexandria Branch.[98] As mentioned earlier, Salem had worked for the Alexandria Special Branch during the 1948 war, where he directed the surveillance and detention of many of the city's Jews. The trial proceedings were heavily publicized in Egypt. Zakaria Muhi al-Din even conducted an interview with the American broadcast organization NBC where he asserted that Cairo had definite proof of the saboteurs' ties to Israeli intelligence. Not only did many of the young Zionists 'confess,' Muhi al-Din observed, the police had also seized wireless equipment used by the Israeli military.[99]

The central role of the Alexandria GID in rolling up the Susannah ring triggered a wave of fear among Alexandria's dwindling Jewish population. When the trial began, the city's Jewish leaders called on the headquarters of the Alexandria GID to proclaim their loyalty to the regime and gain assurances of police protection from mob violence. They said they could not condone what the accused had done, but they hoped a fair trial would determine guilt and innocence.[100]

Verdicts were passed on the defendants in January 1955. Two received death sentences and two were sentenced to life imprisonment. Several received prison terms from seven to 15 years; a few were acquitted.[101] After the sentences were passed, the prisoners were moved to Tura Penitentiary, which one of them later described as a 'huge anthill, with thousands of predatory ants... each one concerned only for itself, always prepared to swoop down on anyone weaker than itself, and cringing in fear and self-abasement before the stronger.'[102]

Operation Susannah had domestic and international implications. In Egypt, it led to new crackdowns on Jews; some 2,000 young men were thrown in jail and sequestrations of Jewish property resumed.[103] Susannah also heightened Nasser's suspicions of Israel and contributed to his growing paranoia of the United States.[104] Tentative peace talks with Israel were put on hold.[105] In Israel, the political aftershocks of the bungled operation led to the resignation of the defense minister and a political scandal that continued to rock the establishment well into the 1960s.

Susannah was also a watershed in Egyptian intelligence. According to one Egyptian official, the sabotage attempts accelerated the expansion of the GID and provided additional impetus for the creation of the Egyptian General Intelligence Service (EGIS).[106] Moreover, Susannah hinted at a growing Egyptian predilection for and expertise in double agent operations. Several Israeli intelligence officials later asserted that the Susannah case officer, Avri El Ad, had been doubled by Egyptians. They point out that Egyptian counterintelligence not only seemed to be on top of the saboteurs from the beginning, it inexplicably failed to apprehend the ringleader, Avri El Ad, who fled the country.[107] Later imprisoned in Israel, Avri El Ad denied working for Egypt's MID, but he did allow that 'there was apparently little that Egyptian intelligence didn't know' about his operation.[108] In any case, the capture of the Susannah ring was a definite success for Egyptian counterintelligence.

Susannah gave Egypt its first real taste of what an adversary's intelligence service could do in the covert action realm. It also marked a transition point when Egyptian intelligence, having overcome domestic opponents, turned to foreign operations with greater interest and capability. The next chapter will examine how Nasser and Zakaria Muhi al-Din created a new intelligence service dedicated to operations abroad.

# 4    General intelligence

At first the Nasser regime pursued a strategy of regime survival in the face of army conspiracies, the communists and the Muslim Brotherhood. But the Free Officers kept an eye on external threats as well and the United Kingdom and Israel were at the top of their list. Cairo regarded the British as the 'main enemy' because of their colonial legacy in Egypt, their presence in the Canal Zone and their occupation of the Sudan.[1] Moreover, Nasser understood that London's dominant role in the Middle East presented a key obstacle to his regional leadership ambitions and his strident brand of Arab nationalism.

Before he could enter the regional stage Nasser had to deal with the British in Egypt or more precisely, the continued British military presence in the Canal Zone. In a bid to pressure London into evacuating from the Canal, Nasser settled on an insurgency organized, trained, armed and led by the MID. Following British withdrawal from the Canal and a separate deal with London over Sudan, Nasser began to flex his muscle in regional affairs. Soon the Egyptian intelligence services were waging subversive operations against British allies in Jordan and Iraq, the French in Algeria and Israel. Egyptian subversion coupled with Cairo's tilt toward non-alignment and Nasser's growing suspicion of CIA activities triggered a significant downturn in Egypt's relations with the West. By 1956 the stage was set for war between Egypt, France, the United Kingdom and Israel.

## Fighting the British

From day one the new *mukhabarat* leadership stressed the British threat. In the MID, for example, it was made clear that the old way of doing business, including the informal passing of sensitive information to British military attachés, would cease immediately.[2] Moreover, the *mukhabarat* doubtless was aware of persistent contacts between British officials in Egypt and disgruntled civilian politicians such as former Prime Minister Ali Maher.[3] Pursuant to a fall 1952 General Staff directive, the MID created a Special Resistance Office whose missions included recruiting, training, arming and leading a guerrilla army against British military units based along the Suez Canal.[4]

But Sudan came first. Egyptian strategists always viewed this country as integral to their national security because of Sudan's upriver access to Egypt's only source of fresh water: the Nile. For these strategists, British control over Sudan meant that London had a lock grip on Egypt's Nile lifeline; dislodging the British from Sudan was a vital Egyptian goal. Cairo believed it took a significant step toward achieving this in February 1953 when it negotiated a deal with London that would give Sudan self-determination and the eventual option to seek either full independence or unity with Egypt.

At first it seemed as if Cairo held most of the cards in Sudan. In addition to historical ties between the two countries, Egypt's new leadership had a popular following among educated northern Sudanese in particular. But over time it became apparent that Cairo's position in Sudan was not as solid as it had seemed, for Sudanese politicians and popular sentiment tended toward independence instead of unification with Egypt. As its position ebbed, Cairo switched to a two track approach where the Egyptian Foreign Ministry endorsed Sudan's right to independence while the *mukhabarat* used covert action to try and keep Sudan in the Egyptian fold.

The MID has long been a key Egyptian player in Sudan given Egypt's long border with Sudan and the close ties between the Egyptian and Sudanese armed forces. Following the July 1952 coup, the MID sent officers to Sudan under cover to recruit spies, build influence, thwart the British and provide arms to pro-Egyptian groups.[5] MID sources offered a window into the thinking of Sudanese military officers on independence; they also gave the MID opportunities to stir up trouble, especially in the south, where the seeds of a civil war were already being laid.[6] One MID spy reportedly obtained sensitive documents on the Anglo-Sudanese negotiating position during high-level talks on sharing Nile waters.[7]

In the end Egypt failed to achieve unity with Sudan. When Khartoum opted for complete independence in 1956, the Egyptians had few alternatives but to accept the fait accompli. One suspects that even the MID, with its intelligence and influence networks, was reluctant to play its covert cards out of fear of Sudanese retaliation. But this was by no means the end of Egyptian clandestine activities in Sudan.

The dispute over the Suez Canal proved more rancorous than Sudan and it was here that Egyptian intelligence used covert action to help force the British to the negotiating table.[8] Nasser himself put it best when he said the insurgency would

> Not be a proper, official war... it will be a commando war, guerilla war... Commando actions will be conducted on such a large scale as to make the British feel they are paying an inordinate price for the occupation of our country.[9]

The MID's Special Resistance Office (SRO) spearheaded the insurgency campaign. Based at MID headquarters in Cairo, the SRO consisted of operations and intelligence departments led by veterans of the 1951 guerrilla campaign against the British in the Canal Zone and frontline offices in Port Said, Isma'ilia, Suez City, and the Canal's east bank.[10] The core of the resistance fighters (or

*Fedayin*) was comprised of elements from the Muslim Brotherhood, Gaza Palestinians, the new National Guard militia, the GID and thieves experienced in stealing weapons and other equipment from the British Canal Zone bases.[11]

In many ways the 1952–1953 MID insurgency campaign in the Canal Zone became the prototype for Egyptian covert action directed against Israel and the Arab states later on. Many intelligence officers who later became prominent in Egyptian subversion such as Mohamed Fa'iq and Kamal Rifa't gained valuable experience in the 1952 campaign. Features of the Canal Zone insurgency included the dissemination of leaflets encouraging British soldiers to desert; infiltrating bases and sabotaging infrastructure; stealing weapons, vehicles and other equipment; sniping at British soldiers; and intimidating and arresting Egyptians who collaborated with the British.[12]

Covert action involved intelligence operations as well. For example, the MID recruited Egyptians employed by the British to obtain maps and other data about British bases, headquarters and arsenals. According to one MID officer, the Egyptians were often pleasantly surprised by the quality of information obtained from the garbage cans of British units. MID counterintelligence engaged in double agent operations by turning spies against their British controllers and feeding them with disinformation. In one case, the MID doubled an Egyptian national who then unraveled several British spy rings operating inside the Egyptian military.[13]

Cairo's strategy of mixing insurgency with a willingness to negotiate over the Canal Zone combined with considerable American pressure on London eventually produced favorable results. With Kermit Roosevelt reportedly mediating behind the scenes, London and Cairo hammered out a deal in October 1954 whereby the British agreed to withdraw their forces from the Canal Zone bases.[14]

## Creation of general intelligence

The Canal Zone deal gave Nasser more flexibility on the international scene. Now that Egypt's 'main enemy' had been pushed out of Egypt, Nasser could devote more attention to the emerging Non-Aligned Movement of African and Asian states. He wrote a book at this time in which he depicted Egypt as a key international player located at the hub of the Arab, Islamic and African worlds.

Nasser stressed in his book that the Arab world still awaited its leader and he left no doubt who this individual would be. In fact, in October 1952, Nasser ordered an infantry officer named Mohamed Fathi al-Dib to organize an Arab Affairs Branch under MID auspices.[15] It was al-Dib and a colleague named 'Izzat Soleiman who put together a plan for liberating the Arabs from both the European colonial powers and conservative regimes like that of the imam of Yemen.[16] The plan's components included a radio station called Voice of the Arabs, which would broadcast Egyptian liberation propaganda to the Arab world; the use of Egyptian educational institutions to promote Cairo's vision of Arab unity; and the recruitment of Arab refugees in Cairo for service in liberating their homelands.[17]

The Arab Affairs Branch was only a half-step toward meeting Nasser's foreign ambitions. Something more was needed: a clandestine service that would not only serve as Egypt's eyes and ears abroad but also facilitate Nasser's Arab liberation agenda through covert action. The current agency undertaking these missions, the MID, had its hands full with army unrest and the Israeli military threat. The only other existing candidate was the Foreign Ministry's Research Department which was created in 1953 to address some of the regime's growing international concerns.[18] But, from the beginning, the Research Department was a small office with an ambitious mandate to provide threat assessments 'bearing on the security of individuals or of the state.'[19] Moreover, the army officers who now ran Egypt did not trust the Foreign Ministry, especially when it came to carrying out sensitive missions. Something else, something new, was needed.

Some suggest that the genesis of the Egyptian General Intelligence Service (EGIS)(*al-Mukhabarat al-'Amma*) date back to late 1952.[20] According to another source, EGIS grew out of the intelligence school that had been established to train new officers and lay the foundations for the Egyptian intelligence community. It was the intelligence school instructors who first proposed the idea of a 'Strategic Intelligence' apparatus to Zakaria Muhi al-Din on 3 December 1953. In March 1954 a Republican decree formally proclaimed the creation of an organization called General Intelligence.[21] Although the intelligence school played a key role in its creation, EGIS was nonetheless the brain child of Gamal 'Abd al-Nasser and Zakaria Muhi al-Din.[22] The latter, in his dual capacities as DMI and interior minister, not only supervised the plans to create EGIS he also served as its first director until he was succeeded by 'Ali Sabri. In many respects, the creation of EGIS was the culminating step in Muhi al-Din's reorganization of Egyptian intelligence.

A future EGIS director named Salah Nasr later observed that prior to EGIS, Egypt had never possessed an organization with the missions of conducting covert action as well as collecting and assessing political and economic intelligence. He admitted that EGIS was deliberately modeled after the CIA in its roles as the supervisor and coordinator of the Egyptian 'intelligence community'; the lead collector of foreign political and economic intelligence; an estimator of political and economic intelligence; and a vital player in counterintelligence. Finally, EGIS was to be the lead agency in planning and executing covert action programs.[23]

Open source intelligence was another important EGIS mission. The Newspapers and Broadcasting Group specialized in the acquisition, translation and analysis of foreign radio broadcasts, newspapers, magazines, and scientific journals. Not surprisingly, many of these documents were published in Israel and acquired through third parties. To accomplish these tasks, the group employed civilians proficient in numerous languages such as Hebrew, English, French, German and Swahili.[24]

It took time before EGIS could undertake all of its missions and it relied heavily on the MID to staff its ranks in the early years.[25] In fact, Salah Nasr asserted that it was not until 1957 – or three years after its creation – that EGIS supplanted the MID in the areas of foreign intelligence collection, analysis and covert action.[26]

## Voice of the Arabs

EGIS played a major role in developing the propaganda arm of Nasser's subversive foreign policy; however, the day-to-day business of radio programming was handled by Egyptian State Broadcasting (ESB), an organization which benefited from CIA-supplied transmitters and anti-communist propaganda.[27] In its early days, ESB could also tap the public relations expertise of the CIA's Cairo station chief, James Eichelberger, and Paul Linebarger, an old OSS expert in 'black propaganda' and author of the 1948 book *Psychological Warfare*.[28]

The Egyptians also turned to former Nazis like Leopold von Mildenstein for advice on improving ESB operations. Joseph Goebbels' propaganda agent for the Middle East during World War II, von Mildenstein was experienced in producing and disseminating anti-Jewish propaganda which the Egyptians valued given their hostility toward Israel.[29] Another Nazi who advised the ESB was the former SS officer and 'expert' on racial issues, Johannes von Leers. Upon arrival in Egypt, von Leers converted to Islam, adopted the name of 'Umar 'Amin von Leers, and became an adviser for the stridently anti-Jewish Voice of the Arabs program.[30]

ESB and Egyptian intelligence worked very closely together. In fact, one could say that the former was an outgrowth of the latter and ultimately subservient to it. As we have seen, it was Zakaria Muhi al-Din, Fathi al-Dib, and 'Izzat Soleiman who first promoted the idea of Voice of the Arabs. Intelligence officers often relied on ESB credentials as cover for their operations overseas. Moreover, ESB correspondents abroad helped the *mukhabarat* monitor Arab popular opinion and recalibrate Egyptian propaganda in response to new regional and international developments.[31] Finally, an EGIS representative sat on the ESB's board of directors.[32]

ESB grew rapidly. In the course of one year – 1953–1954 – it expanded its broadcasts from domestic programs and the Voice of the Arabs to daily broadcasts in eight languages to Africa and Asia.[33] Those broadcasts carried Nasser's message of liberation to the heart of the Middle East and Africa in a highly subversive mix of message and method. For instance, ESB Swahili broadcasts were of particular concern to the British who believed they incited the Mau Mau insurgency in Kenya.[34] As Middle East expert Patrick Seale put it, 'more than any other single factor, Cairo Radio transmissions in Swahili... may be held to account for the early distrust of [Nasser] in London.'[35]

As ESB's influence grew, Washington tried to take advantage of its popularity. For years the US government had tried with limited success to push anti-communist material on Egyptian state media outlets, but it was not until August 1954 that ESB asked the United States Information Service for 'hard hitting anti-Communist scripts for plays, documentaries, [and] editorials' that would be used on local radio and the Voice of the Arabs.[36] By December of that year, ESB was using American material extensively to warn of the threat of international communism.[37] But even as it courted ESB, Washington was starting to have second thoughts about Voice of the Arabs which was not only pouring out anti-British and anti-French vitriol but targeting the Americans as well. At first, the US embassy asked the Egyptian government to tone the message down.[38] When that failed, Washington joined London in setting up rival radio stations to compete with Voice of the Arabs.[39]

In the end, Voice of the Arabs was a cultural-linguistic phenomenon that the United States and others had difficulty comprehending. A 1956 CIA survey fumbled with its explanations for Voice of the Arabs' broad appeal, concluding that the program's 'prolonged effect was a conditioning of Arab attitudes much as is achieved under hypnosis.'[40] Hypnosis or not, Voice of the Arabs was one of the most successful weapons in Egypt's subversive arsenal and, as we shall see, it tended to outshine EGIS-sponsored coups and assassinations in its overall impact.

Voice of the Arabs aside, EGIS was directly responsible for running clandestine ('black') radio stations which attacked neighboring Arab states, Israel and the Western colonial powers. To achieve these ends, EGIS relied on either mobile transmitters that could be deployed by specially adapted vans or more powerful fixed transmitters that broadcast from EGIS headquarters or safe houses in the Cairo area. The Voice of the Arab Nation (*Sawt al-Umma al-Arabiya*) was one EGIS clandestine radio facility that successfully filled the airwaves during the 1956 war when Britain and France had knocked out the overt ESB facilities. Later this clandestine radio station was used to attack the Iraqi regime of 'Abd al-Karim Qassem.[41]

The struggle to oust the British from their Canal Zone bases and Sudan was an early demonstration of Egyptian covert action. After London agreed to evacuate the Canal Zone in 1954, Cairo turned against French North Africa, Israel, Jordan, and Iraq. As with the Canal Zone, covert action was intended to bridge the gap between Nasser's ambitious regional goals and Egypt's limited resources. It was war by affordable means and the *mukhabarat* was very much at the center stage.

## Egyptian intelligence and Algeria

Egyptian meddling in French North Africa preceded the July 1952 coup, but it was under the Free Officer regime that Cairo rapidly expanded its subversive program.[42] Nasser was an early believer in the notion that the liberation of Egypt must be followed by freedom for all Arabs, including those in North Africa.[43] Egyptian strategists also saw France's North African colonies as points of leverage in Egypt's struggle with Israel. They reasoned that if sufficient nationalist pressure was maintained on North Africa, the French might limit their military aid and support for Israel and halt the emigration of Jews from Morocco and Tunisia to Israel.[44]

Zakaria Muhi al-Din exercised overall responsibility for MID operations in North Africa, but most of the work fell on Fathi al-Dib, 'Izzat Soleiman and the

Arab Affairs Branch. Fathi al-Dib played an important role fine-tuning the Voice of the Arabs propaganda assault on France; he also developed contacts with North African exiles in Cairo, including a young Algerian named Ahmed Ben Bella.[45] Fathi al-Dib later recorded that he was much taken with Ben Bella's 'sincerity, his manner of convincing and seducing his interlocutors.'[46] It was Ben Bella who convinced the Egyptians that the seemingly apathetic Algerians were in fact ripe for revolution.[47]

With Ben Bella's help, the MID's Arab Affairs Branch began laying the groundwork for revolution in Algeria. First it helped create the Front de Liberation Nationale (FLN) in October 1954 as an umbrella for the Algerian nationalist groups. This was followed by planning for the FLN's 1 November 1954 revolt in Algeria, the provision of money to buy arms and other supplies and granting the FLN access to Voice of the Arabs.[48]

After the 1 November uprising was launched, Egyptian intelligence faced the problem of sustaining the insurgency with arms and other necessities. Money was not a major problem: MID routinely handled sums from the Saudis and the Arab League for the FLN's use.[49] But buying weapons and getting them into the hands of the Algerian resistance was a more daunting challenge. To overcome this, the MID procured arms from a number of sources, including Egyptian arsenals, Italian and Spanish arms merchants, the Arab League, and illicitly from British soldiers in Libya.[50] Transferring the arms to the FLN was the next hurdle. The best option was funneling them across Libya to FLN camps in Tunisia and Algeria, but this route was subject to the whims of Libyan and Tunisian officials who, although sympathetic to the FLN, were under pressure from the French to stop the arms convoys.[51] Moreover, terrain and sheer distance made it difficult to use the land route to sustain FLN forces in western Algeria. This left the maritime option which was not only free from Libyan and Tunisian interference it also solved the problem of supplying guerrillas in western Algeria. Still, the maritime route required the cooperation of the Spanish and Moroccan authorities since the arms were destined for FLN training camps in Morocco and Spanish Morocco.[52]

The maritime arms supply began once Egyptian naval intelligence had procured vessels that could not be easily traced to Egypt. The first delivery took place in December 1954 and was followed by another to Spanish Morocco in March 1955.[53] Still, neither the land nor the maritime routes could satisfy the FLN's growing demands for arms, and Egyptian intelligence was driven to consider either air drops or deliveries by submarine.[54] But the bottlenecks hampering the arms flow to the FLN were never overcome and this led to criticism by FLN leaders inside Algeria that Cairo was not delivering on its promises of support.

Overall, Egyptian covert action in Algeria was a mixed success. First, the extent to which Cairo in any sense 'controlled' the FLN as a result of its support should not be over-exaggerated. While Egyptian arms, money, safe haven, propaganda and diplomacy bought Cairo some influence with FLN leaders like Ben Bella, that influence never translated to control over operations or the FLN's political goals.[55] Second, as noted, some FLN leaders were perennially unhappy about the MID's inability – or worse, the MID's unwillingness – to provide enough arms to sustain the resistance. Certainly part of this was due to supply problems, but the Algerians also suspected that Egypt kept its distance from the FLN in order to avoid antagonizing the French more than necessary.[56]

Algerian accounts tend to downplay the effectiveness of Egyptian support for the Algerian revolution. Fathi al-Dib's narrative of Nasser's role in supporting the FLN was meant to correct what he saw as a lack of Algerian understanding and appreciation for Egypt's efforts. Thus, al-Dib argues that Egyptian aid to the Algerians was significant; however, given the clandestine nature of the arms deliveries, it was not always apparent to the FLN how much aid Cairo was really providing to the Algerian revolution.[57] On the other hand, French accounts tend to overplay Egypt's role in creating and sustaining the Algerian insurgency.[58] French belief that Egypt was the guiding hand behind the Algerian revolt led to a 1954 decision (the first of many) to assassinate Nasser by means of an agent code-named 'Torpedo.'[59]

## Reconnaissance and guerrilla operations in Israel

Israel was another theater for MID-sponsored subversion, although the initial emphasis was on intelligence collection. The flashpoints of Egyptian–Israeli tensions were the Negev, the al-'Auja demilitarized zone and the Palestinian issue in general, including the status of the refugees in the Egyptian-occupied Gaza Strip. During this period in Gaza, refugees routinely crossed the border into Israel in order to visit family, friends and lost properties. These infiltrations, plus an occasional MID scout, helped generate low grade tensions along the Israeli–Egyptian border from 1949 to 1953.[60] The MID made some effort to inhibit Palestinian infiltration but, as time passed and the refugee problem went unresolved, Palestinian frustration grew and the MID was hard pressed to monitor Gaza let alone clamp down on border infiltrators.

Among the early Palestinian infiltrators was Khalid Wazir (later known by his PLO nom de guerre, Abu Jihad) who organized his first 'commando' team in 1953 at the age of 18 and proceeded to conduct attacks on Israeli settlers and soldiers. The MID finally arrested Wazir; however, he was soon released after a young Palestinian in Cairo named Yasser Arafat appealed to the authorities.[61] As the Wazir story shows, the MID often sought to prevent infiltrations into Israel that were not sanctioned by the MID for its own purposes. MID-sponsored infiltrations in the early 1950s were almost always for intelligence purposes. It used Palestinians, Bedouin and its own scouts to gather information on IDF movements, including potential encroachments on the al-'Auja demilitarized zone or possible raids across the border.[62]

Many MID infiltrations followed a predictable pattern of crossing into Israel, collecting low-grade military intelligence and then exiting into the Jordanian-held West Bank.[63] Later, Egypt's military attaché in Beirut received Lebanese permission to infiltrate Israel from southern Lebanon as well.[64] Key MID players in these missions were Lieutenant Colonel Mustafa Hafez in Gaza and Lieutenant Colonel Salah al-Din Mustafa, Egypt's military attaché in Jordan.[65] One

How intelligence operates when it is weaker.

author described Mustafa Hafez as 'an outstanding soldier – brave, resourceful, and above all a man of high intelligence.'[66] Trained in intelligence by the British, Hafez was assigned to the MID's 'Palestine Intelligence Department' in Gaza in November 1951. He soon built a rapport with the Palestinian population, many of whom he recruited for intelligence missions inside Israel.[67] Since many of his scouts were illiterate, Hafez provided them with pictures of Israeli vehicles and weapons that could be checked off when sighted.[68] Over time, Hafez's infiltrations also included saboteurs who were part of an effort to intimidate and stymie the Israelis from building settlements in the Negev and al-'Auja.[69]

Despite occasional flare ups, the Israel–Egypt border was relatively quiet in 1954, but in early 1955 a new cycle of violence began which was to eventually lead both countries to war.[70] The spark for this new round of hostilities was the death of an Israeli civilian at the hands of Gaza infiltrators in February 1955. This not only forced an Israeli cabinet shakeup and the appointment of David Ben-Gurion as defense minister, it also led directly to Operation Black Arrow, an IDF retaliation raid into Gaza that left 36 Egyptian soldiers and civilians dead and another 30 wounded.[71]

Black Arrow had major consequences for regional security, Egypt–Israel relations and Egyptian intelligence. One historian described the raid as 'a turning point in Israeli–Egyptian relations' where both states 'stopped toying with the possibility of a settlement and plunged headlong down the road to war.'[72] For Egypt, the raid humbled the army and highlighted the Israeli threat. Nasser and his staff now faced dilemmas similar to those during the Canal stand-off with the British: how to retaliate when Egypt's military lacked the means to do so.[73] Acquiring new weapons was one solution, but another was to use insurgents against Israel from bases in Gaza. The guerrilla campaign was intended to help Nasser save face and serve as a deterrent to further Israeli raids while Egypt purchased and absorbed its new weapons. Some optimists in Cairo even believed guerrilla raids would encourage Jewish emigration from Israel by undermining confidence in the Israeli government.[74]

Some accounts assert that Lieutenant Colonel Hafez opened up his Gaza jails and offered Palestinian prisoners their freedom if they joined the guerrillas.[75] He was assisted by an organization called the Arab Nationalist Movement (ANM) which also took part in the recruiting process.[76] Together these elements formed the 141 *Fedayin* Battalion which was trained in MID-run camps by veterans of the guerrilla campaigns against the British.[77] Following their training insurgents were sent across the border in small groups armed with rifles, grenades and explosives for demolition.[78]

Jordan was another player in the insurgency since its extensive border with Israel offered numerous infiltration opportunities. In the summer of 1955, MID's attaché in Amman, Lieutenant Colonel Mustafa, reconnoitered the West Bank for locations to infiltrate guerrillas and store weapons; later he began stockpiling explosives, weapons and propaganda material at his office in Amman.[79] Mustafa's activities were so blatant that the British formally protested to United Nations truce observers with little consequence.[80]

The results of the guerrilla campaign against Israel were mixed. On the one hand, it allowed Nasser to save face with his own people and other Arabs, boosted Egyptian morale and bought Cairo time to purchase weapons from abroad. But in other ways the campaign was a failure. It did not compel Israel to abandon the Negev nor did it demonstrably influence Israeli immigration patterns. It did stiffen the resolve of the Israeli leadership which became convinced that only a shattering military defeat would bring Egypt to its senses. In the end, whereas insurgency tactics succeeded in pushing the British to negotiate on the Canal Zone, they failed in the case of Israel where neither party was much inclined to negotiate their core differences.

## Subverting Iraq and Jordan

Gaza was not the only foreign policy distraction facing Nasser in early 1955. At the same time that Egyptian–Israeli tensions were escalating, Iraq and Turkey forged an alliance viewed by Cairo as a plot to isolate Egypt.[81] Nasser's first response was concluding a defense treaty with Syria and Saudi Arabia. Second, Egypt launched a new Voice of the Arabs radio campaign that was highly critical of the Iraqi government. In April 1955, Iraq retaliated with the clandestine 'Voice of Liberal Egypt' which promised Egyptians that their 'hour of liberation' was near.[82] Iraq then recalled its ambassador to Cairo when Egypt's clandestine Radio Free Iraq called for the overthrow of the Iraqi monarchy.[83] Secretly, Iraq also sought US help in obtaining transmitters to counter Egypt's propaganda assault.[84]

The Egyptian–Iraqi dispute quickly spilled over into Jordan which was under British pressure to join the Turkish–Iraqi Pact. In response, Egypt's intelligence and propaganda apparatus went into high gear with a Voice of the Arabs assault on the Jordanian throne and the pact.[85] In addition, the veteran conspirator Anwar al-Sadat went to Jordan to disseminate subversive pamphlets and money and spur large demonstrations in Amman and other cities.[86] Jordan's King Hussein described the Egyptian propaganda attack in his memoirs: 'Within a matter of hours, Amman was torn by riots as the people, their judgment blurred by propaganda, turned to Nasser, the new mystique of the Arab world. "Hussein is selling out to the British!" screamed Cairo radio.'[87] In the end, Egypt's *mukhabarat* was adept at pouring oil on an anti-Western fire that was already raging within Jordan's political establishment. Under significant domestic pressure, King Hussein not only backed away from the pact he also named a new cabinet opposed to pro-Western regional alliances.

Egyptian intelligence tried imitating its Jordanian success in Iraq; however, Baghdad's January 1956 expulsion of the Egyptian military attaché helped put an end to these efforts. The expulsion underscored several deficiencies in Egypt's covert action program including a lack of Iraqi assets and an over-reliance on military attachés for risky covert action assignments. It would be several years before EGIS officers operating under clandestine covers took control of the covert action mission.

## CIA denouement

It is widely believed that Nasser turned to the Non-Aligned Movement in 1955 in part because of the Gaza raid, the Baghdad Pact and the West's reluctance to sell Egypt arms. But there were other forces turning Nasser from the West including his growing belief that the CIA was intent on overthrowing his government.[88] Nasser's suspicion probably was fueled by his close aides, 'Ali Sabri and Sami Sharaf, who fed him intelligence reports which highlighted the CIA's penetration of the Egyptian army, the police and even Nasser's office.[89]

Nasser raised these concerns in conversations with US Ambassador Henry Byroade during the spring and summer of 1955. But Byroade rebuffed the charges, counseling Nasser against relying on single-source intelligence reports of US malfeasance and asserting that only he, the ambassador, 'was responsible for the United States activities in Egypt.'[90] We do not know what plots Nasser was referring to when he called Byroade to the carpet, although there were rumors at this time of army plotting which the *mukhabarat* may have linked to the CIA.[91] In any case, only weeks after Nasser accused the US labor attaché of espionage, that individual was attacked by an angry mob. The message being sent to Washington was clear.[92]

There were other signs that US intelligence was no longer welcome in Egypt. In August 1955 the GID circulated a memorandum warning civil servants about foreign spies who sought intelligence on Egyptian government and society. It asked bureaucrats to ascertain the motives behind suspicious foreigners and to report all such contacts to the GID within 24 hours. Army officers required permission before attending any events hosted by foreigners.[93]

In a landmark deal that helped reshape the security of the Middle East, Nasser turned to the Soviets in September 1955 for arms. Still, while Egyptian foreign policy was clearly shifting to Moscow there was a sense of 'business as usual' in Cairo's foreign intelligence relationships. For example, in June 1955, an Alexandria GID officer went to the United Kingdom to study the organization and operations of Scotland Yard.[94] A month later, the head of the GID and two senior officers went to London for meetings and training at MI5.[95] In August, yet another GID officer was in the United States for training in investigation techniques.[96] Moreover, Egyptian intelligence continued to procure surveillance equipment from the British and the Americans.[97] It has been said that in the intelligence liaison business there are no enemies or friends only interests. Certainly the West saw no point in declining Egyptian requests for training in intelligence. As one American military attaché put it at the time, training Egyptian officers in the United States provided an 'invaluable source of intelligence.'[98]

By early 1956, Egypt's growing assertiveness on the regional scene combined with its shift towards Moscow was helping forge an unlikely alliance of Britain, France and Israel. As for Egyptian intelligence, its core constituent members – the GID, the MID and EGIS – were now in place. While their missions varied, for many Egyptians, these agencies were synonymous with one dreaded word: *mukhabarat*.

# 5 Egyptian intelligence and the Suez Crisis

With hindsight it seems easy to identify the causes and events that contributed to the 1956 war. Viewed from the broad sweep of history the war was a contest between declining European colonial powers allied with an insecure Israel and an increasingly strident Arab nationalism espoused by Gamal 'Abd al-Nasser. Moving toward specifics, there was Cairo's growing assertiveness on the regional stage, its procurement of East Bloc weapons and Nasser's shift toward non-alignment. For its part, Israel was uneasy about Egyptian military capabilities; it believed it had only a narrow window of opportunity to preempt and arrest Egypt's rise to military parity with or even superiority over Israel. France resented Egyptian covert action in North Africa and its leadership increasingly sensed that Egypt alone was responsible for the Algerian revolt. Finally, the United Kingdom regarded Nasser as a threat to its historic interests in the Middle East including the Suez Canal, the Iraqi and Jordanian monarchies, Aden, colonies in East Africa and protectorates in the Persian Gulf.

The war demonstrated that military victories do not necessarily translate to political success. Although the Israeli army captured the Sinai Peninsula and French and British forces had secured the northern entrance to the Suez Canal, US and Soviet diplomatic intervention forced the allies to relinquish their gains. Because he had survived to witness the retreat of his enemies from Egyptian soil, Nasser's star was to rise even higher in the Arab firmament.

The 1956 Suez war crisis also marked a watershed in the Egyptian intelligence community. While the war found Egypt's intelligence analysis deficient in divining the intentions of its enemies, its counterintelligence enjoyed some success and covert action served as a method of Egyptian retaliation.

## The road to war

Washington had a vital role to play in the brewing crisis since it had close ties with each of the warring parties. Yet, US–Egypt relations were increasingly estranged as a result of Nasser's Soviet arms purchases, his emphasis on non-alignment, his meddling in neighboring states and his suspicion of CIA intentions. American officials were of two minds about Nasser with some warning that the United States should avoid pushing him further into the hands of the

Soviets while others, notably the Dulles brothers at the State Department and the CIA, pressed for Nasser's removal. In fact, the CIA planned to assassinate or oust the Egyptian leader until President Eisenhower at least temporarily ruled out these options in October 1956.[1]

While Washington pondered policy options, US intelligence was definitely interested in the recent Egyptian–Soviet arms deal. On 11 June 1956, a US Navy AJ-2P aircraft departed Athens on a photo-reconnaissance mission against two Soviet-built warships en route to Egypt. But during the flight the plane encountered engine trouble and was forced to land at a base near Alexandria where it was quickly surrounded by *mukhabarat* officers. These security officials resisted all efforts by US diplomats to remove the aircraft's sensitive cameras, code books and other classified material.[2] Moreover, Lieutenant Colonel Mamduh Salem of the Alexandria GID also made it clear that he wanted to question the crew. American officials then escalated the matter to EGIS Director 'Ali Sabri who eventually allowed them to secure their code books and cameras. Sabri's acquiescence aside, this incident only symbolized Egypt's growing estrangement from the United States even at the intelligence level.[3]

On the eve of the Suez crisis, the British and French fretted about Nasser's threat to their colonial possessions in the Middle East and Africa as well as Cairo's warming relations with Moscow. But it was the Israeli leadership that regarded Egypt as an existential threat given Nasser's increasing popularity in the Arab world, his growing arsenal of Soviet-made tanks and his acquisition of bombers that could reach Israeli cities.[4] Then there were the *fedayin* raids which Israeli intelligence had traced to Lieutenant Colonel Hafez in Gaza and Lieutenant Colonel Mustafa in Amman.[5] Israel responded to the *fedayin* by improving internal security and asking the United States to pressure Nasser into halting his guerrilla campaign.[6] When diplomacy failed Israeli intelligence assassinated Hafez and Mustafa with package bombs in July 1956.[7]

There were other factors propelling Cairo, London, Paris and Tel Aviv toward war. When Egypt recognized the People's Republic of China in May 1956, Washington and London withdrew financial support for the Aswan High Dam. Nasser's riposte was to nationalize the Anglo-French Suez Canal Company on 26 July 1956. Although the dispute over the dam provided the trigger, Nasser had been contemplating nationalizing the canal for some time. In the summer of 1955, EGIS director 'Ali Sabri created a secret Suez Canal Office which directed the MID to spy on the Suez Canal Company's financial position while the Foreign Ministry's Research Bureau examined the Company's international links.[8]

Nasser used this information to try and anticipate British, French and Israeli reactions to nationalization. As far as we know, Egypt's Committee of Intelligence Estimates was not asked to assess the British and French courses of action: instead the role of the MID and EGIS was to produce raw intelligence upon which Nasser drew his conclusions.[9] Nasser predicted London would offer the strongest response since it had the most to lose from nationalization. In Nasser's view, the key to handling the British was time: the longer London took to muster a military response the less likely it would use force because of international pressure. Nasser dismissed the possibility of an Anglo-French alliance, believing Paris was too preoccupied in Algeria to handle a canal crisis.[10] The Israeli reaction was the only part of Nasser's paper that was farmed out to the Committee of Intelligence Estimates, and it predicted that Israel would not respond with force.[11]

Since Nasser counted on time to hinder a British military response, he needed to know how long it might take London to put together an invasion fleet and that depended on what British forces were available in theater. The MID dispatched officers to Malta and Cyprus to determine what British forces were available on those islands; it also activated spies to report on British bases in Libya and Aden.[12] It was these sources who confirmed Nasser's assessment that Britain's military response would be delayed because of a lack of forces in the area.

Yet once the canal was nationalized, Nasser's estimates began to fall apart. In fact, his nationalization did something which neither he nor his analysts predicted: it drove his three greatest enemies together. In a secret meeting of French, British and Israeli officials, it was agreed that Israel would invade Sinai first. When Israeli forces neared the canal, Britain and France would issue an ultimatum ordering both Egypt and Israel to withdraw from the canal area to ensure the waterway's protection. Israel would oblige in yielding a few miles of Egyptian territory, but Egypt likely would not, thereby giving the allies the pretext to reoccupy the canal.

But as Nasser had accurately forecasted, the British needed time before the military option could be exercised. This allowed the MID to counter an invasion through the tested strategy of insurgency. On 27 July 1956, one day after Nasser ordered the nationalization of the canal, MID officer 'Abd al-Fattah Abu al-Fadl was ordered to rebuild the insurgent organization that had been used against the British in the Canal Zone two years earlier. Working under the supervision of Zakaria Muhi al-Din, Abu al-Fadl and MID stations in the Canal area recruited guerrillas, established a command and control system and created secret depots for arms and transmitters that would be used in the event of a ground assault.[13]

While the parties prepared for war, Egyptian intelligence continued to supply the Algerian resistance by land and sea; however the FLN had decided at this point to purchase their own ship called the *Athos* in order to increase the amount of arms delivered to western Algeria. While the *mukhabarat* was wary of the *Athos* deal, believing that French intelligence was aware of and monitoring the transaction, the Egyptians nonetheless let the *Athos* sail from Alexandria on 4 October.[14] The ship departed with a lot of eyes on it, including French intelligence stations in Cairo and Beirut, a French SIGINT site in Algeria and Israeli military intelligence.[15] On 16 October, the French Navy intercepted the *Athos* near Oran and seized the ship's cargo of weapons and radio technicians as well as divers trained by the Egyptians to plant sea mines at the French naval base at Mers el-Kebir.[16]

The *Athos* seizure only hardened Paris's resolve to teach Nasser a lesson. Could there have been more tangible proof of Egyptian direction of the Algerian uprising than the *Athos*?[17] For the Egyptians, the *Athos* affair was a minor embarrassment that highlighted the dangers involved in shipping arms to western Algeria. Yet only days after the *Athos* affair, Cairo received another setback when its favored FLN contact, Ahmed Ben Bella, was captured by the French. For a while, Egyptian intelligence contemplated abducting prominent French nationals in Morocco in order to exchange them for Ben Bella. Another plan involved recruiting German mercenaries to free Ben Bella from his French prison, but none of these ventures came to pass.[18]

## Intelligence collection and analysis

On the eve of war Egypt's intelligence collection and analytical priorities included French and British intentions, plans and military capabilities followed by those of the Israelis. But setting priorities was the easy part: actually obtaining the information that Egyptian decision makers required was a more daunting assignment.

Military attachés were Egypt's most important intelligence collectors during the crisis. Attachés in Turkey and France had been reporting on French weapons flowing to Israel and the military buildup on Cyprus, and their data helped the MID assess Israel's order of battle. Unfortunately for the Egyptians, these reports did not alter the MID's low regard for Israel's military capabilities.[19] Tharwat 'Ukasha, the attaché in Paris, ran several sources who reported on French preparations for war with Egypt.[20] Among these was an activist in Egypt's communist movement named Henri Curiel who provided intelligence from French communists opposed to their country's foreign wars.[21] But 'Ukasha's greatest coup may have been a walk-in who in October 1956 provided details on the Anglo-French war plan and the role Israel was to play in it. 'Ukasha sent this crucial information to Cairo by courier, but Nasser dismissed this information as 'impossible': Britain and France would not 'degrade' themselves by an alliance with Israel.[22]

On the eve of war, the MID sent Bedouin scouts into Israel to spy on IDF movements but two were killed and the remainder captured on 14 October near Sde Boker.[23] The problem with these scouts was that their hazardous missions rarely produced more than fragmentary information on Israeli military dispositions. Egypt lacked a deep penetration spy who could report on the intentions of the Israeli leadership. Instead, it had to rely on the Israeli press[24] and assets like Joachim al-Antoni, a Coptic priest who was recruited by EGIS to obtain maps, magazines and Israeli government publications from his home in Jaffa. Unfortunately for Cairo, al-Antoni was arrested on 14 November 1956 at the Mandelbaum Gate in Jerusalem. In his possession was a paper describing the location of Egyptian POWs captured during the recent Sinai campaign as well as the names of his Egyptian controllers in Beirut and Amman.[25]

Despite the growing tension in bilateral relations, the CIA and the State Department passed valuable intelligence to the Egyptians through several channels, including Cairo's ambassador to Washington,[26] the Amin brothers[27] and Cairo Station Chief James Eichelberger. It was Eichelberger who allegedly informed Nasser that the SIS intended 'to do a Mossadeq' on Egypt – that is, remove Nasser either by assassination or an army coup.[28] The CIA also warned Nasser that, given the apparent mental instability of British Prime Minister Anthony Eden, London's behavior was becoming unpredictable even for CIA analysts.[29] The CIA did not pass intelligence to Egypt out of altruism. There were some in Langley who still believed Nasser was the best alternative to communism and that an Egyptian defeat would only pave the way for Moscow's dominance of the Middle East. Moreover, Mustafa Amin later claimed the CIA wanted one of Egypt's new Soviet-made MiGs in return for the information it provided.[30]

In addition to the United States, Egypt had access to intelligence from other parties. India reportedly provided Egypt with information gleaned by its diplomats through contacts with British Labour Party politicians.[31] Egypt also had a routine intelligence exchange with Syria which allowed Syrian intelligence to pass reports on Israel as well as British and French military movements on Cyprus.[32] Even the Jordanians, no friends of Nasser, transmitted warnings to the Egyptians of Israeli assassination plots against the Egyptian president and other officials.[33] Although it was not a classic state-to-state intelligence exchange, Egypt provided the Cypriot resistance group EOKA (Ethniki Organosis Kyprion Agoniston) with arms and cash in return for intelligence on British military preparations on Cyprus.[34] In the end, though, as Nasser was to ruefully note after the crisis, EOKA could not provide him with intelligence on British thinking before the invasion.[35]

With varying degrees of effectiveness HUMINT and foreign liaison partners provided Egypt with its best intelligence on the capabilities and, to a lesser extent, the intentions of its enemies during the Suez crisis. Unfortunately, little is known about Egypt's signals intelligence collection other than a limited capability to monitor Israel's un-enciphered military communications.[36] Egyptian air force Vampire photo-reconnaissance aircraft lacked the range to reach Malta and Cyprus, although they did fly missions over southern Israel as late as 26 October 1956 – three days before the Israeli attack. Apparently these aircraft did not pick up any indications of Israeli preparations for war.[37]

Egyptian intelligence dangerously miscalculated the intent and capabilities of its adversaries. It was Nasser rather than his intelligence officers who tried to predict how London and Paris would react to Canal nationalization. Moreover, he dismissed at least one report that contradicted his assessment. But the biggest flaw in Egyptian assessments was underestimating Israeli intentions and military capabilities. The Egyptians erroneously believed that Israel would avoid war because of Egypt's new Soviet weapons and given the IDF's hitherto limited response to *fedayin* attacks. In pre-hostilities assessments, the *mukhabarat* predicted that even if the IDF conducted a retaliation raid it lacked the ability to go beyond Gaza.[38] The Egyptians also downplayed Israel's air power advantages.[39] In April 1956, the Egyptian air force commander assured a US official that his airfields were invulnerable to attack.[40] In the end, the Egyptians were lulled by a perception that Israel was 'trying to project a picture of itself greater than the reality.'[41]

When known Egyptian assessments before and during the crisis are scrutinized, much of what passed for analysis seemed based on cultural biases (especially toward Israel), overreliance on adversarial behavior patterns, 'guess-timates' and insufficient hard facts. Yet, paradoxically, even though Egypt went into the 1956 war largely blind and deaf to the intentions and capabilities of its adversaries, it emerged from the crisis with a resounding political victory that greatly enhanced Nasser's prestige in the Arab world.

## Counterintelligence

On 26 August 1956, the GID rolled up a British spy network led by an expatriate named James Swinburn. Keys to the GID success were informants who had been carefully monitoring Swinburn's contacts with several Egyptian officials, including a clerk in the GID archives and the former Yugoslav intelligence officer, Milovan Grigorevitch.[42] The *mukhabarat* also successfully created and controlled a 'dissident' group ostensibly led by the head of Egyptian Air Force intelligence which managed not only to secure SIS backing but attract some legitimate dissident Egyptian civilian politicians and former royal family members as well. On the other hand, Egyptian intelligence apparently did not detect another SIS anti-Nasser conspiracy comprised of dissident military officers and former politicians until after the Suez war.[43] In the end, British intelligence never identified a suitable candidate to take Nasser's place.

Ironically, the GID's capture of the Swinburn ring backfired because it forced the British to rely more on SIGINT to address their intelligence shortfalls.[44] And it was in the area of communications security, that is, the ability to safeguard its radio and telephone communications that Egypt encountered some of its biggest problems. Britain's Government Communications Headquarters (GCHQ) and America's National Security Agency (NSA) had broken Egypt's diplomatic cipher before the 1956 war; GCHQ routinely intercepted Egyptian military communications passed by radio and landlines.[45]

Furthermore, Egyptian counterintelligence never discovered the Mossad's pre-war deception plan which involved the use of double agents, diplomats, military attachés and media 'leaks' to convince Cairo that Israel's next attack was aimed at Jordan.[46] Later, as Israel's preparations for war with Egypt became more apparent Israeli intelligence tried to divert Egyptian attention away from the planned assault axis in central Sinai by stirring up trouble in Gaza.[47]

## War and covert action

Nasser learned about Israel's 29 October 1956 invasion of Sinai from MID SIGINT monitoring of Israeli military communications.[48] Further confirmation was provided by Vampire photo-reconnaissance jets.[49] Given what he believed, and what his intelligence people had told him about Israeli intentions, Nasser initially assumed that this was a limited raid, although doubts set in as the hours passed and the Israeli advance continued.[50] Then London and Paris issued their 'ultimatum' which Heikal recorded was 'received with astonishment bordering on disbelief.' Not only did it defy Cairo's predictions of British behavior, Nasser even asked whether the British prime minister had gone mad.[51] Acting on intelligence assessments that the ultimatum was a ruse to get Egypt to withdraw its forces from Sinai, Nasser ordered reinforcements to the peninsula.[52] When Anglo-French forces landed at Port Said on 5 and 6 November, the Egyptians were again taken by surprise since they had assumed the target would be Alexandria.[53]

Nasser understood the limitations of his armed forces, and he always intended to fall back on an insurgency strategy should the European powers invade Egypt.[54] Therefore, once the British and French assault was underway Nasser ordered MID to implement its insurgency plan. Zakaria Muhi al-Din managed the insurgency from MID headquarters in Cairo, but the details were left to local MID officers 'Abd al-Fattah Abu al-Fadl, Kamal Rif'at and Mohamed Fa'iq.[55] While Abu al-Fadl organized the insurgency from the MID base in Isma'ilia, Rif'at directed the guerrilla campaign against the invaders in Port Said and planned to cut off the Anglo-French lines of communication once the invaders had moved into the interior. Among Rif'at's operations was the use of loud-speaker vans which roamed the streets of Port Said, urging inhabitants to resist and assuring them that Soviet military assistance was on its way.[56]

Egyptian intelligence also responded with covert action in Syria, Libya and Lebanon. In pre-war planning, the head of Syria's premier intelligence agency (the Deuxieme Bureau), 'Abd al-Hamid Sarraj, had promised to blow up a vital oil pipeline which originated in Iraq and crossed Syria before terminating in Lebanon. Although Cairo instructed Sarraj to cancel this operation because of American protests, the Syrians blew up portions of the pipeline anyway. In Libya, the Egyptian military attaché handed out guns and money to a 'Front for the Struggle of the Libyan People' and sponsored attacks on oil pipelines. The goal here was to reinforce King Idris's earlier rejection of British requests to invade Egypt from Libyan soil. The attaché was expelled, but a worried Idris sought British military protection in Tobruk just the same.[57] In Lebanon, Egyptian agents bombed oil pipelines and prominent British targets, including the Middle East Centre for Arab Studies and the St George Club. The Lebanon effort came to an end when the Lebanese Surete found explosives and incriminating maps in the car of an Egyptian diplomat.[58]

Covert action was marginally effective as an instrument of Egyptian retaliation during the crisis. On the other hand, there are numerous indications that Cairo's pre-war subversion against its neighbors helped spur the British government (and others) to take military action against Nasser. As Foreign Secretary Selwyn Lloyd noted in October 1956 – before the tripartite attack on Egypt:

> We knew the Egyptians were planning a coup in Libya; they had arms ready there for use and there was a plot to kill the King. King Saud was also threatened. In Iraq Nuri was now in control but there was a dissatisfaction amongst some of the younger officers and this was likely to grow if we continued to do nothing. Jordan was already penetrated and Syria was virtually under Egyptian control.[59]

## Anti-Nasser conspiracies

In the end, a British currency crisis, oil shortages, lack of British popular support, American pressure and Soviet threats combined to force the British and French into accepting a UN ceasefire. Several months later, Israel was compelled by the United States to evacuate Sinai. It was a lucky break for Nasser for, although his forces had been heavily damaged, Suez had nonetheless shifted the regional balance of power in Egypt's favor. While Paris dug in its heels in Algeria and London retained influence in Iraq and the Persian Gulf, a security vacuum had been created in the region which the United States, the USSR and Nasser's Egypt were eager to fill.

On 5 January 1957 President Eisenhower declared that Washington would protect the Middle East from 'international communism' by providing regional states with arms and other assistance. A not so subtle undertone of this 'Eisenhower Doctrine' was that the United States would also block an expansionist Egypt. On 22 March Eisenhower revisited plans to overthrow Nasser in a meeting with Director of Central Intelligence Allen Dulles.[60] Probably as a result of this meeting several plans were put into motion including sending Kermit Roosevelt to discuss a coup with Britain's SIS, exploiting rumored anti-regime unrest in the Egyptian army and examining whether Nasser could be ousted by diverting Nile waters from Egypt.[61]

It did not take long for these CIA plots to reach Nasser. Already critical of the Eisenhower Doctrine, the Egyptian leader ordered the suspension of all contacts between his government and the CIA.[62] On 28 May 1957 Nasser summoned US Ambassador Raymond Hare and confronted him with allegations of American 'conspiracies' toward Egypt. Brushing aside Hare's assertion that American policy was 'straight and above board,' Nasser questioned the extent of US 'hostility' toward his country.'[63] When Secretary of State Dulles ordered his ambassador to inform Nasser that the conspiracy allegations were 'so preposterous that [Washington] does not believe they warrant comment,' Nasser replied that US–Egypt relations were 'in [a] vicious circle.' Cautioning the United States against formulating policies based on questionable intelligence sources, Nasser added that Washington's effort to build up Saudi Arabia as the new Arab leader at Egypt's expense would fail.[64]

In December 1957 Nasser announced that his intelligence services had uncovered a British conspiracy to restore the Egyptian monarchy. This was a complicated case involving SIS contacts with Egyptian exiles and an Egyptian air force intelligence officer named Issam al-Din Khalil before the Suez war. For months, Khalil had taken money from both the British and the Saudis to prepare the plot; however, as Nasser revealed, Khalil had been working for the Egyptian government all along. This was a masterful double agent scheme on the part of Egyptian counterintelligence and an echo of some of the émigré operations run by Soviet intelligence in the 1920s and 1930s.[65]

The suspicion that permeated Nasser's government after Suez began seeping into Egyptian society as well. In December 1956, Alexandria officials quietly confided to US diplomats that MID and the Interior Ministry were the 'real authority' in the city.[66] Other observers noted a spy mania sweeping over some cities, especially Port Said where the GID conducted early morning raids on those British, French and Jewish residents targeted for deportation.[67] In May 1957 the Egyptian government issued amendments to its penal code that now defined secrets as:

> Military, political, diplomatic, economic and industrial information which... should in the interest of the defense of the country remain secret... documents, drawings, maps, plans, photographs... which should in the interest of the defense of the country remain unknown... all matters connected with military affairs.[68]

These amendments spelled out harsh penalties, including prison terms for communicating with foreign powers in a manner 'detrimental to Egypt's military, political, diplomatic and economic position' and death sentences for attempting to disrupt the morale and loyalty of the armed forces. Still other penalties covered unauthorized over-flights of military facilities.[69]

## The rise of Salah Nasr

Coinciding with the rise of the Egyptian police state was Salah Nasr's appointment as EGIS Director. Indeed, for many Egyptians, Nasr is synonymous with the *mukhabarat* excesses of the Nasser era, and he was later immortalized as the corrupt spy boss in Naguib Mahfouz's novel (and film) *Karnak*. A 1939 Military Academy graduate, Nasr was recruited to the Free Officers by 'Abd al-Hakim 'Amr in 1949 and served as 'Amr's Executive Officer from 1953 until his appointment as EGIS deputy director in October 1956.[70]

On the eve of the Suez war EGIS was in urgent need of direction. 'Ali Sabri was its nominal director although Zakaria Muhi al-Din was also very influential in the intelligence community.[71] But Sabri and Muhi al-Din were heavily involved in crisis assignments that drew them away from the day-to-day management of Egyptian intelligence, leaving EGIS without effective leadership at a key juncture in its history.[72] Indeed, President Nasser told Salah Nasr that EGIS was in need of 'reviving.'[73] Salah Nasr wrote that he balked at taking over as EGIS deputy director. He told President Nasser that he lacked experience in intelligence, had concerns about working for Sabri and Muhi al-Din and hesitated to work for an agency that spied on Egyptians. But President Nasser insisted, adding that he would promote Salah Nasr to the EGIS director slot when 'Ali Sabri was appointed prime minister. Nasser also promised that the EGIS director would have direct access to the presidency.[74]

Because of Suez, Salah Nasr did not assume his new position until early 1957; a few months later on 31 May he replaced 'Ali Sabri as EGIS's third director. With his appointment the stage was set for the dramatic expansion in EGIS's capabilities that occurred in the late 1950s and early 1960s.[75] But it was a slow start at first. In his memoirs, Nasr admits that he knew very little about intelligence at first so he studied the American, Soviet, French and Italian services from books in the EGIS library. Following this review, Nasr decided to shape EGIS around the model that appealed to him the most: the CIA. He admired the US intelligence community for the way it parceled out intelligence and security responsibilities among the CIA, the FBI and the military.[76] He also appreciated the fact that the CIA was the principal intelligence and covert action instrument of the US president.

Salah Nasr's intelligence studies at this time paid dividends for him down the road. Both during and after his ten-year EGIS tenure he was a prolific author of books on intelligence and psychological warfare.[77] Many years later, Nasr argued that intelligence services were vital for any country since 'governments these days live in a world resembling a jungle full of beasts [where] the law of the jungle governs international relations: live to eat or be eaten.'[78] In his books, Nasr discussed intelligence analysis which he likened to an 'academy' that collects, classifies and analyzes information; a 'publishing house' that sends out correspondents to gather news that is sent back to editors for processing; and a 'corporation' which is involved in planning, setting deadlines and establishing goals. Nasr maintained that the key to successful analysis was a range of intelligence products – some long, others short – that appealed to the different tastes of decision-makers.[79]

Nasr also analyzed psychological (or information) warfare which he wrote was the field 'affecting the psychology of the enemy and shattering his morale.'[80] Nasr divided psychological warfare into two areas: 'the Battle of the Word' and the 'Battle of the Creed.' For him, the Battle of the Word was fundamental 'whether it is whispered or uttered aloud, whether it is verbal or written' because it is a 'weapon' aimed at 'the heart and mind of man.' Nasr viewed the Battle of the Creed as equally important and no less insidious, for it encompassed foreign efforts to impose religious beliefs, cultural mores and social values on people with the goal of changing their beliefs and making them more malleable to a foreign will.[81]

It took time before Salah Nasr fleshed out his ideas on intelligence and covert action. In fact, during his early years as EGIS Director, he faced several major challenges. The first of these was hiring and training experienced personnel for EGIS's foreign operations. One solution was to send small EGIS teams abroad for training, although Nasr recognized that some of his men might be recruited by foreign services to spy on Egypt.[82] The second challenge was limiting the influence of Nasser, Muhi al-Din, 'Ali Sabri, Sami Sharaf and armed forces chief 'Abd al-Hakim 'Amr in EGIS operations. This required delicate diplomacy and a willingness to be flexible.[83] The third obstacle was acquiring the intelligence technology necessary to win what Nasr later called 'the battle of technology.'[84] Indeed, Nasr and others in the regime were devoted to surveillance technologies of all types: bugs, telephone monitoring instruments and miniature cameras.[85] According to Nasr, EGIS acquired most of this technology on the black market, although he confessed that the CIA and KGB were vital sources of surveillance gear as well.[86]

Salah Nasr's promotion as EGIS director reflected a new Egyptian emphasis on exporting its revolution. Having survived the worst that the British, the French and the Israelis could throw at him, President Nasser was confident he could now step up his efforts to subvert his neighbors and increase his own power. EGIS and its sister agency, the MID, were to play prominent roles in Nasser's 'subversion phase' that extended from 1957 to 1960.

# 6   Unity, subversion and secession

The period following the 1956 war witnessed Gamal 'Abd al-Nasser at the height of his power and confidence. Humbled by its retreat from Suez, Britain was declining as regional hegemon, leaving its allies in Iraq, Jordan and elsewhere vulnerable to revolution and Egyptian subversion. Meanwhile France was increasingly mired in the Algerian morass which threatened its status as the preeminent player in North Africa.

Nasser's Egypt saw an opportunity in the decline of the European powers to assert its own regional leadership. Syria was one of the first fruits to fall in Cairo's lap when it signed a union agreement with Egypt in February 1958. For the first time in over a century Egypt had become a key player in the geopolitics of the *mashreq*, a strategic area that encompassed Lebanon, Syria, Iraq, Jordan and Israel. Another sign of Nasser's ascendancy was increased Egyptian subversion against the conservative Arab states and the British protectorates; however, Cairo's attempts at overthrowing leaderships in Iraq, Jordan, Lebanon and Saudi Arabia were checked by a powerful new player on the regional scene: the United States.

Egypt's regional ascendancy was to be short-lived. By the early 1960s, Nasser's dreams of a pan-Arab union under Egyptian control were crushed first by the isolation his regional subversion engendered and second by the secession of Syria from the union in 1961. Although Cairo retained considerable influence in the Arab world and a strong capacity for clandestine warfare it never again reached the heights of power it enjoyed in the four years following Suez.

## Pathological suspicion

Although Salah Nasr and Zakaria Muhi al-Din were important figures in the development of Egyptian intelligence, it was Gamal 'Abd al-Nasser who created the *mukhabarat* state. Nasser's character was innately conspiratorial and virtually everybody who knew him noted that suspicion defined his personality. UN Secretary General Dag Hammarskjold believed Nasser was 'pathologically suspicious'[1] while Nasser himself once confided to a British diplomat 'that he had been a conspirator for so long that he thought like one and was suspicious of everyone.'[2] And Nasser's suspicions only grew with time. He used the latest bugs and cameras to monitor his colleagues, and all meetings with the president were captured on hidden microphones and cameras. The data culled by these methods, however trivial, was kept in files maintained by 'Ali Sabri and, later, Sami Sharaf.[3]

Allied with Nasser's dominating suspicion was a 'passion for information'[4]. Not only was he a prodigious newspaper reader – he devoted 3–4 hours a day to this alone[5] – the *ra'is* – or 'boss' – also employed a special service that summarized and translated numerous books of interest.[6] As might be expected, the president was an avid consumer of intelligence. One of Nasser's colleagues later revealed that before meeting important guests, the president would ask his intelligence agencies for information on their backgrounds, personalities and political views.[7]

Information reached Nasser through several channels. At first 'Ali Sabri chaired a committee that collated information from the ministries and EGIS in a daily presidential update.[8] Over time this committee produced four morning reports for Nasser: a summary of cables from Egyptian ambassadors; an Interior Ministry update; intelligence reports on army security and counterintelligence; and a financial and economic file.[9]

In many autocratic systems, the gatekeepers to the boss often become important power centers in their own right. This was certainly the case in Nasser's Egypt where first 'Ali Sabri and then Sami Sharaf became powerful, shadowy figures who filtered the president's information and consequently shaped his thinking on key issues. It was Sharaf who was destined to play Iago to the president's paranoid Othello, and the portraits painted of this intriguer are not pretty. One writer described him as a man with 'stooped, round shoulders, bulging stomach, bald head, dark, moony eyes, and drooping moustache [who] looked like a sad pear.'[10] A US ambassador recalled that Sharaf was a 'dirty tricks operator' with a 'serpentine personality.'[11]

By 1959, as Nasser's office chief, Sharaf has expanded his portfolio to include important intelligence matters. Moreover, given his influence over the *ra'is*, Sharaf was a target for foreign intelligence services and the KGB in particular. Indeed, one KGB defector later claimed that Sharaf had been recruited by the KGB in the late 1950s under the unlikely code name 'Asad' ('Lion').[12]

## Egyptian–Soviet intelligence liaison ties

Before examining whether Sharaf was in fact a Soviet agent, it is worth briefly reviewing the broader trends in Egyptian–Soviet relations before and after Suez. Nikita Khrushchev once said that he regarded Egypt's 23 July 1952 revolution as 'just another one of those military take-overs which we had become accustomed to in South America.'[13] In fact, the KGB assumed the CIA was behind Nasser, and the Egyptian regime's crackdowns on communists only reinforced these suspicions.[14] Soviet policies changed once Nasser had drifted toward nonalignment and procured arms from the Eastern Bloc. When the KGB warned Egyptian intelligence of a British plot to assassinate Nasser, the Egyptians responded by requesting KGB assistance in improving presidential security. Moscow responded by sending two officers from the KGB's Ninth Directorate to Cairo where they inspected Nasser's security, identified weaknesses and recommended corrections.[15]

According to Salah Nasr, it was not until Nasser's 1958 trip to the USSR that the Egyptian–Soviet intelligence partnership was firmly established. It was during this trip that Nasr met KGB chief Ivan Serov and concluded an agreement that included intelligence sharing and the KGB's provision of surveillance equipment.[16] Salah Nasr also established a rapport with the KGB's Egypt expert, Vadim Vasilyevich Kirpichenko, a man who reportedly succeeded in recruiting Sami Sharaf as a KGB asset in 1957.[17] It cannot be definitively proved that Sharaf was controlled by the KGB, but he did play an important role in sustaining the relationship between the *mukhabarat* and Soviet intelligence. For example, in 1959 he proposed expanding the EGIS–KGB partnership to include joint operations and training Egyptians in interrogation and counterintelligence.[18]

The KGB found its liaison relationship with the Egyptian services to be a rich source of new agents. As one Cairo *Rezident* counseled a young KGB officer named Lev Alexeyevich Bausin in 1960, Cairo was like a 'big, murky pond. You'll find everyone's trying to fish here.'[19] Bausin's memoirs later recorded some of the challenges of spying in Cairo, including the persistent GID informers who shadowed him. Despite this, Bausin says he recruited one source in the GID who passed intelligence on all known US diplomats and intelligence officers in Cairo at that time.[20]

## Union with Syria

Nasser's victory at Suez was followed by an unprecedented covert action program aimed at bringing the Arab world into the Egyptian fold. One of Egypt's first successes was the February 1958 union with Syria which created Egyptian and Syrian provinces under a United Arab Republic (UAR). The creation of the UAR cemented an already extensive intelligence relationship between Egypt and Syria that included routine intelligence exchanges and joint operations aimed at Jordan and Lebanon. For a while Cairo's most important Syrian ally was 'Abd al-Hamid Sarraj, chief of one of the Syrian intelligence agencies called the Deuxieme Bureau. Sarraj had built up a sinister reputation in the turbulent world of Syrian politics; according to one journalist, he was 'a sallow, taciturn young man with cold eyes and humourless expression... "not an ant moves but Sarraj knows it, the people said." '[21] In short, Sarraj was the perfect Syrian counterpart to the likes of 'Ali Sabri, Sami Sharaf and Salah Nasr.

From its inception, the UAR was a lopsided arrangement that distinctly favored the much larger Egyptian province. Although Nasser had urged the amalgamation of the Syrian and Egyptian intelligence services into one federal entity, this was never really carried out.[22] Instead, Egyptian intelligence officers dominated key management positions in both Cairo and Damascus as well as the station chief assignments abroad.[23] Still, the Syrians were adept at isolating and ultimately marginalizing their Egyptian intelligence managers. According to Salah Nasr, 'Abd al-Hamid Sarraj used his authority as Syrian Province interior minister to limit any Egyptian intelligence inroads in Syria.[24] Evidently, the UAR's intelligence 'partnership' had defined, national limits.

## Unprecedented subversion

The creation of the UAR also upset the regional balance of power. For the first time in nearly a century, Egypt was back in the heart of the Arab east, the *Mashreq,* as a dominant player. One consequence of this was that old alliances were reshuffled so that the Egypt–Syria axis now faced a loosely affiliated league composed of Hashemite Jordan and Iraq as well as Saudi Arabia. The covert battlegrounds of these dueling conglomerates in the so-called 'Arab Cold War' were the relatively weak states of Jordan and Lebanon.

For Nasser, the UAR was a symbol of his rising prestige, power and influence. One diplomat nicely framed this heady moment in Egypt's modern history:

> [Nasser] had become the hero and the architect of Western humiliation and defeat, whose very name struck a magic chord in the heart of every Arab nationalist and whose photograph was to be found in souks, cafes, taxis and shops from the Atlantic to the Indian Ocean. More than ever before, Cairo was now the centre of the Arab world, the fountain-head of the new nationalism.[25]

Nasser had the Arab world seemingly at his feet, but he still faced an old dilemma: how could he reach for regional hegemony when he lacked the military and financial resources to do so? One answer was subversion. The *ra'is* laid out his subversive approach in a secret speech to an Egyptian military audience that was later leaked to an Iraqi newspaper. In his talk, Nasser emphasized the need to match Voice of the Arabs rhetoric with deeds – deeds that could not always be military in nature. He advised that Egyptian officers would have to learn 'the arts of guerrilla warfare and commando operations' in addition to their conventional military studies. Insurgency was only one facet of what Nasser called 'a crooked way for action': radio propaganda was another. According to the *ra'is*, the Voice of the Arabs was 'a weapon in our hands equal in importance to guns and fighter planes.'[26]

This speech offered insights into Egypt's covert action strategy. As we examine case studies of Egyptian covert action, some methods and patterns become readily apparent. In progressive order that approach usually consisted of the following:

1   Undermine the target through Voice of the Arabs radio attacks, subversive leaflets and malicious rumors.

2   Cultivate opponents of the targeted regime at home and abroad, provide them with funds and arm them if they have real or potential subversive forces at their command.
3   Grant the opposition access to Egyptian State Broadcasting to propagate their message.
4   Create pro-Nasser labor unions, student organizations, intellectual groups and political parties in targeted countries.
5   Use exiles or in-country Nasserists (or both) to organize clandestine cells aimed at overthrowing the targeted regime.
6   If local or exile groups prove inadequate, find individuals willing to undertake a sabotage, bombing or assassination campaign.

The Voice of the Arabs was (and remains) a carefully calibrated instrument of Cairo's foreign policy. Under Nasser, daily guidance for radio propaganda came from the president, 'Ali Sabri, Sami Sharaf, the intelligence services and others. It has already been noted how MID officers like Fathi al-Dib could direct the Voice of the Arabs to support insurgent operations in Algeria. In addition, *mukhabarat* entities ran other broadcast operations; for example, Egypt's Hebrew Service was managed by MID using State Broadcasting studios and transmitters.[27]

The Voice of the Arabs was synchronized with Egypt's covert action strategy to divide, paralyze and weaken the opponent. John Bagot Glubb ('Glubb Pasha'), the man who helped create and lead Jordan's famous Arab Legion, grudgingly admired the way Nasser skillfully used radio propaganda to achieve Egypt's national goals. Glubb warned London that radio broadcasts 'constitute the most powerful weapon in this region...ideas are more powerful than weapons.'[28]

## Target: Jordan

Glubb had reason to fret about Voice of the Arabs because Egyptian intelligence focused on Jordan as the weakest link in the conservative Arab states opposing Nasser. Building on the success of earlier covert action to thwart Jordan's entry into the Baghdad Pact in 1955, the *mukhabarat* tried once again in 1957–1958 to subvert Jordan and subordinate that country to Nasser's direction. One method was assassination: King Hussein survived several Egyptian and/or Syrian assassination attempts, including putting acid in his eyedropper and the use of poison.[29] At times, Israel's Mossad warned Hussein of other UAR assassination plots in a bid to keep Jordan out of Nasser's orbit.[30] Army coups were another Egyptian subversive tool. In April 1957, the Egyptian military attaché tried to recruit a Jordanian army officer to serve either as a spy or to foment unrest in the Jordanian army; the attaché was expelled a month later for plotting to murder the Jordanian royal family.[31]

In the spring of 1960 Egypt unleashed a new subversive war against Jordan. In March, Prime Minister al-Majali and King Hussein's uncle narrowly escaped an assassination plot linked to UAR intelligence. But this failure did not deter the Egyptians. On 26 August the Voice of the Arabs urged Jordanians to 'kill al-Majali and drag his body through the streets.'[32] Three days later, al-Majali was killed by a bomb planted in his desk by UAR agents.

### Subversion in Lebanon

While Washington watched Egypt's efforts to subvert Jordan with concern, it was in Lebanon that Nasser overplayed his hand. Like Jordan, Lebanon was a fragile state destined to serve as a battleground for regional power struggles. Moreover, with the creation of the UAR, the Lebanese faced a traditional Syrian adversary whose potential for mischief had been augmented by the union with Egypt. Even before the UAR, Egyptian intelligence had been active in Lebanon by sponsoring the bombings of British targets in Lebanon during the Suez crisis. Miles Copeland later wrote that the Egyptian station chief in Beirut 'was an intelligence officer who would do credit to any intelligence service.'[33]

But it was following the creation of the UAR that Nasser made a concerted bid to pull Lebanon out of the Western orbit. In May 1958 the Voice of the Arabs began to lay the groundwork by urging Lebanese to revolt against their president, Camille Chamoun.[34] Next, MID covert action operatives were dispatched to Damascus to deliver money and arms to the anti-Chamoun opposition and provide guidance for large-scale demonstrations and riots.[35] Lacking military and covert action instruments capable of blunting this offensive Lebanon had to fall back on diplomacy. Throughout the early summer of 1958 Lebanese diplomats pressed their case against the UAR in the Arab League and, eventually, the UN Security Council. A UN fact-finding mission sent to Lebanon to investigate arms smuggling from Syria found 'no tangible evidence of mass infiltration of arms or of UAR nationals'; however, the mission lacked sufficient observers to detect this trafficking.[36]

UAR covert action had gone too far. Working against Lebanon alone, UAR intelligence might have been able to deliver a pliant Lebanon willing to follow Nasser's line. But UAR meddling and a looming Lebanese civil war triggered a larger crisis that attracted outside interest, including US marines who arrived on the beaches of Beirut in July 1958. With this assertion of American power, a truce was eventually worked out between the players in Lebanon where Chamoun stepped down as president, the marines departed and Nasser ordered his *mukhabarat* to cease arming Lebanese insurgents.[37] For all intents and purposes Lebanon was a draw in the Arab Cold War.

### Coup in Iraq

Nasser was flexible on Lebanon because he feared Washington and London would use the Lebanese and Jordanian crises as a pretext to overthrow the new Iraqi republic. On 14 July 1958 Iraqi army officers led by 'Abd al-Karim Qasim overthrew the monarchy and murdered its strongman, Nuri al-Sa'id. Significantly, the new Iraqi leaders had no discernible connections to either Egyptian or

Syrian intelligence but that did not stop the UAR from reaching out to them as a potential new ally.[38] On their side, the Iraqis asked for a UAR military mission and handed over to Cairo confidential files belonging to the now defunct Baghdad Pact.[39] Not long after the Iraqi coup, the Voice of the Arabs commentator Ahmed Sa'id received an envelope from Baghdad that contained a letter and a bone. The letter read in part: 'in appreciation for what you did in helping to make the revolution a success, I send you a piece of the finger of the traitor Nuri al-Sa'id.'[40]

Cooperation in the intelligence field was another sign that a new era could be dawning in Egyptian–Iraqi relations. Barely two weeks after the Iraqi coup, EGIS Director Salah Nasr led a small delegation to Baghdad for talks with the Iraqi leadership and senior intelligence officials. One consequence of this visit was an agreement to share intelligence, Egyptian help in reorganizing the Iraqi intelligence service and the provision of Egyptian technical assistance.[41]

Despite the initial warmth between Baghdad and Cairo, old animosities soon reasserted themselves. In addition to the much older geopolitical tensions between Egypt and Iraq there was a bitter personality rift between Nasser and Qasim. The new Iraqi leader was in no mood to pay obeisance to Nasser's lofty status as idol of the Arabs, while Nasser suspected Qasim of trying to lure Syria out of the UAR. By the fall of 1958 the Iraqis had clamped down on the UAR embassy in Baghdad, expelled its military attaché and begun to arrest pro-Nasser elements in the Iraqi military.[42] Soon, the conflict degenerated into Arab Cold War tactics of radio propaganda and conspiracies. In late 1958 an EGIS assessment on the prospects for an Iraqi coup pondered several important questions: if the UAR successfully removed Qasim, would the USSR intervene to safeguard its new interests in Iraq? Would the Israelis respond by annexing the West Bank? Similar questions were raised concerning Turkish, British and American reactions. But for Nasser there was no debate: the UAR intelligence services had to get rid of Qasim.[43]

The first move was to create a special team within Nasser's personal office that consisted of 'Ali Sabri, Kamal Rif'at, and 'Abd al-Hamid Sarraj.[44] Together, these officers tried to unseat Qasim in March 1959 by backing both an army revolt in the northern Iraqi city of Mosul and an officers' plot in Baghdad.[45] But Qasim moved quickly against the Mosul rebels, relying on communist-leaning officers who were loyal to him not Nasser. The Iraqis also capitalized on what one author later described as a 'surprisingly inept performance by UAR intelligence.'[46] The result was a bitter and bloody defeat for the Nasserists. Still Nasser's *mukhabarat* was not dissuaded and in November 1959 it staged another unsuccessful attempt to assassinate the Iraqi leader. Baghdad responded to Egyptian subversion with Radio Free Damascus which broadcast anti-Nasser propaganda from an Iraqi prison complex called Abu Ghraib.[47]

## Assault on Saudi Arabia

Saudi Arabia was another major target of Egyptian covert action. After Nasser's triumph at Suez, Riyadh swallowed its historical animosity toward the Hashemites and joined Jordan and Iraq in a pact aimed at Nasser. For his part, Nasser knew that Washington was sponsoring King Saud as his rival for Arab leadership and responded with covert action.

The Saudi military was the most likely vehicle for an Egyptian-inspired coup against Riyadh. As early as June 1954 'Ali Sabri told a US diplomat in a moment of candor that Saudi–Egyptian military cooperation was sowing the seeds for a future revolt in the Saudi armed forces. Sabri predicted that Saudi officers who had trained in Egypt would form the nucleus of a Free Officers movement in the Kingdom.[48] In addition to these Saudi officers there were other potential assets for Egyptian subversion. As of 1958 there were over 1,000 Egyptian security personnel in the Kingdom advising the Ministry of Defense and Aviation and helping reorganize the Directorate General of Public Security. Some of these Egyptians were no doubt tasked with identifying and recruiting agents within the Saudi security apparatus.[49]

When Saudi Arabia joined the Hashemite anti-UAR alliance after Suez, Cairo ramped up its subversive war against Riyadh. At first it began with the usual Voice of the Arabs rhetoric (King Saud as 'King of the Jews and the Saxons'[50] etc.) which must have struck a nerve, for not only did the Saudis buy jammers, they also bankrolled several CIA and SIS plots in 1957 against Nasser.[51] Meanwhile, the Egyptian military attaché in Saudi Arabia was smuggling arms for an anti-monarchy conspiracy until he was expelled in April 1957. When 'Ali Sabri was sent to Riyadh to try and mend fences, he was told by King Saud that Egyptian military attachés would no longer be allowed in Saudi Arabia. Sabri assured the king that the attaché would be court-martialed: instead, the officer was sent to Sudan where he was declared *persona non grata* after one week on the job.[52]

King Saud believed he could check Nasser by encouraging dissident Syrian officers to revolt against the UAR. Key to this Saudi plot was 'Abd al-Hamid Sarraj, the Syrian strongman who instead took Saud's money and betrayed the plot to Nasser.[53] Egypt responded to Saudi plots with more conspiracies of its own. In one case, UAR representatives met Yemeni Crown Prince Mohamed al-Badr to discuss sparking a revolt in Saudi Arabia but this never materialized.[54]

Remarkably, the 1956–1960 spike in Egyptian subversion produced only the feeblest of results. Even in relatively weak countries like Jordan and Lebanon UAR covert action produced no lasting consequences while it engendered anti-Egyptian hostility in powerful Arab states like Iraq and Saudi Arabia. Finally, Cairo's efforts at subversion ensured that the United States, Britain (and possibly the Soviets in the case of Iraq) would support local clients against Egyptian subversion. Ultimately, this period marked a high water mark for Egyptian covert action that was never reached again.

## Clandestine wars with Israel

While the late 1950s was a period of heightened tension between Egypt and many of its Arab neighbors, Cairo also prosecuted its anti-Israeli conflict in the espionage arena. Some of the sparks that fed the 1956 war were gone: for example, both Gaza and Sinai were relatively quiet after Nasser turned off the *fedayin* campaign. Egypt also made efforts to curb the enthusiasm of resident Palestinian activists like Yasser Arafat, who eventually moved to a friendlier climate in Kuwait.

But Egypt desperately needed intelligence on Israel and it resorted to questionable agents like Kobruk Yaakovian and Ulrich Schnefft. Yaakovian was an Egyptian-born Armenian recruited by EGIS in 1959 and sent to Brazil under cover as a Jew named Yitzhak Koshhuk. In December 1961, Yaakovian entered Israel as an immigrant, tried and failed to enter the IDF armored corps, and ended up in an IDF logistics company. Shortly after arrival, Yaakovian began sending communications in invisible ink to an EGIS address in Europe. It is not clear how Israeli security uncovered Yaakovian, but he was arrested in December 1963 and jailed until he was returned to Egypt in 1966.[55] Ulrich Schnefft was a German SS veteran who claimed he was a Jew, immigrated to Israel and enlisted in the IDF. At some point he approached the Egyptian military attaché in Paris and offered to spy for Egypt. Eager for Israeli recruits of any kind, Egyptian intelligence sent him to Cairo for interrogation and espionage training. Schnefft returned to Israel before the Suez war where he engaged in minor espionage work until he was arrested in 1957 after revealing his intelligence work to a friend.[56]

At home, Egyptian counterintelligence penetrated several Israeli spy rings in the late 1950s and early 1960s. Among the first was the Goudswaard Ring of European and Egyptian nationals which was recruited in 1958–1959 by Mossad officers posing as members of a 'NATO intelligence service' (a 'false flag operation'). For a while this ring provided political, economic and military intelligence to Israel, but its efforts were detected and the Alexandria GID's Mamduh Salem convinced the Dutchman Meewis Goudswaard to pass disinformation to his 'NATO' controllers.[57] The Goudswaard affair also highlighted the GID's use of torture against Egyptian members of the network. The wife of one suspect was imprisoned with her infant who, in the words of a German diplomat, 'was heard to cry incessantly day and night for three days while [its mother] was undergoing 'interrogation.'[58] A High Court judge told American diplomats that while he did not think torture was used in the Goudswaard case he had heard that 'inflation by air' had been used in the early 1950s as a 'particularly excruciating form of torture.'[59]

Another GID counterintelligence success was the penetration of the Thomas Ring. During the late 1950s Mossad recruited an Armenian named Jacques Leon Thomas who gathered a network that eventually included an agent in the Egyptian artillery training school with access to documents, manuals and maps.[60] As the flow of information from this and other sources increased, Thomas smuggled out microfilmed documents in furniture exported abroad. But Thomas erred when he tried to recruit a Coptic officer who reported the approach to the GID and agreed to pass disinformation back to the ring.[61] Thomas's 'customers' were pleased by the volume if not necessarily the quality of his intelligence and asked for more. They even asked if Thomas could recruit an Egyptian pilot to fly a MiG out of the country.[62] On 6 January 1961, the GID arrested the network and seized thousands of microfilm documents.[63]

## The rise of the GID

The capture of the Goudswaard and Thomas spy rings put a spotlight on the GID which was becoming a powerful actor on the domestic scene. Like its political police predecessor, the GID was a security, intelligence and counterintelligence service subordinated to the Interior Ministry and with branches throughout Egypt. However, unlike the political police, the GID was a more centralized, efficient and ruthless organization that had benefitted greatly from the Nasser regime's single-minded obsession with security.

Port Said offers a good model of how internal security worked in an Egyptian governorate at this time. Although the governor was at the top of the pyramid his internal security responsibilities were delegated to a director of security and the police commandant. This latter official commanded some 1,500 officers and men; he exercised nominal control over the local GID branch which received most of its orders directly from GID headquarters in Cairo. Run by a police colonel, the GID branch was responsible for monitoring and arresting foreigners, communists, Muslim Brothers and other 'subversives.' Given his multiple responsibilities, the Port Said GID Director was described as 'the hardest working man in the Governorate... [he] keeps swarms of informers cruising around Port Said, [and he] knows almost all that happens.'[64]

Informers were the keys to the GID system not only in Port Said but in other governorates as well. Miles Copeland called them the 'City Eye' and they were prevalent around hotels and other sites where foreigners were known to congregate and meet Egyptians.[65] The Israeli spy Wolfgang Lotz described the 'City Eye' system in this way: 'practically every servant, doorman, taxi-driver, shopkeeper, hotel employee, waiter, vendor and beggar was a potential or actual police informer.'[66] The GID's informers were the eyes and ears of the Nasser regime and they were a crucial element in the rise of the Egyptian police state.

The GID developed a predictable pattern when it came to the security side of its mission. Inevitably arrests would occur in the early morning hours when the suspect was disoriented and unable to fight back or escape. Suspects were usually blindfolded and led away to the local GID office for interrogation while their residences were searched, ransacked and sealed.[67] Torture was an integral part of the GID's interrogation-confession cycle.[68]

The GID's anti-communist activities tended to fluctuate depending on the broader Moscow–Cairo relationship. For a brief period after the Suez crisis, when Egyptian–Soviet relations were in a warm phase, the GID eased off on the communists. However when Qasim's communist-backed coup in Iraq raised the specter of a communist resurgence in Syria the GID renewed its attacks on the Syrian and Egyptian communist movements.[69] In November 1958 Nasser met the GID's Communist Section Chief, Major General Hassan al-Musaylihi and peppered him with questions about the communist threat. Al-Musaylihi replied that the threat was indeed 'serious... if we leave them alone, there will be danger for the country and the revolution. They may even succeed in toppling the government. So why don't we have them for lunch before they eat us for dinner?'[70] On 31 December 1958, the GID arrested over 300 communists nationwide.[71] Some were sent to a prison in Upper Egypt which left a terrifying impression on one internee: 'we had terrifying sand-storms, scorpions, tarantulas... conditions were so hard that officers were relieved every three months; the soldiers twice a year. We saw soldiers crack up, go mad.'[72] But it was not all repression: al-Musaylihi later recorded that the GID tried to 'reeducate' imprisoned communists in 'sound political concepts.' He added that some 400 'students' graduated from GID brainwashing and 'not a single one of them [had] relapsed' nearly 20 years later.[73]

Egypt's renewed assault on its communists coincided with a sharp downturn in Cairo's relations with Moscow. Nasser himself was convinced the USSR was engaged in 'flagrant interference in our internal affairs' and he alleged an 'alliance' had been concluded between Egyptian communists and Moscow to destabilize his regime.[74] Yet, just as with the CIA during the worst phases of US–Egyptian relations, the *mukhabarat* did not permit the rift between Moscow and Cairo to upset an otherwise beneficial intelligence liaison with the KGB. For example, only months after the December 1958 GID crackdown on Egyptian communists, Sami Sharaf was in Moscow soliciting intelligence training for his *mukhabarat* officers.

## Syrian secession

Nasser's all-consuming suspicion did not bode well for the longevity of the UAR. The difficulties encountered in combining two very different political cultures were compounded by Egyptian arrogance and Syrian resentment of Egypt's heavy-handed tactics. It was easy for Cairo to blame Syrian grievances on a 'feudal' society or CIA, Iraqi and Saudi machinations, but the roots of the UAR breakup ran much deeper than that. When Nasser tried to graft his one-party police state apparatus onto Syrians who enjoyed a history of dissonant politics, the result was Syrian resentment and the inevitable conspiracies.

Cairo's heavy reliance on veteran Syrian intelligence boss 'Abd al-Hamid Sarraj was another problem since the ambitious Sarraj exploited the grievances of the Syrian *mukhabarat* for his own ends.[75] The Egyptians knew that Sarraj was secretly provoking anti-Egyptian unrest in Syrian intelligence especially when some Syrian *mukhabarat* officers refused transfers to Egypt in September 1961. As a result of this mutiny, Sarraj was summoned to Cairo where he resigned from his posts.[76] But this affair only highlighted the growing discontent in Syrian intelligence at a time when Nasser desperately needed it to foil Syrian plots against his regime.[77]

On 28 September 1961 dissident Syrian army officers captured key points in Damascus and seized both Nasser's viceroy, 'Abd al-Hakim 'Amr and Sarraj who had just flown back to Syria. Almost immediately Cairo began jamming the radio transmissions of the new Syrian junta. It also seemed as if Egypt was going to intervene militarily when Cairo deployed 120 commandos to Latakia.[78] In the end, however, it was clear that Egypt lacked the military means to restore the Union absent broad-based Syrian popular support for Nasser. And, after three years of Union, many Syrians had had enough of an Egyptian-dominated *mukhabarat* state.[79]

The Syrian secession closed one chapter in Nasser's dreams of Arab unity. Yet the era of Egyptian expansion was not quite over: an ill-fated adventure in Yemen was to be the final confirmation that Nasser's ambitions had vastly exceeded the means of his impoverished country and its over-burdened intelligence apparatus.

# 7    Intelligence and the Yemen wars

Egypt suffered a serious setback in the Arab Cold War with the breakup of the UAR. But Syrian secession and failed covert action projects in Iraq, Jordan and Lebanon did not diminish Nasser's appetite for foreign adventures. In fact, the conservative monarchy in Yemen had long been in Nasser's sights and, nearly a year after the demise of the UAR, a coup by Egyptian-backed Yemeni established the Yemen Arab Republic.

Unfortunately for Cairo and its Yemeni allies, the coup did not crush all resistance and, within weeks, an Egyptian army was fighting a bloody counterinsurgency campaign in the mountains of Yemen. Ill-prepared for counterinsurgency on many levels – including intelligence collection and analysis – Yemen proved to be a humbling experience for the Egyptian army.

In many respects, Yemen was a continuation of the Anglo-Egyptian regional power struggle that did not end at Suez. Indeed, shortly after Egyptian troops were sent to prop up the Yemen Republic, the *mukhabarat* began subverting the British presence in neighboring Aden and the South Arabian Federation. While Britain's withdrawal from Aden in 1967 seemed to signal another Egyptian victory, covert action failed to give Cairo any meaningful leverage over the new government in Aden. Moreover, Egypt's defeat in the 1967 war with Israel meant that it had to negotiate its own military withdrawal from the Yemen Republic to the north. In the end, Yemen proved to be a frustratingly bitter experience for Egypt and another symbol of the country's inability to exert meaningful influence over the Arab Middle East.

## Egypt's Vietnam

The war in Yemen stressed Egypt's security apparatus on many levels. Both the MID and the General Staff failed to anticipate or prepare for the rural insurgency that engulfed the Egyptian army in northern Yemen. The result of this failure was a prolonged stalemate that left much of the Yemeni interior in insurgent hands. Just as the United States would fail to do in Iraq and Afghanistan 40 years later, the Egyptians did not predict a long war in Yemen and had adjusted their expectations and strategy accordingly. But in the end Yemen was to preoccupy and overwhelm Egypt's military and intelligence services for the remainder of the 1960s.

Cairo had been planning a coup in Yemen for a long time. According to an Egyptian intelligence officer, the *mukhabarat* had been busy recruiting spies and influence agents among Yemeni students and political exiles in Egypt throughout the 1950s.[1] A 1956 Egyptian–Yemeni defense treaty allowed Egyptian intelligence to identify and recruit agents among Yemeni officers attending Egyptian military schools or receiving training by Egypt's military mission in Yemen.[2] In addition to recruiting Yemeni army officers, the MID also sent its own people into Yemen to determine if and how the imam could be deposed. As early as October 1953 the head of the MID's Arab Affairs Branch, Fathi al-Dib, traveled throughout northern Yemen and parts of the British-controlled Aden Protectorate to appraise the situation. Al-Dib concluded that Yemen was ripe for a pro-Nasser coup and the result was a steady infusion of Egyptian intelligence officers into the imamate throughout the rest of the decade.[3]

There are other examples of Egyptian plotting in Yemen. In 1958, Nasser encouraged the then pro-Egyptian Yemeni Crown Prince al-Badr to overthrow his father.[4] In a possibly apocryphal story from this period the US National Security Agency intercepted a phone call between Egyptian intelligence officers and a servant in the imam's palace who was trying to place a bomb under the monarch's bed.[5] On the eve of the Yemen coup French intelligence intercepted a message from Cairo to an Egyptian agent in Yemen informing him that a bomb had been sent for use against the imam. That plot was foiled by Yemeni security presumably after a French tipoff.[6] Finally, on 13 September 1962 the CIA learned that Yemeni officers were planning to assassinate the Yemeni imam, arrest the crown prince and establish a republic with Nasser's support.'[7] It is not known if the CIA warned its Yemeni counterparts about this plot.

Consistent with Egyptian subversion elsewhere the Voice of the Arabs was employed against the imam even though Egyptian intelligence knew that few Yemenis possessed radios. This propaganda blitz was led by a Yemeni exile whose *Secrets of Yemen* program not only helped instigate student demonstrations in Sana'a in 1962 but also delivered the signal for the coup to begin on 26 September 1962.[8] Not long after that Egyptian forces started flowing into Yemen.

Egyptian special forces began providing security for the new Yemeni leadership within days of the coup. They were soon followed by regular military units intended to help the YAR defeat a tribal insurgency led by the deposed Imam al-Badr.[9] At first the army's progress seemed to vindicate pre-deployment expectations that the Yemen campaign would be a short one.[10] But, as with many insurgencies in mountainous areas, the royalists rebounded by exploiting the difficult terrain to blunt and then throw back successive Egyptian ground offensives.

Nasser had several goals in deploying his soldiers to Yemen, but the most immediate of those was defending the new Yemen Arab Republic (YAR) against a coalition of tribal opponents and monarchists. Then there was prestige: one year after Syria's embarrassing secession from his United Arab Republic Nasser could not allow the YAR to fail.[11] Finally, Nasser and his aides believed there were long term strategic benefits in placing army units on the Arabian Peninsula.

First, a successful Nasserite revolution in Yemen gave Cairo greater control over the strategic Bab al-Mandeb Strait which controlled access to the Red Sea; Yemen also offered a base from which Egyptian intelligence could destabilize the oil-rich Saudis, Aden and the British-protected sheikhdoms of southern Yemen and the Persian Gulf.[12]

## Egyptian intelligence performance

Poor intelligence contributed to Cairo's inability to win the Yemen war. At the strategic level, where the decision to intervene was made, Egyptian intelligence lacked sources with accurate information about Yemeni society, culture, and, most importantly, its complicated tribal structures.[13] Brief MID reconnaissance forays into Yemen before the coup barely scratched the surface of understanding the country's internal dynamics. In some cases, reliable information about Yemen was not distributed because of bureaucratic politics. For example, Egypt's ambassador to Yemen during the critical years 1957 to 1961 sent back useful data on the tribes that never left the Foreign Ministry.[14] Egypt's intelligence deficiencies were such that Nasser sent Sami Sharaf to the US embassy to beg for information on Yemen. Ambassador John Badeau provided Sharaf with an economic report for which Sharaf reportedly was 'very grateful.'[15]

A series of false – and ultimately disastrous – assumptions by Egypt's leadership was directly linked to poor intelligence. When the first units arrived in Yemen to shore up the regime there was a general expectation in Cairo that the war would be short with minimal casualties.[16] No one on the intelligence and planning staffs devoted much attention to how the different elements of the Yemeni population would respond to the ouster of the imam and the influx of Egyptian soldiers. The Egyptians certainly miscalculated Imam al-Badr's ability to rally the Zaidi tribes who proved to be superb guerrilla fighters. The General Staff seemed to calculate that if an insurgency emerged it could be overwhelmed by conventional arms.[17]

Egyptian intelligence was also unable to accurately gauge how outside parties would react to the Yemen crisis. Perhaps anticipating that their intervention would be an easy fait accompli the Egyptians either ignored or downplayed the fact that their bold move in Yemen crossed the strategic 'red lines' of both Saudi Arabia and the United Kingdom. Within weeks of the coup Imam al-Badr was hiding in Saudi Arabia where he received Saudi and Jordanian military assistance and instruction in guerrilla warfare.[18] Meanwhile, as we shall see, London took its own steps to ensure that Cairo's Yemen war would be a protracted and very costly one.

A lethal combination of poor maps, lack of cultural intelligence, faulty assumptions and poor planning led the General Staff to misidentify the type of war it was fighting. In short, Egyptian military units went into Yemen with the training and equipment to fight a conventional war against Israel rather than a dispersed, amorphous insurgency. The breezy assumption that Yemen could be secured within three months undoubtedly was based in part on a failure to understand the type of war that would be fought in that country.[19] Perhaps MID Brigadier General Salah al-Din al-Hadidi put it best when he later likened Egypt's Yemen war to taking a test without studying. The result, he confessed, was that knowledge about Yemen in the General Staff boiled down to the fact that it bordered Saudi Arabia.[20] In fact, some Egyptian officers went to Yemen with only the vaguest idea about whom they were fighting. As one later admitted, 'we were not issued instructions to make war on the Yemenis.'[21]

These strategic intelligence mistakes were compounded and amplified by a lack of accurate terrain maps which impeded military operations. At the operational level plans were drawn up on maps that did not reveal the formidable obstacles posed by rugged mountain passes, flash floods, altitude, dust, and non-existent roads and mountain trails. At the tactical level, soldiers were fighting guerrillas in a harsh terrain that rapidly sapped their energy and morale; units were often lost in a vast labyrinth of defiles and gorges which were poorly charted – if they were mapped at all.[22]

Egyptian fortunes suffered as the war dissolved into a stalemate. Troop numbers increased significantly from 15,000 in December 1962 to 70,000 at the end of 1965, yet even these reinforcements could not alter the stalemate that had settled over the battlefield.[23] Trained and armed by the Saudis, the Jordanians, British-backed mercenaries and others, the royalist insurgents were also growing in numbers and capabilities.[24] More increasingly the Egyptian army found itself relying on firepower and even chemical warfare to preserve a defensive triangle centered on the cities of Ta'iz, Sana'a, and al-Hodeidah.[25]

Stalemate aside, Egyptian intelligence capabilities gradually improved. EGIS and MID had some insights into YAR decision making, although their sources were never as good as one would expect given Cairo's support for the Yemeni regime. Apparently the YAR was just as opaque for the Egyptians as it was for other outsiders.[26] The *mukhabarat* had access to secret communications between Saudi King Faisal and Imam al-Badr, and Cairo later boasted improbably that it could track the imam's movements daily.[27] Egyptian intelligence infiltrated the royalist camp with agents whose missions included sabotage, assassination and spying on the foreign mercenaries.[28] Later in the war MID sent special teams into the rural areas that were educated in local dialects, lived with the tribes and served as focal points for Egyptian civil affairs teams. Over time some of these men earned the trust of local chieftains who proved more willing to offer intelligence on the insurgents.[29]

## Egyptian counterintelligence challenges

But it was an uphill battle, literally and figuratively. The Egyptian military in Yemen faced all the problems of a foreign occupation force trying to impose order on fragmented tribal societies living in mountainous terrain. Despite occasional success in luring a tribal leader to the republican cause Egyptian counterintelligence failed to effectively penetrate and neutralize an elusive enemy that always seemed to be well-informed about Egyptian and republican military movements.[30] Moreover, the insurgents often meted out harsh sentences to those suspected of cooperating with the *mukhabarat*. It was a struggle just to keep intelligence assets alive in a country that already proved to be a lethal place for Egyptian soldiers to live and fight in.[31]

As if the Yemenis were not enough, Egyptian counterintelligence also had to confront the intelligence services of the United States, the United Kingdom, Israel, Saudi Arabia, Jordan, and Iran, all of whom were operating in Yemen with varying degrees of efficiency. The CIA in particular made some early inroads. When Washington recognized the YAR in December 1962, the way was open for the creation of a CIA station in Ta'iz headed by an Arabist named James Fees.[32] Serving under cover as a humanitarian aid officer, Fees had justification to fly throughout the YAR where he met and recruited sources. At some point, Fees recruited at least one spy in Egyptian military headquarters who provided intelligence on upcoming operations as well as the Egyptian and republican order of battle.[33] The CIA passed some of this intelligence on to the British, and from there it presumably made its way to the Jordanians, the Saudis and the Yemeni royalists.[34]

The career of Colonel Mohamed Shawqat offers a window into the work of a senior MID counterintelligence officer in Yemen at this time. From 1964 to 1966, Shawqat served as the 'foreign liaison officer' for the Egyptian army in Yemen, a position which made him the point man for queries from foreign diplomats and military attachés concerning Egyptian military operations. In addition to this overt role, he secretly maintained contact with Yemenis who nursed grievances against the YAR and its Egyptian backers in order to gauge their intent. Shawkat paid tribal leaders for information and organized prisoner exchanges. He also provided political advice to senior Egyptian officers on how to handle Yemen's delicate tribal rivalries. Unfortunately for Shawqat, the more he was asked to deal with foreigners and dissident Yemenis the more he fell under suspicion. When a subordinate formally charged him with revealing secrets to the US embassy, Shawkat had to be accompanied on all his later meetings with foreigners. In summer 1966, he was finally shipped out to Iraq where he served as military attaché.[35]

Communications security was a key Egyptian liability throughout the Yemen war. While field units rarely had encryption and were obliged to broadcast their movements over open channels even encrypted headquarters communications were vulnerable. A big part of the problem was that Egypt still relied on Enigma-based encoders which, still unbeknownst to the world, had been broken by the British in World War II. Consequently, British intelligence had a good read on Egyptian operations based on intercepted communications of Egyptian tactical units and local headquarters.[36] Indeed, both GCHQ and NSA had access to a stream of information on military planning as well as the morale and logistics problems of the Egyptian army in Yemen.[37] In some cases, GCHQ/NSA intercepts picked up the chatter of Russian pilots flying Egyptian air force bomber missions.[38] This SIGINT data was probably shared in sanitized form with Saudi Arabia, Iran, Jordan, Israel and the Yemeni royalists.

## Egyptian covert action

From the outset, Egyptian intelligence viewed Yemen as a base from which to wage covert wars against Saudi Arabia and British Aden. Despite the failure of previous operations to overthrow the Saudi monarchy, the *mukhabarat* was still convinced that Saudi Arabia was vulnerable to subversion staged from Cairo's new base in Yemen.[39] In February 1963 the Saudis discovered 119 containers of weapons and ammunition that had been airdropped on the coast near the Saudi–Yemeni border. Although the arms could not be traced, there was little doubt that they had been dropped by the Egyptians for the use of Saudi dissidents.[40] Sometime in 1963 or 1964 Sami Sharaf reportedly met dissident Saudi officers to discuss a coup.[41] Saudi security investigated separate Egyptian intelligence plots aimed at detonating bombs in the kingdom two years later.[42] In 1967 Egyptian intelligence made one last attempt to destabilize Saudi Arabia starting with an assassination plot against King Faisal followed by the insertion of sabotage teams from Yemen.[43]

Egypt's attempt to subvert Saudi Arabia lasted until its 1967 defeat by Israel forced a realignment of regional alliances and national security priorities. While Cairo's covert action campaign never seriously threatened Riyadh, it sufficiently angered the Saudis to contemplate 'unleashing' a guerrilla war of their own either in Yemen or Egypt itself.[44] Riyadh may also have retaliated by expanding its support for the Egyptian Muslim Brotherhood.

## Problems in the army

As the US military has rediscovered in Iraq and Afghanistan, fighting an insurgency can be an excruciating experience for armies trained to fight conventional wars. The Egyptian soldier in Yemen was no different in this regard, for he faced a punishing terrain and harsh climate as well as tribal adversaries who decapitated or mutilated Egyptian soldiers who fell into their hands.[45] Given this, plus routine hazing by officers and a growing atmosphere of defeat in headquarters, it is no surprise that rumors of army discontent began reaching the *mukhabarat* in 1964 and 1965.[46] In July 1965 the MID began to carefully screen army officers for Muslim Brotherhood and Saudi ties,[47] a year later 20 officers were secretly arrested in an anti-regime conspiracy.[48] Nasser tried to put a brave face on reports of army unrest during a May 1966 speech: 'they say that the Egyptian army is grumbling and might return and stage a coup. But I assure them that they are destined for disappointment and that [their] dreams are unreal.'[49] Yet around this time Nasser confided to the US ambassador that any retreat from Yemen would not only affect army security but the stability of the regime itself.[50] In short, Yemen had become a military and political morass.

## Covert war in south Yemen

Even as it struggled to preserve the Yemen revolution, Cairo was targeting Britain's South Arabian Federation (SAF) and the city of Aden. When the imamate was overthrown in Yemen, the new republican regime inherited historical claims to these British-controlled territories in what would eventually become South Yemen. As for Cairo, its goals for meddling in the SAF were to evict the British; prevent the Saudis from filling the ensuing security vacuum; control the new regime in Aden; and control the Red Sea. But Egypt lacked the military power to achieve these goals given its commitments in the YAR, its defenses against Israel as well as the continued British military presence in Aden. Just as it did in the Canal Zone a decade earlier, the *mukhabarat* turned to covert action to get the British out of Aden.[51]

Named Salah al-Din the first phase of this covert action plan consisted of radio propaganda assaults and the dissemination of rumors intended to break the trust between the British and their south Yemeni subjects.[52] Phase two called for the creation of an anti-British umbrella organization called the National Liberation Front (NLF) which attempted to bridge the deep social and political gaps between the Aden merchants, labor unions and the tribes in the SAF interior.[53] The third phase provided for the training and arming dissident tribes and Aden militants for anti-British operations. Egyptian support included training on the use of explosives, mine laying, ambushes and other insurgency tactics as well as medical assistance for wounded fighters.[54] Formal Egyptian-backed guerrilla operations began in October 1963 with a tribal uprising in the Radfan Mountains. Two months later, the British high commissioner for the SAF narrowly escaped assassination. The war was on.[55]

Britain's response was a covert action campaign of its own. When a Royal Air Force cross-border raid on a suspected Yemeni insurgent camp triggered an international outcry in 1964, London began pondering other options. In a series of secret policy debates in April and May of that year officials decided to distribute money and arms to frontier tribes and royalist insurgents fighting the YAR. They rejected a request by the British Chiefs of Staff to assassinate Egyptian intelligence officers training and directing Aden rebels from the former imam's summer palace in Ta'iz.[56] British policy decisions took tangible form when ex-Special Air Service (SAS) men and French mercenaries began providing training and arms to the royalists.[57] News about these European trainers traveled fast, and it was not long before they were marked by the *mukhabarat* for assassination.

There is no doubt that MID training created a more potent insurgency in the south. In Aden the NLF systematically kidnapped, tortured and murdered Arab Special Branch officers and their informants. Some reports suggest Egyptian intelligence helped identify targets for assassination.[58] The result of this campaign was the decimation of the Special Branch, intimidated informants and a perception that the British were losing the city. In this atmosphere British officials were convinced that Egyptian intelligence was directing the NLF's urban terrorism campaign. One British Special Branch officer put it this way: 'we are fighting a snake – the head of which is in Cairo, the body wriggles down through Yemen, and the tail is right here in Aden.'[59]

As if the loss of their Aden Special Branch officers was not enough, the British also faced an embarrassing spy case involving a non-commissioned officer named Percy Allen who passed sensitive Defence Ministry documents to the Egyptian and Iraqi military attachés. Among other things these papers offered a 'fairly comprehensive picture' of the strengths and weaknesses of the South Arabian Federation's intelligence organization.[60] A damage assessment later tried to put a brave face on this humiliating loss: 'although it is regrettable that so much about our intelligence organization and activities in South Arabia has been disclosed, it is unlikely that our intelligence organization has suffered any real damage.'[61]

## The United Kingdom quits Aden

In February 1966 London announced that it would quit Aden by 1968 without offering any security guarantees to a future south Arabian government. This only emboldened Cairo to step up subversion in a bid to gain de facto control of the entire SAF.[62] Yet, even as the Egyptians were sensing victory in the south, their delicate house of cards began to fall apart. It was the nagging problem of south Yemeni unity and the unwillingness of some elements within the NLF to accept Egyptian direction.

The NLF and another group called the Organization for the Liberation of South Yemen (OLOS) were the main contenders for the allegiance of southern Arabia's population in the mid-1960s. Just as it had done earlier with the creation of the NLF, Egyptian intelligence tried to unite OLOS and the NLF when it established the Front for the Liberation of the Occupied South Yemen (FLOSY) in 1966.[63] But FLOSY was doomed from the start. Not only was its OLOS component declining in influence, fissures had opened within the NLF over whether to join FLOSY. When the NLF broke with FLOSY, Egyptian intelligence responded by redirecting its resources toward creating a FLOSY 'liberation army' for the final victory. Nonetheless, despite this aid, FLOSY never emerged as a credible challenger to the increasingly dominant NLF.[64]

Yet before we turn to the bitter denouement of Egypt's involvement in the Yemen wars, a counterintelligence case involving the CIA in North Yemen is worth examining. As previously described, the CIA had developed a network of sources and contacts in North Yemen who reported on Egyptian military operations and local politics. At some point, however, Egyptian counterintelligence penetrated this network and a decision was made to teach the American spies a lesson. On 26 April 1967 a Yemeni mob attacked and sacked the US Agency for International Development (AID) mission in Ta'iz. Accompanying the looters were Egyptian intelligence officers who opened American safes and seized documents.[65] Two AID officials were arrested and charged with subversion.

In the aftermath of the assault, US officials scrambled to secure the release of these officers and the return of the documents. On 4 May 1967 the State Department ordered its Cairo embassy to deliver a message to Salah Nasr demanding the return of the documents 'uncompromised' to the US government.[66] We do not know what these documents were, although senior White House aide Walt Rostow noted in a memorandum for President Johnson that 'CIA material' was in at least one of the safes.[67] Rostow also noted how Nasser 'sees CIA's hand behind everything that goes wrong for him' even in an AID road project that happened to transit an area where Egypt was training a southern Arabian 'liberation army.'[68] What was not mentioned in the memo was how CIA case officers in Yemen like James Fees were working undercover as humanitarian aid officials.

## The end of Egypt's Yemen wars

The 1967 Arab–Israeli war closed the book on Egypt's military involvement in Yemen. When the last Egyptian troops left Yemen on 8 December 1967 few gave the YAR much of a chance to survive. Nevertheless the royalist insurgency was all but dead by 1970 and a government had emerged in Sana'a that was friendlier to Saudi interests. As for southern Arabia – soon to be called South Yemen or the People's Democratic Republic of Yemen – the British withdrawal led to an NLF regime in Aden. The Egyptian-backed FLOSY was never able to overcome its lack of support in rural areas and, by the fall of 1967, it had been all but defeated.

For the *mukhabarat* the Yemen wars were a protracted trial by fire that strained its resources and revealed serious shortfalls in intelligence collection and analysis. At the same time, Egyptian intelligence had also gained valuable experience in subversive propaganda and aiding insurgencies. Yet in the end, for all the blood and treasure it had expended in Yemen and the SAF, Egypt had accomplished surprisingly little. Neither Yemeni government that emerged after 1967 was in any sense overly partial to Egyptian interests let alone willing to follow a Nasserist line. Nasser's dreams of using Yemen as a base to subvert the Gulf monarchies also proved to be a chimera. Finally, to add insult to injury in the intelligence arena, after independence South Yemen's nascent intelligence services turned to East Germany rather than Egypt for their training and development.[69]

# 8 The Intelligence State

> Everything in the U.A.R. is a State secret and security has become a mania...
> The general atmosphere is one of a complete police State where few people trust
> their friends.
>
> 1963 British Air Attaché Assessment[1]

In his manifesto *The Philosophy of the Revolution* Gamal 'Abd al-Nasser por-
trayed an Egypt at the geopolitical and cultural heart of the Arab, African and
Islamic worlds. For Nasser, this centrality gave Egypt a natural platform to exert
leadership not only over the Arab states but the newly emerging independent
states of Africa and Asia as well. Nasser's support for the non-alignment movement and his friendship with its luminaries like Jawaharlal Nehru and Josip Broz
Tito were intended to demonstrate Egypt's new confidence on the world stage.

We have seen in previous chapters how Nasser's attempts to exert influence
in the Arab world were stymied by regional and external powers that allied
against him. But as *The Philosophy of the Revolution* made clear, Nasser's ambitions were not restricted to the Arabs. In the case of Iran, the Egyptian leader
saw an opportunity to check a powerful rival by promoting separatists and anti-
Shah dissidents. As more African states aspired to and eventually achieved independence, Egypt regarded itself as their natural leader and mentor. It did so not
only with prestige and non-alignment goals in mind, but from a national security
perspective as well, for some states such as Ethiopia were upstream consumers
of the Nile – Egypt's only water source. Thus, for a period in the 1960s, Egypt
fought covert wars in several African states albeit with no tangible results.

On the home front, Nasser used the *mukhabarat* to reinforce his authority,
intimidate his opponents and shield his regime from conspiracies. In addition to
Israeli espionage, Egyptian intelligence was busy in the 1960s fighting the *ra'is*'s
adversaries within the regime itself and a resurgent Muslim Brotherhood.
Egypt's relations with the United States further unraveled and each stepped up
clandestine warfare against the other. This Egyptian–American clash opened the
doors further for Soviet influence and, on the eve of the 1967 war with Israel,
Moscow had become a powerful player in the Egyptian military and security
communities.

## Covert wars in Iran and Africa

In July 1960 Cairo broke diplomatic ties with Tehran over Iran's security ties with Israel, its claims to Bahrain and its support for Yemeni royalists and Iraqi Kurds.[2] From Iran's perspective, Egypt was a subversive state that intended to dominate the Persian Gulf.[3] Iranian intelligence frequently updated the Shah on Egyptian assassination plots against him as well as Cairo's attempts to spur revolts among Iran's minority Arab, Qashqai and Baluch communities. Moreover, in the early 1960s an EGIS-run clandestine radio station called the Voice of Free Iran unleashed a propaganda attack on the Shah that eventually forced American intervention.[4] In March 1962 discussions with the US ambassador Sami Sharaf, and Zakariya Muhi al-Din admitted running this station and stirring up unrest in Iran. But they insisted that their broadcasts were in retaliation for anti-Nasser appeals by Iran and implied that, if Iran stopped its broadcasts, Egypt would follow suit. Although this exchange led to a temporary ceasefire in the radio wars, Egyptian intelligence continued to supply funds to Iranian clerics opposed to the Shah, fund Iranian Arab exiles in Kuwait and smuggle arms into Iranian Baluchistan by way of Pakistan.[5]

In *The Philosophy of the Revolution*, Nasser viewed Egypt as an African player. In patronizing tones, Nasser wrote that 'we will never in any circumstance be able to relinquish our responsibility to support...the spread of enlightenment and civilization to the remotest depths of the jungle.'[6] Its *mission civilisatrice* aside, Cairo's goals in Africa were diverse. In addition to ensuring the free flow of the Nile River, Egypt sought to shepherd the newly independent African states towards non-alignment. Perhaps more importantly, the Egyptians wanted to isolate and contain Israel by asking the new African states to withhold diplomatic recognition of the Jewish state.[7]

To achieve its goals in Africa, Egypt established diplomatic ties with the new states. It also created and/or subsidized several African liberation groups fighting colonial occupation.[8] Just as he had done with the Arab Affairs Branch, Nasser created an African Branch in January 1956 that reported directly to him. Led by a MID officer named Mohamed Fa'iq, the African Branch coordinated Egypt's Africa policies, including the covert action programs of the *mukhabarat*.[9] Key targets at this time were Ethiopia and the Congo.

### Ethiopia

With its mixed Muslim and Christian population as well as its geographical dominance of the Blue Nile, Ethiopia was (and remains) an important factor in Egyptian national security. During the 1950s and 1960s, Egyptian–Ethiopian relations were strained by Nasser's Arab unity agenda and Ethiopia's close relations with the West and Israel. In the regional intelligence wars, Ethiopia was an important base for both Washington and Tel Aviv.[10] When bilateral relations soured after the Suez war, Egypt promoted the independence of Eritrea from Ethiopia by helping establish and fund the Eritrean Liberation Front (ELF) in

July 1960.[11] Moreover, Egypt established a close relationship with the newly independent state of Somalia which had territorial grievances of its own against Ethiopia.[12] The Ethiopians responded by pressing for closer security relations with the West. In November 1956 Ethiopia expelled the Egyptian military attaché for giving guns and money to Eritrean separatists.[13]

## Congo

The difficult circumstances surrounding the Belgian Congo's independence in 1960 offered Cairo another opportunity to influence a key African power. Nasser used the Congo crisis to create a united front with African 'radical' states like Ghana and Guinea who backed the Congo's enigmatic first leader, Patrice Lumumba. In fact, Egypt was one of the first countries to open up a diplomatic mission and intelligence station in Leopoldville; Egyptian aircraft also flew in Ghanaian and Egyptian soldiers to defend the fragile Congolese government against rebels.[14] According to the CIA, Egypt gave a 'large payment' to Lumumba; when the Congolese President was murdered shortly after independence, Cairo extended recognition and support for a rival Congolese regime based in Stanleyville. From 1961 to 1965 Egyptian aircraft ferried arms to airfields in Sudan and later Tanzania for onward delivery to the Congolese rebel leader Antoine Gizenga.[15] Meanwhile, EGIS officials served as advisers and trainers to the Gizenga regime.[16]

Egypt's involvement in the Congo raised American ire. In early 1965, Secretary of State Dean Rusk recorded that Egyptian policies such as support for Congolese rebels were putting Washington on a 'collision course' with Cairo. Both Rusk and his ambassador in Cairo warned the Egyptians that the United States would link wheat deliveries to Egyptian policies in countries like the Congo.[17] Although the Egyptians resented these strong arm tactics they nonetheless began scaling back their covert action project in Congo in April 1965.[18]

Egyptian intelligence funneled arms to resistance movements in Angola, Cameroon, Nigeria and Portuguese Guinea;[19] it also provided military training and intelligence to Congo Brazzaville and Tanzania.[20] Just as Egyptian covert action in the Arab states was often detrimental to Cairo's larger interests, the tendency of Egyptian *mukhabarat* officers to meddle in African states sometimes backfired. In 1966, for example, the government of Malawi closed Cairo's embassy amid allegations that Egyptian intelligence had been interfering in that country's internal affairs. Egypt's expelled ambassador was an MID officer who had been previously declared *persona non grata* by Jordan in 1957 for plotting against the royal family.[21]

Moreover, Egyptian policies did not prevent Israel from gaining the recognition of African states. Even Nasser's erstwhile close ally, Ghana's Kwame Nkrumah, allowed Israel to open an embassy in Accra. Nkrumah also proved to be a receptive customer for Mossad warnings of Egyptian subversion in his country.[22] By early 1966 Israel had diplomatic relations with 29 African states and defense ties with 17.[23] Thus, despite Cairo's perceptions of a 'race' with Israel for the hearts and minds of Africans, there never really was a competition. African leaders were inclined to pick and choose from the best of what Egypt and Israel had to offer but they showed little inclination to extend diplomatic recognition to one state but not the other. If anything, Egypt's penchant for covert action generated unease even among its friends.[24] In the end, Africa was simply too large and its needs too great to serve as a battlefield for the Israeli–Egyptian power struggle.

## Spy wars

Although the Suez war decreased Egypt–Israel border tensions, the intelligence wars continued unabated. The MID led intelligence collection against Israel and, during the 1960s, it relied heavily on groups like the Arab Nationalist Movement (ANM) to conduct reconnaissance missions from Gaza, the West Bank and Lebanon. In late 1965 or early 1966 an ANM infiltrator reportedly succeeded in photographing the Israeli nuclear facility at Dimona, a top MID priority.[25] In addition, the MID relied on Arab fishermen residing in Israel and a pan-Arabist group called *Al-Ard* to obtain public materials like journals, maps and newspapers.[26] But what the *mukhabarat* really wanted were Israeli Jews willing to spy for Egypt and able to operate inside their country without attracting attention. In one case, the Egyptians recruited an agent who not only became a minor international celebrity but also highlighted some of the darker aspects of EGIS operations.

In November 1964 a porter was loading an Egyptian diplomatic trunk onto a United Arab Airlines plane at Rome's Fiumicino Airport when he heard a voice inside the trunk crying for help. When the Italians opened it they found a man strapped to a chair with his head in a helmet and his feet in shoes which had been nailed to the floor.[27] Under police questioning the man revealed that he was a Moroccan Jew named Mordechai Luk who had immigrated to Israel in 1949. In June 1961 Luk crossed into Gaza where he was arrested, interrogated by Egyptian intelligence, recruited as a spy and sent to Naples in January 1963 under cover. But Luk was not a very good spy and, when he failed to produce, the Egyptians drugged him, packed him in the trunk and tried to send him to Cairo for interrogation.[28] Luk apparently was not the only one to suffer the 'trunk' experience: US sources indicated that the box had been used on at least five occasions to deliver heavily sedated defectors and failed spies back to Cairo.[29]

In their spy wars, Israel scored a victory against Egypt by successfully running an agent in Cairo named Wolfgang Lotz. Posing as a German army veteran with an interest in thoroughbred horses, Lotz's mission was to spy on a group of German scientists developing long-range missiles for Nasser. Lotz later described the difficulties he encountered in Cairo with *mukhabarat* informants:

> They sat on every corner, outside every door, outside every ship, idly watching. Their communal retina was something that was intrinsically part of the Cairo streets, the hubbub of the coffee houses, the chatter of the stories, the hustling on the pavements. It was as if the whole city was a slumberous, watching animal.[30]

Lotz learned he could neutralize this surveillance by currying favor with the people who ran it. In fact, it did not take him long to develop a valuable network of contacts in the Egyptian security apparatus as well as the expatriate Germans.[31] In the end though Lotz's cover failed and on 22 February 1965 he was arrested by the GID. What gave him away? One theory is that the frequency and volume of Lotz's radio communications to Israel attracted GID interest which used Soviet radio direction finders to home in on Lotz's transmitter.[32]

EGIS Director, Salah Nasr, claimed that Lotz's arrest was a 'victory' for Egypt, but it is difficult to see why. For several years an Israeli spy enjoyed access to Egyptian security officials not to mention those Germans working on Nasser's secret weapons programs. Indeed, Lotz's capture does not obscure the fact that he was one of the most successful spies of the twentieth century whose activities embarrassed the Arab world's leading counterintelligence officers.

## Regime feuds

The trend in Egypt toward greater police repression accelerated following the Syrian secession. As one US assessment put it, 'an atmosphere of near-panic followed the Syrian coup... a sense of isolation, bordering on claustrophobia.'[33] In this environment rumors of army conspiracies were rampant, and the GID was unleashed again on Egypt's remaining Jewish and foreign communities.[34] Fueling some of Nasser's paranoia was a growing rift with his ambitious old comrade, the *mushir* ('Marshal') of the armed forces, 'Abd al-Hakim 'Amr. It didn't help that the *mushir* also retained considerable influence over the security apparatus: in addition to having a loyal comrade in Salah Nasr at EGIS, 'Amr exercised direct control over the MID and helped select the GID director.[35] But when Nasser learned that his phones were tapped – presumably on 'Amr's orders – he turned on his suspected rival.[36]

In preparing for the showdown Nasser knew he could rely on 'Ali Sabri and especially Sami Sharaf, who supervised a presidential intelligence service which gathered information on Egyptian officials and executed special missions for the president.[37] But this confrontation fizzled: although Nasser hammered out a deal that made him commander-in-chief, everyone knew that 'Amr continued to direct the day-to-day affairs of the military, including the promotion of its officers. The future EGIS director, Amin Howeidy, commented later that the *mushir* remained 'the strongest man in Egypt.'[38]

Nasser tried to curb 'Amr's powers in other ways. In 1962 he presided over the creation of the Arab Socialist Union (ASU), which was intended to serve as the official party for Nasserist ideology. Since intelligence officers like 'Ali Sabri, Kamal Rif'at, Sharawi Goma'a, and Sami Sharaf dominated the ASU leadership from its inception, it is not surprising that this party took on an intelligence hue. Indeed, it was another means to monitor Egyptians and its archives became the depository for files on more than 30,000 officials.[39]

In the end, 'Amr's power was such that Nasser felt compelled to make him first vice president *and* effective commander of the armed forces. The *mushir* made his close associate, Shams Badran, Minister of War and it was Badran who planted supporters throughout the military bureaucracy. Critically, Badran and 'Amr convinced Nasser to give the MID sole responsibility for investigating the loyalties of military officers. This was a big step toward cementing 'Amr's power base since the army was the only institution with a reasonable chance of overthrowing the regime.[40] Furthermore, in 1966 Nasser put 'Amr and his cronies in charge of the Committee for the Liquidation of Feudalism. Intended to crush perceived landowner unrest, the Committee relied heavily on the intelligence services to identify 'feudalists' for midnight arrests, sequestrations and murder. These 'Visitors of the Dawn' soon became notorious for the military police witch hunts which racked the countryside.[41] Eventually, they helped contribute to a growing popular clamor to rein in the secret police establishment.

## Renewed Muslim Brotherhood

'Amr represented one domestic threat to Nasser in the 1960s; the Muslim Brotherhood was another. While some observers viewed the Brothers as a spent force because of regime repression, the organization nonetheless was rebuilding cells and promoting the revolutionary ideas of its chief ideologist, Sayyid Qutb. Qutb had been arrested with other Brotherhood leaders in 1954, tortured by the GID and then sentenced to 15 formative years at the Tura penitentiary. According to one researcher, 'Qutb believed that the guards and torturers in Tura had forgotten God. They no longer worshipped Him but revered Nasser and the state in His stead...In other words, they were pagans.'[42] It was during his imprisonment that Qutb wrote many of his works, including *Signposts*, which still provides an ideological template for the Muslim Brotherhood, Egyptian Islamic Jihad and al-Qa'ida among others.[43]

Qutb was released from prison in May 1964 following an appeal by the Iraqi president. Not long afterwards he was approached by Muslim Brothers who said they had Saudi backing for a coup against Nasser. Although he seemed to be aware that he was under *mukhabarat* surveillance, Qutb agreed to lead them.[44] By May 1965, with the police closing in, the conspirators pondered a range of plans, including machine-gunning Nasser's car on the Alexandria water front, recruiting a fighter pilot to bomb Nasser's residence or assassinating 'Ali Sabri, Salah Nasr, 'Abd al-Hakim 'Amr, and Zakariya Muhi al-Din.[45] But they never proceeded with any of these plans for later that summer the MID arrested Qutb and hundreds of Brotherhood suspects.[46] While the regime publicly alleged that the Brotherhood plot had been sponsored by Western intelligence and the Saudis, privately it was jolted by the fact that the conspiracy included several army veterans of the Yemen war.[47] On 21 August 1966 the Supreme State Security Court sentenced seven Brothers to death and another 100 to extended prison terms. Qutb was hanged eight days later. If the state hoped that Qutb's death would put an end to his ideas they were in for a surprise, for his writings were used by others to justify wars on 'apostate' regimes throughout the Muslim world.

Believing that the GID had failed to warn him of the Qutb conspiracy, Nasser proceeded to overhaul the internal security apparatus. On 1 October 1965 he named Zakaria Muhi al-Din as prime minister and interior minister, and the old security boss lost no time purging the director of prisons, the GID director and senior security officials throughout the governorates.[48] But Muhi al-Din's attempts at reform ran up against powerful bureaucratic players, including 'Amr, who controlled the MID and the military police, Salah Nasr at EGIS and 'Ali Sabri who controlled secret committees in the Arab Socialist Union.[49] Ultimately, Muhi al-Din was eclipsed by these power centers and when he was replaced as prime minister in 1966 this father of the modern *mukhabarat* faded from public view.

## American conspiracies

Egyptian allegations of American involvement in the 1965 Brotherhood plot demonstrated the depths to which US–Egypt relations had declined. At the center of this deterioration was a brooding Nasser who suspected the CIA intended to remove him from power just as it did with Mosaddeq in Iran. As one British diplomat put it at the time, 'Nasser certainly has the C.I.A. very much on his mind and loses no chance to draw attention to their activities.'[50] Despite his misgivings, Nasser nonetheless allowed the EGIS–CIA liaison relationship to continue. Occasionally, the CIA would pass sanitized versions of its intelligence estimates to Egypt; for its part, EGIS stationed a liaison officer in Washington to facilitate what was left of the intelligence partnership. At times EGIS liaison officers tried to create new channels of communication between Nasser and the US leadership.[51]

Intelligence channels could be useful in other ways too. In his memoirs, US ambassador John Badeau recalled how he once asked Zakaria Muhi al-Din to intervene in the case of an Italian national arrested for espionage:

> He [Muhi al-Din] smiled an enigmatic quiet smile, and said 'I think I know all about that case… As a matter of fact, I think that case has been disposed of, just before you came this afternoon.' He picked up the telephone, called the prison, and got the warden. He said, in effect, in good colloquial Arabic, 'you know that damn Dago you've got there? Well, the American ambassador is here asking about him, and I don't want any trouble. I want him out. O-U-T, out. By six o'clock. *Yallah*, get on with it.' He hung up and said to me in English, 'just as I thought. He was released this afternoon.'[52]

In the end, though, EGIS–CIA ties and personal relationships with individuals like Muhi al-Din could not alter Nasser's fundamental apprehensions about the CIA. The *mukhabarat* informed him that the CIA was monitoring his movements; he may also have been aware that nearly a quarter of the US embassy staff in Cairo was composed of CIA case officers in the early 1960s.[53] Then there is the possibility that close aides like 'Ali Sabri and Sami Sharaf deliberately fed

Nasser alarming intelligence reports to aggravate his paranoia. In any case, the *ra'is* believed the United States was out to get him by encircling Egypt with pro-US regimes in Libya, Sudan and Saudi Arabia and backing dissidents like the Muslim Brotherhood.[54]

Nasser's apprehensions contributed to the GID's July 1965 arrest of Mustafa Amin during a meeting with a CIA case officer.[55] What complicated this case was the fact that Amin, an old associate of Kermit Roosevelt, had served for years as one of Nasser's backchannels to Washington through the CIA. The bewilderment Amin felt comes through in his post-arrest 'confession' to Nasser.[56] It seems evident in retrospect that Amin was a pawn in Nasser's game with the CIA, and that his arrest served as a warning to the agency to cease conspiring against the *ra'is*. In fact, even before Amin was arrested the Egyptians had been trying to make it clear that they resented CIA operations in Egypt. For example, Egyptian ambassador Mustafa Kamel kept up a running dialogue with State Department officials about the CIA, warning them 'to stop playing around.' Kamel reiterated that CIA officers in Egypt could not escape surveillance and counseled them to be more discreet.[57] When an Egyptian mob torched a United States Information Service library in November 1964, US officials contemplated retaliating by supporting Nasser's opposition. Although most of the correspondence on this is classified there are hints that US officials contemplated playing 'at chaos for chaos sake' or aggravating Egypt's problems in Yemen.[58]

The 1965 Amin case and the insinuations that the United States was behind the Qutb plot led to additional consultations between Ambassador Kamel and the State Department. Kamel's warnings that Amin was linked to CIA conspiracies were met with claims of innocence and advice not to believe exaggerations of CIA influence. Indeed, one state official even asked Kamel who would take Amin's place at the Egyptian end of the secret channel: Sami Sharaf or Mohamed Hassanein Heikal? In the end, no one in Washington wanted to answer Kamel's question: why was the CIA trying to overthrow Nasser?[59]

In October 1966 Nasser told a visitor that he had 'indisputable evidence' of a CIA plot to assassinate him and asked that this message be delivered to Washington since the US ambassador was apparently oblivious to CIA activities. Secretary of State Rusk responded to these allegations by ordering Ambassador Lucius Battle to 'set the record straight' immediately. Rusk recommended that Nasser's 'evidence' be reviewed by 'competent intelligence technicians' from both sides.[60] For its part, the CIA denied any operations to overthrow Nasser.[61] When Battle approached Nasser with Rusk's recommendations, the Egyptian president unexpectedly downplayed his earlier assertions. This led to the State Department to conclude that either Nasser never had the information or he had changed his mind about sharing it with the Americans.[62]

Even so, Egyptian accusations of American malfeasance continued. In February 1967 Nasser's *éminence grise*, Heikal, alleged that the US government possessed a 'vast secret apparatus' which it used to wage economic and psychological warfare against the Arabs.[63] The following month, when Battle was making his farewell call on Nasser, the *ra'is* informed him that former CIA officers were working with third parties to create problems in the Egyptian army.[64] In similar meetings with 'Amr and Sadat, Battle was struck by the belief among Egyptian officials that the CIA station chief was the de facto 'Super Ambassador' in Cairo.[65]

Some sort of clandestine war was going on between Egypt and the United States during the mid-1960s, but it is difficult to pin down specific operations. Still, some events appear linked to this struggle. For example, on 2 June 1967, amid a spike in regional tensions between Israel and the Arab states, bombs exploded near the US embassy in Riyadh. Hermann Eilts, who was US ambassador to Saudi Arabia at the time, recorded later that the Saudis had 'definitively' linked these bombings to Gaza Palestinians run by Egyptian intelligence.[66] In addition, we have the April 1967 *mukhabarat*-sponsored attack on the US AID (Agency for International Development) mission in Yemen – covered in the previous chapter – as another point of reference.

On the US side of this covert war there are some declassified documents which suggest CIA subversion. In July 1965 the State Department informed the embassy in Cairo that it was concerned 'by evidence that the UAR [as Egypt still styled itself] may believe (rightly or wrongly) that there has been a basic disagreement about UAR policy within the USG [United States Government].'[67] Unfortunately, the remainder of this paragraph is blacked out, although there is an intriguing comment that state officers 'have never felt certain that we have had a full picture of [text not declassified, but undoubtedly refers to CIA] activities.'[68]

State and CIA officers two years later, discussed Egyptian allegations of subversion aired during Ambassador Battle's farewell calls. The CIA denied working with Egyptian army elements to overthrow Nasser, but these protests of innocence did not allay the suspicions of a long-time State Department Egypt hand named Donald Bergus.[69] In a memorandum, Bergus regarded the CIA's denial as 'unsatisfactory...CIA appears to hope that these incidents can be swept under a rug. This should not be allowed to happen.'[70] Bergus then reveals his belief that Egyptian intelligence knew about 'most, if not all' US intelligence operations in Egypt as well as those involving Egyptian nationals in other countries. The United States, he concluded, was running two risks: first, Cairo could blow a CIA operation at any time for propaganda purposes; second, the *mukhabarat* could coach the CIA's doubled Egyptian sources to tell Washington what Cairo wanted it to hear.[71]

## Soviet penetrations

The USSR stood to gain a great deal from the estrangement between the CIA and Egyptian intelligence. While the CIA fought its covert wars against Nasser, the KGB, GRU, and their East European counterparts quietly made inroads in Egypt. The KGB provided EGIS with training and technical support; both services also worked together in joint operations against the West.[72] There is no doubt that Soviet counterintelligence was able to penetrate the Egyptian services at this time.

Eventually all roads on Soviet influence operations in Egypt seem to lead back to the head of Nasser's personal intelligence unit, Sami Sharaf. Whether he was a KGB spy or not, Sharaf was well-placed because he filtered much of what Nasser read in the area of intelligence. There is no question that Sharaf professed a strong sympathy for the Soviet system of government;[73] he undoubtedly put Soviet intelligence reports of CIA malfeasance into Nasser's daily intelligence file.[74] Washington certainly believed the *ra'is* was relying too much on Soviet intelligence reports to shape decisions on US–Egyptian relations. For example, in August 1965 a State Department official told the Egyptian ambassador that Moscow was 'planting false intelligence' on the Egyptian government to 'poison the well' of Cairo–Washington relations. The minutes of this meeting noted that the State Department 'had on various occasions suggested that the Soviets were feeding false intelligence to Nasser; [State Department] thought it possible that someone in the President's immediate staff was providing him with bad advice and false data.'[75]

Just as the Egyptian government relied too much on the CIA for advice, training and equipment in the 1950s, so too did its KGB dependence in the 1960s prove detrimental to some of its interests. The EGIS–KGB relationship gave Moscow opportunities to penetrate the Egyptian military and *mukhabarat* and feed disinformation to an isolated, paranoid leadership. Unfortunately for Egypt that overreliance on Soviet intelligence helped precipitate the worst disaster in the history of modern Egypt: the 1967 Arab–Israeli war.

*[handwritten margin note: Consequences of relying on foreign intel. No source validation.]*

# 9 The 1967 war

No one believed that the Jews would be so capable of undertaking the operation against us because of our superiority in weapons and air force and our excellent plan which would have obstructed any confrontation.[1]

Former War Minister Shams Badran, February 1968

If the 1956 Suez War marked the apogee of Nasser's career as a leader of the Arab world, the June 1967 war marked its nadir. Although he was to survive the shattering defeat of his armies with his presidency intact, Nasser never recovered the regional influence he enjoyed in the years immediately following Suez. Ultimately, the road to the 1967 disaster had multiple causes not the least of which was Nasser himself.

As the shattered wreckage of Egyptian fighters on Egyptian runways attested, the 1967 war demonstrated multiple failures in the country's national security system. On the intelligence front, most Egyptian assessments not only badly underestimated Israeli capabilities and intentions they were also infused with untested assumptions and cultural biases. Moreover, lack of confidence in its own intelligence services drove the Egyptian leadership to rely on erroneous or deliberately false Soviet and Syrian intelligence reports. All the pre-war deficiencies in Egyptian intelligence collection and analysis came to light in the first hours of the war when Israel effectively wiped out the entire Egyptian air force on the ground. It was a humbling experience for an intelligence community that hitherto had prided itself on its professionalism and first rank status in the Arab world.

## Egyptian intelligence on the eve of war

Egypt's road to war was paved with the increased radicalism of the Palestinian movement, a hard-line coup in Syria and intra-Arab bickering. As the summer of 1967 approached, Cairo found itself increasingly hemmed in by a radical Syria, the sniping of smaller states like Jordan, hostility from the United States and periodic Soviet intelligence reports that Israel was preparing for war.[2]

Because Egypt was in a continuous state of war with Israel, the MID was the lead service for collection and especially the analysis of intelligence related to

Israel. The MID director at this time was Major General Mohamed Ahmed Sadiq, a graduate of the Egyptian Military Academy and the Soviet Frunze Academy who, prior to his September 1966 MID appointment, had served as military attaché to Bonn.[3] One contemporary described Sadiq as 'a wary, suspicious man'[4]: these were good traits to have in Nasser's Egypt especially in the *mukhabarat*.

Significantly though, in the lead up to the war, the MID was distracted by internal security missions, including counterintelligence, the Visitor at Dawn raids in the countryside and the 1965 Muslim Brotherhood plot which triggered MID investigations of hundreds of officers. As Sadiq recalled, War Minister Shams Badran was obsessed with ensuring the loyalty of the military to himself and Marshal 'Amr.[5] As a consequence of this fetid atmosphere of fear and suspicion, military intelligence was also plagued by rivalries among the services.[6] For instance, the Egyptian air force Sinai commander, Air Vice Marshal 'Abd al-Hamid al-Dighidi, complained that his intelligence staff spent more time spying on *him* than on the Israelis. Moreover, whatever analysis on the Israeli Air Force (IAF) that did reach al-Dighidi's desk was often contradictory because the military intelligence branches could not resolve their analytical differences. As a result, al-Dighidi ousted his intelligence staff just before the war and put in his own men none of whom was skilled in intelligence let alone the IAF threat.[7] For his part, MID Director Sadiq later complained that the air force not only acted 'in a separatist, independent manner…detached from Military Intelligence' its leadership also ignored 'accurate' MID intelligence of the initial IAF sorties against Egypt.[8]

Human intelligence continued to serve as Egypt's primary source of intelligence on Israel, yet Egyptian HUMINT had not improved much since the 1956 war. While EGIS claims it ran a 'super spy' named Jack Bitton in Israeli before the 1967 war, it is difficult to sort the facts of this man's career from the mythology that has accumulated around him. Indeed, little is definitely known of Bitton's intelligence activities in Israel during his reported residence there in the 1950s and 1960s. Born in Dumyat in 1927, Rifat al-Gamal or Rifat al-Hagan (his real name is not known), was recruited by the *mukhabarat* to undertake a long-term mission inside Israel. Some suggest he was coerced into working for EGIS.[9] In any case, EGIS gave him the identity of Jack Bitton, an Ashkenazi Jew who was born in 1919 in Mansura, Egypt.[10]

Bitton's first assignment was to spy on the Alexandria Jewish community, and it was later claimed that he penetrated the Susannah saboteur ring although this cannot be substantiated.[11] In 1954 or 1955 Jack Bitton immigrated to Israel where he set up a travel agency in Tel Aviv called Cititours.[12] Unfortunately it is at this point that Bitton's story becomes murky. Some claim that Israeli counterintelligence identified Bitton, doubled him and used him to feed disinformation to EGIS over many years.[13] For their part, Egypt argues that Bitton was a spy who warned Cairo of Israel's June 1967 preparations for war through his contacts with Golda Meir, Moshe Dayan and other Israeli leaders.[14] After the war, Bitton repeated requested retirement until the *mukhabarat* let him retire to West Germany where he died in 1982.[15]

If Jack Bitton was an EGIS spy then he probably was the only Egyptian strategic HUMINT asset before and during the 1967 war. Unfortunately, measuring Bitton's impact on Egyptian decision-making requires more verifiable details about him and his reporting than EGIS has so far permitted.[16] For many Egyptians, however, Bitton is Egypt's master spy and the subject of a highly popular television series in the late 1980s.[17]

Other Egyptian HUMINT assets at this time included the military attachés abroad, Palestinian infiltrators and Arab residents of Israel who photographed military facilities and gathered open source literature.[18] MID also relied on reconnaissance bases in Gaza and Sinai, which served as visual observation posts and centers for contacts with Palestinian or Bedouin scouts. These posts housed some of the MID's SIGINT equipment which provided early warning of Israel's 5 June attack until captured by the IDF.[19] Critically, control of the MID's Reconnaissance Branch was transferred from the MID to the General Staff before the war with the result that some tactical intelligence – such as scouting reports of Israeli war preparations – never reached MID analysts.[20]

Egyptian technical intelligence was equally lacking before the war. The air force leadership was reluctant to deploy its photo reconnaissance jets close to or over the border because it feared Israeli retaliation. MID Director Sadiq recalled that the air force flew only two reconnaissance sorties over southern Israel in the days leading up to the war and both photographed the wrong targets.[21] Consequently, Egypt had little or no relevant imagery intelligence of the IDF's peacetime posture let alone wartime deployments. In fact, it has been alleged that much of what passed for Egyptian imagery intelligence of southern Israel dated back to World War II.[22] There is little information on Egyptian SIGINT capabilities before the war. The MID probably intercepted unencrypted Israel tactical communications through its Gaza and Sinai SIGINT sites, but is not clear if Israeli encryption was ever broken. The *mukhabarat*'s abilities to exploit Israeli communications were further limited by its lack of Hebrew linguists and experienced analysts who could put SIGINT data in context.[23]

Just as it did during the 1956 war, Egyptian intelligence relied heavily on foreign partners for intelligence on Israel. The USSR provided imagery-derived intelligence on the IDF order of battle, but Egypt's General Staff believed this over-exaggerated Israel's strength.[24] Unfortunately for the Egyptians, some Soviet intelligence passed through liaison channels was dangerously – perhaps deliberately – inaccurate. This important issue will be examined shortly. Otherwise, the Soviets tended to overemphasize the capability of the weapons they placed in Egyptian hands while underestimating Israel's will and capability to fight.[25] Moscow believed Egypt could win a long war with Israel.[26] In addition to the USSR, Egypt relied on Syria, Jordan and India for intelligence on Israel. For example, Jordan passed intelligence of IDF tactics, order of battle and weapons based upon studies of Israeli raids in the West Bank. Egypt also received electronic intelligence of Israeli Air Force activities collected by Jordan's early warning radars.[27] Both Jordan and India warned Egypt in early June that an Israel attack was imminent.[28]

The record on Egyptian intelligence estimates is ambiguous. On the one hand, the MID provided timely warnings of Israel's ability and intent to initiate war in early June. On the other, inaccurate or erroneous intelligence reports were used to back up assessments of Israeli capabilities that bore little resemblance to reality. Since the MID had no reliable baseline of how the IDF trained – let alone reliable intelligence on Israeli combat doctrine and order of battle – its estimates of IDF capabilities were wildly inaccurate.[29] It seems that the MID swallowed Soviet boasts about the MiG-21 or the MiG-19 without questioning how those capabilities might be influenced by poorly trained Egyptian pilots. Moreover, cultural biases and assumptions of Jewish inferiority were allowed to seep into the estimates. As one observer put it, any assessment had to conform to the Egyptian leadership's belief that Israel was economically weak, unable to mobilize its reserves for a long war and incapable of matching Egypt's Soviet weapons. In brief, it seemed like everyone in the Arab world believed an Arab alliance could defeat Israel without question.[30]

Egyptian security suffered from several deficiencies of its own. Before the war, the Israeli spy Wolfgang Lotz mapped out Egypt's surface-to-air missile (SAM) facilities, the locations of garrisons and the routines and foibles of senior Egyptian officers. Israeli intelligence had other agents like 'Sulayman,' a signals officer who reportedly informed his handlers of the movements of individual Egyptian units during the war.[31] It is possible Sulayman also provided encryption materials to his Israeli handlers for we know that Israeli military intelligence ('Aman') broke the Egyptian army cipher and mapped out Egypt's order of battle and communications networks before the war.[32] This ability to break Egyptian codes was a key enabler of the IDF's victory in June 1967. Finally, the Israelis obtained a trove of sensitive documents, including maps of Egyptian military positions in Sinai, when they captured an MID patrol early in the war.[33]

A key mission for any counterintelligence service is to detect and neutralize the disinformation efforts of its adversaries. Although MID Director Sadiq was to later argue otherwise, the Egyptians came up short in this area as well.[34] Israel's war plan included planting disinformation on the Egyptians through double agents, foreign diplomats and the media. The IDF also created a dummy military unit near Eilat complete with its own encrypted and unencrypted radio traffic and decoys. This ghost unit apparently succeeded in convincing the Egyptians that the Israeli attack on Sinai would come on a north–south axis rather than the east-to-west drive to the Suez Canal that actually occurred. Marshal 'Amr consequently ordered his Sinai army to prepare for an offensive coming from Eilat despite MID reports that the IDF was massing for an attack in north and central Sinai.[35]

Finally, the Egyptian leadership's lack of confidence in *mukhabarat* assessments translated into overreliance on intelligence from foreign sources, particularly the USSR.[36] While policymakers are wise to base decisions on information from multiple sources, Nasser, Shams Badran, and 'Amr relied on intelligence (and, possibly, disinformation) that originated with Soviet intelligence.[37] As we shall see, such was the leadership's reliance on Soviet intelligence that one could say that Egypt entered the worst war in its modern history in large part because of faulty or deliberately misleading Soviet information.

## The road to war

Historians are still trying to trace those factors that pushed Israel and the Arab states into war in June 1967. One factor was the 8 May 1967 dispatch of two Syrian intelligence officers to Cairo with information that Israel was massing forces for a raid on Syria. Confirmation of the Syrian report seemed to come a few days later when the Soviets passed similar warnings of a Syrian attack through several Egyptian channels, including the KGB–EGIS liaison channel and the foreign ministries.[38] It is likely these Syrian and Soviet warnings were based on the same Soviet source. In any case, on 14 May Marshal 'Amr responded by activating the Conqueror war plan which mobilized reserves, deployed reinforcements to the Sinai and raised the alert status across the armed forces.[39] Egypt made no attempt to disguise the mobilization of its reserves and the deployment of regular troops into the Sinai. Israeli SIGINT soon began picking up signs of dislocation and chaos as Egyptian units deployed to Sinai complained of a lack of maps, uniforms, food and water. In the haste and disorganization of the deployment many units were underequipped and understaffed.[40] Faced with a concentration of Egyptian forces on its frontiers, the Israeli leadership was under pressure to respond.[41]

Concurrent with the activation of the Conqueror plan were Egyptian attempts to verify the Syrian/Soviet warnings. 'Amr asked the Soviet ambassador for satellite imagery to clarify the IDF's mobilization only to receive the answer that Moscow could not determine if the Israeli deployment was aggressive or precautionary. It is not known if 'Amr and his staff ever actually saw Soviet imagery prior to hostilities.[42] 'Amr also sent Lieutenant General Mohamed Fawzi and a senior MID officer to Syria to study the situation at first hand. After examining Syrian aerial photographs and surveying the situation from the air himself, Fawzi saw no sign of IDF war preparations. Moreover, much to his surprise, Fawzi discovered that the Syrian military was not in a state of high alert.[43] Meanwhile, the MID sent Palestinian and Bedouin scouts into Israel where they found no indications of mobilization against Syria.[44]

The Israelis and the Americans were aware that the Egyptians had moved to a high alert status. The CIA station chief in Cairo told Salah Nasr and other senior EGIS officers that the United States saw no signs of IDF war preparations but 'the Egyptians seemed uninterested.'[45] Mossad's Meir Amit reportedly tried to revive earlier secret contacts with an Egyptian officer both to ease tensions and relay Israel's concerns about the false mobilization reports.[46]

What is striking is that the MID remained divided about the nature of the Israeli threat even though multiple sources indicated no Israeli mobilization against Syria. While some MID officers assessed that Israel was preparing for a showdown with Syria, MID Director Sadiq told Nasser and others in the leadership that reports of Israeli mobilization were false. Nonetheless, Sadiq's views aside, the Egyptian leadership tended to believe Soviet intelligence while, at the same time, downplaying or denying contradictory information from other sources. The result was a course of action that led directly to war.[47]

In fact, no further attempt was made to confirm the Soviet warning and all attention was now focused on winning a showdown with Israel. On 18 May 1967 Nasser asked the UN Secretary General to withdraw the United Nations Emergency Force that had served as a buffer between Israel and Egypt in the Sinai since the Suez war. At the same time as Egyptian planners contemplated preemptive war the Voice of the Arabs raised its rhetoric against Israel and tried to rally other Arabs to Nasser's cause. On 23 May Nasser announced the closure of the Strait of Tiran to Israeli Red Sea shipping. In an apparent reference to the original Soviet warning of IDF mobilization, Nasser said in his speech: 'The Jews threatened war. We tell them: You are welcome, we are ready for war.'[48] That same day, Marshal 'Amr, surprised by the lack of a prompt Israeli response to the Strait closure, proposed a military operation to seize the Negev. Israeli intelligence picked up this change of orders through one of its sources and warned its leadership on 25 May that an Egyptian attack could come within the next 24 hours.[49] The IDF began to make war preparations of its own.

It is unclear if Nasser knew that 'Amr had now included the Negev in the war plan. Nasser did deliver another bellicose speech on 26 May in which he affirmed that Egypt's 'basic objective will be to destroy Israel... I say such things because I am confident. I *know* what we have here in Egypt and what Syria has.'[50] He also claimed to have seen reconnaissance photographs that showed Israeli forces massing on the Syrian border.[51] Yet even as Nasser focused on an illusory threat to Syria, the MID was starting to notice the IDF build-up on the Gaza and Sinai frontiers.[52] Around this time, War Minister Shams Badran was sent to Moscow to obtain approval for offensive war, returning on 27 May with the message that the Soviets would not support preemption.[53] That same day, Nasser ordered 'Amr to cancel planning for the offensive.[54]

While Egypt backed down from attacking Israel, other changes signified a looming war. On 30 May, Jordan joined Egypt and Syria in an anti-Israel pact. That same day, Menachem Begin and Moshe Dayan entered the Israeli government in a cabinet shuffle that signaled a more confrontational policy toward the Arabs. On 2 June, Nasser discussed these developments with his senior officers. MID Director Sadiq provided an assessment of the Israeli cabinet changes, recent IAF over-flights of the Sinai and new IDF forces detected on roads leading to Gaza and Sinai. Sadiq warned that Israel had completed its military preparations and could attack within 24 hours. He also advised the air force to redeploy aircraft away from their exposed forward bases in Sinai, but Air Marshal Mahmud Sidqi refused, saying that such a move would demoralize his pilots.[55] When Nasser finally spoke up, he predicted accurately that Israel would attack on 5 June. He ordered the strengthening of Egyptian defenses in Sinai to meet the anticipated attack and advised the air force to guard against surprise.

But Air Marshal Sidqi was confident that 80–90 percent of his aircraft would survive an Israeli first strike.[56]

As Sadiq's warnings in the 2 June conference demonstrated, the MID was predicting with greater confidence that an Israeli attack on Egypt was imminent. On 3 June it revised its assessment for the General Staff and warned that an attack could come within the next 48 hours.[57] The following day, the MID commander at al-'Arish sent a warning that IDF forces were massing across the border for a projected attack into Gaza and northern Sinai. These and other last-minute warnings reportedly were disseminated to the armies, but at this point senior Sinai commanders were preparing for a conference with 'Amr that was scheduled for 5 June.[58]

On 5 June 1967 the IAF wiped out the Egyptian Air Force on the ground. That it did so was due in large part to highly accurate intelligence of Egypt's air  order of battle, bases, air defenses, early warning radars, air base command structure even the capabilities of individual Egyptian pilots.[59] Over 200 Egyptian fighters and bombers were destroyed, the bulk of them on the ground where they were parked wing to wing as if preparing for an inspection. Once the Egyptian air force had been destroyed, Israeli ground units could proceed to systematically destroy the Egyptian army on Sinai. For the Egyptian General Staff the situation on the peninsula was perplexing because Israeli aircraft had destroyed key communications links between General Headquarters, the field armies and units in the field. Amid the confusion, on 6 June the MID office at al-'Arish informed its Cairo headquarters that Marshal 'Amr had issued general retreat orders to his Sinai armies to retreat across the Canal. When MID Director Sadiq phoned 'Amr to recommend reversing the order it was too late, for the Egyptian army retreat had now turned into a rout. Two days later, as Israeli forces halted on the east bank of the Suez Canal, Egypt was out of the war.[60]

## Assessing Egyptian intelligence at war

The intelligence collection and assessments problems that plagued Egypt before the war were aggravated by combat. While the MID began to comprehend the gravity of the situation in the hours immediately preceding the Israeli attack, there was insufficient time to warn the leadership. Just as it had in 1956, the *mukhabarat* went to war without really understanding its adversary. When he later analyzed the defeat, Zakaria Muhi al-Din believed 'lack of intelligence was the problem. While the Israelis knew the name of every Egyptian on relief, and his wife's too, we didn't even know where Moshe Dayan's house was.'[61]

Intelligence collection seems to have broken down completely under the pressure of combat. There was no imagery intelligence since most of the photo reconnaissance aircraft were destroyed, disabled or chased from the skies. Electronic intelligence disappeared as soon as the early warning radar network was jammed or bombed while ground reconnaissance collapsed with the rout of the retreating armies. Any useful intelligence about the enemy that was collected during this period – such as the results of an interrogation of an Israeli pilot captured near Gaza – never reached headquarters.[62]

While Egypt lost her eyes and ears at the very beginning, Israel retained its intelligence capabilities throughout the war. Its SIGINT stations monitored the chaos of the retreating Egyptian armies by intercepting their panicked calls for instructions and support.[63] Perhaps the most damaging example of Egypt's poor communications security practices came on 5 June when Israeli intelligence intercepted a phone conversation between Nasser and Jordan's King Hussein. Significantly, this conversation was not secure because of incompatible encryption equipment in Cairo and Amman. The SIGINT transcript of this conversation was later publicly used to refute Nasser's insistence that Washington and London had joined the war on Israel's behalf. In March 1968, the Egyptian president himself withdrew this accusation, saying it was due to 'suspicion and faulty information.'[64] The MID committed a significant security breach of its own when it failed to destroy its files before evacuating Gaza. As a result, Israel obtained a valuable archive of documents on MID's Palestinian infiltrators as well as Egypt's war plans.[65] Over the long term, the information contained in these files no doubt helped the Israelis establish what was to be a decades-long occupation of the Gaza Strip.

It is noteworthy that Cairo began preparing for an insurgency-based defense of the west bank of the Canal almost immediately after the war began. The natural model for this was the 1956 war; in fact key intelligence officials like 'Abd al-Fattah Abu al-Fadl and Kamal Rifa't were once again enlisted to organize the planned insurgency. In the end though the IDF wisely did not cross the Suez Canal and denied Egypt the opportunity to use its insurgency strategy.[66]

## Postmortem questions

The war ended with a shattering defeat for the Arab armies. In addition to Egypt's loss of Gaza and Sinai, Syria lost the Golan Heights, and Jordan had been pushed out of the West Bank and East Jerusalem. Still, there are numerous unanswered questions about why Nasser and his military behaved the way they did. According to one school of thought, Nasser thought that in a showdown with Israel he could gain a political victory without jeopardizing his regime. After all, this had worked in 1956 so why not try again? Due to faulty intelligence and/or disinformation as well as a cultural bias against Jews, the Egyptians were confident that a weak and demoralized Israel would back down from war with the Arabs and let a victorious Nasser dictate the peace. Indeed, Salah Nasr told the CIA station chief before the war that Egypt was in the driver's seat in this crisis.[67] According to US Special Envoy Robert Anderson who was dispatched to the region to try and halt the slide to war, Nasser 'seemed confident of both his intelligence and of his military capability... he stated that his target system was prepared and that this time he would be ready.'[68] On 9 June, that is shortly after Egypt was knocked out of the war, Nasser still defended the performance of both his intelligence services and his military:

Our estimates of the enemy's strength were precise. They showed us that our armed forces had reached a level of equipment and training at which they were capable of deterring and repelling the enemy. We realized that the possibility of an armed attack existed, and we accepted the risk.[69]

Moreover, Nasser confronted senior officers critical of the MID's performance by comparing the MID's pre-war assessments of Israel's order of battle with that of a foreign (possibly Soviet) source. As MID Director Sadiq later related, the two reports were largely consistent leading Nasser to admonish the military not to 'mistreat Military Intelligence.'[70] In fact, Sadiq attributed some of the post-war criticism of the *mukhabarat* to senior Arab Socialist Union officials who were trying to salvage what was left of their pride.[71]

Then there is the question of the Soviet warning which sparked the conflagration. There are some who believe Moscow fed disinformation into the intelligence liaison channel to escalate a round of tensions between the Arab powers and Israel.[72] According to a CIA intelligence cable from this time, the Soviets hoped that a Middle East crisis would further exhaust a United States that was already overwhelmed in Vietnam.[73] Others argue that Israel instigated the crisis to pummel the Egyptian militarily before it could absorb its new Soviet weapons. This school believes that Israel planted intelligence on the Soviets either by double agents or false radio messages that indicated the IDF was massing for an attack on Syria. Unfortunately, neither claim can be substantiated.[74] It is nonetheless clear though that the Egyptian leadership and the MID investigated the Syrian/Soviet warning and concluded it was false. In the end, one is left with the impression that Egyptian leaders rejected the MID's (correct) assessments because they had greater confidence in the Soviets. Alternatively, Cairo used a warning it knew was dubious to spark a crisis from which it expected to make political gains.

The 1967 war is an excellent case study of the pitfalls of foreign intelligence liaison, particularly where one partner's espionage capabilities are vastly superior to the other. The Egyptian leadership put far too much confidence in Soviet intelligence reports. At a minimum that trust created an excellent opportunity for disinformation that Moscow would have found difficult to ignore.

Some observers have asked how a suspicious leader like Nasser could be taken in by an intelligence report from a foreign power that he often viewed with guarded reserve. As one of Nasser's biographers put it, how could 'this formidable manipulator of records and rumors let himself be fooled like a child by the information provided by the Soviet and Syrian service [?]' The biographer concludes that, in the end, Nasser could not distinguish reality from illusion.[75] But that seems to underestimate Nasser's penchant for seizing an opportunity – in this case tensions sparked by the Syrian/Soviet report – to try and humiliate Israel. One thing was clear though: Nasser had now entered the twilight years of his political career. Gone were the days of regional ambition: a new, much weaker Egypt had to adjust to the harsh realities of a new Middle East.

# 10 Nasser's twilight

In the immediate aftermath of the 1967 defeat, Nasser's top priorities were internal security and maintaining control of his presidency. Given his doubts about the loyalty of his internal security apparatus and the army, the *ra'is* gave Salah Nasr's EGIS unprecedented new powers on the domestic front. Salah Nasr was also instructed to open a secret channel to Washington in order to gauge American views on the Nasser regime, war termination and future Egyptian–Soviet relations. At the same time, Nasser took advantage of the defeat to finally turn on his old colleague and rival, Marshal 'Amr.

The grim political and economic realities of the 1967 defeat forced Egypt to reexamine its national security strategy as well. Consequently, new emphasis was placed on accommodation with the conservative Arab powers like Saudi Arabia and exploiting the Palestinian resistance as leverage over Israel. Cairo also turned to Moscow for new weapons and advice in restructuring its military and internal security apparatus. Finally, Nasser initiated a 'War of Attrition' on the Suez Canal front to try and raise international pressure on Israel to cease its Sinai occupation.

The 1967 defeat also triggered reforms in the Egyptian intelligence community. First, Israel was finally given the priority it deserved in the areas of collection and analysis. Second, the Egyptians reorganized their technical intelligence effort and acquired new surveillance capabilities from the Soviet Union. Together these changes were instrumental to early Egyptian success in the 1973 war.

Unfortunately for Egyptian society, Nasser's post-war promises to dismantle what he called the 'Intelligence State' were not kept. When Nasser died in September 1970 the *mukhabarat* state proved to be as strong and resilient as ever. Even so, the 1967 humiliation and the failure of Arab Socialism had released new Islamist forces within Egypt that were to impact heavily on domestic security in coming decades.

## Salah Nasr's cryptodiplomacy

Nasser must have had misgivings about Salah Nasr that predated the June war, for the EGIS boss was a boon companion of 'Amr and participated in many of the *mushir*'s nocturnal debaucheries. Either Nasser pushed his suspicions aside or, more likely, he followed the old adage of keeping your friends close but your enemies closer. For why else would Nasser rely on Salah Nasr for his security in the crucial weeks after the 1967 war? On 7 or 8 June 1967 the *ra'is* informed Salah Nasr that he would be a member of a new committee to purge military officers and have expanded responsibilities in the internal security arena. Internal security was to be EGIS's top priority: Nasser demanded 'constant reports' about public opinion in Egypt. Salah Nasr said he balked: this was a GID responsibility. But the president said he was not confident the GID could carry out its responsibilities in present circumstances.[1] Thus EGIS entered the fragile postwar period with a new mission where, as Salah Nasr noted, the organization shifted from an 'information' to a 'security apparatus' responsible for policing internal opposition to Nasser's rule.[2]

Nasser also asked the EGIS chief to represent him in a backchannel to Washington. Accordingly, on 8 June Salah Nasr told a US diplomat/CIA case officer that Cairo could not accept a ceasefire with Israel because of the external and internal implications for Egypt of surrender. 'What would we tell the people?' Nasr asked rhetorically.[3] Insisting that Egypt's military position was 'not too bad' Nasr hinted that Cairo might accept the status quo ante: i.e. an Israeli withdrawal from Sinai and Gaza in return for placing the Straits of Tiran under the UN's temporary supervision. He also tried to assure the United States that Egypt would not request Soviet military aid.[4] But Nasr's initiative was dead on arrival for, the same day that he met the American, Israeli forces had reached the Suez Canal. That evening, Egypt accepted a ceasefire.

The ceasefire was accompanied by conspiracy rumors in Cairo and it seemed for a while as if everyone was connected to one plot or another: 'Amr and his cronies were plotting at General Headquarters; 'Ali Sabri was in contact with Moscow.[5] Then came Nasser's 9 June bombshell when he declared his resignation as president in favor of Zakaria Muhi al-Din. The next day, amid massive street demonstrations in support of the *ra'is*, the National Assembly unanimously voted that Nasser must retain the presidency. As if on cue, he agreed and all talk of resignation vanished.

Even as these dramas were being played out, Salah Nasr met again with US officials to discuss the war and US–Egyptian relations. In a 9 June meeting, Salah Nasr offered his 'personal' views of the war, noting that his adversaries would depose him if they knew he was talking to the Americans. Warning that pro-Soviet forces were gaining the upper hand in Nasser's inner circle, Salah Nasr urged Washington to take 'pro-Arab' actions or risk losing Egypt to Moscow.[6] The United States was cautious in its response. It told Nasr that it was prepared to ease tensions with Egypt and that the US ambassador to Italy would facilitate high-level talks. Shortly after this, Italian intelligence entered the picture as a mediator between Washington and Cairo.[7]

On 24 June the United States passed a more detailed message through the Italian channel, reaffirming its interest in meeting Salah Nasr in Rome and facilitating direct talks between Egypt and Israel. The United States proposed a peace treaty that would include Egyptian recognition of Israel in return for the withdrawal of the IDF to pre-1967 boundaries. Israel would also be given free passage through the Straits of Tiran while Egypt would obtain some compensation for war damages.[8] In response, Salah Nasr said he would not be allowed to go to Rome; however, he wanted to continue communications with Washington through CIA or Italian intelligence channels regardless of Nasser. According to one US intelligence assessment, Salah Nasr voiced 'disdain' for Nasser for the first time.[9]

On 26 June, Salah Nasr used the backchannel again to convey information and his perspectives. He said he had advised Nasser to extend de facto recognition to Israel but the *ra'is* had 'flinched.' More significantly, Salah Nasr confided that he was in league with 'Amr, Muhi al-Din and others in the military and *mukhabarat* to get rid of Nasser.[10] As might be expected, Salah Nasr's latest proposals put US officials in a quandary. Were they genuine? What were Nasr's motives? To what extent was Nasser aware of his spy chief's dealings with Washington? The State Department's Bureau of Intelligence and Research (INR) counseled that Salah Nasr's 'anti-Nasser sentiments... should be received with caution' since the approaches to the United States were conducted with the full knowledge and approval of the *ra'is*. Furthermore, INR stressed that any US aid offered to Egypt under Salah Nasr's terms would only 'perpetuate' Nasser's rule.[11] If Salah Nasr was acting on President Nasser's instructions, the purpose of this mission is not entirely clear. Given his suspicious nature Nasser may have 'dangled' the alleged 'Amr-Muhi al-Din 'conspiracy' to see if the CIA would rise and take the bait. In any case, as far as is known, the Egyptians ceased using this channel by the end of June.

## The 'Amr conspiracy

While Nasser pondered American intentions, he had other more pressing concerns particularly the suspicious behavior of Marshal 'Amr and his clique. Just before the 8 June ceasefire took effect, the *mushir* had departed General Headquarters for one of his villas where he reportedly began stockpiling arms. The next day both 'Amr and War Minister Shams Badran resigned and were replaced by Mohamed Fawzi and Amin Howeidi respectively. At the same time a purge committee led by Zakaria Muhi al-Din forced the resignations of other senior officers, many of whom were 'Amr acolytes.[12] In his planning against 'Amr, Nasser relied on Sami Sharaf, War Minister Howeidi and Interior Minister Sharawi Guma'a in addition to MID Director Sadiq who supervised surveillance of the 'Amr group.[13] Some EGIS officials joined in the anti-'Amr operation even though the *ra'is* had already decided to remove Salah Nasr as well.[14]

The plan was implemented on the evening of 25 August when 'Amr was invited to Nasser's personal quarters and was confronted by the *ra'is*, Zakaria Muhi al-Din, Anwar al-Sadat and others. According to some accounts, it was during this meeting that 'Amr first tried to poison himself when he learned he was under house arrest.[15] A few weeks later, on the night of 14–15 September, the *mushir* was either murdered or committed suicide by swallowing a poison called Aonitine.[16] The evening of the *mushir*'s arrest, the security services rounded up Shams Badran, Salah Nasr and some 50 senior officers and civilians and charged them as accomplices in 'Amr's plot. Nasser was done toying with his director of general intelligence, and he refused any further contact with Salah Nasr to discuss the affair.[17]

Salah Nasr was quickly indicted on the charges of false arrests, use of torture to extract confessions, blackmail and embezzlement. There were also allegations that Nasr had given 'Amr the poison to kill himself.[18] Salah Nasr eventually received a sentence of life in prison for his involvement in the 'Amr plot and 15 years for the intelligence deviations. He did not serve the full term of either sentence.

We do not know if Salah Nasr was involved in 'Amr's conspiracy or whether such a plot even existed. But there were other reasons that called for Nasr's removal, not the least of which was an Egyptian public that had grown weary of the excesses of the *mukhabarat*. The *ra'is* was aware of this disenchantment, and it is likely that Salah Nasr was offered up as a scapegoat to public opinion. In November 1967 Nasser gave a public speech in which he explained Salah Nasr's role in the 'Amr conspiracy. The *ra'is* tried to reassure the public that not only had *mukhabarat* 'irregularities' been detected and stopped but the 'Intelligence State' itself was going to be dismantled. Nasser said that the powers of the security services had been 'one of the most important negative aspects which we dispensed with in our bid to purge public life in Egypt.'[19]

Nasser may have proclaimed the end of one Intelligence State but another was already taking its place. A new 'power triumvirate' was on the rise and each member had control of his own intelligence organization: Nasser's long-time aide, Sami Sharaf, controlled the small but powerful presidential intelligence apparatus; Amin Howeidi commanded MID and EGIS; and Sharawi Guma'a supervised the GID. Together these individuals ensured that the *mukhabarat* would flourish during Nasser's last years in power.

## New strategic environment

Although Nasser tried to focus on his domestic battles, Egypt's foreign commitments began to claim more of his time. The 1967 war left Egypt overextended, battered, humiliated and isolated. Its foreign policy was blunted by defeat, poor relations with key Arab states like Saudi Arabia and the abrogation of diplomatic ties with the United States. Egypt had no military means of evicting the Israelis from Sinai since its weapons had been destroyed or abandoned in the war and the rest of its army remained tied down in Yemen. The economy was all but dead.[20]

Egypt's core dilemma after the war was recalibrating its national security strategy to the circumstances of its defeat. As one of Nasser's biographers put it, the 1967 war raised the question of 'whether a country as materially weak and geographically exposed as Egypt could afford a foreign policy which tried to combine non-alignment and reliance on foreign economic development aid with a militant anti-imperialism.'[21] Set on healing the rift with the conservative Arab states, Cairo quickly dropped the strategy of subverting its Arab neighbors; on 31 August 1967 Egypt announced the withdrawal of its army from Yemen, a move which pleased the Saudis.[22]

Nasser also changed his approach to the Palestinians. Before the war, Egypt's policy had been one of endorsing the restoration of Palestinian lands while, at the same time, exercising tight control over Palestinian activities in Gaza and Egypt proper. Such was the case with Yasser Arafat, who was arrested by the GID in 1956 or early 1957 and forced to resettle in Kuwait.[23] It was there that Arafat and other Palestinian exiles founded a party called Fatah, although for security reasons they initially named it 'Asifa ('Storm'). Cairo regarded the creation and subsequent growth of Fatah with concern for a number of reasons. First there was the fear that Fatah militants would embroil the Egyptians in an unwanted war with Israel. Second, Nasser heard from his intelligence staff that Arafat was either a secret member of the Muslim Brotherhood or a hired asset of Syrian intelligence.[24] The MID made it clear that Fatah was not welcome in Gaza by monitoring and cracking down on the organization's cells.[25] On one occasion Nasser even ordered EGIS to hunt down and execute the Fatah leadership.[26]

But Egyptian attitudes began to thaw, in part because of Fatah's growing appeal among young Palestinians; by 1966, the relationship had improved to the point that Salah Nasr hosted Arafat and another Fatah leader named Faruq Qaddumi in Cairo. According to one account, EGIS lodged the Fatah delegation at an upscale Cairo hotel where the Palestinians were offered their pick of Egyptian women. But this only irritated Qaddumi who burst out: 'We are the representatives of a revolutionary movement on which the fate of an entire people depends! It isn't with favors and loose women that you can establish relations with us!' Needless to say, neither Qaddumi nor Arafat was inclined on this occasion to answer Egyptian questions about Fatah operations, finances and membership.[27]

After the 1967 war Fatah and the *mukhabarat* mended ties. As the shock of Israel's occupation of Gaza and the West Bank set in, more Palestinians were searching for radical and violent solutions to their crisis. Meanwhile, shorn of its weapons, Egypt regarded Fatah as a useful lever against Israel. As General Mohamed Fawzi put it, '*fida'i* [guerrilla] action was very important to us... because we were at point zero, especially in the Air Force. We needed to "heat up" the other fronts so as to be able to rebuild our strength.'[28] Accordingly, in fall 1967, EGIS Director Howeidi invited a Fatah delegation to Cairo. According to one version of what followed, Howeidi introduced the delegation to Nasser who said that Fatah could serve as the Arabs' 'irresponsible arm' or as an Arab version of Israel's pre-independence Stern Gang.[29] In another account offered by Fatah intelligence chief Salah Khalaf (Abu Iyad), there was no meeting with Nasser, only an encounter with Mohamed Hassanein Heikal who opened the meeting by saying: 'We know very little about you... Our intelligence file on al-Asifa is virtually empty. Your mystery intrigues us, and in the last analysis your capacity for dissimulation is no doubt an indication of your seriousness.'[30]

While accounts differ over who met whom there is little disagreement over what followed. Shortly after the meeting, Egypt reportedly flew in at least two planeloads of arms to Fatah guerrillas in Jordan.[31] On the intelligence front there were major developments as well, for the *mukhabarat* needed a new generation of Palestinian scouts who could penetrate Israel from bases in Jordan. Fatah held out some promise in this regard and in 1968 Egyptian intelligence trained Fatah intelligence officers in recruiting and controlling assets; reports writing; intelligence evaluations; interrogations and surveillance; and the use of small arms.[32] The partnership also included intelligence sharing and joint asset recruiting. An MID officer was posted to Amman to liaise with the various Palestinian groups including Fatah.[33] When the MID received Soviet intelligence about a pending IDF raid across the Jordan River in 1968, it transmitted this warning to Jordan and Fatah who prepared for the ensuing Battle of Karameh.[34] Egyptian intelligence also helped Fatah recruit assets. For example, in November 1969 the Egyptian military attaché in London recruited two British nationals and sent them to Cairo where they were trained by Fatah in sabotage, hijacking and kidnapping. The operation was derailed when one of the recruits informed the British police.[35]

Another consequence of the 1967 defeat was Egypt's increased reliance on the USSR for arms and military training. Indeed, the dust had hardly settled on the war when Moscow began to rapidly make up Egypt's losses in weapons and equipment.[36] The Soviets also sent a team to analyze the MID's performance. In an unusual move, the MID granted the Soviets access to daily and weekly intelligence reports that it submitted to the Egyptian leadership immediately prior to the war. According to MID Director Sadiq, the Soviets generally supported the MID's assessments of Israel before the crisis. This may account for the fact that Sadiq survived the war with his job intact.[37]

The dramatic increase in the official Soviet presence in Egypt after the war meant new recruiting opportunities for Soviet intelligence officers. According to one estimate, there were as many as 50 KGB and GRU officers in Cairo alone who were focused on recruiting spies in the Egyptian military, security forces, government and media circles.[38] Nonetheless, although he permitted the Soviets to assess the MID's wartime performance, General Sadiq argued successfully that his agency should be shielded from Soviet advisers given the potential for espionage.[39] In addition to the Soviets, Interior Minister Guma'a pressed for an intelligence exchange with the East German Stasi as well as Stasi assistance in investigating Israel's penetration of the Egyptian government. Apparently Guma'a was convinced that Israeli spies were responsible for Egypt's defeat in June 1967. Although the East Germans protested that they had little or no intelligence on Israel's security services, they did help the GID set up an improved telephone monitoring system.[40]

In the months following the June war, US–Egypt relations had plummeted even further. Not only were diplomatic ties cut but, for a while at least, Nasser persisted in his belief that the US military had attacked Egypt during the war. In the intelligence field Egyptian hostility manifested itself by aggressive human and technical surveillance of American officials working in the US Interests Section at the Spanish Embassy; they also used agents provocateurs against US missions overseas.[41] Such may have been the case with Egypt's ambassador to the Netherlands, 'Uthman Husein Fawzi, who approached his American counterpart in March 1970 and offered to help overthrow Nasser. Fawzi's proposal drove American intelligence analysts to their files where they learned that this Egyptian diplomat had previously served in the MID and EGIS. Indeed, one of his duties at EGIS in 1955 was collecting intelligence on Americans.[42] The US embassy in the Netherlands was advised by Washington to be in a non-committal listening mode should Fawzi approach the United States again. According to the State Department, Fawzi's was only the latest in a series of recent efforts by Egyptian officials to commit Americans to subversive action against the Egyptian government. Indeed, State believed that all of these approaches were 'likely provocations by the UAR intelligence apparatus.'[43]

Yet even during this period, at the worst of times in US–Egyptian relations, the old EGIS–CIA backchannel was used to provide some semblance of communications between Cairo and Washington. Assessments, reports and diplomatic communications were quietly passed even as Cairo and Washington jousted on the international scene.[44]

## Reforming intelligence

After the 1967 defeat Cairo's need for intelligence on Israel was greater than ever, for the Israelis now occupied Sinai, blocked the Suez Canal and were in a good position to dictate humbling peace terms. One major fear in Cairo was that the shattered state of the Egyptian army might invite IDF incursions across the canal itself. It was in this context that Egypt began to reorganize the *mukhabarat*.

Amin Howeidi's three-year tenure as both war minister and EGIS director gave him a unique opportunity to overhaul and realign the missions of the MID and EGIS. Educated at the Egyptian Military Academy and later at the US Army's Command and General Staff College, Howeidi had previously served as director of EGIS's Research Department, ambassador to Iraq and commander of Egyptian forces in Yemen.[45] Undoubtedly with the Soviet 'warning' of May 1967 in mind, EGIS Director Howeidi made it clear he wanted 'confirmed' and 'validated' intelligence instead of 'news' from his intelligence services.[46] The MID in particular was ordered to downgrade missions like spying on Egyptian officers and focus on the Israeli threat.[47]

MID intelligence officers were now given the green light to study Israel in all its facets from topography and meteorology to politics, society and psychology. New efforts were made to produce a reliable baseline of Israeli military capabilities and order of battle. Perhaps most importantly, MID officers were allowed to study the once taboo subject of the Hebrew language.[48] This alone must have paid some impressive dividends when both countries returned to war in 1973. Indeed, by analyzing press interviews given by Israeli commanders after the

1967 war, the MID learned a great deal about how the IDF fought, the IDF's perception of its own and Egypt's strengths and weaknesses and future Israeli intentions.[49]

Given the new circumstances, MID operations were now directed against Sinai instead of Israel proper. Fortunately for Egypt the 8 June ceasefire left it in possession of the city of Port Fuad on the east bank of the Canal. This toehold in Israeli-occupied Sinai was used as an infiltration point for MID scouting and special forces missions behind Israeli lines.[50] The main goal of these missions was to gather intelligence on the IDF, its transportation networks and fortifications. In February and November 1968 Israeli security uncovered Egyptian networks in Sinai which revealed the MID's modus operandi at this time. In the earlier case, Bedouin agents were apprehended along with a radio and over 200 cables sent to the ring by MID case officers since November of the previous year. In the later raid, Israeli security apprehended a 27-year-old Bedouin who carried photographs and documents of airfields, military installations and IDF units in Sinai. The detainee said he was controlled by a MID case officer based in Port Said.[51]

But Egyptian military planners required detailed order of battle intelligence and for this they turned to air force photo reconnaissance jets which began flying missions over the Sinai within days of the 8 June ceasefire.[52] As a measure of Egyptian anxieties at this time, the MID ordered one over-flight just after the ceasefire to determine if the IDF was preparing to invade the west bank of the canal.[53] But the reconnaissance missions were very risky and many pilots did not survive Israel's air defenses. If Egypt was to ever conduct a cross-canal assault and expel Israel from the Sinai it required more imagery intelligence. Only the Soviet Union could fill this need and, over time, the MID was granted greater access to Moscow's satellite imagery.[54] In addition, in April 1968, Soviet aircraft began to stage out of Egyptian airfields both to monitor the US Sixth Fleet and to fly along and sometimes over the Sinai shoreline. Some of these planes bore Egyptian markings and their photographs of Israeli positions were shared with the MID.[55]

The 1967 war taught the Egyptians valuable lessons in electronic intelligence (ELINT) and electronic warfare. In 1969 the military reorganized its existing ELINT capabilities – i.e. the ability to intercept electronic emissions from aircraft and ground radars in order to counter, avoid or destroy them – and placed them under a new Electronic Warfare Directorate. As in other fields the Soviets were the key to Egypt's future ELINT capabilities since only they could supply the necessary early warning radars and electronic countermeasures (ECM) equipment.[56] The Electronic Warfare Directorate staffed and serviced the new ELINT and ECM equipment while the MID compiled and interpreted the data.[57] But progress in the highly technical (and expensive) ELINT and ECM fields was slow, and in December 1969 Cairo was humiliated by an Israeli raid on an early warning facility which resulted in the theft of a sophisticated new radar.[58]

Egypt's signals intelligence (SIGINT) capabilities during the crucial period between the 1967 and 1973 wars are a mystery. The emphasis on training

Hebrew linguists must have paid off handsomely in the SIGINT arena if only to expedite the analysis of intercepted unencrypted Israeli military communications. In addition, the MID built a large SIGINT facility on Jebel 'Ataqa just west of the city of Suez, which collected Israeli military communications throughout the Sinai.[59]

Egypt also tried to improve its intelligence assessments process. Not surprisingly, the emphasis was now on a more accurate estimate of how Israel prepared for, fought and won its wars.[60] According to one source, an Egyptian Staff College instructor was told to back off when he proposed analyzing the IDF in depth before the 1967 war.[61] That situation had now changed as the MID began producing assessments on IDF capabilities, strengths and weaknesses.[62] No doubt these estimates benefited greatly from a cadre of military officers who were now trained in Hebrew and conversant with the latest open source intelligence on the Israeli military. For the Egyptian intelligence services this was a big step forward.

## Attrition war

While the *mukhabarat* struggled to reform itself, the country's leadership grappled with the problem of ending Israeli occupation of Egyptian lands. The fact was that Cairo had no military means to expel Israel from Sinai, and its diplomacy was hampered by Egypt's isolation, weakness, the humiliation of defeat and its economic problems. Not long after the 8 June ceasefire went into effect Egypt began to conduct commando raids and fire sporadic artillery shells at Israeli positions in Sinai. These pinpricks, designed to raise Egyptian morale and remind Israel that the war was not over, often sparked a disproportionate Israeli response. In 1968 the MID followed its tradition of creating guerrilla groups against foreign occupiers when it set up the Arab Sinai Organization; unfortunately for Cairo this group had a negligible impact on the battlefield.[63] Therefore, faced with few alternatives except a peace deal he could not entertain, Nasser settled on an attrition strategy in March 1969.

One US intelligence agency called the 1969–1970 Egyptian–Israeli Attrition War a '*danse macabre*.'[64] This is a good description of the process where Egypt would fire artillery shells onto Israeli positions only to invite disproportionate Israeli retaliation. Cairo would view Israel's response as a humiliation, and retaliate with another round of artillery shells that would initiate the cycle again. One September 1969 Israeli raid on an Egyptian coastal district resulted in a shake-up of the Egyptian high command. Nasser promoted MID Director Mohamed Ahmed Sadiq to Armed Forces Chief of Staff. Sadiq's replacement was Major General Mihriz Mustafa 'Abd al-Rahman, a long-serving military intelligence officer who had served as Sadiq's deputy. A military attaché to Beijing from 1960–1963, Mihriz was described in one report as 'quiet, carefully spoken, courteous and shrewd.'[65]

On 7 January 1970, the Israelis escalated the attrition war when the IAF conducted deep penetration raids in the Nile Valley and expanded their targets to include civilians. This shift led many observers to believe that Israel was intent on overthrowing Nasser by highlighting his inability to protect his people from Israeli attacks.[66] It was only when the Soviets provided new SAMs, aircraft and even air defense crews that the tide began to turn. On 22 July 1970 Nasser felt secure enough to support a 90 day renewable ceasefire plan proposed by US Secretary of State William Rogers.

## Internal unrest

It was probably inevitable that the 1967 defeat would provoke internal unrest in Egypt. Although the Interior Ministry's legions of informants and secret police officers were watching for dissent, they were caught off guard by worker and student demonstrations that rocked the country in February and November 1968. The February riots were sparked by public outrage over the lenient sentences passed on senior military officers tried for the June war. The demonstrations, the largest in over 14 years, started in Helwan and then spread to Cairo and Alexandria where they attracted university student support as well. Among the demands of these loosely coordinated rallies were harsher sentences on the military officers, removal of the secret police from university campuses and free elections.[67] Indeed, one popular student cry at this time was: 'Down with the Intelligence State!'– mocking Nasser's vague promises to dampen the excesses of his secret police.[68]

But these protests and riots could not be sustained. The internal security apparatus was soon humming in high gear, arresting leaders and spreading stories that 'reactionary elements' were provoking the unrest. Even so, in November 1968 a new round of student protests was ignited in several universities forcing the government to temporarily shut down several campuses.[69] The 1968 protests may have been inspired by similar student unrest sweeping across Europe and North America, but they were also firmly rooted in an angry rejection of the police state and frustration at Egypt's Sinai defeat. Rather than address the causes of discontent, the regime cynically linked the student leaders to Israeli intelligence, whipping up a new atmosphere of spy mania.[70]

But regime repression could not combat the tectonic shifts that were occurring in Egyptian society as a result of the 1967 war. The humiliation of defeat combined with police state excesses had gutted the appeal of Nasser's Arab Socialism for many Egyptians, especially the youth. Many returning soldiers and angry students believed their country had lost its spiritual moorings by chasing the materialistic Western chimeras of Arab Socialism. The Muslim Brotherhood's mantra that 'Islam is the Solution' was gaining more adherents than ever before. The full implications of this new emphasis on Islam was not to be felt until the next decade, but there was little doubt that it had its roots in the soul-searching that followed the 1967 debacle.

## The death of Nasser

Nasser's death by heart attack on 28 September 1970 marked the end of a tumultuous period in Egyptian history. From an intelligence perspective, his personality shaped the nature and behavior of the Egyptian intelligence state. Habitually suspicious, Nasser created an elaborate internal security apparatus that shielded him from army plotters and the Muslim Brotherhood; it monitored subordinates and dissidents and tackled foreign espionage. The creation of EGIS coincided closely with Nasser's growing ambitions in the international arena in the 1950s and early 1960s. EGIS not only served as a subversive instrument of Nasser's foreign policy, it also spied on Nasser's growing list of foreign enemies.

Nasser was an avid intelligence consumer. He understood the need for reliable estimates but, at the same time, he did not – or could not – prevent the dangerous politicization of intelligence assessments in 1956 and 1967. At the same time, Nasser was an introvert who increasingly relied on the sycophants Sharaf and Sabri and less on the grounded advice of Zakaria Muhi al-Din or other old colleagues. In fact, by the mid-1960s, Nasser was falling prey to a venal clique of yes-men who fed him stories of threats to his throne that only confirmed his worst suspicions. The intelligence clique of Sharaf, Nasr and Sabri no doubt validated their own worth by constantly reminding Nasser of their ability to shield him from plots, conspiracies and assassination.

It is not surprising then that the Egyptian regime reflected the character of its founder. There was a strong sense of siege by conspiracies emanating from within Egypt and abroad. An elaborate, sophisticated and brutal *mukhabarat* apparatus was created to neutralize these conspiracies and export the Nasserist revolution abroad. It did irreparable damage to Egyptian society. When Nasser publicly criticized the Intelligence State in late 1967, it was already far too late to do anything about it. As one US intelligence assessment put it in October 1969: 'Nasser has organized an extensive and efficient intelligence and security apparatus which reaches into almost every corner of Egyptian society.'[71] What remained to be seen was how the new leadership would manage the *mukhabarat* state that Nasser had created.

# Part III
# Intelligence under Sadat

# 11 Power struggles

He devoured them for lunch before they could eat him for dinner.

Egyptian saying

When Vice President Anwar al-Sadat announced Nasser's death there was an outpouring of mass grieving that surprised many foreign observers by its scale and fervor. Yet while millions mourned Nasser's death, a power struggle was already underway within the Egyptian government to anoint his successor. Acting President Sadat was one possibility, but it was widely believed in Egypt and abroad that he lacked the clout and ruthlessness of his rivals to assert a credible claim to Nasser's mantle. Indeed, in the early days of his presidency, Sadat appeared at times to be emasculated by more powerful and well-connected political players such as Interior Minister Sharawi Guma'a, 'Ali Sabri, Sami Sharaf and Mohamed Fawzi.[1]

Yet Sadat survived the ensuing power struggle in large part because his rivals erroneously judged him to be a weak, pliable, transition figure. How mistaken they were, for behind Sadat's complacent exterior lurked a raw cunning and iron will that none of his adversaries apparently anticipated.[2] Sadat slowly and quietly built his powerbase by shrewdly reaching out to powerful military and *mukhabarat* figures. At the same time, he proved adept at manipulating his opponents, playing on their weaknesses and undermining their confidence in each other. There are also indications that Sadat's links to US intelligence helped bolster his hold on the presidency even though many in Washington suspected he would not last long.

The early months of Sadat's presidency were also marked by a growing estrangement with the Soviet Union. Part of this was based on Soviet awareness of the new Egyptian leader's clandestine contacts with the Americans; however, Moscow also erred badly by backing Sadat's political opponents in the post-Nasser power struggle. When Sadat expelled most of his Soviet military advisors in 1972 he did so with two objectives in mind: (*a*) to remove an obstacle to his plans for war with Israel; (*b*) to lay the groundwork for a new, pro-Western foreign policy.

## Sadat and intelligence

Apart from his dealings with German spies, British intelligence and the political police during World War II, Sadat's experience with intelligence was limited. In fact, he used this inexperience to his advantage. According to one account, Sadat refused to look at Sami Sharaf's daily compilations of intercepted telephone calls unless they pertained to state security. He then insisted that all phone tapping cease absent a court order.[3] Sadat tried to portray himself as Nasser's 'clean' successor who did not share the *ra'is*'s suspicious nature and who was willing to truly shut down the Intelligence State. Yet appearance was frustrated by reality.

Sadat did not share his predecessor's penchant for reading and absorbing detailed information. An 'ideas man' rather than a devotee of details, Sadat reportedly balked at the 'mountain of paper' that was heaped on his desk during his first days in office.[4] Not for him were the *mukhabarat* files, the embassy reports, the transcriptions of tapped phone conversations: Sadat had neither the inclination nor the time for this. Yet Sadat knew how to get intelligence that was essential for his personal and political survival. Moreover, his influential wife, Jehan, read many of the intelligence reports that crossed his desk and passed the gist of them to her husband.[5]

## Power struggles

Few in Egypt and abroad gave Sadat's presidency much staying power. In one of its earliest assessments of his rule, the CIA commented that Sadat did not 'carry much political weight' and that it was 'doubtful' he could retain the presidency 'for more than [an] interim period.' Instead the CIA – and many others – predicted Sadat would be a 'figurehead president' fronting for an inner ring of men like 'Ali Sabri, Sharawi Guma'a, Sami Sharaf and Mohamed Fawzi.[6] It was clear that these men were powerful challengers for the throne; moreover, each had deep roots in the *mukhabarat*.[7]

It was not long before EGIS was mired in the power struggle. In November 1970 its director, Mohamed Hafiz Isma'il, was replaced by Ahmed Kamel, a former artillery officer who thought he was going to be Sadat's Minister of Youth.[8] Although a member of the ASU apparatus, Kamel was not trusted by any of the players and marginalized from the start. In fact, Sadat met him only two or three times and directed that EGIS reports were only to reach him through Sami Sharaf.[9] This lack of access to Sadat must have demoralized Egypt's premier intelligence service which historically served at the behest of the president. Kamel later recalled that he entered his office with 'conflicting views' – a euphemism for recognizing and fearing the by now notorious behavior of the *mukhabarat*.[10]

Sadat spent the beginning of his presidency sizing up his opposition and preparing for a showdown. What the president counted on was that his relative lack of stature in Egyptian politics would be outweighed by the notoriety and lack of popularity of his opponents. Perhaps an anonymous Egyptian worker summed this up best when he said that, although he did not particularly like Sadat, he '*hated* Sharawi Guma'a, 'Ali Sabri, etc., who acted like...only they understood socialism and spoke for the people.'[11] Sabri was regarded as Nasser's likely heir; however he had an unattractive 'secretive' personality and his prospects were badly tarnished by the opposition of many senior military officers.[12] Interior Minister Sharawi Guma'a was another contender. A former army officer with an EGIS background, Guma'a was unpopular because he had presided over some of the most ruthless purges of public life in Egypt's recent history.[13] Then there was Sami Sharaf, the head of the small but powerful presidential intelligence apparatus who also enjoyed de facto control over EGIS. A man of the files, Sharaf collected information on all senior officials; presumably he had a file on Sadat, too.[14] But Sharaf was a rather dull, faceless but ruthless functionary hated by those who had the misfortune of crossing his path.[15]

As he plotted strategy, Sadat knew he had to maintain the loyalty of those Republican Guard officers who were responsible for presidential security.[16] Sadat also made a point of courting armed forces chief of staff Lieutenant General Mohamed Ahmed Sadiq and military officers embittered by the post-1967 purges of the ranks.[17] Sadat also found *mukhabarat* allies even though his opponents exercised direct control over the intelligence services. For example, Sadat maintained the loyalty of Hafez Isma'il despite the fact that he had turned a blind eye to – or was powerless to prevent – Isma'il's removal as EGIS Director the previous year. According to one account, Isma'il tipped off Sadat to the conspiracy that was building against him in April 1971.[18] Sadat also recruited MID Director Mihriz Mustafa 'Abd al-Rahman and Alexandria Governor, Mamduh Salem, an individual with deep roots in the secret police and the ASU.[19]

## The corrective revolution

By April 1971 it was apparent to most observers of Egyptian politics that things had reached a boiling point. Not only did Sadat show no inclination of playing a figurehead role, his opponents were growing impatient with a president who refused to fit the mold they had created for him.[20] They also were suspicious of Sadat's secret dealings with foreign powers, for EGIS bugs had captured clandestine discussions between US diplomats and Sadat's emissaries on a possible peace deal with Israel.[21] Sadat's rivals made their move on 17 April 1971 when they rejected the president's proposal for a paper union with Libya and Syria. 'Ali Sabri alleged the unity deal was concluded without the ASU's consent while Interior Minister Guma'a secretly deployed the GID to state radio and television facilities to block Sadat from making a direct appeal to the people.[22] At the same time Minister of War Fawzi organized Cairo-area military units for a coup and instructed the Electronic Warfare Department to prepare jamming foreign embassy communications.[23] But this crisis passed without resolution.

Then Sadat struck back. On 2 May he announced 'Ali Sabri's removal as vice president. By acting against Sabri, Sadat was not only confronting the most credible of his opponents, he also knew that Sabri was mistrusted and disliked by his fellow conspirators. Sadat counted on them to remain passive and that is exactly what happened.[24] Things went into a tense lull again until the crucial morning hours of 10 May 1971. According to the first – and more widely known – narrative, a GID major approached Sadat with secret tapes of senior ASU members discussing future moves against the president.[25] The second account lacks corroborating sources, although it suggests an intriguing dimension of the CIA–Sadat relationship that has never been examined. According to this narrative, US intelligence picked up indications of an anti-Sadat conspiracy from both a KGB asset named Vladimir Sakharov and intercepted phone conversations. A CIA case officer in Cairo named Thomas Twetten then conveyed this intelligence to key Sadat aide Ashraf Marwan.[26] If this second account is accurate it could help explain why Sadat turned so decisively to the Americans for diplomatic, security and intelligence assistance after the 1973 war.

On 13 May Sadat replaced his most powerful adversary, Interior Minister Guma'a with Mamduh Salem. Upon assuming his new position, Salem sacked the GID director and replaced him with an ally from the Alexandria GID.[27] On the night of 13 May the remaining conspirators – Sharaf, Fawzi and Mohamed Fa'iq – tried to force Sadat's hand by collectively resigning from their posts. But Sadat did not let these resignations deter him: the core conspirators were arrested without resistance while the MID was instructed to be on the watch for further plotting.[28] Although he had no apparent ties to the plot, EGIS boss Ahmed Kamel was jailed for his alleged failure to warn Sadat of the conspiracy. He was replaced by Ahmed Isma'il.[29] In this way EGIS underwent another leadership change – its fourth since 1967.

On 25 August 1971, 91conspirators were put on trial and charged with attempting to overthrow the government and thwarting the president from exercising his powers. The main evidence used against the defendants was 185 taped telephone conversations that had been found in the GID and EGIS repositories.[30] When the verdicts were announced in December 1971, Guma'a, Sharaf and Sabri received death sentences; however, these were commuted to life with labor at the Abu Za'abal penitentiary. With these sentences all domestic opposition to the Sadat presidency had been effectively crushed for the moment.

## Reform

Sadat tried to shore up public support for his regime by reforming the secret police. On 31 May he participated in the public destruction of thousands of GID wiretap tapes at the Interior Ministry.[31] Sadat also promised to cease wiretapping without judicial oversight, end press censorship, close concentration camps and make it easier for Egyptians to travel abroad.[32] A few weeks later Mamduh Salem announced the release of most political prisoners and the abolition of the university police whose tasks had included spying on student leaders.[33]

Yet Sadat was careful not to go too far in alienating the *mukhabarat*. In a speech delivered at MID headquarters on 12 August 1971, Sadat attributed the

1967 defeat to the military's senior officers not the fighting soldiers. He infamously declared that 1971 was to be the 'decisive year' for Egypt in her confrontation with Israel.[34] Sadat also issued a decree that renamed and partly reorganized the GID and its Interior Ministry supervisors. Stripped of its remaining military officers, some of whom were holdovers from the 1950s, the GID was renamed the General Department of State Security Investigations and, eventually, the State Security Investigations Service (*Jihaz Mabahath Amn al-Dawla*) (SSIS). But these changes did not affect the SSIS's core missions of intelligence collection, counterintelligence and internal security.[35]

Sadat also overhauled his national security team. The most prominent of these changes was General Mohamed Sadiq's promotion to War Minister. A former EGIS officer who was related to Nasser by marriage named Ashraf Marwan replaced Sami Sharaf in the role of presidential gatekeeper.[36] At least two sources indicate that Marwan warned Sadat of the mounting conspiracies against him in May 1971.[37] As we have seen, Sadat replaced the unfortunate Ahmed Kamel at EGIS with Ahmed Isma'il, the first Egyptian to graduate from the Soviet Frunze military academy in the 1950s.[38] Unfortunately for the demoralized EGIS, Isma'il also came with the humiliation of having been dismissed from command after a September 1969 Israeli raid. Sadat rewarded former EGIS Director Mohamed Hafiz Isma'il (no relation to Ahmed Isma'il) with the newly created post of Adviser to the President for National Security Affairs in September 1971. Presumably because Isma'il had warned Sadat of the looming April 1971 conspiracy, his new assignment included some of Sharaf's old intelligence oversight responsibilities.[39]

## Sadat and the Americans

Although Washington did not give Sadat much chance of surviving his first months in office it did see an opportunity to forge a new relationship with Egypt. Reflecting the precedent set by Nasser, US–Egypt relations were conducted in separate channels: conventional diplomacy and a more secret dialogue run by CIA. According to one account, it was a CIA Free Officer contact from the 1950s named 'Abd al-Mun'im 'Amin who first convinced Sadat that a harshly anti-American line was counterproductive. Sadat agreed to let 'Amin establish a discreet dialogue with US intelligence officers working at the Interests Section, including station chief Eugene Trone. On the other side of this quiet exchange were Richard Nixon and eventually Henry Kissinger, no strangers to secret channels in their own right.[40] It is not clear what role the weakened EGIS played in this, especially in the beginning when Sadat still doubted its loyalties.[41]

There were dangers for the United States in conducting secret diplomacy with an Egyptian regime torn by intrigue and whose intelligence services were under the control of the president's enemies. In late 1970 the MID was conducting radio security checks in Cairo when it came across a series of suspicious signals emanating from inside the city. Eventually, the MID determined that they were coming from Sadat's villa in Giza. In January 1971 War Minister Fawzi had the somewhat awkward mission of approaching the president and suggesting that he move the transmitter out of the residence. It was in fact moved to 'Abdin Palace downtown.[42] Sadat probably was using this transmitter for secret negotiations with the United States.

The delicate and clandestine minuet between Cairo and Washington never disguised the fact that the CIA and EGIS were at this point still adversaries. Indeed, in September 1971 the *mukhabarat* arrested an alleged CIA spy named Tanashi Randopolo who worked near the Gianaclis air base outside Alexandria. In addition to the Egyptian Air Force, Gianaclis also served Soviet reconnaissance aircraft monitoring the US Sixth Fleet in the Mediterranean. According to one official, Randopolo used his friendly ties with some Soviet officers to gain access to Gianaclis, where aircraft, radars, air defenses and other features were monitored.[43]

It is not clear how the *mukhabarat* was first put Randopolo's trail. Soviet counterintelligence at Gianaclis may have been suspicious of the garrulous Egyptian who was often seen at the base. Alternatively, Egyptian counterintelligence may have been monitoring Randopolo or, more likely, his CIA case officers. Just as they did with Mustafa Amin several years earlier, the spy catchers pounced on Randopolo during a meeting with his case officer. The American pleaded diplomatic immunity and was released but Egyptian intelligence also arrested another suspected CIA officer named Sue Ann Harris who was taken to EGIS headquarters.[44]

The head of the US Interests Section fired off an angry letter to the Foreign Ministry, arguing that EGIS had acted on faulty intelligence, but this only enraged EGIS Director Ahmed Isma'il who summoned the CIA station chief, Eugene Trone, to deliver a formal complaint. Trone reportedly tried to dampen the crisis by assuring Isma'il that the United States was spying on the Soviets – not Egyptians – and that Randopolo information would not be shared with Israel.[45] It was a delicate moment in the new relationship between EGIS and CIA. For her part, Harris refused to confess to spying and she was released after the CIA threatened to cut the secret channel between Sadat and Washington.[46] Randopolo's fate is not known, although there are rumors that he died of a 'heart attack' while under interrogation.[47]

EGIS–CIA spy wars did not end with Randopolo. In early 1972 Egyptian intelligence arrested a retired general officer and ambassador named Muhab 'Abd al-Ghafar and accused him of espionage. According to the *mukhabarat*, the general reportedly had met with US officials in the casual setting of the Ma'adi Club and agreed to gather information for the United States. Although US diplomats insisted Ghafar was not an American intelligence asset, the Egyptian press reported in November that he had been sentenced to ten years for divulging secrets and communicating with a foreign power.[48] The Egyptians also responded to the Randopolo and Ghafar affairs by ordering a reduction in the official US presence in Egypt.[49]

## A Saudi spy?

Anwar al-Sadat was not immune from espionage rumors during the highly charged period between the 1967 and 1973 wars. Indeed, given his preference for clandestine talks with foreign powers, it is not surprising that stories circulated that Sadat was a spy for one or more powers, including the United States and Saudi Arabia. Evidence is lacking to back these allegations, although Sadat's dealings with the Saudis do merit a closer look.

At the heart of the Saudi-Sadat story was a former head of Saudi intelligence named Kamal Adham.[50] Sadat first met Adham during the early 1950s and by 1955 their relationship was such that Sadat stood witness for Adham's marriage.[51] During the 1950s, or perhaps the early 1960s, Sadat reportedly began accepting Saudi 'gifts.'[52] According to one source, Kamal Adham had 'extremely close' ties to Sadat which he cultivated during the Yemen war period 'with a steady income.'[53] It is impossible to verify these claims. What is known is that after Nasser's death Adham was a frequent visitor to Egypt where his agenda included improved Egyptian–Saudi relations and convincing Sadat to evict the Soviet military advisers.[54] Adham not only established a secret link between Sadat and King Faisal, he also mediated between Cairo and Washington in a process that culminated in a de facto alliance after the 1973 war.[55]

Rich gifts from Saudi emissaries were (and are) a common feature of Middle East politics and it is plausible that Sadat accepted periodic Saudi 'gifts' with no concrete quid pro quo expected. Moreover, as president, Sadat certainly recognized that Kamal Adham could bring Egypt a badly needed boost of foreign currency – some say up to $200 million a year.[56] At the same time, the Saudis provided Sadat with an entrée to the United States and some shelter from the Egyptian president's fiercest critics in Libya, Iraq, Syria and South Yemen.

Kamal Adham was also linked to stories that Sadat may have been a CIA contact as well. For example, Sami Sharaf later alleged that Sadat began receiving payments from the CIA in 1966.[57] If Sharaf was speaking the truth (or perhaps recalling an intelligence report or two from this time) it is surprising that neither Sharaf nor Nasser did anything about Sadat's seeming treachery. Yet, as Mustafa Amin learned in 1965, the *ra'is* had no tolerance for unauthorized contacts between presidential acquaintances and American intelligence.

## Soviet troubles

No country stood to lose more in post-Nasser Egypt than the USSR. Unfortunately for Moscow, Sadat never showed the same inclination toward Soviet communism as Sami Sharaf or 'Ali Sabri did. When the Soviet leader Aleksei Kosygin came to Nasser's funeral he reportedly urged Sadat to preserve the policies of his predecessor:

> Let me tell you how we used to deal with things when Nasser was alive… We never had any secrets from him, and he never had any secrets from us. It is essential that each of us tell the other everything.[58]

But sharing secrets with Moscow was never in Sadat's playbook, especially when he learned that Sabri, Sharaf and Guma'a were in secret contact with the Soviet ambassador before May 1971.[59] For its part, Moscow was aware of Sadat's backchannel communications with Washington either through access to *mukhabarat* wiretaps or a KGB SIGINT station located at the Soviet embassy in Cairo.[60] The mere existence of Sadat's secret talks must have sent tremors through Moscow. Having invested a lot in Egypt, Moscow was determined to preserve its gains in what was still the most important country of the Arab world.

The KGB and GRU presence in Egypt was a large one at this time. Some of the Soviet intelligence officers were declared – that is, the Egyptians knew their identity and that their purpose for working in Egypt included liaison with Egyptian intelligence. At the same time, there were numerous clandestine Soviet intelligence officers who tried to infiltrate the Egyptian services and spied on Egyptians and foreign diplomats. These were the case officers that the *mukhabarat* had to worry about.

From 1970 to 1974 the most senior KGB officer ('*Rezident*') in Egypt was Vadim Vasilyevich Kirpichenko, a veteran case officer with previous experience in the country.[61] By the time Kirpichenko became *Rezident*, the KGB had a stable of Egyptian assets many of whom were recruited from the minority Armenian, Coptic, Syrian and Lebanese communities. Others were officers recruited during the war in Yemen.[62] The KGB had also successfully penetrated Egyptian counterintelligence and one of its agents was an SSIS officer named 'Abd al-Maqsud Fahmi Hasan with access to thousands of files on foreigners still resident in Alexandria.[63] These must have been a boon for KGB recruiters looking for new agents in Egypt.

Soviet intelligence was thrown off stride by Sadat's May 1971 move against his opposition. In the purges of Egyptian officials and security personnel that followed, the KGB lost several of its best access agents. Hitherto routine clandestine contacts between Soviet case officers and their spy networks were broken and several agents refused to continue spying for the USSR.[64] Moreover, Egyptian counterintelligence stepped up its harassment of Soviet intelligence officers and disrupted their meetings with agents and contacts.[65] In April 1972, the SSIS replaced its Stasi telephone surveillance advisory team with a French mission.[66]

Sadat believed that Soviet interference would block any attempt by Egypt to resume hostilities with Israel, and in July 1972 he used Moscow's refusal to sell Cairo ballistic missiles and fighters as a pretext to terminate the Soviet military mission in Egypt. Within weeks most of the Soviets were gone and with them went their aerial reconnaissance assets like the Tu-16 and MiG-25. For the conspiracy minded, the presence of Kamal Adham and the Saudi Defense Minister in Cairo at the same time that Sadat made his announcement provided ample fodder.[67] Although he certainly did not burn all his crucial security bridges to the USSR, Sadat felt that the drastic reduction in the Soviet military presence in Egypt helped clear the way for his much discussed and often mocked 'decision war' with Israel.

# 12  Grand deception in the 1973 war

By the end of 1972 Sadat had shored up his domestic front by disposing of his opponents, implementing reforms, appeasing his military and security constituencies and expelling the unpopular Soviet advisors. But Israel's occupation of Sinai continued to cloud Egypt's (and Sadat's) horizon. Sadat's periodic proposals of peace with Israel in return for a Sinai withdrawal lacked credibility absent a rearmed, highly trained Egyptian military. Indeed, Sadat's negotiating position seemed to have been made worse by his 1972 decision to expel the Soviet advisors.

Sadat went to war in October 1973 with only a limited military objective in mind: to capture all or part of the east bank of the Suez Canal and then weather the anticipated Israeli retaliatory assault. He pinned his hopes on the anticipation that a successful canal crossing – even if for limited territory on the other side – would improve his negotiating position such that the Israelis would agree to withdraw from Sinai. That this is in fact what ultimately occurred is due in no small part to the increased effectiveness of the Egyptian intelligence community in both war and peace. Indeed, strategic deception combined with improved technical intelligence collection, better analysis and quite possibly a highly-placed double agent all contributed to early Egyptian success on the battlefield.

Although Egyptian (and Syrian) fortunes waned in the latter days of the war, Sadat continued to pursue his limited war strategy much to the consternation of his Syrian ally. In the end, despite its military defeats on the west bank of the canal, Cairo was able to convert its limited hold on the east bank of the canal into a deal under which Egypt regained the Sinai in return for recognizing the state of Israel. It was a diplomatic tour de force.

## Military unrest

Prior to the 1973 war, many experts believed the Egyptian military was not prepared for any major confrontation with Israel, especially after Sadat expelled the Soviet advisors. They also cited simmering army unrest symbolized in October 1972 by an army captain's decision to lead a military convoy to the al-Hussein Mosque in Cairo and demand 'immediate war' with Israel. Indeed, although this officer and his followers were promptly arrested, the incident was nonetheless a troubling sign of larger problems between Sadat and his military.[1] Not long after this incident, Sadat fired his Minister of War, Mohamed Ahmed Sadiq. While numerous reasons were offered to explain this move, it seemed evident that Sadat was uncomfortable with Sadiq's popularity in the army.[2] Another factor may have been EGIS chief Ahmed Isma'il who had reportedly warned the president that Moscow was grooming Sadiq to be Sadat's replacement.[3] Perhaps not surprisingly, Sadat put Ahmed Isma'il into Sadiq's job while the EGIS director's chair went to Ahmed 'Abd al-Salim Tewfiq in March 1973.[4]

Sadat then moved against Sadiq's powerful patronage network, including MID Director Mihriz Mustafa 'Abd al-Rahman. There are two different accounts linked to Mihriz's dismissal. According to the first, Mihriz took the fall for failing to warn the president of discontent brewing at Beni Suef air base. When Sadat visited this base he reportedly was angry at the poor reception that he received there.[5] The second explanation comes from Lieutenant General Saad al-Shazly who recalled that a MID captain discovered an anti-Sadat plot among senior officers. Concerned that Mihriz might be part of the conspiracy the captain went directly to Sadat with his warning. A subsequent EGIS investigation confirmed that pro-Sadiq officers had been meeting and contemplating moves against Sadat as part of an organization called Save Egypt. Whether Mihriz was part of this conspiracy or was dismissed for failing to report it is not clear.[6]

## Denial and deception

The Sinai problem was never far from Sadat's mind. After his tentative peace feelers were rejected by the Israelis, Sadat believed that war was the only option left. Given Egypt's lack of military means that war would have to be a limited one: gone were the days of declaring wars to wipe Israel off the map. In Sadat's view, Israel needed a psychological blow that would convince it to negotiate with Egypt on the return of the Sinai. As for Egypt, it needed a victory, *any* victory that would let it save face and overcome its own aversion to peace with Israel.[7] This was the strategic worldview. At the operational level, Egypt's General Staff developed plans to cross the Suez Canal under fire, assault Israel's Bar Lev line of canal-edge defenses and set up a defense perimeter capable of withstanding the anticipated Israeli counter-attack. The generals understood that surprise, speed and stealth were the keys to a successful canal crossing, because, in the end, the Egyptian army needed to attack the Bar Lev line and establish defensive positions before the IDF could deploy reserves to battle area.

At this point denial and deception entered the Egyptian war plan. Using the British deception plan before the Battle of al-Alamein as a model, the Egyptians hoped to convince the IDF that a cross canal assault was unlikely even in the face of indications to the contrary. To that end, Egypt's denial and deception plan was built around five interlocking goals: (*a*) lulling Israel into a false sense of security; (*b*) reinforcing Israel's belief in its superior combat arms and intelligence capabilities; (*c*) augmenting Israel's perceptions of Egyptian military ineptitude; (*d*) disguising Egyptian military preparations; and (*e*) deceiving Israel, the Americans and the Soviets as to what Sadat really intended to do. The plan was developed by the General Staff's Operations and Intelligence Directorates. Indeed, the MID appears to have been given the lead in developing and implementing key aspects of the plan, including assessments of how the Israeli leadership assessed its own and Egyptian strengths and weaknesses. It can be assumed that EGIS fed disinformation to media sources, foreign diplomats, military attachés and double agents.[8]

The denial aspect of the plan boiled down to preventing foreign intelligence services from obtaining clues that would reveal Cairo's intent to go to war. To accomplish this, Egypt built and then gradually raised a huge sand and rock berm along much of the west bank of the canal to disguise its steady infusion of soldiers to the front. In addition, underground bunkers were built close to the berm to hide the growing numbers of men, weapons and bridging equipment from Israeli reconnaissance flights.[9] Egypt also relied on information barriers, including compartmenting sensitive information, particularly war plans. Acutely aware of Israel's proven – and publicized – SIGINT capabilities, the Egyptians decreased their use of radios, telephones and the telegraph for close-hold information.[10] Cairo also coordinated its canal deployments of men and materiel to avoid the transit patterns of American imagery satellites.[11]

Information denial was not enough: the Egyptians had to convince the Israelis that Egypt would not – in fact could not – go to war absent a major improvement in its military capabilities. The Egyptians used leaks, brinksmanship, confusion and other means to shape Israel's perceptions of Egyptian capabilities and intent. For example, Cairo leaked seemingly useful yet often deceptive information about the poor maintenance practices of its military, its failure to repair damage caused by the Attrition War and its decisive air defense weaknesses. It was suggested that since Egypt and Syria were at eternal loggerheads the prospects for a united Arab front were as dismal as ever.[12] Vehicles for the dissemination of deceptive information included Egyptian military communications known to be vulnerable to Israeli interception, double agents and suspected Israeli spies.[13] Cognizant that many Western intelligence services shared information with Israel, the Egyptian military invited Cairo's military attaché community to war games that deliberately exaggerated Egyptian battlefield incompetence.[14]

More importantly, the Egyptians used brinksmanship to create a predictable pattern of calm-alarm-calm. The intent was to convince Israel that Egyptian mobilization and crisis escalation was aimed at appeasing Sadat's critics even though the Egyptian president had no intent of going to war. Between 1970 and 1973, there were four major escalations on the canal front during which the IDF partly mobilized its reserves at considerable cost to the Israeli economy. Each time nothing happened.[15] And then there were the frequent military exercises: according to one researcher there were at least 22 such exercises in 1973 alone. Over time, Israeli (and American) intelligence became complacent as Egypt mobilized and demobilized, fought and trained in a seemingly endless series of drills and exercises.[16]

At times Cairo tried to sow confusion about its intentions. Sadat frequently hinted at a peace deal with Israel while at the same time he belabored the

Palestinians and other Arabs for their aggressive rhetoric. As late as 28 September 1973, Sadat delivered a public speech in which no reference was made to liberating occupied Arab lands by force. This strategy was designed to ease Israeli fears and instill a sense that this Egyptian president really had no intention of going to war despite his anti-Israeli rhetoric.[17]

As Egypt approached the date for its canal assault, other aspects of the deception plan were brought into play. The war commenced at the end of a heavily publicized military exercise which not only provided suitable cover for the large-scale movement of men and equipment, it also allowed the General Staff to make visible preparations for the end of the training cycle. As the exercise wound down, reservists were demobilized and regular officers and conscripts permitted to take leave. As late as 6 October, the day of the assault, unarmed Egyptian soldiers were seen fishing and swimming in the canal.[18]

## Improved intelligence capabilities

Denial and deception played a vital part in Egypt's war plans, and intelligence was, in turn, integral to the success of the denial and deception plan. It has already been noted how the *mukhabarat* tried to improve its collection and analytical capabilities after the 1967 war. Perhaps the single greatest improvement was the MID's emphasis on understanding Israel's history, culture, politics, military and language. For example, after the 1973 war, Israeli soldiers discovered a Hebrew primer published by the MID's Military Intelligence College.[19] No doubt a better understanding of Israel helped the MID assess how religious holidays like Yom Kippur could impact on the IDF's ability to mobilize.[20]

Egypt also improved its HUMINT capabilities with the aid of the USSR and its Eastern Bloc allies. Even so, there is no indication that Egypt penetrated Israel's political or military leadership before the war. This was a major shortcoming since EGIS could not gauge how the denial and deception scheme was influencing Israeli decision making.[21] At the operational level, MID regional offices at Suez, Isma'ilia, Port Said and Port Fuad trained Bedouin agents, equipped them with cameras and other surveillance gear and infiltrated them behind Israeli lines.[22] Occasionally, the MID would send Egyptian scouts and special forces units across the canal. For example, in the days leading up to the war, MID's Reconnaissance Branch inserted several patrols into Sinai to ascertain Israeli military preparedness. Such patrols were risky since the MID did not want to alert Israel to the possibility of attack, but the need for intelligence trumped even this concern.[23]

Egyptian intelligence scored several successes in the HUMINT arena, including access to parts of the IDF's Dovecote plan which provided for the rapid deployments of tanks to the Bar Lev line in the event of attack. This knowledge, combined with observations of IDF exercises, allowed Egyptian planners to frame an assault plan with precisely those Israeli tanks in mind. Indeed, as the canal crossing unfolded, the Egyptian army's use of anti-tank guided missiles helped neutralize Israel's early advantages in armor.[24] At some point before or during the early hours of the war, Egyptian intelligence also obtained an IDF map that included the secret code names and locations of every Israeli unit on Sinai. The capture of this map – of which only nine copies were said to be in existence – allowed Egyptian intelligence officers to track the location and status of individual IDF units as they reported to headquarters. It was an operational coup that the Egyptians never adequately exploited.[25]

Although General Sadiq had kept Soviet advisors out of the MID, there are indications that Soviet intelligence trained and provided surveillance equipment to MID's SIGINT agency.[26] In addition, Soviet ELINT/SIGINT ships supplemented whatever intelligence the MID gleaned from its SIGINT stations on Jabal 'Ataqah, the Suez Canal and the Red Sea.[27] No doubt SIGINT and ELINT provided valuable insights into IDF command and control procedures; they also facilitated planning and targeting.

Imagery intelligence (IMINT) was crucial for the MID's understanding of the IDF order of battle. Although the USSR provided Egypt with some imagery, IMINT was a constant bone of contention between the MID and Soviet intelligence. For example, while the Soviets based MiG-25 reconnaissance aircraft at Cairo West Air Base in 1970, these aircraft were targeted against the US Sixth Fleet.[28] As one Egyptian officer recalled in 1975,

> The Russians would come in and show us their pictures of the Sixth Fleet and say 'aren't these wonderful?'... But when we asked them for reconnaissance of Israel or Sinai, they would say, 'we are too busy in the Mediterranean.'[29]

What Egyptian planners really wanted was high-resolution Soviet satellite imagery of the Sinai. In November 1971 the Soviets granted the MID limited access to this, but the Egyptians were not allowed to keep or copy it.[30] Still, occasional access to satellite imagery must have allowed military planners to update and refine their estimates of IDF units along the Canal and in rear echelon areas.

Open source intelligence (OSINT) was perhaps the single most important source of strategic information on Israel. As noted earlier, EGIS dedicated a department exclusively to the acquisition and analysis of publicly available information on Israel, including war memoirs, journals, newspapers and maps.[31] In a process that began after 1967, intelligence analysts carefully monitored what Israeli leaders said about the IDF's strengths and weaknesses, Egyptian military capabilities and, most importantly, Israel's estimate of Egyptian intentions.[32] All the material gathered from OSINT was fed into Egypt's denial and deception scheme. Since Egypt lacked strategic HUMINT assets, OSINT was the only way Egyptian planners could gauge the impact of their denial and deception campaign on the Israeli leadership. It was probably through OSINT that Egypt learned the broad outlines of 'The Concept' – the prediction by Israeli intelligence that Sadat would not go to war until he had some means to deter and, if necessary, retaliate for IAF raids on Egyptian population centers. Once The

Concept became generally known in Cairo, it was only natural that Egyptian intelligence would try to reinforce these views by playing them back to Israel through the media, double agents and other sources.[33]

Given Egypt's disastrous underestimation of Israeli capabilities before the 1967 war, it is not surprising that the pendulum swung in the opposite direction before the 1973 war. In his memoirs, Saad al-Shazly, records his frustration with conservative MID estimates of Israel. Not only was the MID warning that Israeli military capabilities dangerously exceeded Egypt's, the MID Director Fuad Nasir predicted that Israel would have at least 15 *days* of warning prior to the commencement of hostilities. This would give the IDF ample time to mobilize its reserves and block a cross-canal assault. As al-Shazly recalled, 'the Director of [MID] was guarding his rear. If anything went wrong, he was not going to carry the can.'[34] Still, the MID's amplification of the Israeli threat did benefit the armed forces in some ways. For instance, MID warnings about Israel's ability to rapidly mount a counteroffensive forced planning changes that included arming the initial assault wave with anti-tank guided missiles and man-portable air defense systems.[35]

Al-Shazly's frustration at his lack of control over MID operations probably contributed to his critique of MID assessments. In one jab at the MID, he noted that 'every agent... simply reports any rumor, tidbit, snippet of gossip he hears.' As a result, the 'mélange is served up, on the desk of the President as "opinion in the armed forces."'[36] Very likely such criticisms were legitimate, but al-Shazly's status as a persistent MID critic and his ambitions to include MID in his personal empire did not make him an unbiased evaluator of MID assessments.

Al-Shazly's criticisms aside, there were good reasons for the MID's analytical pessimism before the 1973 war. In part, this organization was trying to compensate for its failures in 1967, but Egyptian intelligence also had a much better understanding of its enemy through experience, open source information and intelligence sources. The cultural and political blinders had been lowered: echoing conventional wisdom among international military observers and exploiting Israeli open source materials, the MID could not see how Egypt could win a war given: (*a*) the effectiveness of the IAF; (*b*) the absence of adequate Egyptian air power to protect the assault; (*c*) Egypt's lack of retaliation weapons to hit the Israeli homeland; and (*d*) Israel's excellent indications and warning system.

## The Ashraf Marwan case

Another key to Egypt's deception plan was the ability of its counterintelligence services to detect, neutralize and, in some cases, turn Israeli spy networks. Israel's greatest spy in Egypt at the time of the 1973 war may have been Ashraf Marwan who was a close aide and intelligence adviser to his father-in-law, Gamal 'Abd al-Nasser and later Sadat. Marwan's career as a spy must be questioned, for although it seems clear that he spied for one or more parties it is much less clear who those parties were. The Israelis claim that their 'Top Source' – Marwan – was recruited in 1969 in London when he approached the Mossad with top secret Egyptian documents.[37] Although the Mossad questioned Marwan's motivations, its concerns were mitigated by the quantity and quality of Marwan's information on Egyptian power struggles, foreign relations and war plans. Significantly, he also passed documents that reinforced Israel's belief that Egypt would not go to war until she had obtained advanced fighter-bombers and/ or ballistic missiles.[38]

At the same time, Marwan frustrated his Israeli handlers by issuing false warnings of immediate Egyptian attacks. In April 1973 he alerted Mossad that Egypt and Syria intended to start a war on 15 May, beginning with a five-division Egyptian assault across the Suez Canal. As a consequence of what turned out to be a false alarm, Israel mobilized its army at a cost of $35 million to its treasury.[39] In mid-September 1973, Marwan predicted that although Cairo and Damascus planned to fight by the end of that year, Sadat still wanted three more years of peace.[40] This mixed prognosis was changed yet again, on 4 October, when he warned Israel again of immediate war.[41] During the early morning hours of 6 October, the day the Egyptian–Syrian assault actually commenced, Mossad chief Zvi Zamir debriefed Marwan personally in London. During this conversation the spy said the attacks would take place at sunset that day. They actually began at 13.55 local time.[42]

After the war, a secret debate began in Israeli intelligence concerning Top Source. Convinced that Marwan was an Egyptian double agent, the head of Israeli Military Intelligence, General Eli Zeira, argued that Top Source deceived Israel by warning of attacks that never came. And when the assault finally did occur, Marwan erred in giving the actual time of the attack by several crucial hours. Others weren't so sure: Mossad reportedly conducted an investigation and concluded that Top Source was a bona fide spy for Israel. Later, Zeira all but directly revealed Marwan's identity as Top Source to a journalist, an act for which the former Mossad chief Zamir took him to court.[43]

So was Ashraf Marwan Israel's best spy before the 1973 war? While there is no definitive answer it is useful to examine some aspects of the case. First of all, when the story linking Marwan to Top Source first emerged in 2002, Marwan, then living in London, denied that he was a spy for Israel or an Egyptian double agent. It was all 'an absurd detective story' he said.[44] But evidence seems to suggest that Marwan was indeed Top Source. The question then centers on Ashraf Marwan's ultimate controller: Israel or Egypt? If Marwan was an Israeli asset he would have been one of the top spies of the twentieth century. An Israeli official once described Top Source as a 'miraculous source'; given his close proximity to Nasser and Sadat, Marwan would have been a dream recruit for any case officer. Privy to many secrets, it is conceivable that Marwan had access to the date – if not the precise time – of the 6 October assault on Israel. It is equally possible that Egypt and Syria *did* intend to attack Israel earlier in May 1973 but were forced to call off their assault.

Alternatively, Marwan could have been a double agent, a vital part of Cairo's denial and deception plan to lull Israel into a false sense of security about Egyptian intentions. Supporting this argument is the fact that on at least two occasions

Marwan warned of attacks that did not occur.[45] Moreover, Marwan passed information confirming Israel's false Concept that Egypt would not resume hostilities until she possessed the requisite retaliation weapons.[46] After he died of an apparent suicide in London in 2007, Ashraf Marwan's funeral was attended by President Husni Mubarak's son (and heir presumptive), Gamal, and the Director of General Intelligence, 'Umar Soleiman. When President Mubarak was queried about the Marwan case, he replied that Marwan 'carried out patriotic acts which it is not yet time to reveal.'[47]

If Marwan was a double agent, then his was a truly remarkable achievement. EGIS had demonstrated some skill in running double agents before, but Marwan was an altogether different and far more complex challenge.[48] Perhaps the greatest obstacle confronting EGIS was the same one faced by any double agent operator: how much 'legitimate' intelligence must be passed to the adversary to build up the double agent's credibility? In Marwan's case, the high stakes game played by Cairo involved warning the Israelis of Egyptian war preparations including the actual date (if not the hour) of the final cross-canal assault. One key to assessing whether Marwan was a double agent is his warning to Israel that 6 October was the date for the attack. In passing this warning through Marwan the Egyptians must have assumed that the IAF could have acted on the information and delivered a devastating preemptive strike as it did in 1967. It seems unlikely that Cairo would have taken such a risk.[49]

Examining the Marwan case is complicated by the smoke and mirrors of the intelligence business. The protagonist is now dead under somewhat mysterious circumstances. One side generally claims that the individual was one of their most valuable spies while the other elliptically hints that he was a true patriot. No doubt both Mossad and EGIS have a lot symbolically at stake here, for this is a case pitting the vaunted prestige of Israel's premier espionage service against its often underrated Egyptian rival.

## Security problems

The challenges for Egyptian security were not limited to the Israeli services. Indeed, the integrity of the Egyptian war plan and its critical denial and deception components was built on denying information to multiple foreign intelligence services. When it came to the Soviets, Sadat and his advisors calculated that if the KGB learned of the seriousness of Egyptian and Syrian plans to go to war, Moscow would act to prevent the Arabs from doing so.[50] Al-Shazly noted that Moscow was a key obstacle to Egyptian war planning in the months leading up to the war. In an attempt to justify apparent Egyptian war preparations, MID Director Fuad Nasir told the senior Soviet military liaison officer that Egypt was organizing its defenses for an anticipated IDF raid across the canal.[51] But Soviet sources were warning that something much bigger was coming and on 4–5 October they evacuated their remaining military advisors from Egypt and Syria. Soviet imagery satellites certainly monitored the war in all its phases.[52]

In the lead-up to the war Egypt continued to suffer from one major weakness: communications security. One consequence of the 1967 war was that Israeli SIGINT stations could reach deeper into Egypt from stations along the banks of the Suez Canal. In addition, Israel planted bugs on communications lines used by Egypt's Center 10 General Headquarters complex.[53] At times, intercepts of Egyptian communications seemed to confirm Israel's Concept about Egyptian capabilities and intent, although it is not clear if this was disinformation planted by Egypt. For example, Israel's Military Intelligence Unit 848 reportedly intercepted a communication in which Sadat pressed Soviet leader Leonid Brezhnev for 'deterrent weapons,' namely ballistic missiles and survivable bombers.[54] Critically, by late 1972, Unit 848 had acquired valuable intelligence on how the Egyptian military intended to cross the canal.[55]

Egypt was aware of Israel's prowess in SIGINT. For example, in the early 1970s Egyptian security discovered that Israel was tapping military communications between bases on the Red Sea and Cairo by using hollowed-out telephone poles with battery-powered bugs inside.[56] And then there was the publicized Israeli interception of the 1967 war-time conversation between Nasser and King Hussein. According to one Israeli intelligence officer, Israel's SIGINT take from Arab sources declined by 60 percent after the Nasser–Hussein intercept was published.[57] Egypt tried to compensate for its communications security weaknesses by using couriers and landlines. Moreover, pre-war meetings between the Egyptians and the Syrians were handled under conditions of the greatest secrecy in rooms that were frequently swept for electronic surveillance devices.[58] As the deadline for war rapidly approached and tight schedules prevented face-to-face meetings the Egyptians transitioned from radio communications to passing heavily encrypted messages through landlines.[59]

## Intelligence and war

A combination of Israeli complacency and Egyptian deception created the optimal conditions for tactical surprise when the Egyptian armies crossed the canal on 6 October 1973. At first the Egyptian Second and Third Armies achieved victories that vastly exceeded the MID's pre-war expectations. Through the use of surface-to-air missiles and anti-tank guided missiles the Egyptians successfully repelled Israel's initial air and armor counteroffensives. But then the tide began to turn when the IDF began pushing the Syrians out of the Golan. In a move that was opposed by General al-Shazly, Sadat ordered units to capture the Sinai mountain passes and take some pressure off Syria. By using bugs planted in or near Egyptian General Headquarters, the Israelis learned of the pending Egyptian attack, set a trap, and on 14 October the Egyptians were badly mauled in a failed bid to seize the passes.[60] Meanwhile, IDF scouts had discovered a crucial seam between the Second and Third Armies at a place called Deversoir and exploited it. Soon IDF forces were on the west bank of the canal and rapidly moving south on the port city of Suez. When a ceasefire was finally called on 24 October, the IDF had a virtual stranglehold on both Suez City and the Third Army.

Although it enjoyed success early in the war, Egyptian intelligence was soon overwhelmed by problems it could not resolve. Perhaps the greatest of these was getting intelligence to headquarters and the front. As the future Defense Minister, 'Abd al-Halim Abu Ghazala recalled, 'one of our greatest points of weakness in October 1973 lay in the spread of information.'[61] He noted how Egyptian scouts had reported back to headquarters as early as 7 October that the Sinai passes were clear but either this information never reached the right people or it was never exploited by them. Abu Ghazala attributed Egypt's failure to close the Deversoir seam to poor transmission of reports from the front, although it could also be argued that it was a failure of Egyptian army scouts and aerial reconnaissance.[62]

Given Egypt's air power weaknesses, it is not surprising that aerial reconnaissance contributed little to Cairo's war time intelligence posture. Abu Ghazala later admitted that if Egypt had more aggressively conducted aerial reconnaissance within its protective SAM belt it might have been able to detect and neutralize the Deversoir bridgehead.[63] As it was, the Egyptians had to rely almost exclusively on Soviet satellite imagery to detect and track the IDF's west bank breakout.[64]

Some have posited that Egypt's loss of the Jabal 'Ataqa SIGINT post to Israeli commandos was a key turning point in the war. Before its loss, Jabal 'Ataqa had provided Egyptian commanders with accurate intelligence on Israel's efforts to muster a counteroffensive. After the station's seizure, Egyptian headquarters was forced to rely on local commanders for intelligence yet those commanders lacked reconnaissance teams and communications to transmit reliable data to headquarters. As a consequence, 'after the loss of [Jabal 'Ataqa], confusion mounted throughout the chain of command as field officers increasingly misled their superiors about the condition of their forces and the disposition of the enemy.'[65]

In looking back at the performance of Egyptian intelligence during the 1973 war it is necessary to reexamine the role that denial and deception played in the Egyptian and Syrian surprise attacks. On the one hand, the plan's effectiveness was mitigated by the fact that seemingly everyone from the Israelis and the Soviets to the Jordanians and the Americans had indications of Egyptian and Syrian war preparations.[66] Israel even had a source who accurately reported the date of the attack, if not the exact hour. On the other hand, the denial and deception plan apparently was sufficient to cast just enough doubt that Israeli and American intelligence still believed Cairo and Damascus would not attack Israel.[67] In fact, neither Israeli nor US analysts could fathom why Sadat risked his military in a seemingly futile bid to recapture the Sinai. After the war Moshe Dayan supposedly told one Egyptian officer that 'no sane person would have launched an offensive with such a capability as yours, but you went against all logic and indulged in war.'[68] With greater insight, Secretary of State Henry Kissinger rephrased Dayan's statement in a different way:

> [Sadat] overwhelmed us with information and let us draw the wrong conclusion. October 6 was the culmination of a failure of *political* analysis on the part of its victims... Our definition of rationality did not take seriously the notion of starting an unwinnable war to restore self-respect.[69]

## The road to peace

With his self-proclaimed 'victory' in hand along with an improving relationship with Washington Sadat believed he now had a foundation from which to negotiate peace with Israel. This was eventually achieved through confidence building steps that began with the disengagement of the armies from the canal and the eventual redeployment of the IDF east of the Sinai passes. Then there were secret talks between Egyptian and Israeli emissaries in Morocco that helped pave the way for Sadat's historic 1977 trip to Jerusalem.[70] The culminating point in this process was the peace treaty of March 1979. A key aspect of the Sinai disengagement process was the creation of SIGINT/ELINT facilities on Sinai that provided information to both sides.[71] Although the relevant documents have not been declassified yet, it is likely that EGIS emissaries helped facilitate the secret dialogue between Egypt and Israel that eventually led to peace.

The year 1979 opened a brave new world for Egyptian intelligence. While it is true that Egyptian–Israeli espionage wars continued after the peace, the bilateral intelligence relationship became more or less 'routine'; that is, both sides found it in their best interests to occasionally meet and discuss shared security concerns. In fact, although it cannot be proved, some believe that an intelligence-sharing agreement between Egypt and Israel was included in secret codicils to the Camp David agreement. Ironically, given all that has happened in the Middle East since 1948, the focus of Egypt–Israel exchanges was – and remains to this day – the Palestinians.[72]

The peace treaty generated considerable anti-Egyptian animosity in the Arab world and the *mukhabarat* now faced threats from Syria, the PLO, Iraq, Libya and eventually Iran. At home, Sadat and his security services were slow to recognize a growing challenge posed by Egypt's resurgent Islamist movement.

# 13 Rejectionists

There were early signs that Anwar al-Sadat planned on reorienting Egyptian foreign policy away from the Soviet Union; however it was not until after the 1973 war that he moved his country into a close alignment with the West. This fundamental shift was reflected by changes in Cairo's intelligence liaison relationships. For the first time since the mid-1950s the CIA enjoyed close ties with EGIS that included intelligence exchanges, technology transfers, training and joint operations. On the other hand, as Egypt's relations with the USSR continued to deteriorate, Sadat began directing his secret police against alleged Eastern Bloc espionage rings inside the country.

In addition to Moscow, Sadat earned another set of enemies. By pursuing peace with Israel, the Egyptian president was opposed by former allies Syria and Libya who resented Egypt's retreat from the Arab cause. Libya in particular used subversion and violence to destabilize Sadat's regime and this sparked a border war with Egypt in 1977. Finally, the 1979 revolution in Iran and the radical shift in that country's policies created a new long-term security challenge for Egypt and its peace treaty with Israel.

The year 1979 was also a year of opportunity for Sadat. Increasingly isolated in the Arab world, Sadat saw an opportunity to burnish his Islamic credentials by opposing the December 1979 Soviet invasion of Afghanistan. In fact, Egypt was one of the first countries to sign on to Washington's plan to arm and train the mujahedin resistance.

Despite his many foreign supporters, Sadat never enjoyed much popularity inside Egypt. Moreover, as the 1970s progressed, his regime was increasingly isolated from a population embittered at its lack of economic opportunity, the corruption of the political establishment and the increasingly dictatorial habits of the president. Islamist trends accelerated with the encouragement of Sadat himself who saw the Islamists as a counter to his Nasserite and leftist opposition. But the president underestimated his opposition and on 6 October 1981 a small cell of Islamist revolutionaries successfully carried out his assassination. It was one of the biggest failures in the history of Egyptian intelligence.

**Some new allies**

Although Sadat intended to reorient Egypt's foreign policy when he expelled the Soviet advisers in 1972, it was not until after the 1973 war that Egypt's relations with the West began to blossom. This shift manifested itself in new and expanded intelligence ties between Egyptian intelligence and the CIA such that, by the mid-1970s, Egypt became a top CIA priority for espionage, influence operations and liaison.[1] James Fees, a CIA case officer who had previously spied on the Egyptians in Yemen, was named Cairo station chief. Soon CIA contract employees were training Sadat's bodyguards and a new counterterrorism unit while CIA officers provided Sadat with threat briefings on Libya, Ethiopia, Syria and eventually Iran.[2] The new partnership included technical support as well. According to one report, US surveillance technology allowed the *mukhabarat* to increase its telephone-tapping capabilities from 1,200 lines in 1971 to 16,000 lines by the late 1970s.[3] In return, EGIS helped the CIA collect military and political intelligence in countries of joint concern like Libya.[4]

Still, liaison has its limits and the CIA, uncomfortable with granting Egypt access to advanced technology, turned to contractors like Frank Terpil and Martin Kaiser to provide training and equipment to defeat electronic surveillance.[5] In his memoirs, Kaiser detailed some of the technical deficiencies in Egyptian counterintelligence including poor technical knowledge of Israel's latest surveillance equipment. For instance, the Egyptians did not understand how transmitters could carry conversations on a beam of light even though 'Israel and other countries had used that type of attack for more than a decade.'[6] Moreover, from Cairo's perspective, liaison offered the CIA more clandestine opportunities to recruit Egyptians as spies. In fact, US intelligence penetration in Egypt reportedly had reached a point by the early 1980s where it had the country 'wired electronically [with] agents from top to bottom.'[7] For Egyptian intelligence, the risk of penetration was another cost (albeit a high one) of doing business, but US espionage recruiting must have been galling just the same.

Egyptian intelligence also expanded its ties with other intelligence agencies by participating in a coalition of French, Saudi, Iranian, and Moroccan intelligence agencies called the Safari Club. Conceived by the head of French intelligence, Comte Claude Alexandre de Marenches, the club shared a fear of Soviet expansionism in Africa and the Arabian Peninsula after the US defeat in Vietnam.[8] For its part, Cairo saw the Safari Club as a way of alleviating Egypt's isolation in the Arab world.[9] When they first convened on 1 September 1976, Safari Club members agreed that Cairo would serve as base for an operations center which assessed intelligence and developed courses of action. Egypt provided the office space while France supplied secure communications and other equipment.[10]

From its inception the club focused mainly on Africa. In 1977 it provided funds, intelligence and Moroccan forces to help Zaire's strongman Mobutu Sese Seko counter Katanga separatists.[11] In Somalia, Saudi money paid for the Egyptian arms that helped lure strongman Siad Barre away from Soviet influence while the club also helped Djibouti confront a threat from Moscow-aligned Ethiopia.[12] There are indications that Cairo facilitated Safari Club money and arms to anti-Qadhafi groups in Libya and Egypt.[13]

How effective was the Safari Club? While the journalist Mohamed Hasanein Heikal called it an 'opera bouffe,' the club seems to have served a useful purpose for its members at a critical time when pro-Soviet regimes were taking power in Ethiopia and the former Portuguese colonies.[14] French researchers assert that the Safari Club helped facilitate the Egyptian–Israeli peace process by using club member Morocco as an intermediary. The club also coordinated lethal aid to the Afghan resistance after the 1978 communist coup in Kabul.[15] In the end, whatever its shortcomings, the Safari Club represented Egypt's first experience with a multilateral intelligence coalition that involved more than just Arab members.

## Some new enemies

At the same time that Cairo was mending fences with the West in the 1970s its relations with the Eastern Bloc were taking a turn for the worse. It was inevitable that Moscow would react negatively to its rapid loss of influence in a country that had benefited from Soviet largesse for so long. On the one hand, Moscow joined Libya, Syria, Iraq and South Yemen in condemning Egypt for its dealings with Israel and 'abandonment' of the Palestinian cause. On the other, although the Soviets ran spies in the Egyptian military and even Sadat's office, they did so cautiously presumably out of fear that a blown spy ring would only depress Egyptian–Soviet relations yet further.[16] For instance, in May 1976 the KGB rejected a request by its case officers to recruit a MID contact code named Gerald.[17]

The *mukhabarat* was well aware of the threat posed by Eastern Bloc diplomats residing in Egypt. Indeed, years after the Egyptian–Soviet relationship had soured Moscow's embassy in Cairo was staffed by over 60 accredited diplomats of whom a substantial number worked for Soviet intelligence.[18] Starting in March 1979, when a Soviet military attaché was expelled for espionage, Egyptian counterintelligence waged a covert war against the Soviet and East European services[19] SSIS claimed two months later that it had uncovered a Bulgarian intelligence network that was attempting to infiltrate the Egyptian Foreign Ministry and presidency.[20] In September 1981, the Soviet ambassador and several Soviet and Hungarian diplomats were expelled after the *mukhabarat* unveiled a spy ring that was allegedly inciting sectarian unrest.[21] Shortly after this, Moscow retaliated by expelling several Egyptian military attachés.[22] The key to breaking the September 1981 spy ring was the use of an Egyptian double agent who had originally been recruited by the KGB in the mid-1970s until he was turned by the Egyptians.[23]

Libya was one of the first countries to 'freeze' relations with Egypt as a result of Camp David. At the intelligence liaison level, EGIS and SSIS probably helped train the Libyan services after the 1969 coup in Tripoli; however, their marriage of intelligence interests ended when the broader Cairo–Tripoli political relationship collapsed in the mid-1970s. After years of waging covert wars against other Arabs, including monarchist Libya, Egyptian intelligence now found itself battling Libyan-sponsored subversion at home. Imitating the Voice of the Arabs, Libyan radio began denouncing the Egyptian president as a 'Zionist tool' while Libyan intelligence officers tried to recruit assassins for operations against Sadat. Tripoli revived old claims to parts of Egypt's Western Desert and tried spurring Bedouin unrest there.[24]

In 1976, after SSIS linked Libyan intelligence and Palestinian extremists to a series of bomb attacks in Egypt, the *mukhabarat* was given the go-ahead to assassinate Qadhafi or oust him in a coup.[25] But Egypt's instruments for covert action against Libya were modest: in addition to arming Chadian dissidents (Libya was involved in a border dispute with Chad at this time), EGIS worked with French intelligence to set up a Libyan opposition party called the National Democratic Union.[26] But Egyptian leaders were considering more than just covert action to punish Libya. In the summer of 1976, two army divisions and several squadrons of combat aircraft were moved to bases near the Libyan border.[27] Tensions were already high in the early summer of 1977 when Egypt received intelligence from Israel of another Libyan plot against Sadat.[28] According to one account, the Israelis warned that Qadhafi's plot against Sadat was part of a broader conspiracy aimed at Sudan, Chad, Egypt and Saudi Arabia.[29] When Egyptian intelligence verified this information through other sources a decision was made to launch a border war in late July.[30]

Very little is known about the Egyptian intelligence component of this short-lived conflict. According to one account, EGIS and French intelligence helped sponsor a Libyan insurgency as well as commando raids against targets in eastern Libya.[31] In the end, Sadat called for a ceasefire even though his army had not achieved any of its goals. This inconclusive end to the war certainly did not deter Qadhafi from subverting Egypt. In May 1978 SSIS uncovered a clandestine Libyan-backed Front for the Liberation of Egypt which intended to 'liberate' Egypt through sabotage and assassinations.[32] The following year the *mukhabarat* announced that Libya was infiltrating 'terrorists' across the border and sponsoring sabotage missions against railroads and public utilities in western Egypt.[33] In addition, Libyan intelligence agents were periodically caught crossing the border to spy on the Egyptian military.[34]

Beyond the Arab rejectionists, Iran was another new regional enemy. Cairo's close ties with Tehran combined with a close Egyptian–Iranian intelligence relationship all ended with the fall of the Shah in 1979. Although the new Iranian regime took several years to sort out its internal power struggles, it did replace the defunct SAVAK with new intelligence services run by the Islamic Revolutionary Guard Corps (IRGC) and a separate Ministry of Intelligence and Security (MOIS). Both the IRGC and MOIS had the mission of exporting the Iranian revolution and it was here that they were to clash with Egypt frequently in coming years.[35]

Egypt was an early Iranian target because of its peace treaty with Israel and Sadat's offer of safe haven to the Shah. As early as December 1979, the SSIS had arrested a suspect who claimed to be a member of a revolutionary organization called the *Fedayin-e Islam* and headed by Iran's notorious 'hanging judge' Sheikh Mohamed Salih Khalkhali. In an eerie replay of the 1950s Susannah plot, the suspect said that the *Fedayin*'s mission was to undermine the Egypt–Israel peace process by sparking a series of arson and bomb attacks in Cairo, Alexandria and Aswan.[36] This arrest was only the first salvo in a cold war between Tehran and Cairo that persists to this day. Iran shall be revisited frequently in coming chapters.

## Anti-Nasser campaign

The title of Sadat's memoirs, *In Search of Identity,* appropriately describes a man who struggled to emerge from the legacy of his charismatic predecessor. One sign of Sadat's new identity was his repudiation of Nasser's Intelligence State. Another was the decision to free Mustafa Amin and permit him to publish memoirs of his experiences at the hands of the *mukhabarat*. Even Salah Nasr was freed in January 1974 only to face torture charges from Amin and others.[37] In addition to freeing some political prisoners, Sadat encouraged newspapers like *al-Musawwar* to attack the Nasser period. As one pro-Sadat commentary put it at the time, Nasser's Arab unity, Arab Socialism and anti-imperialism were little more than a 'brilliant façade' which veiled 'torture and oppression,' 'centers of power,' and 'weak, corrupt, and dissolute commanders.'[38]

As is often the case, some of the most eloquent and sophisticated indictments of Nasser's *mukhabarat* state came from authors and filmmakers. In *Karnak*, the Nobel Laureate Naguib Mahfouz wrote about the rampant suspicion, fear, corruption and spying in Nasser's Egypt. Gamal Ghitani set his novel *Zayni Barakat* in sixteenth-century Mameluke Egypt where the proliferation of spies, plots, torture, deception, betrayal and intrigue offer a dark allegory for the Nasser period. Even more than novels, Egyptian films like *The Sparrow*; *The Night Visitors* and an adaptation of *Karnak* reached audiences eager for a cathartic break with the recent past.[39]

## An Afghan adventure

Even as Egyptians struggled with the political and social impact of the Nasser period, their government was revisiting Nasser's covert action strategy – only this time in Afghanistan. While Egypt and Afghanistan were separated by geography, culture and history, they did share some recent ties particularly in the area of religious education where al-Azhar, Egypt's leading institution of Islamic studies, helped sponsor Kabul University's Faculty of Islamic Law. This link facilitated an exchange of students and teachers that was to have a significant impact on Afghanistan's future.[40]

Sadat's interest in Afghanistan took shape after a 1978 coup in Kabul brought Soviet-backed communist factions to power.[41] His concerns were no doubt shared with Safari Club partners Iran and Saudi Arabia who were equally troubled by events in Afghanistan and the prospects for that country entering the Soviet orbit. In the period immediately before and after the Soviet invasion of 1979, the Safari Club probably helped Egypt funnel arms to the Afghan resistance. Cairo also relied on its own intelligence officers in Pakistan who met Afghan resistance leaders in Peshawar and Islamabad in the late 1970s. Naturally, the Egyptians gravitated to Afghans who had studied at al-Azhar, including Burhannudin Rabbani and 'Abd al-Rasul Sayyaf, a Pashtun warlord who had extensive dealings with the Saudis as well.[42]

When the USSR invaded Afghanistan on 25 December 1979, Sadat saw an opportunity to boost his Islamic credentials and Egyptian national prestige while also solidifying his close ties with Saudi Arabia. At the same time, by aiding the Afghan insurgents, the *mukhabarat* collected intelligence on Soviet arms and tactics which could be shared with the Safari Club, the Americans and other partners. Then there was the domestic element: Sadat was under pressure from the al-Azhar sheikhs, a reinvigorated (but banned) Muslim Brotherhood and other Islamist organizations to do something about Afghanistan. In January 1980 al-Azhar and Brotherhood leaders staged large rallies demanding that Egypt sever all ties with the USSR.[43] At the same time, Cairo used the Afghan war to facilitate the travel of Egyptian Islamists to Pakistan.[44]

Following a 6 January 1980 meeting between Sadat and his national security team, the Egyptian government agreed to reduce the size of the Soviet diplomatic mission in Egypt, provide military training and financial aid to the Afghan mujahedin and host an Islamic summit to discuss the situation.[45] In addition, the Egyptians likely agreed to increase intelligence cooperation with the United States, step up arms shipments to the Afghan resistance in concert with the CIA and the Saudis, and harass Soviet intelligence personnel in Egypt. Finally, the United States probably was offered access to Egyptian ports and airfields to facilitate the delivery of arms and other supplies to the rebels. The 6 January 1980 initiative was likely developed in response to the CIA's plan to secretly funnel Soviet-origin weapons to the mujahedin. Egypt's ample stockpile of Warsaw Pact weapons – and the capability to produce more – dovetailed nicely with the CIA's goals. Soon US and Saudi money was purchasing Egyptian AK-47 rifles, SA-7 surface-to-air missiles and anti-tank weapons for delivery to the guerrillas via Pakistan.[46]

While Egypt made some half-hearted attempts at disguising its role as an arms merchant, it was quite open in its decision to provide food, money, blankets, clothing and medical equipment to the Afghan refugees in Pakistan.[47] Moreover, in late January 1980, the Egyptian defense minister publicly revealed that Cairo would provide army training camps and instructors to the mujahedin.[48] For his part, Sadat proposed that Egypt serve as a base for an Afghan government-in-exile; he frequently urged resistance leaders to unify their efforts against the Soviets.[49]

In this way, Egypt entered her first major covert action operation since the 1960s. While he would not live to see the outcome of the Afghan war, Sadat would no doubt have been shocked at how the Afghan jihad boomeranged against Egypt in the 1990s when many of Egyptian veterans of Afghanistan tried to bring the Afghan jihad home to Egyptian soil.

## Al-Jihad

Another important Egyptian player in Afghanistan was the Muslim Brotherhood which worked closely with the government to identify volunteers and arrange their transportation to Pakistan. This quiet cooperation signaled a change in the Egyptian government's approach to the Brotherhood. While Sadat made it clear he would not tolerate a direct challenge to his authority, he did ease *mukhabarat* pressure on Brotherhood activities in order to counterbalance his still powerful Nasserist and leftist opposition. The Muslim Brothers also benefited from major shifts that had taken place in Egyptian society since the 1967 war. In the wake of that defeat, many Egyptians questioned the spiritual hollowness of Arab Social-ism and the lack of religion in official life.

After the 1973 war, Egyptian Islamists began to fragment with a new genera-tion condemning the evolutionary approach adopted by older Muslim Brother-hood leaders toward the regime. Loosely called the Islamic Associations (*Jama'at al-Islamiyya*) these activists included university students and profes-sors who agitated against the preponderance of leftist thinking on the campuses in the early 1970s. Consonant with the regime policy of cultivating the religious right, the SSIS not only eased its harassment of the Islamists it even quietly sup-ported them in their on-campus battles with the left.[50] As one activist put it, 'the truth is we found [the regime] to have a rare faith, with their offices decorated with Qurans... even in the Mabahith Amn al-Dawla! [SSIS]'[51]

What Sadat apparently did not understand was that the most militant Islamists regarded him and the *mukhabarat* as the embodiment of a *jahiliya* ('ignorant') apostate government that stood in the way of an Islamic state based on *sharia* law. Even so, there were some early signs of trouble. In April 1974 Islamists staged an attack on the Technical Military Academy with the goals of seizing the school's arsenal, killing Sadat and establishing an Islamic state. Fortunately for the regime, an Alexandria university student warned the SSIS of what was being planned and the conspirators were either killed or captured by alert guards. The authorities later linked the failed uprising to Libya.[52]

The Islamist organizations also exploited the growing socio-economic inequalities in Egyptian society that had been created as a result of Sadat's eco-nomic liberalization. In January 1977 this simmering resentment fueled large-scale riots that overwhelmed the police and forced the government to call in the army to restore order. Sadat was not only surprised by the unrest, he also seemed bewildered by the young demonstrators who chanted 'Nasser! Nasser!' In response, Sadat called the riots an 'uprising of thieves.' He used the excesses of Nasser's *mukhabarat* state as a reminder of darker times: 'Is surveillance what you want, expropriation, detention camps, Arab Unity, the Nasser way, turning Egypt into a loudspeaker for the Arabs?'[53] After the demonstrations were crushed, the internal security apparatus arrested over 3,000, alleging that the riots were masterminded by communists. Another result of the 1977 unrest was augmenting the capabilities of the SSIS and an internal security police called the Central Security Forces.[54] Interestingly, the lesson that Moscow took from the riots was that the Egyptian communists had been penetrated by the security services. The KGB responded by training three Egyptian communists in establishing an effective counterintelligence service.[55]

By the late 1970s, the fissures within the Egyptian Islamist movement had grown wider. Still dominant was the Muslim Brotherhood, a large 'establishment' organization with an aging leadership that was committed to the long-term peaceful transformation of Egypt into an Islamic state. Some Brotherhood leaders at this time collaborated with the *mukhabarat* against the more radical groups like the *jama'at*.[56] Although more militant than the Brotherhood the *jama'at* were themselves divided over whether to confront the regime with violence. Within these associations was a much smaller, more disciplined and clandestine cadre of activists who espoused a Leninist-style *coup d'état*. This latter group eventually was called al-Jihad.

Among the leading al-Jihad thinkers were a young doctor named Ayman al-Zawahiri, 'Abd al-Salam Farag, and 'Abud al-Zumur, a retired Lieutenant Colonel from the MID's Reconnaissance Branch.[57] Al- Zumur was not only a hero of the 1973 war with a Cairo street named after him, he also possessed an insider's knowledge of the regime's security apparatus.[58] As one researcher put it, al-Zumur 'evince[d] a methodical mind capable of coldly evaluating a plan in terms of its risks and results... [he] seems much like a free officer 30 years on.'[59] In other words, al-Zumur represented everything that the security organs feared most: an intelligent, motivated, disciplined retired army officer who would use violence to effect regime change.

Like the Free Officers before him, al-Zumur's coup plan involved seizing key regime security and telecommunications facilities. Any successful coup, he counseled, would have to control the Defense Ministry and the General Staff, the Interior Ministry and the SSIS headquarters, the telephone and telegraph buildings, and state radio and television. Unlike the Free Officers, the al-Jihad plan also rested on the assassination of senior regime figures. Al-Jihad reasoned that once they had seized the key levers of power they could proclaim an Islamic state and rally the public behind them.[60] But what Farag and al-Zumur still needed were foot soldiers and they found one in a 24-year-old lieutenant named Khaled Ahmed Shawki al-Islambuli. Al-Islambuli had begun reading Islamist books on his own but what really galvanized him was the arrest and torture of his brother in a September 1981 security sweep. Al-Islambuli wanted revenge (and an Islamic state) and al-Jihad seemed to be the ideal vehicle to achieve that goal.[61]

## What did the security services know?

The clandestine cellular nature of al-Jihad's structure thwarted surveillance until June 1981 when the police began monitoring a key al-Jihad suspect named Nabil

'Abd al-Magid al-Maghribi. The SSIS learned that al-Maghribi was part of a cell that was acquiring arms, training youth in desert camps and spreading seditious propaganda. More alarming still for the authorities was the fact that al-Maghribi was in contact with a former MID officer named Abud al-Zumur.[62] On 21 September 1981 the SSIS secretly taped meetings in which al-Maghribi and other al-Jihad militants discussed the need to obtain more arms. During one session, al-Maghribi was seen inspecting a rifle and commenting how he could put a bullet through Sadat's heart.[63]

SSIS confronted a dilemma: should it act now or hold back and see if al-Maghribi would lead the police to more members of the ring? The decision was made to strike. On 26 September the *mukhabarat* arrested al-Maghribi and an associate. They also searched a Giza apartment belonging to al-Zumur where they found encoded messages, guns, ammunition, photographs of regime leaders and a schedule of Sadat's public meetings until 9 November.[64] Under interrogation, al-Maghribi revealed Abud al-Zumur's role as the cell's leading planner and weapons expert. The results of the investigation were given to Sadat but he did not appear especially concerned. Whether he was overly confident of his security or perhaps just fatalistic is something that will never be known. In any case, the remaining members of al-Jihad who were still at large had not abandoned their plan to kill the president.[65]

On 29 September the Interior Ministry declared that the SSIS knew everything about the 'underground organization' which it linked to the Muslim Brotherhood.[66] Yet behind this brave front the regime was betraying some anxiety too. In a speech delivered only days before his assassination, Sadat warned al-Zumur (whom he did not mention by name) that the *mukhabarat* was closing in: 'I know that there is one officer left at large, and he must be watching me now... He will be listening to me, and I warn that we will catch him too.'[67] But Sadat's confidence was misplaced. For reasons that have never been adequately explained – and which have nurtured numerous conspiracy theories – the MID apparently investigated Khaled al-Islambuli in the weeks before the assassination but found nothing alarming.[68]

On 6 October 1981 Egypt suffered one of the worst intelligence failures in its modern history when an army officer named Khaled al-Islambuli, who had been under surveillance for ties to an extremist organization, breached all the defenses surrounding the Egyptian president. The assassin managed to replace regular conscripts in his truck with his al-Jihad associates. He convinced others that his associates were 'intelligence' officials checking parade security.[69] Although MID regulations prohibited live ammunition on the parade route, no one bothered to inspect the loaded rifles and grenades carried by the team.[70] Images of the assassination were caught on film: a truck swerves from the parade route and halts near the presidential review stand. Sadat rises from his chair as if expecting a salute. Then the bullets and grenades are thrown. All is in confusion. And the president's CIA-trained security guards are nowhere to be seen.

## Intelligence and the Sadat presidency

Egyptian intelligence played an important role in sustaining the Sadat presidency. In 1970 and 1971 the MID helped Sadat retain power in the face of powerful competitors with direct access to the civilian intelligence agencies. The *mukhabarat* also helped Sadat secure his political victory in the 1973 war where improved collection and a much better understanding of the enemy helped produce a deception plan that facilitated the crossing of the Suez Canal. After the war, and during the period in which Egypt pursued peace with Israel, the Egyptian services protected Egypt and Sadat from a number of external and internal adversaries. But this record is tarnished by the fact that the *mukhabarat* failed to roll up the conspiracy to murder Sadat. Although SSIS had partially penetrated the al-Jihad group and had even warned the president of the extremist threat, it could not arrest key conspirators like al-Zumur and al-Islambuli in time. Still, most of the blame should fall on the MID which failed to monitor extremism in the military or even enforce its own security regulations during the 6 October parade.

Under Sadat, the trend in Egyptian intelligence was toward internal instead of external operations. With the exception of Afghanistan, covert action had been dramatically curtailed from its peak in the late 1950s and early 1960s. This was of course due to a fundamental shift in national goals and foreign policy that dropped Nasser's expansive ambitions for greater cooperation with the Arab moderate states. Closely paralleling the change in goals and strategy was a shift in the relative influence of the individual Egyptian intelligence services. Whereas Salah Nasr's EGIS was preeminent up to the 1967 war, the MID prevailed from 1967 to 1973 in large part because of the wars with Israel. However, after the 1973 war, when Egypt began to pursue peace with Israel, the MID's influence started to fade. By the late 1970s, the internal security mission was preeminent and the SSIS assumed the post of leading agency of its day.

Sadat's assassination dramatically emphasized the serious deficiencies in Egypt's internal intelligence apparatus. It was up to his successor, former Commander of the Air Force Husni Mubarak to decide if and how that apparatus should be reformed and reorganized. One thing was clear though: al-Jihad had become the primary enemy of the Egyptian state.

# Part IV
# Intelligence under Mubarak

# 14 Troubles at home and abroad

Sadat's 1981 assassination made the former air force general, Husni Mubarak, Egypt's fourth president in 30 years. Given the circumstances of Sadat's murder, it is not surprising that Mubarak's early days in the presidency were marked by conspiracy rumors, much uncertainty and secret police investigations into the loyalty of the armed forces. Mubarak tried to project an aura of calm leadership, but the maelstrom surrounding his early administration suggested otherwise.

Mubarak did not make any major alterations to his predecessor's foreign policy particularly with regard to Egypt's relations with the West. The American–Egyptian intelligence alliance weathered several crises in the 1980s, including some espionage cases and Cairo's involvement in the notorious *Achille Lauro* hijacking. In fact, the United States delivered advanced intelligence technologies to Egypt such as unmanned aerial vehicles and ELINT collection aircraft. While Mubarak downplayed Egypt's public role in Afghanistan, his government continued to quietly sell arms and other supplies to the mujahedin. Its motives in doing so were not altruistic: in addition to the infusions of American and Saudi cash into the Egyptian arms industry, Mubarak's security men viewed the Afghan jihad as a useful lure for the regime's most vociferous Islamic opponents. Finally, Washington and Cairo cooperated closely on the diplomatic and security fronts in combating the threat posed by the Libyan leader, Mu'ammar al-Qadhafi.

## Who is Mubarak?

Unlike his predecessors, Husni Mubarak shuns publicity. We know he was born in the Nile Delta in 1928, graduated from the Military Academy in 1949 and piloted World War II-vintage Spitfires as well as Il-28 and the Tu-16 medium bombers.[1] After flying Tu-16 missions over Yemen and training in the USSR, Mubarak was promoted to air marshal and supervised Egyptian air operations during the 1973 war. Following the war, Sadat groomed Mubarak as his successor by giving him assignments in the ruling party and eventually making him his vice president.[2] In this latter capacity, Mubarak reportedly coordinated Egypt's intelligence community for Sadat in the late 1970s.[3] This assignment must have given the future president valuable insights into the missions and capabilities of the *mukhabarat*.

Although Mubarak never served in the MID or EGIS, he was surrounded by advisors with considerable experience in the intelligence business. His *eminence grise* and lead foreign policy expert, Usama al-Baz, previously directed Sami Sharaf's office in the late 1960s where he witnessed the inner workings of the intelligence community at first hand.[4] Another important advisor was Safwat al-Sharif who served in the MID and cultivated close ties with Salah Nasr. Named Mubarak's information minister after the Sadat assassination, al-Sharif held this position for more than two decades.[5] Like his predecessors, Mubarak established an Office of the President for Information that reportedly coordinated intelligence activities and prepared a daily assessment for Presidential Counselor for Security Affairs, Dr Mustafa al-Fukki. It was Fukki's responsibility to keep Mubarak informed about the latest intelligence developments.[6]

## Early days of the Mubarak presidency

The early days of the Mubarak presidency were shaky. In the immediate aftermath of Sadat's murder, the Egyptian leadership feared a larger military conspiracy and quickly imposed a state of emergency. All military participants in the 6 October parade were returned to garrison for inspections while the roads to the Canal were blocked to prevent any rebellious units from entering Cairo.[7] Given leadership doubts about the MID's reliability, the SSIS played an important role in the hours following the assassination. Under the Interior Ministry's Plan 100, the SSIS worked with the Republican Guard to secure critical Nile bridges, the larger mosques, state radio and television and the presidential residences in Cairo.[8] Rounding up Sadat's assassins was a top priority: Khaled al-Islambuli and an accomplice were wounded, another was dead while a fourth was rounded up later that day by the police.[9] But the dust had barely settled in Cairo when a Jihad cell in the upper Egyptian city of Asyut staged an uprising on 8 October that had to be crushed by military force.[10]

It was a difficult start for Mubarak's reign. The new president tried compensating for the uncertainty and fear by projecting a military image of discipline and fortitude in media interviews. But it was clear that the security services had no idea of the identities and goals of the conspirators.[11] Although the assassins were accounted for, the *mukhabarat* nonetheless faced several pressing questions: how and why did presidential security fail?To what extent had the conspirators penetrated the military? Had they infiltrated Military Intelligence? Where would they strike next? Presidential security received immediate attention.[12] Publicly, the regime asserted that the Republican Guard was reliable; however, privately the MID and SSIS arrested the Republican Guard commander as well as several soldiers who were near the reviewing stand when Sadat was killed.[13] In fact, responsibility for Mubarak's protection was transferred to a special air force detail pending an investigation into the Republican Guard's possible role in the assassination.[14]

Next to presidential security the biggest question mark was the loyalty of the armed forces. Foreign observers noted in the days after the assassination that soldiers were not seen on the streets of Cairo even though a nationwide state of emergency had been declared. This was interpreted as a sign that the regime lacked confidence in the military.[15] Some attention was focused on the MID director too since it was his job to probe the loyalties of officers like al-Islambuli and ensure proper security procedures were followed during the parade. It turned out, however, that the MID chief was on pilgrimage to Mecca when the assassination took place. A few weeks later, the government denied rumors that the MID director had been dismissed.[16] Still, it was embarrassingly clear that this key *mukhabarat* component had failed in its core security responsibilities.

Given the uncertainties surrounding the MID, a specialized SSIS counter-terrorist team called Intelligence Unit 75 was given the delicate mission of investigating the military's possible role in the assassination.[17] While the regime publicly asserted that the intelligence services were cooperating closely there was a behind-the-scenes struggle over the investigation which the MID ultimately won.[18] The potentially embarrassing results of this inquiry have never been made public; however, the military was obviously sensitive to criticism and even Defense Minister Abu Ghazala was forced to publicly deny that he was under investigation.[19] On 25 October, in another sign of the post-Sadat intra-*mukhabarat* feud, the SSIS Director was relieved of his command.[20] Naturally, the secrecy surrounding the investigation has provided fertile ground for conspiracy theories about the military's role in Sadat's murder.

Despite their internal battles, the SSIS and MID successfully hunted down most of the al-Jihad leaders. From the outset, the emphasis was on capturing or killing the former MID officer, Abud al-Zumur, whose photograph was posted on television and in newspapers along with demands for public assistance in his apprehension. Yet even as the security forces closed in on him, al-Zumur was plotting at least two new conspiracies against the government. The first was supposed to coincide with Sadat's funeral when al-Jihad would try to kill Mubarak and foreign dignitaries while the second involved capturing the SSIS municipal headquarters in Giza, seizing weapons and then leading a coup against Mubarak.[21] Fortunately for the new regime, al-Zumur and his brother were arrested by the SSIS before they could carry out their plans.[22]

The universities were another target for *mukhabarat* investigators. Armed with lists of names, the secret police began arresting suspected militants and imposing tighter security restrictions on the campuses. New student identity cards were issued to assist the police in investigating dissident activity.[23] Hundreds of students were thrown into prisons where they were tortured for confessions and information on the conspiracy. Among those jailed at this time was the 31-year-old future al-Qa'ida leader, Ayman al-Zawahiri, who was to allege torture in the prisons during his 1982 trial:

> There they kicked us, they beat us, they whipped us with electric cables, they shocked us with electricity!They shocked us with electricity!And they used the wild dogs!And they used the wild dogs!And they hung us over the

edges of the doors with our hands tied at the back!So where is the democracy?Where is freedom?Where are human rights?Where is justice? Where is justice?We will never forget!We will never forget!   [24]

Despite its extensive use of physical and mental coercion, Egyptian intelligence never seemed to get a good handle on the al-Jihad group. While it executed al-Islambuli and others for their roles in the assassination, the regime sentenced other important extremists like al-Zawahiri and 'Umar 'Abd al-Rahman to short, three-year prison terms. Both were freed in 1984 only to end up in Afghanistan where their anti-Mubarak zeal metastasized and contributed directly to the violence that plagued Egypt in the 1990s. It seems plausible that their release was contingent on their agreeing to go to Afghanistan.

## US–Egypt intelligence relations

No agency in the US government was more surprised by the Sadat assassination than the CIA. According to one report, when news of the murder filtered in, Director of Central Intelligence William Casey feared that Mubarak would punish the CIA for failing to adequately train Sadat's bodyguards.[25] A CIA team was sent to Cairo to find out what went wrong; fortunately for Langley, if Mubarak had any grievances against the CIA he never aired them publicly.[26] The CIA's key concerns at this time were securing the confidence of the new president, maintaining the relationship with the *mukhabarat* and ensuring that Egyptian arms continued flowing to the Afghan mujahedin.[27] In return, the CIA likely reaffirmed its commitment to helping Egypt neutralize threats to Mubarak from Libya, Syria, Iran and Palestinian extremists.

There is no doubt that Washington fretted about Egypt's future. Was the country headed toward an Iranian-style Islamic revolution?How stable was the Mubarak regime? To what extent were the army and security services infiltrated by extremists? Answering these difficult questions required unilateral espionage operations aimed at Egypt's political and military leadership. The *mukhabarat* was well aware of CIA spying on Egyptian soil; however it handled American espionage cases with greater discretion than in the past. The only notable exception was the November 1988 publicized arrest of a dual Egyptian–American national, Dr Sami Yusef Ibrahim Wassif who allegedly passed information to the CIA on the PLO, Egyptian politics and Islamic extremists.[28] For its part, the United States was equally careful not to publicize Egyptian intelligence operations discovered on American soil. Only one arrest from the 1980s received any major press attention and this involved another dual national named 'Abd al-Kader Helmy who was paid by EGIS to procure sensitive ballistic missile technology. Given the similar timeframe of these incidents, it is likely that Egypt seized Dr Wassif in retaliation for Helmy's arrest.[29]

The Egypt–US intelligence partnership has had its ups and downs. But it came close to breaking point in October 1985 when Palestinian terrorists hijacked an Italian cruise ship called the *Achille Lauro*, killed an American Jew named Leon Klinghoffer and demanded the release of Palestinian prisoners in Israel. When the hijackers steered the ship into Egyptian waters, Cairo negotiated a secret deal with the PLO which released the hostages in return for Egyptian assistance in spiriting the terrorists out of the country. Meanwhile, the Americans were leaning on the Egyptian regime to hand over Klinghoffer's murderers only to be told that the terrorists had disappeared.[30] Yet once again Cairo's communications security problems came back to haunt it, for the National Security Agency 'listened in' on phone calls between Mubarak and his foreign minister as they discussed what to do about the terrorists who were still under Egyptian protection. It was through these intercepts that the United States learned that the terrorists had boarded an Egyptair 737 bound for Tunis.[31] When US fighters forced the plane to land in Italy and the terrorists were discovered on the manifest, Egyptian duplicity was made embarrassingly clear.[32]

While the *Achille Lauro* affair put a great strain on US–Egyptian relations, the intelligence partnership nonetheless prospered in the 1980s with a routine exchange of intelligence on countries and issues of mutual interest, including Libya, Iran and terrorism. Egypt's acquisition of unmanned aerial vehicles (UAV) was another area of bilateral cooperation. In the years following the 1973 war both the air force and the MID sought a long-range aerial reconnaissance capability, but it was not until the mid-1980s and successive crises with Libya that UAVs were put on the front burner of Cairo's acquisition plans.[33] At that time, Egypt acquired both the jet-powered Scarab and Skyeye UAV systems which it used on the Libyan and Sudan border to monitor military forces and counter militant infiltration and arms smuggling.[34] Egypt also acquired two EC-130 electronic intelligence/electronic counter measures aircraft (ELINTECM) and four Beech Guardrail ELINT platforms. These aircraft gave Egypt an advanced airborne ELINT capability that it previously did not possess; their acquisition from the United States was probably justified by the need to monitor the modernization of the Libyan armed forces.[35]

The *mukhabarat* acquired other surveillance technologies during the 1980s such as video cameras to monitor the major thoroughfares and public areas of Egyptian cities, enhanced telephone tapping capabilities and mobile listening posts. Each of these technologies augmented the City Eye informant system and substantially improved the regime's ability to monitor and harass its opposition. The Egyptians undoubtedly used this technology against foreigners as well.

## Afghanistan

The Sadat assassination coincided with a dramatic increase in US covert aid to the Afghan mujahedin. Although Egypt was an early source of weapons for the resistance, Husni Mubarak was more cautious than his predecessor when it came to the Afghan project.[36] Still, Mubarak was receptive to the CIA's Afghan project since it entailed American and Saudi cash infusions into the Egyptian arms industry and an opportunity to direct domestic Islamist discontent away from the regime and toward Afghanistan.[37]

Mubarak and his security chiefs recognized that the Afghan jihad was a source of fascination for hundreds if not thousands of Egyptian Islamists.[38] In the mid-1980s, a number of militants like Ayman al-Zawahiri were released from prison and either volunteered or strongly encouraged by the *mukhabarat* to go to Pakistan and assist the mujahedin. At that time an 'Arab Afghan' contingent in Peshawar was gathering around a Palestinian al-Azhar graduate named Shaykh 'Abdallah 'Azzam who raised funds and recruited Arabs for the Afghan war.[39] Among 'Azzam's associates were such future al-Qa'ida luminaries as Usama Bin Laden, al-Zawahiri, 'Umar 'Abd al-Rahman, Mohamed 'Atef and Mohamed Shawki al-Islambuli. Like the CIA the Egyptian security services evidently did not understand the nature of the monster they were creating when they encouraged Egyptian Islamists to fight in Afghanistan. Indeed, the early- to mid-1980s represents a critical development phase in the history of the Egyptian jihadist movement when militants gained valuable experience in Afghan guerrilla warfare.[40]

Sometime in 1988 or 1989 bin Laden and a small group of Egyptian al-Jihad associates founded the transnational terrorist organization called al-Qa'ida – or 'The Base.'[41] The al-Jihad group was pivotal to al-Qa'ida's birth for it was commanders like Abu 'Ubayda al-Banjshiri, Abu Hafs al-Misri, Mohamed 'Atef and Mohamed Makkawi (aka Seif al-'Adl) who first aired the concept of a transnational organization dedicated to using violence to create a new Islamic state.[42] The 1989 Soviet withdrawal from Afghanistan provided additional impetus for al-Qa'ida's creation. Faced with the anticipated collapse of the communist government in Kabul (it did not in fact fall until April 1992) and the denouement of the Afghan jihad, many Arab Afghans were in a quandary about what to do next. Some favored the peaceful promotion of Islam in their home countries while others advocated using their Afghan experiences to export jihad abroad. The Egyptians were prominent in this latter group.[43]

When one phase of the Afghan conflict wound down in the early 1990s another one was ramping up as new jihadists arrived in Pakistan and Afghanistan for training and combat experience.[44] They joined a hardened core of veteran Egyptian, Syrian, Algerian, Tunisian and Libyan fighters who risked imprisonment or worse if they tried to openly return to their homelands.[45] Many Egyptians with Afghan experience later moved to Sudan where they established a base for igniting an Afghan-style insurgency in the Nile Valley.

## Libyan subversion

While al-Jihad and the evolving Islamic Group were being energized and radicalized by their Afghanistan experience, the *mukhabarat* was focused on a challenge that seemed much closer to home: Mu'ammar al-Qadhafi's Libya. Even after the Sadat assassination – which he applauded – Qadhafi was an erratic and angry adversary who was as dismissive of President Mubarak as he had been of Sadat; however, unlike Sadat, Mubarak showed more patience in his dealings with the Libyan leader. Still, Libyan provocations reached a point on several occasions in the 1980s when both countries nearly came to blows, for Libyan intelligence was at the center of a multi-faceted attack aimed at Egypt. In addition to supporting anti-Cairo Palestinian terrorist groups like the Abu Nidal Organization, Tripoli sheltered prominent Egyptian exiles and fomented conspiracies against Cairo and its allies in Sudan and Chad.

In 1983, Qadhafi's intelligence services attempted to overthrow Sudanese President Ja'afar al-Nimeiri. There are two accounts of the role that EGIS played in thwarting this plot. In the first version, EGIS and its Sudanese counterpart foiled a Libyan plan to assassinate Nimeiri and install a pro-Libyan government in Khartoum. As soon as EGIS learned of this plan, Mubarak asked for and received US AWACS surveillance aircraft to patrol southern Egypt.[46] When the US media exposed the AWACS mission in Egypt in mid-February, Qadhafi reportedly was deterred from his Sudanese project.[47] According to the second account, Sudanese intelligence set up a fake rebel group that asked Libya for help in overthrowing Nimeiri.[48] Then the Sudanese brought in the CIA and Egypt's MID to draw up a plan that would lure the Libyan air force into northern Sudan where it could be attacked by Egyptian fighters working closely with US AWACS. US imagery satellites even reportedly picked up signs of a large Libyan air force deployment to al-Kufa before Qadhafi called off the operation for unknown reasons.[49]

Throughout the remainder of 1983 and 1984 Egyptian security continued investigating alleged Libyan rings aimed either at overthrowing the Egyptian government or infiltrating Libyan dissident organizations headquartered in Cairo.[50] In November 1984, the *mukhabarat* scored a victory in a case involving exiled former Libyan Prime Minister 'Abd al-Hamid al-Bakush. As with most of his prominent Libyan opponents, Qadhafi wanted al-Bakush dead and he sent an assassination team to do the job.[51] While *mukhabarat* officers quietly rounded up the would-be assassins, others ensured that photographs of a supposedly dead Bakush ended up in Libyan hands. Almost immediately, Libyan radio began to proudly announce that the 'stray dog' Bakush had been murdered because he had 'sold his conscience to the enemies of the Arab world.'[52] Shortly after, the Egyptians held a press conference where they unveiled a Bakush who was still very much alive.

Egypt–Libyan tensions continued into 1985. The *mukhabarat* helped sponsor and support a Libyan exile organization called the National Front for the Salvation of Libya (NFSL). When the NFSL tried to assassinate Qadhafi in April 1985 the Libyans retaliated by sending a team to Cairo to blow up the US embassy; however, that plot was foiled by Egyptian intelligence.[53] Then Libya began expelling thousands of Egyptian guest workers, generating fears in Cairo that Qadhafi might be infiltrating terrorists among the Egyptian returnees.[54] The crescendo of Libyan-sponsored terrorism peaked in late November with the hijacking of an Egyptair 737 by the Abu Nidal group. After the terrorists forced the plane to land in Malta, an Egyptian military counter-terrorism squad called Unit 777 tried to assault the aircraft with disastrous results. Altogether, 57 were killed in the attack; only 25 passengers survived the smoke, fire and bullets.[55] Nonetheless, despite these and other provocations, Mubarak resisted US pressure to join in a military plan against the Libyan leader.[56]

The extent of EGIS–CIA cooperation against Qadhafi is secret. Given Egypt's espionage networks inside Libya, the CIA probably relied on its Egyptian counterpart for intelligence on Qadhafi, his internal security apparatus and his military. It is safe to assume that the United States shared intelligence on Libyan intelligence activities aimed at Egypt. For example, we know that NSA was intercepting some Libyan intelligence communications during this time, and some of this may have been passed to Egypt in a sanitized form.[57] EGIS–CIA cooperation against Libya probably included supporting anti-Qadhafi dissident groups like the NFSL. At a minimum, the *mukhabarat* would have been aware of and condoned CIA cooperation with Libyan opposition groups based on Egyptian soil.[58]

On 14–15 April 1986, US aircraft struck targets in Tripoli and Benghazi in retaliation for a Libyan-backed terrorist campaign in Europe. Following the air raids Libyan security announced the arrest of a three-man 'espionage and sabotage network' that was allegedly run by Egyptian Military Intelligence. The Libyans also declared that this spy ring had planted beacons to guide the US aircraft to their Libyan targets.[59] It is not clear if this was a real spy ring or unfortunate Egyptian laborers rounded up by the Libyan secret police; however, Cairo did demand their release during negotiations with Tripoli the following year.

Throughout this period of Libyan–Egyptian tensions, both sides waged radio wars reminiscent of decades past. As one October 1986 broadcast demonstrates, the venerable Voice of the Arabs had not lost its tone, even if it had lost a few listeners: 'O free men of Libya…We must all shoulder our responsibility with regard to this calamity called al-Qadhafi…Undoubtedly, it would only take one courageous move by the [Libyan] army to send this…al-Qadhafi to his destiny.'[60]

The *mukhabarat* was watching closely when Qadhafi blundered into northern Chad in the 1980s. When the Libyan army began to get bogged down in inconclusive fighting, Egyptian intelligence picked up signs of lagging Libyan morale, poor training and shoddy staff work. Yet, lest the Americans believe these problems could ultimately unseat Qadhafi, the *mukhabarat* assessed that the Libyan leader would survive even a humiliating defeat in Chad because of his control over the Libyan security forces.[61] This assessment – and others like it – was most likely based on intelligence gleaned from Libyan defectors, Egyptian laborers in, Libya, spy networks and foreign liaison. The Egyptians probably were also collecting SIGINT on Libya at this time.

In 1988 and 1989, Egyptian–Libyan tensions began to ease as a result of Saudi mediation and increased Islamist activism in both countries. Egyptian intelligence was certainly monitoring unrest in Libya quite closely: according to one Egyptian report, Libyan security forces crushed a 1989 mutiny in Tobruk that involved Islamist-influenced army units.[62] Still, what is striking about the Egypt–Libya cold war of the 1980s is Cairo's forbearance in the face of repeated provocations. This patience was probably due to fear of Libyan retaliation through Palestinian extremists; it was also motivated by Cairo's desire for reintegration into the Arab world. In any case, Egyptian intelligence consistently bested its Libyan rival and the sources of this success were a productive partnership with the United States and the skill of the security apparatus in neutralizing Qadhafi's plots.

# 15 State security

The Egyptian security apparatus was preoccupied with multiple threats throughout the 1980s and into the early 1990s. We have already seen how the Libyan challenge waxed and waned, but the *mukhabarat* was also focused on Israel – despite the peace treaty; revolutionary Iran and its support for militant Islamist groups; and a new regime in Sudan that began harboring Egyptian extremists. Another regional threat was Iraq, whose 1991 defeat in Kuwait by a multinational coalition helped facilitate Egypt's reintegration into the Arab world.

But victory against an external adversary like Iraq did not buy Egypt more security at home. In 1986, the regime was badly shaken by a mutiny within its premier civilian police force. This was followed a few years later by the so-called 'Arab Afghan' phenomenon which involved attempts by Egyptian veterans of the Afghan jihad to ignite a Nile Valley revolt. By 1992 Egypt faced an unprecedented urban and rural insurgency that fed off growing discontent over social and economic inequalities, official corruption and the embarrassing inability of the authorities to provide basic social services. To combat this insurgency, the Egyptian government turned to the SSIS whose brutal interrogation tactics proved controversial in human rights circles. But secret police torture and intimidation were matched by militants who showed no hesitation in systematically killing government informers and police officials. Even so, the regime began gaining the upper hand by the mid-1990s, and its success was based on *mukhabarat* informers, the arrest of key militant leaders and a growing public backlash against militant excesses.

## The Israel threat

Despite – or because of – their formal peace treaty, Egypt and Israel continued to wage spy wars against each other throughout the 1980s and 1990s. Indeed, the *mukhabarat* aggressively monitored Israeli diplomatic officials after Israel opened its embassy in Cairo. As one Israeli diplomat assigned to Cairo put it, Egyptian intelligence

> Literally established a blockade on the chancery, the ambassador's residence and diplomats' houses and openly shadowed all their movements. Alto-

gether, 700–1,200 (depending on the political situation) personnel of all categories, uniformed and plain-clothed, were involved in this major operation.[1]

It was not just the persistent surveillance but intimidation as well. Any Egyptian visitors to the embassy who did not clear their visit first with the *mukhabarat* faced interrogation at SSIS headquarters. They were also pressured to report on their Israeli contacts. The security services forced the Israelis to live in certain Cairo suburbs like Ma'adi where they could be better monitored and protected.[2]

The *mukhabarat*'s repression of Egypt's once large Jewish population continued. According to former Israeli ambassador Ephraim Dowek the SSIS Department of Jewish and Zionist Affairs was the 'real boss' of Egypt's remaining Jews by exercising control over Jewish communal properties and spying on community meetings. Dowek recalled that SSIS men were 'present at every celebration, religious or secular, and [sat] in the most central seats…It was pathetic to see the marks of submission to these officers by their victims and the words of praise poured on them on every occasion.'[3]

There have been several prominent espionage incidents between Egypt and Israel since 1979, but, by and large, the covert action programs, border infiltrations, sabotage, assassinations, and radio propaganda that once characterized their relations have receded into the past. As we shall see, both countries cooperate extensively in areas of shared concern like Palestine.

## Revolutionary Iran

Although Iran was embroiled in a war with Iraq for much of the 1980s its intelligence services nonetheless continued their clandestine war against Egypt by initiating contacts with and extending support to al-Jihad and the Islamic Group (IG).[4] For its part, Cairo was not only closely allied with Baghdad against Tehran its intelligence services reached out to controversial Iranian dissidents like Manuchehr Ghorbanifar. Not surprisingly, given its experience in this field, Egypt funded an anti-Tehran black radio station.[5] Like its allies in Riyadh and Kuwait, the Egyptians feared that an Iranian victory over Saddam Hussein would destabilize the region by emboldening Shi'a in the Gulf and energizing Sunni extremists like al-Jihad. Finally, the Egyptian economy relied heavily on the remittances of nearly two million guest workers in Iraq as well as an estimated $2 billion in arms sales to the Iraqi military.[6]

During this period, US intelligence was feeding the *mukhabarat* intelligence of Iranian activities against Egypt. Indeed, the CIA was the likely source of a report published in the Egyptian media detailing a February 1987 meeting in Tehran between Iranian Ministry of Intelligence and Security (MOIS) officials and Egyptian militants. Initiated by an Iranian cleric with MOIS ties named Ayatollah Mohamed 'Ali Taskhiri, the meeting discussed the formation of an 'Egyptian Hizballah' organization. The report also detailed how MOIS officers assigned to the Iranian special interests section in Cairo monitored the Suez

Canal and plotted the assassination of key Egyptian officials.[7] Reports like this probably convinced the Egyptians to expel two Iranian diplomats and temporarily shut down the special interests section in May 1987.

In June 1988 the *mukhabarat* announced the discovery of another Iranian-backed network that intended to trigger a Khomeini-type revolution in Egypt through sabotage, bombings, assassinations and subversive literature. The police alleged the network was linked to MOIS, Lebanese Hizballah and the Iraqi al-Dawa party although it was not clear how a Khomeini revolution could succeed in a country with a miniscule Shi'a population.[8] Indeed, the network reportedly turned to Sunni groups like al-Jihad for support.[9]

### Troubles to the south

Egyptian fears of a rising Iran were aggravated by growing links between that country and Sudan that included intelligence cooperation and support for Egyptian extremists. When a 1989 coup in Khartoum brought 'Umar al-Bashir and National Islamic Front (NIF) leader Hasan al-Turabi to power, Cairo tried to curry favor by dispatching the EGIS director as Mubarak's personal envoy to Khartoum. But the bilateral relationship quickly frayed as Turabi established ties with Iran, Lebanese Hizballah and Arab fighters returning from Afghanistan.[10] More alarming still was evidence that the NIF and Sudanese intelligence were providing training camps, funding and ideological support for the Islamic Group and al-Jihad.[11] In December 1991 Iranian president 'Ali Akbar Hashemi-Rafsanjani concluded military agreements with Khartoum under which Tehran agreed to help rebuild the Sudanese navy and train and supply the Sudanese army in its war against southern rebels.[12] Another secret deal reportedly involved Hizballah training of Pakistani, Egyptian, Algerian and Tunisian militants at camps in Sudan.[13] From Cairo's perspective, the nexus between Sudan, Iran and Egyptian militants represented a national security threat of the first order.[14] The *mukhabarat* responded by improving border security and developing espionage networks to monitor the training camps.

### The Gulf War

When Egypt signed its peace treaty with Israel in 1979, Iraq tried to assert its leadership over the Arab world in Egypt's place. Cairo–Baghdad ties were acrimonious until the early 1980s when the Iran–Iraq war forced the Iraqis to turn to Egypt for diplomatic support, weapons and technical expertise. It is likely that bilateral intelligence cooperation resumed at this time as well. According to one report, EGIS agreed to cease intelligence collection in Iraq in return for a cessation of Iraqi rhetoric against the Egypt–Israel peace treaty.[15]

When the Iran–Iraq war ended in 1988 it was assumed that Saddam would focus on rebuilding his country; however, he defied predictions and instigated a crisis with Kuwait in the spring of 1990. When Iraq invaded Kuwait in August 1990 Egypt and its allies faced a new and unexpected security challenge that could reorder the regional balance of power. Should Saddam occupy Saudi Arabia as well he would dominate the bulk of the world's energy supplies. Given these fears (as well as Gulf Arab money) Cairo contributed two divisions to the US-led multinational coalition against Iraq.[16]

The *mukhabarat* confronted new challenges with the Kuwait crisis, including collecting intelligence on Iraq's leadership, military and opposition while also monitoring pro-Iraqi Palestinian extremists. Undoubtedly, US–Egyptian liaison channels were very busy at this time passing assessments and other information on Iraq. Indeed, given the NSA's reported success in intercepting and breaking Iraqi intelligence communications during this period, it is possible that sanitized SIGINT was passed to the Egyptians and used in their subsequent operations against Iraqi intelligence officers.[17] For its part, the MID focused on protecting Egyptian forces in Saudi Arabia by preparing assessments of Iraqi military capabilities and infiltrating scouts into Kuwait and possibly Iraq.[18] In conversations with foreign journalists Egyptian intelligence officers anticipated a quick victory over Iraq.[19]

Egyptian intelligence contributed to the coalition in other ways as well. For example, EGIS worked with the Saudi General Intelligence Department (GID) to develop a psychological warfare plan against Iraq. An Egyptian intelligence officer named Amin Sultan, later described as 'one of the most expert officers' in the field of information operations, worked with the Americans and Saudis to develop anti-Iraq clandestine radio stations and leaflets urging Iraqi soldiers to surrender. The psyop plan also tried to reinforce Saddam's conviction that the coalition would liberate Kuwait without invading Iraq.[20]

The *mukhabarat* was at work inside Egypt as well where the primary threat was posed by Iraqi Intelligence Service (IIS) officers working alone or in concert with Palestinian terrorists. In September, Egypt and Iraq traded tit-for-tat expulsions of military attachés and suspected intelligence officers.[21] Around the same time the SSIS declared that it had discovered an Iraqi plot aimed at sabotaging the tourism infrastructure and assassinating Egyptian officials.[22] There were also fears that IIS officers might try delaying coalition deployments to Saudi Arabia by sinking cement-laden ships in the Suez Canal.[23]

The March 1991 liberation of Kuwait was a mixed blessing for Cairo and other Arab states. Although the Iraqi military had been weakened, Saddam was still in power and embittered at those who had fought against him. Not long after the cease fire, EGIS met other Arab services and proposed overthrowing the Iraqi leader by providing arms and other support to the Iraqi opposition.[24] EGIS found one interested partner in the Saudi GID which had already begun pressing the CIA for help in overthrowing Saddam.[25] In February 1992, US Director of Central Intelligence Robert Gates visited Cairo and Riyadh with proposals to remove Saddam Hussein through economic and diplomatic pressure as well as covert action.[26] Although this was publicly denied in Cairo, it is likely that Egypt contributed to the anti-Saddam planning that followed.[27]

The Gulf War showcased Egypt's reemergence on the Arab scene after a decade of Camp David isolation. Throughout the 1980s, Mubarak sought to reintegrate Egypt into the Arab fold even if this occasionally conflicted with Cairo's relations with Israel and the United States. Intelligence liaison was one approach taken by Egypt to restore ties with the other Arab states; Egyptian officials often highlighted intelligence cooperation as a sign that their country was not as isolated as it seemed. For example, in December 1987, Interior Minister Zaki Badr argued that 'despite the absence of relations between Egypt and other Arab countries, security cooperation was not completely cut off. There were contacts, mostly unpublicized, involving coordination, cooperation, and the exchange of intelligence with Arab security services.'[28]

Zaki did not elaborate, but it is likely that Egypt shared intelligence on Iran and terrorism with Iraq, Jordan, Israel, Saudi Arabia and other Gulf Arab states. As is often the case in the world of intelligence exchanges, the Egyptians felt that they were giving more than they received. In August 1989, one official lamented that 'although we supply these countries with all kinds of information, we do not get 1 percent of what we offer. Egypt does not conceal anything and relays every single fact it receives to competent security agencies for appropriate action.'[29]

Egypt's intelligence partnerships with the Arab states had a darker side as well. After Kuwait was liberated in 1991, reports surfaced that an unspecified Egyptian intelligence service was training its Kuwaiti counterpart in interrogation and torture techniques.[30] No doubt there are other cases like this.

## Internal problems

The nature of internal threats to the regime shifted over time. In 1986 the government faced a mutiny by the Interior Ministry's Central Security Forces (CSF), a pivotal player on the domestic scene. If the SSIS comprised the eyes, ears and interrogator of the regime, the CSF was its instrument of brute force.[31] When some 17,000 CSF recruits rioted in February 1986 over rumors that their conscript term would be extended by one year, the shaky foundations of the regime were highlighted in bold relief. Eventually, Mubarak had to call in the army to restore order.[32]

The riots and their aftermath rocked the Interior Ministry and the secret police. Mubarak's first move was to sack the interior minister and the SSIS chief. A few weeks later an influential editor penned a blistering critique which alleged that the SSIS knew about brewing CSF unrest but failed to warn the regime for unknown 'political reasons.' The article also confirmed what many Egyptians already knew or strongly suspected: the SSIS had informants at all levels of government and the public sector.[33] This commentary also signaled Mubarak's intent to trim the sails of the secret police.[34] His new Interior Minister, Zaki Badr, forced the retirement and transfer of hundreds of SSIS officers, restricted payments to informants, and named a new SSIS chief with a reputation for repressing internal dissent.[35]

The CSF riots raised some awkward questions about the reliability of the police, but it was the militants who posed the most enduring threat to the regime. As we have seen, the early days of the Mubarak presidency were marked by assassination plots, unrest in Upper Egypt and fears that extremists had penetrated the army and *mukhabarat*. After several al-Jihad leaders were executed or incarcerated in the early 1980s, extremist activities seemed to recede. But this calm was deceptive, for Egypt's chronic poverty and unemployment created fertile ground on which the Islamists could carry out their 'revolution by stealth.'[36] In impoverished urban areas the Islamic Group (IG) was creating a veritable 'state within a state' where militants imposed their ideas of Islamic morality on the populace.[37]

But coercion was not the only – or even the most important – factor behind the Islamists' influence. Both the IG and the Muslim Brotherhood provided valuable social services like schools, charities, health clinics and community centers in areas where government services were deficient or nonexistent.[38] At the same time, many observers were struck by *mukhabarat* complacency when Islamist imams openly denounced the 'apostate' regime and its policies.[39]

The secret police finally began to take action when the more radical IG began to assert itself on the domestic scene. An outgrowth of the religious student organizations of the 1970s, the IG was an amalgamation of societies led by local 'emirs' who exercised considerable autonomy.[40] Only gradually did some of those emirs coalesce around an ideology emphasizing the overthrow of Egypt's 'secular' state through violent means.

Then there was al-Jihad. Perhaps the regime's greatest single national security mistake was letting al-Jihad leaders like Ayman al-Zawahiri go to Pakistan in the mid-1980s. Safe in the tribal areas along the Afghanistan–Pakistan border, al-Zawahiri and others recreated al-Jihad, although they retained its small size and centralized decision-making as well as its doctrine of creating an Islamic state through a military-led coup. Entering the 1990s, al-Jihad was focused on regime change in Egypt; however, its growing ties to Usama Bin Laden generated a new emphasis on other targets like the United States. Finally, al-Jihad's chronic funding problems created an opportunity for cash-rich al-Qa'ida to exert more influence over the veteran Egyptian terrorist group. By the late 1990s, al-Jihad's identity had been largely subsumed by al-Qa'ida.[41]

## Spotlight on the SSIS

On the frontlines against the IG and al-Jihad was the SSIS. A lineal descendant of the old political police, the SSIS is still responsible for the core missions of intelligence, counterintelligence, counterterrorism, and combating 'political crime.' Located in Lazoghly Square in downtown Cairo, the SSIS has a military-type command structure headed by a major general who responds directly to the Interior Minister and the Deputy Minister for State Security. In addition to Lazoghly, the SSIS possesses large facilities in Nasr City near Cairo as well as offices in every governorate and major municipality. Unlike their predecessors, governorate level SSIS offices report directly to Cairo rather than provincial governors or the local police apparatus. In a centralized state like Egypt the secret police is a national rather than a provincial asset.[42]

Today's SSIS is a formidable instrument of state repression. Its size in terms of budget and personnel is a state secret, but it is clear that this organization has a nationwide presence with an officer cadre numbering in the many thousands. Significantly, those officers are not Copts even though that community represents anywhere from 6–10 percent of Egypt's estimated 75 million people.[43]

Informants are vital to the SSIS mission and they come from all walks of life. They include doormen at hotels and apartment complexes and sweepers who keep a sharp eye out for the suspicious and unusual. They might be any of Cairo's numerous taxi drivers who swarm in the traffic circles, hand on horn and foot on pedal. Additionally, the SSIS recruits informants from the legions of unemployed young men who lounge at cafés or on the streets near major hotels, tourist sites and foreign diplomatic facilities.[44] Sometimes the informants are ordered to maintain an overt presence to deter and intimidate their targets. As one mosque imam told a human rights group:

> I know the mukhbireen [informers]... there are three main mukhbireen in my district. I see them in my mosque and in front of my house. They monitor lectures and prayers in the mosque. They're there all the time, twenty-four hours a day, openly, like my shadow.[45]

The secret police supplements its informants with computer network monitoring, audio-visual surveillance, opening mail and tapping telephones.[46] Legally, the SSIS must obtain judicial authorization before it can tap any telephone or fax line; however, Egypt's emergency laws grant the *mukhabarat* unlimited authority to monitor any Egyptians it deems suspicious.

In addition to espionage, SSIS authorities include harassment, arrest, interrogation, prolonged detention and torture. It often conducts its arrests in the early morning hours when suspects are roused from sleep in a disoriented state and incapable of offering much resistance. While detainees are shoved into squad cars, the secret police search their premises and seize documents, audio-visual materials and computers.[47] Suspects are usually taken to a regional SSIS office, Lazoghly or to special detention camps where they can be detained incommunicado for days or even weeks. It is in these 'interim' detention areas that most torture takes place.

As we have seen, the use of torture is not a new phenomenon in Egypt; however, it subsided under Sadat only to return under Mubarak with a vengeance.[48] Indeed, in the panic following Sadat's assassination, the *mukhabarat* used torture extensively to extract information about al-Jihad and the threat it posed to the government. Although Egypt acceded to the UN Convention against Torture and Other Forms of Cruel, Inhuman or Degrading Treatment or Punishment in 1986, human rights groups continue to document numerous cases of torture in *mukhabarat* prisons. According to one organization:

> The detailed testimony of torture victims persuades Middle East Watch that the methods of torture in Egypt are rigorous yet predictable, indicating that

a system appears to be in place to train [SSIS] personnel in torture techniques and that the use of torture is directed and supervised by officers in the [SSIS].[49]

As human rights reports like this one detail, there is a systematic approach to the use of torture. When a detainee enters the prison complex, he or she is usually blindfolded and handcuffed to intimidate, disorient and protect police identities.[50] Some handcuffs automatically tighten with any movement of the hands.[51] Stripped down to their underwear, detainees are often subjected to insults, curses and threatened sexual abuse directed at the prisoner and his or her family members. Some detainees have endured prolonged taped sessions of human screams to further 'soften' them up.[52] Physical torture is part of the routine with detainees frequently beaten or kicked with sticks or batons. Some are hung by their wrists for extended periods with their feet barely touching the floor. Electric shocks to the genitals seem to be part of the torture routine.[53]

Its use of torture has definitely contributed to the *mukhabarat*'s notorious reputation for shock, pain and terror. Moreover, there are indications that torture in Egyptian prisons has produced unforeseen and unintended consequences. For example, in his studies of incarcerated religious extremists, the sociologist Sa'ad al-Din Ibrahim concluded that torture reinforced an already potent martyrdom complex, sharpened hatreds and intolerance and contributed to a worldview shaped by conspiracy and suspicion.[54] An Islamist lawyer believed that Ayman al-Zawahiri's messianic rage stems from the humiliation of being forced to divulge incriminating information about colleagues to the *mukhabarat*.[55]

Once the SSIS has obtained its information, confession or perhaps recruited an informant through coercive means, it releases some with an admonition to stay silent about their ordeal; others are transferred to the larger prisons like Tura or Abu Za'abal where they await trial.[56] Significantly, from a legal and human rights perspective, the date of the prisoners' entrance into these larger prisons usually marks the time when they are *officially* detained. In other words, the government maintains no public record of the days or weeks the detainees have already spent being tortured at an SSIS facility.[57]

## Tremors

But informants, torture and a reputation for brutality could not forestall the rising tide of unrest that swept over Egypt in the 1990s. Much of that violence was fueled by al-Jihad and IG veterans of the Afghan war who began infiltrating Egypt from Sudan after the Soviets withdrew from Afghanistan in 1989.[58] The radicalization and militarization of the IG was another factor. In 1989 the IG created a military branch led by Tala'at Mohamed Yasin Hammam, a man who had been arrested by the SSIS in the early 1980s for his suspected involvement in the Sadat assassination. Released in the late 1980s, Hammam returned to the IG where he was so successful in evading surveillance that SSIS officers called him 'the Ghost.' He eventually fled Egypt and resided for a time in Pakistan before returning to lead the IG's new military wing.[59]

In December 1989, Hammam's organization tried to assassinate Interior Minister Zaki Badr. While Badr escaped, the attack heralded a period of sustained jihadist violence in Egypt that was fueled by Arab Afghan veterans. While it did not take the *mukhabarat* long to assess the importance of the Afghanistan link to the violence, Egyptian officials admitted that identifying the names of specific Arab Afghan jihadists was another challenge altogether.[60] What little they did have was exchanged with the CIA, the Algerians and others to better understand the nature of the new threat.[61] When they could, the security services arrested and interrogated those Arab Afghans who had returned to Egypt. According to one defense lawyer with an exaggerated appreciation for the *mukhabarat*'s prowess, 'the police know everything about those who have gone to Pakistan and Afghanistan. As soon as they return they are arrested.'[62]

Several developments enabled Egyptian intelligence to arrest some of the early 'returnees from Afghanistan.' One was the establishment of an EGIS station in Kabul in 1992 or 1993 which established a liaison relationship with the new Afghan government. According to a source with good insights into the Afghan–Egyptian intelligence relationship at this time, EGIS felt that the Afghans were not doing enough to interdict arms transfers to militant camps in Sudan.[63] Intelligence cooperation with Pakistan, Algeria and the Saudis was another useful instrument. Working with Algeria's Securite Militaire and Pakistan's Inter-Services Intelligence (ISI), EGIS built a 'census' of Arab Afghans resident in Pakistan that included the names of the 30 most dangerous individuals to Egyptian and Algerian security. In April 1993, an Egyptian air force plane sat for two weeks at Peshawar airport while EGIS sought extradition rights from the ISI and the Pakistani judiciary. Unfortunately for Cairo, many of those sought for extradition were likely tipped off by the ISI and had fled to Afghanistan.[64] Yet Pakistan showed its penchant for playing both sides when an ISI tipoff led to the arrest of two jihadists upon their return to Cairo.[65]

Although the December 1989 assassination attempt on Interior Minister Badr marked the start of the new jihadist offensive, it was not until a year later that the campaign began in earnest with the murder of an IG spokesman by a probable *mukhabarat* agent.[66] The IG retaliated one month later by assassinating the Speaker of the National Assembly outside the Semiramis Hilton in Cairo.[67] Meanwhile Algeria faced a sharp spike in Islamist violence of its own after the Algerian military outlawed Le Front Islamique du Salut (FIS) in early 1992. In January 1992 an Egyptian counterterrorism team was sent to Algiers to assist the security forces in combating anticipated Islamist violence as well as offering information on those Algerians who had fought in Afghanistan and trained in Sudan.[68] But the *mukhabarat*'s main concern in 1992 was the IG's targeting of the tourism industry, senior political leaders, so-called 'secularist' thinkers, and Copts. Millions were lost to the economy as a result of canceled tourist reservations alone.[69]

## Insurgency

When the IG ramped up its campaign against the government, the al-Jihad leadership was under pressure by its rank-and-file and foreign supporters to initiate an offensive of its own. In August 1993 al-Jihad failed in an attempt to assassinate Interior Minister Hasan al-Alfi with a suicide bomber. An al-Jihad car bomb aimed at the Egyptian Prime Minister killed a schoolgirl instead three months later; her death triggered widespread outrage in Egypt.

The *mukhabarat* quickly developed an appreciation for its opponents' skill in monitoring the routines of their intended targets. There was even speculation that the jihadists could tap phone lines.[70] One captured IG member described how his group copied the secret police by employing informers in government ministries and on the streets to monitor targets:

> Shop owners and sandwich or fruit juice sellers there talk without anyone asking them. I knew from their remarks and gossip that the education minister and a judge in the military courts who sentence the brothers to death lived in that building.[71]

This militant explained how the assassination team would conduct discreet but comprehensive surveillance of the victim, including an analysis of his physical characteristics, daily routine and residence.[72] Moreover, the IG had a good understanding of the *mukhabarat*'s technical capabilities and enjoined its members to practice rigorous counterintelligence and communications security practices. During their trials, many militants revealed that they had received counterintelligence training at camps in Sudan or Yemen.[73]

In March 1993, the IG murdered a senior SSIS officer and his son even though the identities of most SSIS officials were supposedly secret.[74] Senior officials downplayed suggestions that the security services had been penetrated, but these assertions were found wanting when the IG successfully assassinated the Director of the SSIS Religious Extremists Department, Major General Ra'uf Khayrat in April 1994. Investigators later concluded that someone inside the SSIS had tipped off the IG to Khayrat's identity and his residence.[75]

Khayrat's murder spurred a renewed SSIS drive to penetrate and destroy the extremist movement; however, unbeknownst to the secret police, the head of the IG's military wing, Hammam, was living in the Cairo suburb of Hada'ak al-Kubbah – literally within sight of EGIS headquarters and a presidential palace.[76] For some time, he had used an apartment there to plan operations including the assassination of Khayrat. Eventually the SSIS succeeded in penetrating Hammam's network through informants and communications intercepts of his associates.[77] In the early morning hours of 25 April 1994, SSIS officers burst into Hammam's apartment and shot him several times in the head. Afterward the Interior Ministry praised its officers, noting that Hammam was 'the most dangerous of terrorists because he alone occupied the strategic position of having experience in all elements of the terrorist organization including the military wing.'[78]

In addition to eliminating part of Hammam's network, the *mukhabarat* got another big break in 1993 with the arrest of al-Jihad's membership director. In his possession was a computer containing the names, addresses and aliases of the entire al-Jihad network.[79] It was an unprecedented coup that no doubt helped the security services infiltrate and dismantle al-Jihad cells inside Egypt and disrupt al-Jihad activities abroad.

Successes like these were directly tied to the intensive use of informants. The security services routinely updated the Egyptian press on their success in planting agents inside the extremist groups.[80] For their part, the militants understood the importance of informants to the security organs and, as a result, they intimidated and often murdered suspected government collaborators.[81]

For its part, the regime used intimidation and fear as key elements of its counterterrorism campaign in the 1990s. Part of this intimidation strategy was the construction of new prisons with tighter security and more sinister reputations such as the Scorpion. Completed in May 1993 and housed within the Tora prison complex, the Scorpion is a 320-cell facility that is reportedly controlled by the SSIS instead of the Prisons Authority. According to human rights groups, no visitors are allowed inside the Scorpion despite Egyptian court judgments that this practice is unconstitutional.[82] Ironically, one of the lawyers who won a court case regarding the status of Scorpion prisoners became himself a *mukhabarat* victim. In April 1994 'Abd al-Harith Madani, was arrested by SSIS officers who took him to their municipal office in Giza. But only a few days after his arrest he was brought to a special ward reserved for SSIS detainees at Qasr al-'Aini hospital where he died within an hour of admission. Madani had been beaten to death, although the authorities insisted he had died of asthma. His coffin was delivered to his family along with an SSIS escort, but no one was allowed to open it.[83]

Secret police repression did not deter further IG and al-Jihad violence. In October 1994, the Nobel Prize Laureate Naguib Mahfouz was stabbed because the IG objected to the depiction of revered Islamic figures in one of his novels. In April 1996, 17 Greek tourists were murdered in Cairo. In September 1997, IG terrorists killed nine German tourists outside the Egyptian Museum in Cairo; two months later the IG staged another horror at the Hatshepsut Temple in Luxor where it killed another 58 tourists. Neither the Egyptian government nor the international community knew it yet, but the Luxor massacre marked the high tide of the IG's terrorist campaign in Egypt. As a wave of revulsion undercut support for the IG in Egypt, the *mukhabarat* was beginning to focus more increasingly on al-Qa'ida operations abroad.

# 16 General intelligence wars

Repeated SSIS successes against Islamic Group insurgents combined with a growing public outcry against militant atrocities meant that Egypt's war on terrorism was shifting overseas by the late 1990s. This period might well be called the General Intelligence Era in Egyptian security for EGIS had once again become the preeminent player in the Egyptian intelligence community.

The 1995 assassination attempt on President Mubarak in Ethiopia was another factor in the EGIS ascendancy, for the assassins were thwarted at least in part by some critical advice from EGIS Director 'Umar Soleiman. A politically savvy former military officer with previous experience leading the MID, Soleiman fundamentally enhanced and redefined EGIS's liaison relationship with the CIA. New emphasis was placed on intelligence sharing and joint operations against al-Qa'ida and its powerful Egyptian affiliates; Egypt was also one of the first countries to participate in Washington's controversial policy of 'extraordinary rendition' whereby alleged militants were kidnapped by the CIA in third countries and shipped to states like Egypt for interrogation and incarceration. Indeed CIA renditions helped the Egyptian government capture, interrogate, convict and execute several Egyptian jihadist leaders.

On the eve of the 11 September 2001 terrorist attacks in the United States, 'Umar Soleiman had positioned EGIS as a pivotal member in a growing US-led international intelligence coalition against terrorism. In addition to its vital American connections, Cairo forged closer security ties with several important Arab states including Saudi Arabia, Yemen, Algeria and the United Arab Emirates.

## The rise of 'Umar Soleiman

The escalating violence in Egypt during the early 1990s combined with the growing threat posed by the Arab Afghans convinced President Mubarak to appoint former MID chief Major General 'Umar Soleiman as Director of General Intelligence in 1993. Soleiman is easily the most influential EGIS chief since Salah Nasr and, like Salah Nasr, Soleiman's tenure as Egypt's top spy chief has been an enduring one. It used to be that the identity of the general intelligence director was a closely kept secret; for his part, Soleiman really did not emerge in public until the late 1990s when he began mediating between Israel and the Palestinian Authority. Just the same, Soleiman is not a publicity hound, a trait that no doubt endears him to his power-sensitive boss, Husni Mubarak.[1]

According to the few details of his public biography, Soleiman was born in Qena in Upper Egypt in 1935. He graduated from the Egyptian Military Academy in the mid-1950s and received training in the USSR. A veteran of Egypt's wars with Israel in 1967 and 1973, Soleiman transferred to the MID in the mid-1980s and served as MID Director during the first Gulf War.[2] Soleiman's reticence probably accounts for the contrasting public descriptions of him. In one profile, the Israeli journal *Maariv* noted that Soleiman 'looks like a classic spy – balding, chubby, of medium height, a person who draws no particular attention.' Still, the *Maariv* article cautions, 'on second glance... you notice his dark eyes and piercing gaze. He does not speak much.'[3] Former Director of Central Intelligence George Tenet described Soleiman as 'tall and regal looking, a very powerful man, very deliberate in his speech... In a world filled with shadows, he is straight up and down.'[4] An Israeli politician who had many dealings with Soleiman offers this description:

> He is an impressive man, but free of a ruler's mannerism... he creates an air of intimacy already in your first meeting with him, and your conversation runs smoothly so you feel like you have known him for years... he is not pompous at all.[5]

Given his extensive experience interacting with Palestinian factions over the years, Soleiman is particularly knowledgeable about Palestinian affairs. As another Israeli Knesset Member noted,

> I was most impressed with his vast knowledge of and familiarity with all the strata on the Palestinian street. He knows subgroups and leaders of all levels. As a rule, his command of what goes on in the Arab world is most unusual. He is one of the most successful secret service chiefs in the region.[6]

'Umar Soleiman's worldview is summed up in the motto 'Stability Above All.' Stability for Soleiman begins at home: Egypt's powerful Islamist groups must be contained yet, according to prominent Egyptian lawyer Muntasir al-Zayat, Soleiman believes some Islamists should be allowed to participate in politics provided they pay due regard to the institution of the Egyptian presidency.[7] Given the nature of the agency he runs Soleiman intrinsically understands the myriad links between regional crises and domestic stability. In the Palestinian arena, for example, Soleiman and his subordinates realize that escalating unrest in the Palestinian arena could generate regional unrest that ultimately embroils Egypt in a war with Israel.[8]

'Umar Soleiman sees Iran as a pressing challenge especially now that Saddam is gone and the Shi'a have power in Iraq. The image of a waxing Iran armed with nuclear weapons combined with Tehran's historical links to al-Jihad, the IG and Hizballah haunts the Egyptian leadership and influences its relations with other moderate Arab states. While Iran is an abiding concern, Soleiman is pre-occupied these days by the al-Qa'ida threat. In fact, EGIS has had a prominent role in US strategy against al-Qa'ida before and after 11 September 2001.

## 1995 Mubarak assassination attempt

'Umar Soleiman's influence increased dramatically after the June 1995 IG assassination attempt on President Mubarak in Addis Ababa. The plot was the result of an April 1995 meeting in Khartoum between al-Jihad and the Islamic Group in which the participants decided that a high-profile assassination could reignite the flagging insurgency in Egypt.[9] When the IG volunteered for the mission, Sudanese intelligence reportedly provided Sudanese passports and stored weapons at the Sudanese embassy in Ethiopia where the assassination was to take place.[10] Two months later, in an Egyptian cabinet meeting, Soleiman insisted over Foreign Ministry objections that the president take his armored limousine on an official visit to Ethiopia.[11]

On 26 June 1995, Mubarak landed at the airport near the Ethiopian capital, transferred to his armored car and headed toward the conference site. Not far from the airport, his convoy was blocked and then fired on at close range by 11 IG assailants. But the attackers fired on the lead vehicle which turned out to be an unarmored limousine provided by the Ethiopian government for Mubarak's use. Mubarak's armored vehicle, situated at the rear of the procession, spun around and immediately carried the president back to the airport where he was bundled aboard his jet and returned to Egypt.[12]

Cairo almost immediately accused Khartoum and Tehran of backing the attempt. No doubt these charges were backed by intelligence reports linking the Sudanese government to Egyptian terrorists, al-Qa'ida and Iranian-sponsored terrorist training facilities. A spate of Egyptian government-sanctioned press reports detailed how Sudanese intelligence officers provided al-Jihad and the IG with finance, training and arms as well as assistance infiltrating into Egypt.[13] There was also a good deal of saber-rattling in the Egyptian press hinting of Egyptian air force retaliation strikes against Sudanese terrorist camps, sending EGIS after militants abroad and providing support for Sudanese rebels.[14] While much of this turned out be talk, the Egyptians did send forces into the Halaib Triangle, a strip of desert in dispute with Sudan.[15] Egyptian intelligence also made a point of harassing Sudanese diplomats in Cairo.[16]

In the months following the assassination attempt Egypt improved the security of its border with Sudan. After desert training and familiarization with local dialects, SSIS officers were dispatched to the border where they began patrolling, developing agent networks and setting up infrared cameras to monitor suspected infiltration routes. Not long after these procedures were put in place, the SSIS began reporting the capture of militants.[17]

Egyptian intelligence responded in other ways too. The most notorious involved the 13-year-old son of a senior al-Jihad official who was captured by

EGIS agents in Sudan, given drugs and then photographed while he was being sodomized. The photographs were used to blackmail the boy into becoming an EGIS informant. Unbeknownst to this unfortunate victim and his Egyptian handlers, Sudanese intelligence grew suspicious of the boy, monitored his contacts with Egyptian embassy officials and then arrested him carrying explosives that were to be used against al-Zawahiri. After the Sudanese authorities handed the boy over to al-Jihad, al-Zawahiri convened a court, convicted the boy of various crimes and had him executed. This execution enraged the Sudanese government which responded by expelling al-Zawahiri and al-Jihad from the country.[18]

## An embassy bombing

Despite its relative lack of success inside Egypt, al-Jihad maintained a formidable apparatus abroad including Afghanistan and Sudan. When EGIS sponsored several assassination attempts against Usama bin Laden and al-Zawahiri in 1994 and 1995, al-Jihad retaliated in November 1995 with a suicide car bomb attack on the Egyptian embassy in Pakistan that killed 15 and wounded more than 80. EGIS quickly dispatched a security delegation to Pakistan to investigate the attack and share intelligence with the Pakistani services.[19] Pakistan's Inter-Services Intelligence (ISI) and police promised to apprehend the attack planners; however, acting on probable ISI tip-offs, the suspects fled either to Pakistan's tribal areas or neighboring Afghanistan.[20]

Today, the multinational coalition fighting in Afghanistan is frustrated by ISI's complicity in sponsoring Taliban fighters and other extremists based in Pakistan's Federally Administered Tribal Areas. Similarly, in 1995 and 1996, Egyptian intelligence allowed its criticism of ISI to surface in the press where it chafed at ISI inaction in extraditing identified Egyptian militants to Cairo and leaking Egyptian-sourced intelligence.[21] Despite these tensions, both sides later signed a security agreement that included the exchange of intelligence on counterterrorism cases as well as cooperation in the areas of narcotics smuggling, counterfeiting and extortion.[22]

In the wake of the embassy bombing, the Egyptian government set up a committee consisting of representatives from the Foreign Ministry, EGIS and SSIS to investigate how the security of Egyptian embassies could be improved. In addition to physical security measures, the committee also pressed for stepped up liaison with foreign governments to share intelligence on militants. The overriding objective was extraditing to Egypt those individuals deemed dangerous to national security; the al-Jihad leadership was at the top of the list.[23]

In 1996 the Sudanese government, under increasing pressure from Washington, Cairo and Riyadh, expelled al-Qa'ida, forcing the organization and its leadership to return to Afghanistan. For his part, after his expulsion from Sudan, Ayman al-Zawahiri managed to elude his EGIS pursuers by traveling a circuitous route through Switzerland, Bosnia, Bulgaria, Malaysia, Taiwan, Singapore, Hong Kong and even Chechnya (where he was imprisoned by the Russians for a while) before he finally joined bin Laden in Afghanistan.[24]

As the al-Jihad leadership began to disperse from its base in Sudan, the IG was waging a losing terror campaign in Egypt. A combination of security measures, including repression, torture and infiltration by the security forces was eroding the IG's underground networks. At the same time, secret contacts between Interior Ministry representatives and imprisoned IG and al-Jihad leaders eventually induced the militants to call for a unilateral ceasefire. But the incarcerated leaders did not speak for their respective organizations as a whole. Al-Jihad militants abroad, including those clustered around al-Zawahiri, rejected the ceasefire out of hand. As for IG militants still at liberty, they responded with the infamous November 1997 massacre of tourists in Luxor that triggered widespread Egyptian public revulsion.[25] By March 1999 it was clear that IG ceasefire proponents had won out and most of the organization's emirs agreed to cease 'armed operations.'[26] In return, the government released an estimated 6,000 Islamists from its prisons, the bulk of whom were alleged IG members.[27]

## The rise of general intelligence

The end of the IG terror campaign inside Egypt ushered in a new era in the Egyptian intelligence community. Confronted by dispersed al-Jihad cadres in Afghanistan, Pakistan, Albania and other countries, Egypt moved its war on terrorism overseas and EGIS was the lead agency in that fight. Headquartered in the Cairo district of Hada'ak al-Kubbah, EGIS is the preeminent intelligence agency in Egypt today for not only does it enjoy the prestige associated with its ties to the CIA, European and Arab secret services, EGIS also benefits from the trust that Mubarak places in its powerful director, 'Umar Soleiman.

Unfortunately for the researcher, little is known about EGIS except that its very existence supposedly is secret by law. This secrecy extends to memoirs, 'literary words' and 'works of art' which may not be published except with EGIS permission.[28] Despite these limitations, historical sources, memoirs and newspaper articles offer insights into general intelligence as it is constituted today. Above all, EGIS is responsible for collecting intelligence via its human assets abroad. While MID runs spies in neighboring countries of military concern, EGIS is dominant in the foreign espionage arena. EGIS also plans and implements covert action operations ordered by the national security authorities.

EGIS is the key liaison partner for foreign intelligence agencies like the CIA. Although details are lacking, EGIS seems to be the primary Egyptian beneficiary of CIA largesse and shared intelligence. This would certainly be in keeping with historical precedent. The close relationship with the CIA, and the benefits it brings, no doubt enhances the prestige of EGIS within the Egyptian intelligence community. Another important factor is the proximity of EGIS to the real center of power in Egypt. Unlike the SSIS or the MID, which are subordinate agencies of the interior and defense ministries respectively, EGIS takes its orders directly from the president. In a system as centralized as Egypt's, the presidency is the undisputed fulcrum of decision-making.

While EGIS directs most of its resources abroad, the agency also has an important counterintelligence role at home. If the past is any guide, it is safe to assume that General Intelligence is a lead agency for offensive operations aimed at foreign intelligence agencies, including penetration, running double agents and disseminating disinformation. Still, the main challenges for EGIS today are combating the threats posed by al-Jihad and, more prominently, al-Qa'ida. Another pressing EGIS concern is containing Palestinian unrest. Unlike the Nasser period when EGIS often single-handedly carried out intelligence and covert action missions abroad, Soleiman's General Intelligence is not much of a unilateral actor these days. On the contrary, intelligence liaison is at the center of two EGIS strategies against terrorism. The first is promoting greater international cooperation against religious extremism. The second involves the extradition – or rendition – of suspects from European and other countries.

Throughout the 1990s, General Intelligence knew that al-Jihad and Islamic Group militants were taking refuge in several Arab countries like Sudan and Yemen. In the case of the latter country, *mukhabarat* officers were often irritated by the close relationship between extremists and Yemen's intelligence service, the Political Security Organization (PSO).[29] Indeed, not only did the Yemeni government have a record of using Arab Afghans to fight southern separatists in 1994, PSO officers maintained cordial ties with both al-Jihad and al-Qa'ida.[30] Still, despite these concerns, Egypt signed an intelligence sharing arrangement with the PSO in 1995.[31]

EGIS understood that eliminating safe havens was crucial to defeating the jihadist threat. This was particularly true of Sudan, Yemen and several Gulf Arab states where extremists found refuge and financial support. To counter this trend, the Egyptians concluded bilateral security arrangements with several Arab states that included intelligence exchanges and the extradition of suspects.[32] These deals produced some tangible benefits: in 1994 and 1995 Egypt extradited 68 suspects from three (unnamed) Arab states.[33] Moreover, Egyptian (and American) pressure finally convinced the Saudi government to revoke bin Laden's citizenship in March 1994.[34]

But the Arab states were not the only safe havens for Islamists. Throughout the 1990s, EGIS appealed to its European counterparts to extradite, arrest or at least monitor alleged Egyptian extremists residing abroad. Many of these appeals went unanswered.[35] For instance, the United Kingdom was one important refuge for Egyptian Islamists such as Yasser Tawfik 'Ali al-Sirri whom the *mukhabarat* had linked to al-Jihad and several assassination plots. Although Egyptian intelligence continued to pass information on al-Sirri's jihadist links, the British government refused to extradite this individual to Egypt.[36] In addition to al-Sirri, EGIS repeatedly emphasized the danger posed by al-Jihad and al-Qa'ida but these warnings apparently had little impact.[37] When London turned down Egyptian extradition requests for humanitarian and legal reasons, the Egyptian services grew frustrated with the British and their lack of reciprocity.[38]

The British were not alone in receiving *mukhabarat* requests for cooperation. France also helped track militants during the 1990s. According to one source,

French technical experts assisted in an early 1990s reorganization of EGIS.[39] Although there are conflicting stories surrounding the arrest of terrorist Carlos the Jackal in Khartoum in August 1994, at least one account states that EGIS helped the French locate and extradite Carlos.[40]

Given Cairo's problems in extraditing alleged terrorists from Britain and other countries, rumors began to circulate in the mid-1990s of EGIS 'hit squads' who were sent abroad to hunt down and kill Egyptian extremists.[41] Apparently some émigré Egyptian Islamists were sufficiently alarmed by these reports to take action of their own: in November 1995, an Egyptian diplomat in Geneva was gunned down amid suspicions that he was an undercover EGIS officer whose mission was to monitor political exiles in Europe.[42]

## The rendition era begins

As more countries became aware of the Arab Afghan threat, bilateral and multilateral intelligence cooperation increased markedly. Such was the case with the CIA's liaison relationships with EGIS and SSIS during the early 1990s where some of the CIA's best intelligence on Arab extremists reportedly originated with the North African services. The Egyptian *mukhabarat* certainly used the CIA channel to air their concerns about the jihadists, their Gulf Arab funding networks and European unwillingness to cooperate in extraditing them.[43]

But it was the 26 February 1993 terrorist bombing of the World Trade Center in New York City which opened a new phase in the already close partnership between Egyptian and American intelligence. The *mukhabarat* assisted the CIA and the FBI in several facets of the investigation, including locating and extraditing a key suspect in the case named Mahmud Abu Halima.[44] Egyptian intelligence also provided information on a mastermind of the plot named Ramzi Yusef who had fled to Pakistan. Similar intelligence was passed to the Americans in April 1993 when Director of Central Intelligence James Woolsey led a team of 20 CIA regional and terrorism experts to meetings with EGIS and SSIS in Cairo.[45] Significantly, this was the same month when Mubarak was pushing Pakistan to be more cooperative on extraditing Egyptian extremists like al-Zawahiri. In fact, according to one report, a joint EGIS–CIA team went to Pakistan at this time to press ISI for information on over 300 Egyptians resident in Peshawar.[46]

American and Egyptian intelligence services benefited from their stepped-up cooperation after the 1993 World Trade Center bombing. Even so, the relationship was not without some awkward moments. For example, during an April 1993 interview with the *New York Times*, President Mubarak claimed that his intelligence services had warned the CIA of militant plans to blow up the World Trade Center. Later, under White House pressure, Mubarak backtracked by admitting that the *mukhabarat* did not have 'definitive information' on the plot.[47] For his part, President Bill Clinton said that a US investigation was underway to see if Egyptian intelligence could have prevented the bombing.[48] So what did the *mukhabarat* know about the plot? It is plausible that the Egyptian services had intelligence on extremists discussing upcoming operations against the United States but nothing specific. Curiously, the Egyptians later claimed they had a detainee who 'confessed' to an Iranian role in the World Trade Center attack but nothing more was heard in public concerning this.[49]

The 1993 World Trade Center bombing led to a renewed CIA emphasis on combating transnational terrorism. On 23 January 1995, President Clinton signed Executive Order 12947 which designated several terrorist organizations as a threat to the United States including the Islamic Group and al-Jihad.[50] This order, combined with Presidential Decision Directive (PDD)-39, framed the legal basis for the US government's 'extraordinary rendition' policy under which the United States reserved the right to covertly seize and transport alleged extremists to third countries like Egypt without obtaining permission of the countries in which the suspects resided.[51] The motivations for this new policy are complex and multifaceted. On the one hand, the United States wanted to 'neutralize' identified terrorists even if it lacked the evidence to convict them in US court. On another level, the policy tacitly acknowledged that some foreign security services – such as the Egyptian *mukhabarat* – not only had a better understanding of the culture and history of the jihadist groups they also had greater 'latitude' for detaining suspects and 'extracting' information.

Up until this point, EGIS–CIA cooperation included a routine intelligence exchange and the provision of US expertise and technology. Both services not only worked closely in identifying and locating jihadists (especially those with Egyptian backgrounds), they also researched the financial links to extremists and the growing role of Usama bin Laden as a terrorism facilitator. For instance, in the early 1990s EGIS cooperated with the CIA station chief in Khartoum by monitoring bin Laden terrorist training camps in Sudan. The CIA even approached EGIS on at least two occasions to see if the Egyptians would accept bin Laden for trial and/or imprisonment. Although EGIS was wary of a public trial, they did offer to kill the Saudi terrorist. In addition, according to former US Ambassador to Cairo Edward Walker, the CIA trained an Egyptian special forces unit in counterterrorism until the program was shut down in 1998.[52] While Ambassador Walker and the CIA were wary of training special forces – Walker likened them to a 'hit squad rather than an arrest squad'[53] – the United States was nonetheless keen on recruiting Egyptian intelligence for its extraordinary rendition program. In the summer of 1995, the CIA station chief concluded an agreement with 'Umar Soleiman that covered EGIS's role in identifying and receiving Egyptian nationals 'rendered' to Egypt by the CIA. Soleiman later secured SSIS cooperation in the program.[54]

Egyptian intelligence was very receptive to extraordinary rendition. As the June 1995 assassination attempt against Mubarak had demonstrated, while the danger posed by Islamists on Egypt's home front might be waning, the same was not true of Egyptian militants abroad. The *mukhabarat* had previously encountered difficulties getting the Europeans to extradite alleged Egyptian extremists who had sought asylum overseas. From 'Umar Soleiman's perspective, the CIA's proposal must have been a sign that the Americans had finally 'seen the light.'

Although details of the EGIS–CIA agreement are still secret, several elements of the pact have emerged in public. First, EGIS would work with the CIA to locate Egyptian jihadists abroad. The CIA (and occasionally EGIS) would then either approach the host nation's security services for help in extraditing the suspects to Egypt or, alternatively, unilaterally abduct suspects and transport them to Cairo on a chartered jet. Upon landing in Egypt, EGIS or SSIS representatives would take custody of the prisoners. The most important suspects were delivered to EGIS headquarters or a safe house where they would be interrogated and undoubtedly tortured for confessions and information. Once EGIS was finished with them, the suspects were often transferred to SSIS for further interrogation. According to former CIA counterterrorism expert Michael Scheuer, the CIA cooperated closely with EGIS in the interrogation of prisoners even if it was not allowed direct access to them. The Cairo station and Langley analysts would produce a list of questions which would be submitted to EGIS for follow up; often EGIS came back with 'answers' the same day.[55]

The earliest known example of a joint EGIS–CIA rendition involved Abu Talal al-Qasimi, an IG spokesman who had been granted asylum in Denmark. The Egyptians wanted al-Qasimi for his alleged involvement in the Sadat assassination for which he had been sentenced to death *in abstentia*. In September 1995, al-Qasimi was arrested by Croatian intelligence and handed over to the CIA for interrogation on a ship in the Adriatic. After they were done with him, the CIA transferred al-Qasimi to EGIS; it is believed that he was executed after his rendition to Egypt.[56]

Another rendition involving Egypt occurred in July 1998 when a CIA-Albanian intelligence team apprehended an al-Jihad cell that was raising money, counterfeiting passports, and setting up a training camp in Albania.[57] At least four al-Jihad members were eventually transferred to the *mukhabarat* which interrogated and presumably tortured them before showcasing them and several other alleged extremists in the so-called 'Returnees from Albania' trial.[58] Among the more interesting trial revelations was an al-Jihad plan to land a special team with hand gliders onto the roof of the Scorpion prison where they would stage an inmate revolt.[59] In another story from the trial, the IG allegedly tried to convince bin Laden to move to Upper Egypt after undergoing plastic surgery to disguise his features. But Ayman al-Zawhiri successfully counseled against this after highlighting the capabilities of the Egyptian *mukhabarat* especially when it was fighting enemies on its own soil.[60]

The July 1998 arrest of the al-Jihad network in Albania upped the ante in the growing war between al-Qa'ida and the CIA. On 4 August, al-Zawahiri sent a warning to the United States: 'a reply is currently being written. We hope they read it well, as God willing, we will write it in the language they understand.'[61] Three days later US embassies in Kenya and Tanzania were hit by suicide car bombs that left 257 dead and an estimated 5,000 injured. The United States retaliated with cruise missile attacks on al-Qa'ida camps in Afghanistan and an alleged bin Laden-affiliated chemical warfare plant in Khartoum. The attack on this latter facility triggered international criticism after the Sudanese government successfully convinced many that the chemical weapons factory was in fact the al-Shifa pharmaceutical plant. Later, stories emerged that EGIS might have played a part in the al-Shifa attack by providing an asset to the CIA who collected soil samples near the facility. When the samples were tested in a US laboratory they allegedly revealed traces of a precursor for a nerve gas called VX.[62]

The third example of EGIS–CIA cooperation involved the arrest of two of Ayman al-Zawahiri's brothers. In 1998 or 1999, Mohamed al-Zawahiri's wife surrendered to EGIS officers in Yemen and revealed her husband's whereabouts. In March or April 1999, Mohamed al-Zawahiri – at one time an al-Jihad deputy leader and financial expert – was captured in the United Arab Emirates and either extradited or 'rendered' to Egypt with CIA assistance. He was presumed dead for several years until a London newspaper revealed in 2003 that he was detained at Tora prison. Allowed to speak to a relative, Mohamed al-Zawahiri revealed that he had spent more than four years in an EGIS underground prison before he was transferred to the SSIS for further interrogation.[63] Mohamed al-Zawahiri's wife also disclosed the location of another Zawahiri brother. Although the timing is not clear, Hussein al-Zawahiri was arrested by Malaysian intelligence and transferred to the custody of a joint CIA/EGIS team. After six months of interrogation by General Intelligence, this al-Zawahiri brother was released into house arrest with a warning to remain silent about his *mukhabarat* experiences.[64]

The extraordinary rendition program is the most visible aspect of EGIS-CIA cooperation in recent years but another element of their partnership was the role General Intelligence played in infiltrating terrorist groups. Since the CIA lacked many case officers experienced in the languages and cultures of the Arab Middle East, services like EGIS were often called on to fill the gap. The Egyptians had extensive experience dealing with the al-Jihad group which was probably the single most important element of al-Qa'ida. As a result, the CIA provided funds, intelligence and undoubtedly surveillance technology to help EGIS penetrate al-Qa'ida.[65]

As EGIS agents nibbled around the edges of al-Qa'ida, Usama bin Laden, al-Zawahiri and others were planning an operation against the United States that easily dwarfed anything they had done before. On 11 September 2001, al-Qa'ida terrorists hijacked four US passenger planes and flew them into the World Trade Center, the Pentagon and a Pennsylvania field. These attacks heralded a new phase in the EGIS–CIA partnership.

# 17  11 September 2001 and beyond

For the *mukhabarat*, 9/11 was a grim vindication of sorts for all the warnings about al-Qa'ida that had been passed to the Americans and Europeans in the 1990s. But 11 September also gave EGIS the opportunity to build upon its alliance with the CIA. One consequence of America's post-11 September 'global war on terrorism' was greater *mukhabarat* access to US intelligence and analytical training, the CIA's extensive hub of international contacts, and surveillance technology. Indeed, Egypt's secret services became part of an intelligence network of over 100 nations whose primary goal is the destruction of the al-Qa'ida network. All of this was something the *mukhabarat* had been fervently pressing for in the 1990s but with limited success.[1]

In addition to its war on al-Qa'ida, EGIS has enjoyed a high profile (for an intelligence service) in ameliorating the Israeli–Palestinian conflict and mediating between competing Palestinian factions. But when the internal Palestinian conflict devolved into de facto civil war in 2006, some of the shortcomings of using EGIS 'cryptodiplomacy' in peace building were exposed. Nonetheless, Cairo views stability in the Palestinian territories as integral to Egyptian national security, and EGIS's continued involvement in this arena is a given.

As Egypt entered the first decade of the twenty-first century (CE), uncertainties persist regarding its future stability. Mubarak's age and the sclerosis afflicting his regime are damaging enough; however, Egypt's burgeoning population, glaring socioeconomic inequalities, corruption and lack of democratic institutions raise further doubts about the longevity of the 'army republic.' One thing is clear though: the three organizations that comprise the Egyptian intelligence community will continue to serve as the eyes, ears and, ultimately the shield, of the Egyptian state.

## 9/11

What did the Egyptian intelligence services know about the 9/11 plot? In the months after 11 September this question was raised in US national security circles for, just as he did with the 1993 attack on the World Trade Center, President Mubarak alleged that EGIS had provided crucial warnings to the CIA prior to 9/11. According to Mubarak, from March to May 2001 EGIS penetration agents had reported that al-Qa'ida was planning a major attack on the United States. While Mubarak admitted that EGIS did not know the intended targets or the scale of the planned attack, he insisted the *mukhabarat* had warned Washington that something big was in the works.[2] For the Bush administration, Mubarak's assertions were an annoyance that had to be laid to rest quickly. The White House quickly claimed that Washington did not receive any specific warning prior to 11 September; a CIA official noted that while Egypt had provided intelligence 'of possible attacks against US or Egyptian interests... there was nothing about hijackings, nothing about an attack inside the US.'[3] Was Mubarak exaggerating? While *mukhabarat* reports passed to the Americans before the attack are classified there are a few sources which hint at the information being shared.

One of the intelligence assessments declassified by the 9/11 Commission was a 4 December 1998 Presidential Daily Brief (PDB). The PDB, which was based in part on a source with access to Islamic Group discussions, referenced an al-Qa'ida plan to hijack an aircraft in order to obtain the release of 'Umar 'Abd al-Rahman, Ramzi Yusef and other terrorists held in US prisons. The PDB warned that al-Qa'ida was exploring the use of a man-portable surface-to-air missile system like the SA-7 to bring down an Egyptian or US aircraft.[4] Although the evidence is not conclusive, the discussion of IG-related intelligence and planned attacks on Egyptian targets suggests that Egyptian intelligence was the origin of at least some of the information found in this document.

Director of Central Intelligence George Tenet later told the 9/11 Commission that the warning 'system was blinking red' in the summer of 2001.[5] Some of those warnings were spurred by Egyptian intelligence reporting. In June the *mukhabarat* warned the United States that al-Qa'ida intended to attack President Bush and other world leaders during a G8 Summit in Genoa. Although Mubarak later claimed that this intelligence referenced planes filled with explosives, an unnamed US official insisted the warning was too vague to be useful.[6] On 5 July 2001 Egyptian intelligence reportedly warned that al-Qa'ida was planning to attack US interests in the Persian Gulf.[7] Although it is unlikely that the Egyptians had detailed intelligence of the 9/11 plot it is clear from the foregoing that EGIS had passed to the Americans several intelligence warnings of pending al-Qa'ida attacks against US interests.

In the end, despite the efforts of EGIS, CIA and other security services, al-Qa'ida proved to be a very elusive target. Acting on an EGIS tip that Ayman al-Zawahiri was at a hospital in Sana'a, Yemen, CIA put surveillance on the al-Qa'ida leader in the summer of 2001. Unfortunately for EGIS and the CIA, either the Yemeni security services tipped off al-Zawahiri or his security detected the CIA surveillance, for he managed to escape to Afghanistan.[8]

There is no doubt that US–Egyptian intelligence cooperation was taken to a new level after 11 September. The Chairman of the US Joint Chiefs of Staff praised this cooperation during a January 2002 visit to Cairo: 'we could not ask for more support from the Egyptian government. They have supported us in essentially every way we've asked and we've also shared with them what we have in terms of intelligence.'[9] Certainly, in the aftermath of 9/11, the FBI and presumably the CIA probed their Egyptian partners for information on the hijackers. For example, on 13 September 2001 the FBI legal attaché in Cairo obtained information from probable SSIS contacts on the 9/11 ringleader Mohamed Atta. This information was sent to FBI headquarters where it was incorporated into a timeline on the hijackers and their activities in the lead-up to 11 September.[10] For its part, EGIS reportedly gained access to Arab detainees captured by the United States in Afghanistan. Perhaps more importantly, the *mukhabarat* was able to exploit CIA's global reach to locate wanted Egyptian exiles, liaise with foreign intelligence services and press for the extradition of alleged Egyptian terrorists.[11]

## Post 9/11 renditions

The extraordinary rendition program continued after 9/11 albeit with greater urgency. In many cases, Egyptian nationals captured in Afghanistan or in CIA snatch raids in other countries were rendered to Egypt for interrogation and prosecution. In December 2001, the Swedish security police, SAPO, delivered two Egyptian asylum seekers named Mohamed al-Zery and Ahmed Agiza to CIA and EGIS agents at an airport in Sweden.[12] Both were then stripped, given sedatives and flown to Cairo on a CIA-chartered jet. Upon arrival they were taken to EGIS headquarters where they were blindfolded, handcuffed and tortured with electric shocks and freezing treatment.[13] Agiza eventually received a 15-year sentence for his involvement in the bombing of the Egyptian embassy in Islamabad. As for al-Zery, he was released without any charges being brought against him, although he was warned against talking about his experience with others.[14]

The second prominent rendition case involving the *mukhabarat* after 9/11 was that of 'Usama Mustafa Hasan Nasr – also known as Abu 'Umar. Nasr was an alleged former IG member living in Italy when he was snatched off a Milan street by a CIA team in February 2003. After he was delivered to Egypt, Nasr was sent to EGIS headquarters where he was interrogated, placed in a tiny cell with poor ventilation, and tortured with electric shocks, beatings and threats of sexual assault. Although EGIS interrogators sought information on the IG, Nasr says the *mukhabarat* also used torture to persuade him to become an informant.[15] After four months of interrogation, Nasr was handed over to the SSIS for another round of questions and torture. Yet after all this, the *mukhabarat* concluded that Nasr was not the man they were looking for and released him on 19 April 2004. He was warned not to go to any mosques suspected of IG affiliations and to avoid contact with anyone in Europe or Italian embassy officials. Indeed, everything that happened to him while in EGIS and SSIS custody was to be kept secret. Despite these injunctions, Nasr called his wife in Milan shortly after his release and told her what had happened; this only angered the security services who rearrested Nasr on 12 May. He was not released until February 2007.[16]

Although the majority of those rendered to Egypt appear to have been Egyptian nationals, there were a few exceptions such as 'Ibn al-Shaykh al-Libi. One of the first alleged al-Qa'ida officials to be captured by the United States after 9/11, al-Libi – a Libyan national – was first interrogated by the FBI then handed over to the CIA who flew him to Egypt for interrogation by the *mukhabarat*. Among al-Libi's controversial revelations, presumably extracted under torture, was an allegation that Iraq had offered to train al-Qa'ida in the use of chemical and biological weapons. Some of the al-Libi material was incorporated into Secretary of State Colin Powell's February 2003 UN speech that tried to justify the subsequent US–UK invasion of Iraq.[17] Significantly, al-Libi later retracted this statement.[18]

The CIA was not directly involved in all renditions to Egypt. For instance, in October 2001 Azerbaijan's Ministry for National Security transferred an Egyptian national to EGIS custody at Cairo's request.[19] Another case was that of 'Abd al-Salam 'Ali 'Abd al-Rahman al-Hilah, a Yemeni intelligence officer who landed at Cairo International Airport in September 2002, checked into the Semiramis Hilton and then vanished. Although 'Abd al-Rahman reportedly was a partner in an Egyptian contractor firm, it later transpired that he was an expert on Arab Afghans at Yemen's Political Security Office (PSO).[20] The Egyptians regarded him as a jihadist sympathizer and he had been under EGIS surveillance from the moment he landed in the country. 'Abd al-Rahman's brother believes he was arrested by the Egyptians and handed over to the CIA for interrogation.[21]

Yemen was a country of particular interest for the *mukhabarat* after 9/11. Most important from Cairo's perspective was the presence of Egyptian extremists on Yemeni soil and a strong suspicion that the PSO was sympathetic to al-Qa'ida. Even so, in February 2004, the PSO secretly transferred to Egypt six alleged al-Jihad operatives in return for a Yemeni general who had fled to Egypt after backing the secessionists during Yemen's 1994 civil war. In fact, Egypt and Yemen continued to exchange intelligence on religious extremist groups throughout this period.[22]

## The home front

Although the Bush Administration urged Cairo toward greater democratization and respect for human rights, the security services continued to harass and intimidate Mubarak's domestic opposition. Egyptian and international organizations have catalogued an extensive list of human rights abuses in Egypt, most of them linked to the *mukhabarat*. The most visible of these are the arrest of regime opponents like Ayman Nur, prolonged detention under emergency laws, detentions without trial and the use of torture for confessions and other purposes. Human rights groups continue to criticize the Egyptian government for its use of state security and military courts to try detainees.[23]

The *mukhabarat* persists in targeting the Muslim Brotherhood and the radical Islamist organizations for intimidation and incarceration. In May 2004, the regime conducted a broad crackdown on the Brotherhood that included the arrest of more than 50 and the shutdown of Brotherhood websites and affiliated companies. According to the Egyptian government, the Brotherhood was recruiting volunteers for wars in Iraq, Chechnya and Palestine.[24] Clearly, the regime is troubled by the Brotherhood's enduring popularity and relevance as a dynamic social, cultural and political force. Given the persistent appeal of Islamist ideologies for many Egyptians the SSIS monitors controversial imams, censors their sermons as necessary and harasses those who step out of line.[25] The same is true of Coptic churches and priests.

After the 1997 Luxor massacre a combination of public outrage and regime repression put a lid on jihadist violence in Egypt for a while; however, on 7 October 2004, terrorism returned to Egypt when a car bomb exploded at the Taba Hilton in Sinai killing more than 30. The attack, which was aimed at Egypt's burgeoning Red Sea tourism industry, triggered an aggressive SSIS crackdown that included mass arrests in al-'Arish. But repression did not neutralize the threat, for on 23 July 2005 suicide bombers struck again, killing more than 60 in an attack on a hotel in Sharm al-Shaykh. On 24 April 2006, another series of bombs exploded at a Sinai resort, killing 18.[26] These attacks no doubt were inspired – if not planned and led – by al-Qa'ida. Nonetheless, as of late 2009 no group has emerged on the domestic scene that is willing to take up where the IG left off in the late 1990s by instigating a nationwide campaign of assassinations, anti-Copt violence and general unrest.

## Peacemaker

The unrelenting clandestine struggle against al-Qa'ida often obscured EGIS efforts to nurture and sustain the fragile Israeli–Palestinian peace process that began in the mid-1990s. At the dawn of the new millennium, 'Umar Soleiman had gained control over key foreign policy portfolios, including Sudan and the Palestinians in addition to his usual duties as EGIS Director. It is ironic that EGIS has become a peacemaker in Sudan and Palestine when we consider its previous role in subverting Israel and the Arab states during the 1950s and 1960s. Nonetheless, Cairo's emphasis on peace in these countries clearly reflects national priorities and strategies under Mubarak. Egypt's overarching goal is preserving domestic and regional stability by isolating religious extremists, helping the Palestinians acquire a state in the West Bank and Gaza, and working with other Arab moderates like Saudi Arabia to limit Iranian inroads in the Arab Middle East.

Mubarak probably relies on EGIS to help facilitate the Arab–Israeli peace process because of that organization's long-standing contacts with Palestinian factions. As we have seen, EGIS spearheaded Cairo's rapprochement with Fatah in the late 1960s. Later, it built and expanded upon a web of relationships with other Palestinian groups, including the Popular Front for the Liberation of Palestine (PFLP), Hamas, Palestine Islamic Jihad (PIJ) and even the Abu Nidal organization. At the same time, EGIS also had extensive ties to the Israeli, Syrian, Lebanese and Jordanian secret services. In short, EGIS was in an excellent position to serve as mediator between the various countries, parties and factions to the Palestinian dispute.

Moreover, the use of EGIS as Cairo's primary interlocutor on Palestine reflects Mubarak's desire to conduct 'cryptodiplomacy' outside of routine

Foreign Ministry channels. Unlike the Egyptian Foreign Ministry EGIS offers a smaller, more streamlined and secretive bureaucracy that is directly subordinate to the president. In addition, cryptodiplomacy allows EGIS to secretly pursue the full range of what is politically possible with the Palestinians, Israel, the United States and the other Arab states without paying the necessary obeisance to Arab nationalist rhetoric. Finally, EGIS often delivers when others cannot. When the Palestinian track of the Arab–Israeli peace process languished in the late 1990s, the role of Mubarak's personal advisors like 'Usama al-Baz was deemphasized in favor of Soleiman since EGIS had the contacts and inducements to help get all sides back to the table.

But, above all, Soleiman controls Egypt's Palestine file because of Mubarak's fear that Palestinian instability could spark regional conflict.[27] After all, tensions on the Gaza–Israel border helped set the stage for the 1956 Suez war. More recently, the rise of Hamas and its close ties with Egypt's Muslim Brotherhood have only accentuated the imperatives of stabilizing the Palestinian conflict from Cairo's perspective. As one Egyptian official observed in March 2006, 'from the beginning our role was based on the principle that Gaza is key to Egypt's national security, we must be involved.'[28]

That involvement began with the 1993 Oslo Agreement between Israel and the Palestine Liberation Organization which traded recognition of the state of Israel in return for defining a future Palestinian state. Once Oslo was signed, EGIS promptly set up a formal relationship with the new Palestinian Authority (PA) under which it passed technical and political assistance as well as intelligence.[29] Unfortunately for regional moderates like Egypt, Oslo proved to be a false dawn and the agreement broke down because of disagreement over the status of Jerusalem and the right of return for Palestinian refugees, the 1995 assassination of Israeli Prime Minister Yitzhak Rabin, a Likud victory in subsequent Israeli elections, and Palestinian terrorism. In September 2000, the second Intifada was launched after Yasser Arafat turned his back on a deal that reportedly would have left him with more than 90 percent of the West Bank and all of Gaza. It was around this time, when the potential for regional instability was high, that 'Umar Soleiman stepped in. As a result of his frequent shuttles between Israel, Hamas and the PA, Soleiman laid the ground work for the October 2000 conference at Sharm al-Shaykh where the leaders of Israel, the PA and Egypt along with George Tenet and Soleiman tried to negotiate a deal that would end the Intifada and nudge the peace process forward.[30]

When Sharm al-Shaykh failed, Soleiman was sent again to Israel in 2002 to try and mediate between the Palestinians and the Israelis. Under one proposal, the IDF would withdraw from certain areas of Gaza with their positions filled by Palestinian Authority (PA) security units. The idea was to give the Palestinians an expanded role in maintaining security and to help the PA reestablish its fading presence in Hamas-leaning Gaza.[31] In December 2003, as the peace process languished, EGIS hosted meetings in Cairo that were attended by several Palestinian factions. The purpose of the meetings was to discuss a National Project Plan that would include a one-year truce with Israel, the acceptance of Israel's right to exist and a two-state solution to the Israeli–Palestinian conflict based on the pre-1967 borders. While Fatah and the PA were on board with the plan, Soleiman and his lieutenants could not obtain the agreement of Hamas and Palestine Islamic Jihad.[32]

A few months later, in March 2004, Soleiman ignored the objections of Hamas and the others and concluded a security agreement with the Fatah-dominated PA. Motivating this new EGIS drive was an Israeli announcement that it would unilaterally withdraw from the Gaza Strip in 2005 and tear down the Jewish settlements that had been built there. From Egypt's perspective, Israel's withdrawal created an unwanted security vacuum in Gaza that probably would be filled by Hamas. Since Hamas refused to acknowledge Israel's right to exist, Egypt feared the stage would be set for a new round of Israeli–Palestinian violence. The key elements of Soleiman's new deal involved improving the capabilities of the Palestinian security services so they could police Gaza after the withdrawal. The plan envisaged the creation of a unified Palestinian police headquarters and a media campaign that would emphasize the rule of law, security and stability. Mosque imams would be urged to echo these themes in their sermons.[33]

Another aspect of Soleiman's March 2004 plan was Egyptian help in reforming the PA's security services. The first goal was to reduce the number of Palestinian intelligence agencies from 12 to perhaps three or four following which EGIS would begin training PA security officers in July 2004.[34] As a result of this arrangement the number of EGIS officers in Gaza on overt business increased to about 40 with most training Yasser Arafat's Presidential Guard – Force 17.[35] Others undoubtedly monitored Hamas, the IDF withdrawal and collected intelligence on local politics and security.

Egypt sent more delegations to PA after the Israelis completed their withdrawal from Gaza in 2005. The first, a political team, was put in place to monitor the ceasefire, maintain contact with the PA, Hamas and the other factions, and generally nudge the radical groups toward reconciliation. A security delegation led by a senior EGIS officer was sent to Gaza to work with the PA's Interior Ministry and security services; another 15 EGIS officers were sent to 'rebuild the Palestinian soldier' through training and new equipment. The goal of both missions was to help the PA preserve the peace and deny the IDF justification for future incursions into Gaza.[36] Unfortunately for nearly all concerned, Palestinian infighting ultimately wrecked Egypt's hopes of creating a stable, prosperous Gaza Strip. When a civil war erupted between the PA and Hamas in 2006, the Egyptians first withdrew their security advisory teams and then tried to forge a new ceasefire among the factions. In December 2006, Cairo showed which side it favored by providing 2,000 assault rifles and ammunition to the PA security forces.[37]

The role of General Intelligence as a would-be peacemaker in Gaza highlights the limitations of cryptodiplomacy in resolving highly complex, seemingly intractable political problems like the Israeli–Palestinian conflict. While EGIS officers could mediate local crises and defuse some flare-ups, they lacked the political, economic and security clout to impose durable, long-term solutions. As the events of 2006 in Gaza demonstrated, EGIS's efforts to create a PA security force capable of policing Hamas were no more than a house of cards.

A much less visible EGIS peacemaking role was in Sudan. After Egyptian–Sudanese relations reached their nadir in 1995, 'Umar Soleiman began reconciliation talks in 1997. The process was facilitated by the decline in influence of al-Turabi's National Islamic Front and Khartoum's decision to quietly render 12 Egyptian militants to Cairo.[38] After bilateral relations improved, Soleiman began mediating between the Sudanese government and the opposition National Democratic Alliance coalition in 2004.[39] This peace-making not only solidified Soleiman's already influential role in formulating Sudan policy, it also highlighted the *mukhabarat*'s continued prominence in shaping Egypt's policies toward its southern neighbor.

At the end of the first decade of the twenty-first century, the Egyptian republic created by Nasser faces an uncertain future. First there is the uncertain succession that will follow the departure of an aging Mubarak. Second is the sclerosis paralyzing the Egyptian government from undertaking any meaningful action to alleviate the country's chronic economic disparities and burgeoning population. Although the Islamic Group and al-Jihad have been disbanded or politically marginalized, the Muslim Brotherhood waits patiently in the wings with an ideology that has yet to be tested in government despite its wide popular appeal.

Amid the many unanswered questions concerning Egypt's political future it is evident that the Egyptian security services – the *mukhabarat* – will continue to serve as the ultimate shield of the Egyptian state. Moreover, the Egyptian intelligence community has reached a mature point in its development built around three agencies with unique missions and responsibilities. EGIS is the most important intelligence service today by virtue of its foreign liaison ties, size, technical sophistication and the prestige that goes along with its close proximity to Mubarak. In addition to its pivotal role as a covert action player and collector of foreign intelligence, EGIS has responsibility for developing and executing important foreign policies toward Sudan and the Palestinians.

Sometimes vying with EGIS for leadership of the Egyptian intelligence community is the SSIS. Directly subordinate to the Interior Ministry, the SSIS enjoys the distinction of being the oldest intelligence service in Egypt; it can trace its pedigree back to the earliest years of the twentieth century when the British created a security service to monitor Egypt's nascent nationalist and pan-Islamist movements. Roughly equivalent to the FBI, the SSIS is largely focused on Egypt's domestic scene where it has responsibilities for internal security, counterterrorism and counterintelligence. Under Egypt's emergency laws, the SSIS has wide-ranging powers of surveillance and detention. It is often linked to torture allegations by Egyptian and international human rights organizations.

The MID is the third and final agency of the Egyptian intelligence community. Today's MID is but a shadow of the powerful organization which helped run Egypt in the 1950s. Its decline in relative status is due to the changing nature of the threats confronting Egypt: with no significant military threat in sight, the MID has been largely overshadowed by EGIS and SSIS as they battle religious extremism at home and abroad. Nonetheless, the MID's importance should not be underestimated for, in the end, it is the organization that monitors the loyalty of the armed forces. For a would-be conspirator hoping to unseat the Mubarak regime, Ayman al-Zawahiri got one thing right: the only way to overthrow this nearly coup-proofed regime is by recruiting within the military officer establishment. And the only way that could happen is by subverting and neutralizing the *mukhabarat*.

# Conclusion

> Intelligence pervades and dominates statecraft. All intelligence stands for 'knowing the enemy.' Since knowing the enemy is tantamount to fighting him, the conclusion is tenable that intelligence stands for warfare of one kind or another....Counterintelligence is subsumed in all statecraft, and covert action is the name of the game in domestic and international affairs.[1]

The introduction to this history proposed six questions to guide our analysis of the historical evolution of the Egyptian intelligence services. The purpose of this concluding chapter is to answer each of those questions in turn and in doing so derive some conclusions about intelligence studies in general and Egypt's historical and political development in particular.

## Threat perceptions and the intelligence community

The continuity and change in Egypt's national security threat perceptions was the first 'lens' through which we examined the *mukhabarat*. As this history shows, the nature of those threats and how they were perceived by the Egyptian government had a direct bearing on the evolution of the Egyptian intelligence community and the status of its constituent parts. Many of those threats have come and gone; only a few have endured to the present day.

The ancestors of today's *mukhabarat* – the Special Branches of the city police and the Central Special Office – investigated the dangers posed by the early nationalist and Islamist movements. Indeed, the genesis of the Cairo Central Special Office, arguably the grandfather of the modern intelligence apparatus – was the assassination of a Coptic prime minister at the hands of a young nationalist. Over time, the list of threats expanded to include native fascists, Italians, Germans, communists, Zionists and others, although the British assumed responsibility for protecting Egypt from external actors. This alignment was a reflection of Britain's colonial domination of Egypt; it persisted into the 1940s and helps explain the domestic missions of Egypt's political police apparatus. It was not until after World War II, the creation of the Arab League and the establishment of the state of Israel that the political police and military intelligence really began to focus on external challengers such as Israel, the Soviet Union, France and the United Kingdom

The foundations of the modern Egyptian intelligence community were laid in the years immediately following the July 1952 Free Officers coup. The first step in that process was the creation of the General Investigations Directorate (GID), which was built upon and significantly expanded the old political police apparatus. The second step was to reorganize and centralize military intelligence by giving the Military Intelligence Department (MID) greater responsibilities in the areas of intelligence collection, analysis and covert action. The GID and MID were very much creatures of their times. In the early days of the Free Officers regime, they were oriented against the communists, dissident military officers and the Muslim Brotherhood. At the same time as they imposed their rule at home, the Free Officers created the Egyptian General Intelligence Service (EGIS). An important player in Gamal 'Abd al-Nasser's vision of Egypt's unique place in the Arab, African and Islamic worlds, EGIS was the country's first dedicated civilian foreign intelligence and covert action arm.

The intelligence community that was created by Nasser and his associate, Zakaria Muhi al-Din, remains largely unchanged today. Yet, at the same time, Egypt's national security threats have been marked by continuity and change. While some challenges like those posed by Israel, Libya, the Soviet Union, domestic communism and even Iraq have diminished or faded altogether, the most enduring threat to the regime is posed by Egypt's homegrown Islamists. Politically, socially and culturally, the Islamists enjoy a much broader appeal than communism or Arab Socialism ever did. The only saving grace for a ruling system that is embarrassingly bereft of any popular ideology is that Egyptian Islam is multifaceted, diffuse, and subject to numerous and often conflicting interpretations. Indeed, there is no single voice speaking for anything remotely resembling a unified Islamist ideology in Egypt today. Even so, the alternate vision for Egypt proposed by the Muslim Brotherhood will continue to challenge a regime that is widely perceived as corrupt, inefficient and uninspiring.

## Intelligence collection and analysis

Intelligence collection and analysis constitute the second lens through which the Egyptian intelligence community was examined. In many respects collection, analysis and counterintelligence are the 'bread and butter' – the core missions – of a modern intelligence agency. By identifying and infiltrating its domestic and foreign enemies, the Egyptian security services are fulfilling a vital part of their 'coup proofing' mission.

The *mukhabarat*'s emphasis on human intelligence operations in general and informants in particular has been a consistent trend over the last 100 years. From the city police Special Branches to today's technically sophisticated State Security Investigations Service (SSIS), the 'City Eye' has been a vital tool in intelligence collection, counterintelligence, counterterrorism and other internal security missions. Built around a legion of street kids, merchants, doormen, hotel employees, civil servants, taxi drivers and others, the City Eye is a formidable obstacle for any regime opponent to overcome. Indeed, the informants are the key to Egypt's well-deserved reputation as a secret police state.

While the historical emphasis has been on human intelligence operations, Egyptian intelligence has also acquired formidable skills in the technical areas of intelligence collection. As we have seen in this history, over the course of many decades the *mukhabarat* has dramatically improved its capability to tap telephone lines, plant sophisticated listening devices and conduct other forms of technical surveillance. MID has acquired SIGINT and photo-reconnaissance capabilities of increasing sophistication by acquiring aircraft like the Scarab, the Skyeye and the EC-130. Unfortunately, public information on Egypt's SIGINT capabilities is scarce; unclassified sources do not even indicate if there is a separate SIGINT agency in Egypt today or if this function still falls under the control of the MID.

Assessments are an often overlooked aspect of the intelligence process. This history has examined some of the earliest intelligence assessments prepared by the modern *mukhabarat*. It has also noted how the CIA helped Egypt develop a Committee of National Estimates which provided a national level, presumably consensus-driven, analytical product on major threats of the day. As an engaged consumer of intelligence products, Nasser recognized the need for a true, all-source intelligence estimates process even if in reality that analysis was often flawed or ignored. After the 1967 debacle Nasser vigorously defended the pre-war intelligence estimates in front of his senior commanders.

The estimates process did not always live up to expectations. In both the 1956 and 1967 wars, Egyptian intelligence tragically underestimated the intentions and capabilities of its enemies. Still, the fault often lay with the intelligence consumer as well as the estimator. In 1956, Nasser himself developed the erroneous assessment of the intentions of his British and French adversaries. In 1967, the Egyptian leadership ignored reasonably accurate assessments from some of its intelligence agencies and favored erroneous or deceptive Soviet reports that helped propel Egypt to war with Israel. In some cases, cultural and political bias was allowed to influence the estimates process; however, as the recent US war in Iraq demonstrates, Egypt is by no means alone in this. Certainly what some experts observed of the Soviet intelligence system is equally true of the Egyptian one:

> Because analysis in all one-party states is distorted by the insistent demands of political correctness, foreign intelligence do more to reinforce them than to correct the regime's misconceptions. Though the politicization of intelligence sometimes degrades assessment even within democratic systems, it is actually built into the structure of all authoritarian regimes.[2]

Improvements were made to the intelligence assessments process in Nasser's later years and under Sadat. Important steps were taken to improve the quality of analysis by ensuring that estimators had a better understanding of Israeli politics, culture, religion and the military. The result was a more realistic appraisal of Israeli military capabilities even if those estimates were criticized by some in Cairo as going too far in the other direction – i.e. inflating IDF capabilities. In any case, the improved estimates contributed to the success of Egypt's pre-war denial and deception scheme against Israel and its crossing of the Suez Canal.

Unfortunately for the researcher, publicly available information on Egyptian national intelligence estimates starts to drop off significantly after the 1973 war. It is known that Egyptian estimators correctly gauged Mu'ammar al-Qadhafi's survivability and the likelihood of a rapid Iraqi military collapse in 1991. Still, there is insufficient information to examine how President Mubarak organizes and utilizes his national intelligence estimates or the extent to which Mubarak is influenced by those estimates.

## Counterintelligence

Counterintelligence has been a *mukhabarat* concern from the beginning. The pattern in Egyptian counterintelligence has been one of trying to mitigate the opportunities for foreign espionage in Egypt that are created when foreign services provide training, intelligence and equipment to the *mukhabarat*. The pattern started with the United Kingdom, which used its dominance of the Egyptian political police to cement its imperial hold on Egypt in the first half of the twentieth century. Next were the Americans who, while they helped Nasser reorganize the Egyptian intelligence community, also used their access to identify and recruit agents. Eventually, CIA influence-making had reached a point where a suspicious Nasser substituted the KGB, GRU and their Eastern Bloc brethren for the CIA. Throughout the 1960s, the Soviets not only helped train and share intelligence and technology with the *mukhabarat,* they also developed their own assets within Egypt. The pendulum swung back under Sadat. Only this time the CIA was able to step in and become a more or less permanent *mukhabarat* ally. No doubt CIA case officers today are spotting and recruiting spies within the Egyptian services even as they train Egyptian intelligence cadres, share intelligence and provide advanced technology. It seems to be a never ending cycle.

One scholar puts a finer point on the counterintelligence dilemmas associated with intelligence liaison:

> The first risk [of liaison relationships] is that one is identifying some of one's intelligence personnel to the other intelligence service (so as to conduct liaison) and one is giving them and the other service justification for considerable contact. Obviously one is somewhat exposing them to being recruited by the other service as its moles. The other service may also get leads for direct and indirect recruitment of one's personnel; perhaps other fellow-citizens, in and out of government.[3]

As former Mossad officer Yaacov Caroz noted in 1978, counterintelligence has been a 'central' mission of the Egyptian *mukhabarat*. He goes on to note wryly that the British were not only the first instructors of the Egyptian counter-intelligence apparatus they were 'also among the first victims of the Egyptians.'[4] Historically, informants known to some as the City Eye have played a critical role in Egyptian counterintelligence. Former Israeli, American and Soviet intelligence officers have all noted how proficient the City Eye informant system is at foiling intelligence operations. It is no exaggeration to suggest that counterintelligence is an Egyptian forte and that pervasive human and technical surveillance are fundamental to that success.[5]

## Covert action

Although some researchers question whether covert action is truly an intelligence discipline, the fact is that in Egypt – as in many other countries – covert action is an intrinsic function of its intelligence services. Covert action was a very prominent feature of Nasser's foreign policy in the late 1950s and early 1960s, for it represented a strategy that helped bridge Nasser's ambitious regional goals with Egypt's limited resources. Under Nasser's guidance, the MID and later EGIS were the planners and implementers of subversive policies aimed at destabilizing the conservative monarchies of Jordan, Iraq, Yemen, Saudi Arabia and Libya. The *mukhabarat* also employed covert action against the British and the French in North Africa, the Middle East and sub-Saharan Africa.

In Egyptian terms, covert action embraced activities which were intended to lower public confidence in a targeted regime, boost opposition forces and ultimately force the creation of a new government that would be more partial to Egyptian interests and influence. To achieve this the *mukhabarat* employed assassination; black radio stations; overt but highly critical and defamatory radio stations like Voice of the Arabs; support for insurgency groups, including providing weapons, the granting of safe haven, propaganda, funding and diplomatic support; promoting Nasserist policies in local student groups and trade unions by distributing money and propaganda; cultivating Free Officer-type cells in Arab military establishments; and sponsoring bombings of civilian and military targets.

Despite the resources that were invested in it, Egyptian covert action produced only mixed results. In the case of Algeria, Egyptian arms, diplomatic and propaganda support to anti-French nationalist insurgents were not decisive in the liberation of that country nor did they buy Cairo much influence in independent Algiers. Similarly, although Egyptian-fueled unrest ultimately convinced Jordan's King Hussein to renege on his country's participation in the Baghdad Pact, it did not fundamentally realign Jordan's foreign policies toward Egypt. Finally, covert action did not supplant any of the Arab monarchies with the exception of the imamate in Yemen. Yet even there, Egypt's substantial investment in blood and treasure never bought Nasser the influence in Sana'a that he desired.

Why did Egyptian covert action fail more often than it succeeded? Part of the problem lay in Nasser's high expectations that covert action would buy influence over neighboring states at relatively little cost and without committing the army. Yet while covert action could achieve some tactical victories – like convincing Jordan to stay out of the Baghdad Pact – it could not purchase the more ambitious goals that Nasser had in mind for the region. On another level, Egyptian covert action often failed because it could not overcome the resistance of local security forces either working alone or in concert with the United States, United Kingdom, France or even Israel. Finally, the *mukhabarat*'s early lack of trained covert action operatives resulted in operations that often seemed amateurish and poorly planned.

If there is one distinguishing feature of Egyptian covert action under Nasser it is the skillful use of overt radio like Voice of the Arabs for subversive purposes. Perhaps more than any other weapon in Egypt's covert action arsenal, Voice of the Arabs instilled fear in targeted regimes, aroused passions among Arab citizens of other countries, and generated unrest and instability. While its 'magic' lasted, the Voice of the Arabs could command an audience of millions throughout the Arab world even if its rhetoric was often crude and its message overblown. Voice of the Arabs is truly Egypt's dubious – if unique – contribution to the art of covert action, although it is unlikely that this model, a creature of its time and circumstance, could be easily transferred to other countries and societies.

## Intelligence liaison

Liaison with foreign intelligence services has been fundamental to the evolution and growing sophistication and capability of the Egyptian *mukhabarat*. It was the British who provided the early cadres, training and other forms of support to make modern Egypt's political police apparatus work. Later, under Nasser, the CIA stepped in to provide training, intelligence and other assistance to the General Investigations Directorate (GID), the MID and EGIS. Indeed, both the GID and EGIS were intentionally modeled after their respective American counterparts in the FBI and CIA. As we have seen, when Nasser grew suspicious of the CIA liaison relationship he replaced it with an equally over-weaning Soviet one. One former CIA official has noted that intelligence relationships often have more staying power than conventional diplomatic ones.[6] Continuity rather than change certainly seems to be true of the US–Egyptian intelligence partnership where the EGIS–CIA relationship was quietly allowed to persist even after Nasser had turned to the Soviets for intelligence and training.

Clearly, the nature of Egypt's intelligence liaison has varied widely in terms of partners and the depth and types of cooperation over time. Intelligence scholar H. Bradford Westerfield's matrix of intelligence liaison relationships is useful in studying how Egyptian intelligence has interacted with foreign partners. In Westerfield's framework, 'full-fledged' liaison characterizes a very close intelligence relationship between one or more powers. It consists of common classifications and code words; often each intelligence service hosts at its headquarters liaison officers from the partner service for a constant give-and-take of intelligence. Full-fledged liaison appears to best characterize the historical relationships between EGIS and the CIA and EGIS and the KGB/GRU. It certainly appears to be emblematic of the liaison arrangements between EGIS and CIA today.

Other important facets of intelligence liaison are intelligence sharing and joint operations. Intelligence sharing has been a standard feature of Egypt's liaison partnerships with the United States, Russia, and numerous other Arab, Asian and European states. Joint operations were a prominent feature of the relationship between the British security agencies and Egypt's political police in the late 1930s and 1940s. For its part, the CIA worked jointly with the *mukhabarat* against Soviet targets in Egypt during the 1950s. More recent examples of Egyptian joint intelligence operations include the Safari Club of the 1970s, EGIS cooperation with the Saudi General Intelligence Directorate against Iraq in the 1990–1991 war, and EGIS–CIA joint rendition operations. Egypt strongly values the joint operations aspect of its foreign intelligence partnerships. As one Egyptian intelligence officer noted in 2003, joint operations are 'the highest degree of intelligence cooperation.'[7]

Intelligence liaison can also include support functions such as training and the provision of technology. As this study demonstrates, the Egyptian intelligence services have relied heavily on Western and Soviet sources for the training of Egyptian cadres, the supply of surveillance technology and even the training of presidential bodyguards. There can be no doubt that foreign training and technology have increased *mukhabarat* capabilities in the areas of intelligence collection, counterintelligence and assessments. The Egyptian services have passed on some of these skills to other, primarily Arab, parties.

The final area in Westerfield's intelligence liaison scheme is cryptodiplomacy, that is, the area where intelligence services substitute for conventional diplomacy in particularly sensitive negotiations. Cryptodiplomacy has often been the instrument of choice for Egyptian presidents; Nasser, Sadat and Mubarak all leaned heavily at times on their intelligence services to conduct secret diplomacy. This preference for the *mukhabarat* stems from a desire for discretion and deniability as well as a lack of trust in traditional Foreign Ministry diplomats. In recent years, cryptodiplomacy has characterized the prominent role EGIS plays as a mediator in Palestinian affairs.

Given Egypt's extensive intelligence partnerships with many foreign powers, it is clear that liaison has been central to the *mukhabarat*'s development and its ability to carry out many of its missions. Indeed, the Egyptian experience as outlined in this book offers researchers a superb example of how liaison relationships have influenced the development of a major non-Western intelligence service.

## Intelligence and Egyptian democracy

From the beginning the *mukhabarat* has been a major impediment to the development of democracy and human rights in Egypt. One of the unfortunate legacies left by the British after their 70-year occupation of Egypt was the creation of a secret police system to monitor, harass, intimidate torture and even extort money from the Egyptian population. In the 1920s and 1930s, the Egyptian monarchy and its chosen cabinets of the day used and abused the political police apparatus to suppress dissent and stifle Egypt's fragile experiment with liberal democracy. Indeed, the *mukhabarat* was (and still is) handmaiden to the suppression of Egyptian aspirations for a more representative government.

Despite its early promises of reform, the Nasser system relied heavily on a new political police system with dramatically enhanced repressive capabilities. Indeed, ever since the 1952 coup, Egyptian governments have used the *mukhabarat* continuously to silence competing voices from the liberal opposition, the communists, the Muslim Brotherhood and others. Under Nasser and his heirs, the intelligence apparatus reinforced one-party rule in Egypt through the systematic elimination of any rival claims to power. As intelligence scholar Christopher Andrew notes, intelligence communities in one-party authoritarian states like Egypt are different in at least two respects from their counterparts in democracies:

> 1. The intelligence community is central to the structure of the one-party state and to the systems of repression and social control which seek to suppress all challenges to its authority; 2. It also acts as a mechanism for reinforcing the regime's misconceptions of the outside world.[8]

One argument repeatedly advanced by the Egyptian government and its supporters is that a secret police apparatus contributes to stability and security at a time when Egypt is threatened by external adversaries or terrorism such as occurred in the 1990s. The regime's alluring message of 'stability and order' certainly resonates in many sectors of Egyptian society which do not want to see their country go the way of Iraq, Algeria or Lebanon. But 'stability and order' is a Faustian bargain, for as researchers Thomas Plate and Andrea Darvi assess:

> In the end, of course, citizens will get far more than they bargained for. The tragedy of the secret police solution is that it is such a blunt and crude instrumentality that in the name of preserving paradise it winds up creating hell... And even when the moderate critics of the regime are eliminated, incarcerated, exiled, or intimidated, the secret police machine rolls on.[9]

Can the secret police apparatus in Egypt be reformed? Can we envisage a future SSIS with sharply curtailed powers of surveillance, detention and no torture? Unfortunately, the record of reforming the SSIS and its antecedents is not a very inspiring one. In the earliest days of the Free Officer regime, the authorities promised to eliminate the political police. Technically they did so, but they replaced it with a much more formidable and efficient apparatus that survives to this day with all of its powers intact. After the 1967 war, Nasser promised to eliminate some of the more flagrant excesses of what he himself called the 'Intelligence State.' But the security organs continued to enjoy expansive powers just the same. Anwar al-Sadat promised to curtail torture, reform the secret police and make it more responsive to the judiciary and the constitution. But the apparatus survived those promises. Under Husni Mubarak, there was a brief moment following the 1986 Central Security Forces riots when it seemed as if broad and fundamental reforms would be made to the SSIS, including its widespread use of informers. But the secret police survived that period too.

Reform of the security apparatus is fundamental to the creation of a stable, healthy Egyptian democracy. At a minimum, that reform process would have to include the following:

1   Fundamental overhaul of the secret police organs, including circumscribing their powers to conduct extra-judicial surveillance of Egyptians, greater controls over their powers of arrest and extra-judicial detention and the elimination of any forms of torture as defined by the United Nations Convention.

2   Revoking the emergency laws is crucial to undercutting the quasi-legal basis for secret police abuse of the Egyptian constitution. These laws have been in place for the entire Mubarak presidency, and their existence is a grim testimony to the abject emptiness and paucity of ideology that constitutes the core of the modern Egyptian polity.

3   Parallel to the revocation of the emergency laws and the throttling back of the powers of the *mukhabarat* must be the restoration of Egypt's judiciary as an independent voice in the legal structure. On a positive note, the judiciary can tap into a rich legacy when it enjoyed a more influential role in national political life during the liberal democratic experiment of the 1920s and 1930s. Even today some Egyptian judges demonstrate a willingness to stand up to the regime and its flouting of constitutional norms. Only an empowered judiciary can ameliorate the abuses in places like the Scorpion.

4   Egypt would have to hold free and fair elections that are unfettered by secret police harassment. The Egyptian government and its supporters often invoke the specter of a Muslim Brotherhood-dominated government to postpone democratic reform. But not only does this argument reveal an embarrassing lack of trust in the ability of the Egyptian voter to decide what is best for the country, it also ignores the incredible diversity of thought in Egyptian Islam today. It downplays Egypt's legacy of liberal democratic experimentation and fails to offer the Muslim Brotherhood an opportunity to govern and abide by its promises.

5   Additional reforms will have to be made to the Egyptian presidency. If democracy is to take root in Egypt, it must be accompanied by a marked reduction in the extensive powers enjoyed by Egypt's imperial presidency. Any such move of course would cut against a legacy of strong, centralized rule in Egypt; however, it is difficult to envisage a democracy thriving in the shadow of a quasi-king.

6   A final step toward democratic reform is an example offered by another country which successfully navigated a transition from the rule by a few to a rule for all: South Africa. A truth and reconciliation commission might be critical if a fragile Egyptian democracy is to survive its early years. Certainly there are thousands in Egypt who have suffered at the hands of the *mukhabarat* and who must be heard if the country is to proceed on the path of democratic reform. As South Africa seems to demonstrate, a country that publicly investigates the darker closets of its past is better equipped to handle the challenges of a democratic future than one that does not.

In the end, all roads to democracy in Egypt seem to stem from the premise that fundamental reforms will have to be made to the intelligence apparatus of the state. As one astute observer put it recently:

> Unless the security services are reined in, real political change and efforts to implement 'reform from within' will continue to be blocked in Egypt and across the Middle East. The enlightened political elite will remain powerless, individuals who can make genuine contributions will be systematically targeted, moderate groups and trends will continue to be excluded, and most citizens will remain absent from political life... in a word, the political arena will still echo only one voice.[10]

A lot is riding on Egypt these days. Because of its size, location and historical exposure to and acceptance of foreign ideas, Egypt has always been a trendsetter for the Arab world. Given that one in four Arabs is Egyptian, it follows that Egypt's choice of democracy or dictatorship will help determine if the future of the Arab world will be shaped by coup-proofed *mukhabarat* regimes or something more inspiring, tolerant, responsive, and peaceful. In any case, the Egyptian intelligence services and their reform will be a key barometer of Egypt's progress in building a stable, enduring democracy.

# Notes

## Introduction

1 J. Quinlivan, 'Coup-Proofing: Its Practice and Consequences in the Middle East,' *International Security* 24, fall 1999, 131–165. I use the US intelligence community's definition of intelligence: 'a body of evidence and the conclusions drawn therefrom that ... is often derived from information that is concealed or not intended to be available for use by the acquirer,' Intelligence Community Staff, *Glossary of Intelligence Terms and Definitions*, June 1989, 18.
2 T. Plate and A. Darvi, *Secret Police*, Garden City, NY: Doubleday & Company, 1981, 9.
3 R. Godson, ed., *Comparing Foreign Intelligence*, Washington, DC: Pergamon-Brassey's, 1988, 3–4.
4 US National Security Council Document 10/2 defined covert action as:

> Any covert activities related to propaganda, economic warfare; preventive direct action, including sabotage, anti-sabotage, demolition and evacuation measures, subversion against hostile states, including assistance to underground resistance movements, guerrillas and refugee liberation groups.
>
> (T. Weiner, *Legacy of Ashes*, New York: Doubleday, 2007, 533n29)

## 1 *Mamur Zapt*

1 Telegram from Fish (Cairo) to DOS, 'Transmitting Text of Lecture on the Police System of Cairo,' no. 471, 19 November 1935, NARA, 883.105/9.
2 B. Carman and J. McPherson, eds., *Bimbashi McPherson: A Life in Egypt*, London: BBC, 1983, 207–208.
3 M. Thomas, *Empires of Intelligence*, Berkeley, CA: University of California Press, 2008, 111.
4 Quoted in H. Tollefson, *Policing Islam*, London: Greenwood Press, 1999, 152–153.
5 P.J. Vatikiotis, *The History of Modern Egypt*, Baltimore: Johns Hopkins University Press, 1992, 203.
6 D. Reid, 'Political Assassination in Egypt, 1910–1954,' *International Journal of African Historical Studies* 15, 1982, 627; E. Tauber, 'Egyptian Secret Societies, 1911,' *MES*, 42, 2006, 603–604.
7 G.W. Harvey, 'Note on the Special Political Office of the Cairo City Police,' 25 October 1915, BNA, FO 141/474/1.
8 J. Salim, *Al-Būlīs Al-Siyāsī Yaḥkum Miṣr, 1910–1952*, Cairo: al-Qāhirah lil-Thaqāfah al-'Arabīyah,1975, 27; Tauber, 'Egyptian Secret Societies,' 605; G.W. Harvey, 'Note on the Special Political Office.'
9 M. Badrawi, *Political Violence in Egypt 1910–1924: Secret Societies, Plots and Assassinations*, London: Curzon, 2000, 88n47.

10 *Baedeker's Egypt 1929,* London: George Allen & Unwin, 1974, lxiv.
11 G.W. Harvey, 'Note on the Special Political Office.'
12 Carman and McPherson, *Bimbashi McPherson,* 205.
13 G.W. Harvey, 'Note on the Special Political Office'; Correspondence from Thomas Russell, Commandant, Cairo City Police, to the Director General, European Department, Ministry of the Interior, 10 June 1925, BNA, FO 141/474/1.
14 Ibid.
15 Badrawi, *Political Violence,* 84.
16 Ibid.
17 Thomas, *Empires,* 110.
18 Tauber, 'Egyptian Secret Societies,' 605.
19 Ibid.
20 Badrawi, *Political Violence,* 132n65; Tollefson, *Policing Islam,* 169.
21 G. Clayton, *An Arabian Diary,* ed. by Robert Collins, Berkeley, CA: University of California Press, 1969, 303.
22 L. Grafftey-Smith, *Bright Levant,* London: John Murray, 1970, 103–104; G. Perrault, *A Man Apart: The Life of Henri Curiel,* trans. by Bob Cumming, London: Zed Books, 1994, 86.
23 A. Sansom, *I Spied Spies,* London: George G. Harrap, 1965, 196; J. Lacouture, *Nasser,* trans. by Daniel Hofstadter, New York: Knopf, 1973, 249.
24 G.W. Harvey, 'Note on the Special Political Office.'
25 G.W. Harvey, 'Note on the Special Political Office'; Correspondence from Thomas Russell.
26 Salim, *al-Būlīs,* 27; Tauber, 'Egyptian Secret Societies,' 610.
27 G.W. Harvey, 'Note on the Special Political Office'; Telegram from Knabenshue (Cairo) to Secretary of State, 'Plot to Assassinate High Personages in Egypt,' no. 232, 12 July 1912, 883.00/41, NARA; Note by 'R.G.' 9 July 1912, BNA, FO 141/746/1.
28 Badrawi, *Political Violence,* 87.
29 Telegram from American Embassy (Constantinople) to Secretary of State, no. 276, 16 September 1912, 883.00/43, NARA; Badrawi, *Political Violence,* 86.
30 G.W. Harvey, 'Note on the Special Political Office.'
31 Correspondence from Thomas Russell.
32 Badrawi, *Political Violence,* 110n62.
33 R. Seth, *Russell Pasha,* London: William Kimber, 1966, 105–106.
34 Russell, *Egyptian Service,* 164–165.
35 Russell, *Egyptian Service,* 165–170; Seth, *Russell,* 105–123.
36 Seth, *Russell,* 121–122.
37 Badrawi, *Political Violence,* 91.
38 Carman and McPherson, *Bimbashi McPherson,* 204.
39 Ibid., 205.
40 Ibid., 208–209.
41 Ibid., 210, 235.
42 Ibid., 210.
43 J. Lacouture and S. Lacouture, *Egypt in Transition,* trans. by Francis Scarfe, New York: Criterion Books, 1958, 82–83; Mansfield, *British in Egypt,* 211, 220–221; Seth, *Russell,* 136.
44 Mansfield, *British in Egypt,* 211.
45 Ibid., 223.
46 Carman and McPherson, *Bimbashi McPherson,* 231.
47 Seth, *Russell,* 143.
48 Carman and McPherson, *Bimbashi McPherson,* 237, 259–260; Seth, *Russell,* 132.
49 Correspondence from Allenby to Curzon, FO, 13 May 1922, no. 381, BNA, FO 141/474/1.

50  Clayton, *Arabian Diary*, 71–73; Correspondence from Allenby to Curzon.
51  Donald Reid, 'Political Assassination,' 629; Yunan Labib Rizk, 'The Great Conspiracy,' *Al-Ahram Weekly* 5–11 August 1999. Online, available at: http://weekly.ahram.org.eg, accessed 12 October 2006; Badrawi, *Political Violence*, 139–140.
52  Badrawi, *Political Violence*, 149; Rizk, 'The Great Conspiracy.'
53  Badrawi, *Political Violence*, 152; Rizk, 'The Great Conspiracy;' Seth, *Russell Pasha*, 150.
54  Correspondence from Clayton to Thomas Russell and Two Other Addressees, 20 November 1919, BNA, FO 141/474/1.
55  Correspondence from Ryder to Selby, 4 April 1921, BNA, FO 141/793/7.
56  Clayton, *Arabian Diary*, 346–347; Correspondence from Ryder to Selby.
57  Correspondence from Ryder to the British High Commission, 4 July 1922, BNA, FO 141/793/7; Correspondence from Ryder to the British Residency, 8 June 1922, BNA, FO 141/793/7; Correspondence from Ryder to Selby.
58  Correspondence from Ryder to the British High Commission.
59  Correspondence from Ryder to the British Residency; Correspondence from Ryder to Selby.
60  Correspondence from Ryder to Selby.
61  Correspondence from Ryder to the British Residency.
62  Correspondence from Ryder to the British Residency.
63  Thomas, *Empires*, 119, 143.
64  Salim, *al-Būlīs*, 161–162; Abd al-Wahhab Bakr Muhammad, *Al-Būlīs al-Miṣrī, 1922–1952*, Cairo: Maktabat Madbūlī, 1988, 292.
65  Badrawi, *Political Violence*, 190n8.
66  Ibid.
67  Correspondence from Furness to High Commissioner, Cairo, 16 July 1922, BNA, FO 141/793/7.
68  'Political Crime Department,' *Egyptian Gazette*, 26 July 1922, NARA, 883.01/420; Muhammad, *Al-Būlīs al-Miṣrī*, 35.
69  'Political Crime Department,' *Egyptian Gazette*, 27 July 1922, NARA, 883.01/420. Correspondence from Furness to High Commissioner; Correspondence from Allenby, High Commissioner, to Balfour, 24 July 1922, no. 594, BNA, FO 141/446/9; Telegram from Howell (Cairo) to DOS, no. 275, 10 February 1923, NARA 883.00/444.
70  Correspondence from Russell to the Director General, European Department, 10 June 1925, BNA, FO 141/474/1; Correspondence from Henderson (Cairo) to Austen Chamberlain, no. 547, 24 July 1925, BNA, 141/793/7; Correspondence from Bland to Henderson (Cairo), 17 August 1925, BNA 141/793/7.
71  Badrawi, *Political Violence*, 200.
72  Badrawi, *Political Violence*, 185; Correspondence from Courtney to British High Commission, 'Italian Activities of the Ex-Khedive,' 19 October 1920, BNA, FO 141/648/1; Correspondence from Ablitt to Director General, PSD, 20 August 1924, BNA, FO 141/793/7; Correspondence from Archer to the Director General, European Department, 1 July 1924, BNA, FO 141/508/1.
73  Perrault, *Man Apart*, 63–64; Telegram from Ives (Alexandria) to DOS, 'Communism and the Beginning of an Era of Industrialism in Egypt,' 11 April 1924, NARA 883.0013; Telegram from Johnson (Alexandria) to DOS, no. 514, 1 August 1924, 883.00/40, NARA.
74  *Journal Officiel*, no. 64, 28 June 1923, NARA 883.01/27.
75  Salim, *al-Būlīs*, 105–115; Telegram from Howell (Cairo) to DOS; Badrawi, *Political Violence*, 184.
76  Grafftey-Smith, *Bright Levant*, 103–104; Russell, *Egyptian Service*, 149.
77  Badrawi, *Political Violence*, 2224n59; Seth, *Russell Pasha*, 150; Muhammad, *Al-Būlīs al-Miṣrī*, 40.

78  Seth, *Russell Pasha*, 159–160.
79  Ibid.
80  Ibid., 160–161.
81  Telegram from Howell (Cairo) to DOS.
82  Correspondence from Zaki to the Assistant Commandant, CCP, n.d., BNA, FO 141/474/1.
83  Ibid.
84  Muhammad, *Al-Būlīs al-Miṣrī*, 32–33; Telegram from Winship (Cairo) to DOS, 'Annual Report of Cairo City Police for 1926,' no. 72, 26 September 1927, NARA, 883.105/21.
85  'Annual Report of Cairo City Police for 1926,' 55.
86  Ibid.
87  Ibid.
88  A. McGregor, *A Military History of Modern Egypt*, Westport, CT: Praeger, 2006, 230.
89  'Young Egypt Society,' Special Section, 2 June 1935, no. S.2 (102), BNA, FO 141/618/6; Correspondence from Keown-Boyd to Smart, British Residency, 16 November 1935, BNA, FO 141/618/6; Intelligence Report, Special Section, 3 July 1935, BNA, FO 141/618/6; Minute from Smart to High Commissioner, 15 April 1935, BNA, FO 141/618/6.
90  Telegram from Morris (Cairo) to DOS, 'Attempt to Assassinate the Egyptian Prime Minister,' no. 1141, 6 December 1937, NARA 883.00/991.
91  Muhammad, *Al-Būlīs al-Miṣrī*, 293.
92  Perrault, *Man Apart*, 94.
93  R. Mitchell, *The Society of the Muslim Brothers*, New York: Oxford University Press, 1993, 14.
94  Mitchell, *Society*, 24.
95  Correspondence from Haldrett-Jays to Amin Osman Pasha, 14 October 1937, BNA, FO 141/546/1.
96  Salah Nasr and 'Abd Allah Imam, *Al-Thawrah, Al-Naksah, Al-Mukhabarat*, Cairo: Dar al-Khayyal, 1999, 23.
97  Mansfield, *British in Egypt*, 265–266.
98  F.H. Hinsley and C.H.G. Simkins, eds., *British Intelligence in the Second World War, Volume IV: Security and Counter-Intelligence*, New York: Cambridge University Press, 1990, 150; Minutes, British Residency, 'Police Force, Egyptian,' no. 9/521/37, 8 August 1937, BNA FO 141/546/1.
99  Correspondence from G. Haldrett-Jays to Amin Osman Pasha.
100 Telegram from Fish (Cairo) to DOS, 'Political Report for July 1939,' no. 1763, 12 August 1939, NARA 883.00.
101 Ibid.
102 Hinsley and Simkins, *British Intelligence in the Second World War, Volume IV*, 150.

## 2 Decline and fall of the old regime

1  Abd al-Wahhab Bakr Muhammad, *al-Būlīs al-Miṣrī, 1922–1952*, Cairo: Maktabat Madbūlī, 1988, 295.
2  A. Sansom, *I Spied Spies*, London: George Harrap, 1965, 10–11; L. Mosley, *The Cat and the Mice*, New York: Harper & Brothers,1958, 122–123.
3  J. Salim, *al-Būlīs al-siyāsī yaḥkum Miṣr, 1910–1952*, Cairo: al-Qāhirah lil-Thaqāfah al-'Arabīyah, 1975, 157–159.
4  A. Sadat, *In Search of Identity*, New York: Harper & Row, 1979, 23–24.
5  Ibid., 30.
6  F. Hinsley and C. Simkins, eds., *British Intelligence in the Second World War*, vol. IV, New York: Cambridge University Press, 1990, 163.

7 M. Heikal, *Autumn of Fury*, London: Corgi, 1986, 22; A. Sadat, *Revolt on the Nile*, New York: John Day, 1957, 38.
8 Sansom, *I Spied Spies*, 68.
9 Ibid., 70–71.
10 Sadat, *Revolt on the Nile*, 51.
11 H. Dovey, 'Operation Condor,' *INS*, 4, 1989, 363; Sadat, *In Search*, 35–36.
12 Dovey, 'Operation Condor,' 336; R. Stephens, *Nasser*, New York: Simon & Schuster, 1971, 58.
13 Sansom, *I Spied Spies*, 102–103.
14 Correspondence from G.J. Jenkins to F.H. Tomlyn, 23 July 1942, BNA, FO 141/841.
15 Telegram from Lampson (Cairo) to Eden, FO, no. 2298, 29 September 1942, BNA, FO 141/841.
16 Office Memorandum from Ingersoll (DOS) to Mr. Jenkins (DOS), 6 December 1948, NARA, 883.002/12–648.
17 Muhammad, *al-Būlīs al-Miṣrī*, 300.
18 M. Heikal, *Sphinx and Commissar*, New York: Harper & Row, 1978, 48; Intelligence Report, SSU, USWD, 'Anti-Communist Drive,' 27 August 1946, A-70298, NARA, RG 226.
19 *Al Ahram* (19 March 1957).
20 *Annual Report of the Cairo City Police for the Year 1945*, Cairo, 1946, 51–58; R. Mitchell, *The Society of the Muslim Brothers*, New York: Oxford University Press, 2003, 30–32; Sansom, *I Spied Spies*, 190, 208.
21 Mitchell, *Society*, 39; Intelligence Report, Strategic Services Unit, US War Department, 'Labor Organizations and Labor Unrest,' 23 July 1946, A-69511, NARA, RG 226.
22 M. Laskier, 'Egyptian Jewry under the Nasser Regime, 1956–70,' *MES*, 31, 1995, 575–576; A. Abdel-Malek, *Egypte Societe Militaire*, Paris: Editions du Seuil, 1962, 35.
23 A. Golan, *Operation Susannah*, trans. by P. Kidron, New York: Harper & Row, 1978, 13.
24 Quoted in K. Kyle, *Suez*, New York: St Martin's, 1991, 30.
25 G. Nasser and W. Khalidi, 'Nasser's Memoirs of the First Palestine War,' *Journal of Palestine Studies*, 2, 1973, 10–11.
26 Nasser and Khalidi, 'Nasser's Memoirs,' 5n4; L. Collins and D. Lapierre, *O Jerusalem!*, New York: Simon & Schuster, 1972, 418.
27 Nasser and Khalidi, 'Nasser's Memoirs,' 10.
28 L. Nordeen and D. Nicolle, *Phoenix over the Nile*, Washington, DC: Smithsonian Press, 1996, 60–61, 67, 89; J. Lacouture, *Nasser*, trans. by Daniel Hofstadter, New York: Knopf, 1973, 138; Nasser and Khalidi, 'Nasser's Memoirs,' 27.
29 Salim, *al-Būlīs*, 189; D. Raviv and Y. Melman, *Every Spy a Prince*, Boston: Houghton Mifflin, 1990, 215.
30 Laskier, 'Egyptian Jewry,' 575–576; Airgram from Patterson (Cairo) to DOS, 23 November 1948, no. 5538, NARA, 883.014/11–2048; Telegram from Caffery (Cairo) to DOS, 'Report of Geographic Attaché for Period April 25 – May 31 1954,' 1 June 1954, no. 2811, NARA, 774.022/6–154.
31 J. Shields, 'Jewish Refugees from Arab Countries,' Jewish Virtual Library. Online, available at: www.jewishvirtuallibrary.org/jsource/history/jewref.html, accessed 4 May 2006.
32 Sansom, *I Spied Spies*, 224.
33 Airgram from Ernst (Port Said) to DOS, A-111, 22 July 1948, NARA, 883.00/7–2248.
34 E. Dowek, *Israeli–Egyptian Relations, 1980–2000*, London: Frank Cass, 2001, 1.
35 Mitchell, *Society*, 67n90.
36 Mitchell, *Society*, 55, 72, 205–206; Sansom, *I Spied Spies*, 225.

37  Sansom, *I Spied Spies*, 196.
38  D. Reid, 'Political Assassination in Egypt, 1910–1954,' *International Journal of African Historical Studies*, 15, 1982, 635; Mitchell, *Society*, 58, 67; Sansom, *I Spied Spies*, 226.
39  Mitchell, *Society*, 67, 69; Sansom, *I Spied Spies*, 227.
40  Airgram from Patterson (Cairo) to DOS, 18 February 1949, no. A-211, NARA, 883.00/2–1849; J. Heyworth-Dunne, *Religious and Political Trends in Modern Egypt*, Washington, DC: Self published, 1950, 76; Sansom, *I Spied Spies*, 227–228; Salim, *al-Būlīs*, 208–211.
41  Y. Caroz, *The Arab Secret Services*, London: Corgi, 1978, 39.
42  Sansom, *I Spied Spies*, 226–227.
43  Telegram from Williamson (Rome) to DOS, 'Memorandum of Conversation with Ex-King Farouk,' 8 November 1955, no. 898, NARA, 774.11/11–855.
44  *British Intelligence in the Second World War*, volume IV, 150; S. Dorril, *MI6*, New York: Free Press, 2000, 538.
45  Dorril, *MI6*, 601.
46  Telegram from Griffis (Cairo) to DOS, 23 September 1948, no. 1371, NARA, 883.00/9–2348.
47  'Obituaries – Kermit Roosevelt,' *The Times*, 16 June 2000. Online, available at: www.flyingfish.org.uk/articles/rushdie/00–06–16tim.htm, accessed 22 February 2007.
48  M. Copeland, *Game Player*, London: Aurum Press, 1989, 144.
49  M. Copeland, *The Game of Nations*, New York: Simon & Schuster, 1969, 62–63; Copeland, *Game Player*, 145–146. B. Hersh, *The Old Boys*, St Petersburg, FL: Tree Farm Books, 2002, 309–310.
50  Hersh, *The Old Boys*, 309–310.
51  Airgram from Webb (DOS) to Amembassy Cairo, 14 November 1949, A-581, NARA, 711.85/10–1245.
52  Telegram from Caffery (Cairo) to DOS, 'Communism in Egypt,' 17 March 1950, no. 479, NARA, 774.001/3–1750.
53  Telegram from Caffery (Cairo) to DOS, 'Anti-Communist Campaign,' 7 April 1950, no. 697, NARA, 774.00/4–750.
54  'The Espionage Case,' *Al Ahram*, 19 March 1957.
55  Telegram from Caffery (Cairo) to DOS, 'Egyptian Request Re Police Mission to Study US Counter Espionage Methods,' 1 May 1953, no. 2304, NARA, Microfilm.
56  A. Nutting, *Nasser*, New York: E.P. Dutton, 1972, 7.
57  K. Mohi El Din, *Memories of a Revolution*, Cairo: American University in Cairo Press, 1995, 25, 32–33; Lacouture, *Nasser*, 68.
58  K. Wheelock, *Nasser's New Egypt*, New York: Praeger, 1960, 8.
59  Sansom, *I Spied Spies*, 259–260.
60  Telegram from Caffery (Cairo) to DOS, 'The Place of King Farouk I in the Political Life of Egypt,' 28 October 1949, no. 952, NARA, 883.001 FAROUK/10–2849.
61  Salim, *al-Būlīs*, 163.
62  M. Naguib, *Egypt's Destiny*, New York: Doubleday, 1955, 81.
63  P. Mansfield, *The British in Egypt*, New York: Holt, Rinehart and Winston, 1972, 298.
64  Sansom, *I Spied Spies*, 260–261.
65  Copeland, *Game Player*, 156.
66  Mohi al-Din, *Memories*, 96; J. Gordon, *Nasser's Blessed Movement*, New York: Oxford University Press, 1992, 52; 'Abd al-Fattāḥ Abū al-Faḍl, *Kuntu nā'iban li-ra'īs al-mukhābarāt*, Cairo: Dār al-Ḥurrīyah,1986, 101.
67  Copeland, *Game of Nations*, 80–81.
68  Mohi al-Din, *Memories*, 87–89; Mitchell, *Society*, 106; Telegram from Caffery (Cairo) to DOS, 'The Military Take-over in Egypt,' 30 July 1952, no. 151, NARA, 774.55/7–3052; Telegram from Caffery (Cairo) to DOS, 25 July 1952, no. 183, NARA, 774.00/7–2552.

69 Telegram from Creswell (Alexandria) to FO, no. 1094, 25 July 1952, BNA, FO 371/102703.
70 Ibid.
71 Quoted in Lacouture, *Nasser*, 153.
72 Telegram from Caffery (Cairo) to DOS, 'Biographic Data – Members of Military High Committee,' 4 October 1952, no. 602, NARA, 774.521/10–452.
73 Telegram from Caffery (Cairo) to DOS, 23 July 1952, no. 140, NARA, 774.551/7–2352.
74 Naguib, *Egypt's Destiny*, 107–108; Telegram from Caffery (Cairo) to DOS, 'The Military Take-Over in Egypt'; M. Heikal, *The Cairo Documents*, New York: Doubleday, 1973, 34.
75 Telegram from Caffery (Cairo) to DOS, 25 July 1952, no. 178, NARA, 774.00/7–2552.
76 Telegram from Wright (Alexandria) to DOS, 26 July 1952, no. 31, NARA, 774.00/7–2652.

## 3 Creating a new intelligence community

1 Memorandum from Tamlyn, Assistant Military Attaché, British Embassy, Cairo, 19 September 1952, BNA, FO 371/165345.
2 Memorandum from Evans, Oriental Counsellor, British Embassy, Cairo, 20 September 1952, BNA, FO 371/165345.
3 Memorandum from Burroughs, British Embassy, Cairo, 19 September 1952, BNA, FO 371/165345.
4 Telegram from Caffery (Cairo), 'Military Junta Around General Naguib: Lieutenant Colonel Zacharia,' 2 September 1952.
5 K. Mohi al-Din, *Memories of A Revolution*, Cairo: American University in Cairo Press, 1995, 245.
6 'Leading Personalities in Arab Republic of Egypt 1972,' Foreign and Colonial Office (hereafter FCO) 39/1205; Airgram from Rogers (DOS) to Amembassy Belgrade, 'UAR Ambassador-Designate to Belgrade, Sa'd 'Abdallah Hasan 'Afra,' 23 July 1971, no. CA-3449, NARA, Box 2642, POL 17 UAR-YUGO; Y. Caroz, *Arab Secret Services*, London: Corgi, 1978, 41.
7 'Abd al-Fattāḥ Abu al-Fadl, *Kuntu nā'iban li-ra'īs al-mukhābarāt*, Cairo: Dār al-Ḥurrīyah, 1986, 103.
8 Telegram from Caffery (Cairo) to DOS, 18 August 1952, no. 383, NARA, 774.00/8–1852.
9 Telegram from Caffery (Cairo) to DOS, 5 September 1952, no. 574, NARA, 774.00/9–552; Telegram from Caffery (Cairo), 'Confidential Biographic Data – Lt. Col. Zakaria Muhieddin,' 6 September 1952.
10 Telegram from Caffery (Cairo) to DOS, 1 August 1952, no. 238, NARA, 774.00/8–152.
11 Minutes by African Department, FO, 'Communist Activities,' 20 August 1952, BNA, FO 371/96884.
12 Telegram from Stevenson (Cairo) to FO, 'Communist Activities,' 19 August 1952, no. 1240, BNA, FO 371/96884.
13 Ibid.
14 Telegram from Caffery (Cairo) to DOS, 2 August 1952, no. 248, NARA, 874.501/8–252; Caroz, *Arab Secret Services*, 44; K. Wheelock, *Nasser's New Egypt*, New York: Praeger, 1960, 22.
15 Telegram from Stevenson (Cairo) to FO, no. 1228, 15 August 1952, FO 371/102703; K. Beattie, *Egypt during the Nasser Years*, Boulder: Westview, 1994, 107n96.
16 Caroz, *Arab Secret Services*, 45; J. Baud, *Encyclopedie du Renseignement et des Services Secrets*, Paris: Editions Lavauzelle, 1997, 183.

17 Caroz, *Arab Secret Services*, 55; Telegram from Caffery (Cairo) to DOS, 'Members of Egyptian Military High Committee,' 26 September 1952, no. 535, NARA, 774.00/9–2652; Airgram from Byroade (Cairo) to DOS, 'Stability of the Military Regime in Egypt – An Evaluation,' 29 April 1955, no. 2040, NARA, RG 59, 774.00/4–2955.

18 Telegram from Caffery (Cairo), 'Egyptian Request Re Police Mission to Study US Counter Espionage Methods,' 1 May 1953.

19 Telegram from Caffery (Cairo) to DOS, 'Chief of the General Investigations Department, Ministry of the Interior, Explains Functions of His Department at Press Conference,' 4 June 1954, no. 2829, NARA, 774.13/6–454; Abū al-Faḍl, *Kuntu nā'iban*, 108.

20 Telegram from Caffery (Cairo), 'Egyptian Request Re Police Mission to Study US Counter Espionage Methods.'

21 Ibid.

22 L. James, *Nasser At War: Arab Images of the Enemy*, London: Palgrave Macmillan, 2006, 23; Mustafa 'Amin expressed similar suspicions in his 1965 'confession' found in S. Nasr and 'Abd Allah Imam, *Al-Thawrah, Al-Naksah, Al-Mukhabarat*, Cairo: Dar al-Khayyal, 1999, 234; M. Copeland, *Game of Nations*, New York: Simon & Schuster, 1969, 75; Telegram from Caffery (Cairo), 'Military Junta Around General Naguib: Lieutenant Colonel Zacharia.'

23 M. Heikal, *Cutting the Lion's Tail*, New York: Arbor House, 1987, 35; A. Nutting, *Nasser*, New York: E.P. Dutton, 1972, 57–58; when President Eisenhower later asked Roosevelt 'if he had the right to make decisions on subjects that should properly be in the [Anglo-Egyptian] treaty,' Roosevelt 'replied, rather annoyed, "Why yes – eh, yes"': W.S. Lucas, *Divided We Stand*, London: Hodder & Stoughton, 1995, 16.

24 Nutting, *Nasser*, 45–46.

25 Nutting, *Nasser*, 45–46; D. Neff, *Warriors at Suez*, New York: Linden Press, 1981, 87.

26 Neff, *Warriors at Suez*, 87.

27 M. Copeland, *Game Player*, London: Aurum Press, 1989, 25, 129.

28 W. Eveland, *Ropes of Sand*, New York: W.W. Norton, 1980, 96; Heikal, *Cutting the Lion's Tail*, 41–42.

29 Eveland, *Ropes of Sand*, 103; Copeland, *Game Player*, 161.

30 Heikal, *Cutting the Lion's Tail*, 90.

31 Abū al-Faḍl, *Kuntu nā'iban*, 207–209.

32 J. Gordon, *Nasser's Blessed Movement*, New York: Oxford University Press, 1992, 168.

33 K. Kyle, *Suez*, New York: St Martin's, 1991, 52; Copeland, *Game Player*, 165; S. Shpiro, 'Intelligence Services and Political Transformation in the Middle East,' *International Journal of Intelligence and Counterintelligence* (hereafter IJIC),17, 2004–2005, 577.

34 R. Gehlen, *The Service*, trans. by David Irving, New York: World Publishing Co., 1972, 260.

35 Gehlen, *The Service*, 260; E. Cookridge, *Gehlen: Spy of the Century*, New York: Random House, 1971, 352; H. Hohne and H. Zolling, *The General Was a Spy*, New York: Coward, McCann and Geoghegan, 1971, 220.

36 R. Breitman *et al.*, *US Intelligence and the Nazis*, New York: Cambridge University Press, 2005, 404–405, 417n66.

37 Telegram from Stevenson (Cairo) to FO, 'Germans Employed by Egyptian Government,' no. 156, 26 January 1952, BNA, FO 371/102869; John Starr, 'Rommel Men Helping the Egyptians,' *Daily Mail*, 14 February 1952; Telegram from Caffery (Cairo) to DOS, 'German Advisors with Egyptian Armed Forces,' 20 December 1952, no. 1211, NARA, 774.5/12–2052.

38 Telegram from Holloway (Bremen) to DOS, 'Egyptians Recruit Former German

Paratrooper for Training Job,' 20 December 1951, no. 262, NARA, 774.55/12–2051; Telegram from Caffery (Cairo), 'German Advisors with Egyptian Armed Forces,' 20 December 1952; A. El-Ad, *Decline of Honor*, Chicago: Regnery, 1976, 107.
39 Cookridge, *Gehlen*, 352, 353; A. Sabit, *A King Betrayed*, London: Quartet Books, 1989, 170.
40 Cookridge, *Gehlen*, 353.
41 R. Breitman *et al.*, *US Intelligence and the Nazis*, 169n69, 267n29; Caroz, *Arab Secret Services*, 77; Cookridge, *Gehlen*, 353; C. Simpson, *Blowback*, New York: Collier/Macmillan, 1988, 247; Central Intelligence Agency, Intelligence Report, Subject Redacted, from Chief of Station, Munich to Director, 25 April 1961, National Security Archive (hereafter NSA). Online, available at: www.gwu.edu/~nsarchiv/nsaebb/ nsaebb150/box15_do_file_vol. 3/doc35.pdf, accessed 2 April 2007.
42 R. Fisk, *Pity the Nation*, New York: Nation Books, 2002, 180; Telegram from Schultz, DOS to Amembassy Damascus, 'Nazi War Criminal Alois Brunner's Presence in Damascus Hits the Papers Again,' 5 November 1987, no. 345288, NSA. Online, available at: www.gwu.edu/~nsarchiv/nsaebb/nsaebb150/box14-d1-file/ doc04/pdf, accessed 2 April 2007.
43 Cookridge, *Gehlen*, 354; Simpson, *Blowback*, 247; Fisk, *Pity the Nation*, 180. Brunner ended up in Damascus where he trained Syrian intelligence under the alias Georg Fischer: Fisk, *Pity the Nation*, 179; Telegram from Schultz to Amembassy Damascus, 'Nazi War Criminal Alois Brunner's Presence in Damascus,' 5 November 1987.
44 Caroz, *Arab Secret Services*, 77; Sanche de Gramont, 'Nasser's Hired Germans,' *Saturday Evening Post*, 28 July 1963, 60–64.
45 Copeland, *Game of Nations*, 105; Eveland, *Ropes of Sand*, 103.
46 Abū al-Faḍl, *Kuntu nā'iban*, 213–214.
47 Copeland, *Game of Nations*, 105–106.
48 Abū al-Faḍl, *Kuntu nā'iban*, 214–216.
49 M. Copeland, *Beyond Cloak and Dagger: Inside the CIA*, New York: Pinnacle Books, 1975, 212–213; Heikal, *Cutting the Lion's Tail*, 41–42 and Abū al-Faḍl, *Kuntu nā'iban*, 215.
50 Copeland, *Game Player*, 180–181; Cremean's role was confirmed in 1 October 2007 e-mail correspondence with former CIA Case Officer, Ray Close. C.D. Cremeans authored *The Arabs and the World: Nasser's Arab Nationalist Policy*, Oxford: Praeger, 1963.
51 Heikal, *Cutting the Lion's Tail*, 41–42.
52 J. Alterman, 'American Aid to Egypt in the 1950s: From Hope to Hostility,' *MEJ*, 52, 1998, 57.
53 Copeland, *Beyond Cloak and Dagger*, 227–228; Ernest Volkman, *Spies: The Secret Agents who Changed the Course of History*, New York: John Wiley, 1994, 146.
54 Correspondence from Trevelyan (Cairo) to CAE Shuckburgh, FO, 10 November 1955, no. 20, BNA, FO 371/113591.
55 Nutting, *Nasser*, 45–46; Copeland, *Game of Nations*, 138; Lucas, *Divided We Stand*, 62.
56 The *Saturday Evening Post* mentioned Roosevelt's role in Mossadeq's overthrow; Roosevelt was a former reporter for this newspaper.
57 Eveland, *Ropes of Sand*, 137–138; Copeland, *Game of Nations*, 138.
58 Hersh, *Old Boys*, 310; James, *Nasser at War*, 3; Heikal, *Cairo Documents*, 36–37; Shpiro, 'Intelligence Services,' 577.
59 Serge Kovaleski, 'The Most Dangerous Game,' *Washington Post*, 15 January 2006, p.W16.
60 Heikal, *Cutting the Lion's Tail*, 91; Shamir in *Suez 1956*, eds. W.M. Roger Louis and Roger Owen, Oxford: Oxford University Press, 1989, 95–96; Copeland, *Beyond Cloak and Dagger*, 216, 227, 278.
61 Correspondence from Stevenson (Cairo) to African Department, FO, no.

1011/276/52, 12 September 1952, BNA, FO 371/102703; Telegram from Caffery (Cairo) to DOS, 4 September 1952, no. 555, NARA, 774.00/9–452; Telegram from Gifford (London) to DOS, 5 September 1952, no. 1301, NARA, 774.00/9–552; Gordon, *Nasser's Blessed Movement*, 111.

62  Memorandum from Burroughs, British Embassy, Cairo, 19 September 1952.

63  Telegram from Caffery (Cairo) to DOS, 'Arrest of Air Force NCO's,' 23 December 1952, no. 1241, NARA, 774.551/12–2352.

64  K. Beattie, *Egypt during the Nasser Years*, Boulder: Westview Press, 1994, 107n104; Muhi al-Din, *Memories*, 154.

65  Mohi al-Din, *Memories*, 118,143; Gordon, *Nasser's Blessed Movement*, 128–129; R. Stephens, *Nasser*, New York: Simon & Schuster, 1971, 126; M. Naguib, *Egypt's Destiny*, New York: Doubleday, 1955, 200, 299–300; Beattie, *Egypt during the Nasser Years*, 93.

66  Gordon, *Nasser's Blessed Movement*, 129.

67  Ibid., 139.

68  Airgram from McClintock (Cairo) to DOS, 'Views of Director of Military Intelligence on Communist Activity,' 27 December 1952, no. 1265, NARA, 774.001/12–2752; Abū al-Faḍl, *Kuntu nā'iban*, 103.

69  Telegram from Payne (Cairo) to DOS, 'Creation Against Communist Literature,' 17 April 1953, no. 2167, NARA, 974.63/4–1753; Telegram from Payne (Cairo) to DOS, 'Creation of Anti-Communist Bureau under Chief of Military Intelligence of the Armed Forces,' 6 February 1953, no. 1569, NARA, 774.1/2–653.

70  Telegram from Payne (Cairo), 'Creation Against Communist Literature'; Caroz, *Arab Secret Services*, 20.

71  Telegram from Caffery (Cairo) to DOS, 'Police Chief of Anti-Communist Section Discusses Communist Activities,' 30 April 1953, no. 2308, NARA, 774.001/4–3053; Telegram from Lunt (Cairo) to DOS, 'Federation of Trade Unions Movement Expected to be Revived,' 8 December 1952, no. 1083, NARA, 874.062/12–852; Telegram from Caffery (Cairo) to DOS, 'Labor Leaders Among Communists Recently Arrested,' 15 September 1953, no. 735, NARA, 774.001/9–1553; Telegram from Lunt (Cairo) to DOS, 'Request for Permit to Hold Peace Conference in Cairo and Other Communist Activities,' 7 May 1954, no. 2645, NARA, 774.00/5–754.

72  Telegram from Caffery (Cairo) to DOS, 'Chief of the General Investigations Department, Ministry of the Interior, Explains Functions of His Department at Press Conference.'.

73  Ibid.

74  Gordon, *Nasser's Blessed Movement*, 31; J. Lacouture, *Nasser*, trans. by David Hofstadter, New York: Knopf, 1973, 263.

75  S. Botman, 'Egyptian Communists and the Free Officers: 1950–54,' *MES*, 22, 1986, 364; Wheelock, *Nasser's New Egypt*, 42.

76  Abū al-Faḍl, *Kuntu nā'iban*, 213.

77  Gordon, *Nasser's Blessed Movement*, 98.

78  Mohi al-Din, *Memories*, 171.

79  Bureau of Intelligence and Research (INR) 'The Muslim Brethren in 1968,' Research Memorandum, 15 May 1968, no. RMA-20, NARA, POL 27 UAR; Airgram from Payne (Cairo) to DOS, 'Army's Counter-propaganda Campaign against Ikhwan and Commies,' 25 March 1954, no. 2291, NARA, 774.00/3–2554.

80  Telegram from Caffery (Cairo) to DOS, 'Transmitting Memorandum of Conversation Concerning Moslem Brotherhood,' 6 December 1954, no. 1102, NARA, 774.00/12–654.

81  Telegram from Caffery (Cairo) to DOS, 'Senior Police Officers Dismissed,' 4 October 1954, no. 604, NARA, 774.00/10–454.

82  The Brotherhood asserted this was a *mukhabarat* operation: A. Golan, *Operation Susannah*, trans. by P. Kidron, New York: Harper & Row, 1978, 129. In 1978,

   Hasan al-Tohami claimed Nasser survived because of a bullet-proof vest provided by CIA: Gordon, *Nasser's Blessed Movement*, 180; D. Little, 'Mission Impossible: The CIA and the Cult of Covert Action in the Middle East,' *Diplomatic History*, 28, 2004, 678; others doubt al-Tohami's story: James, *Nasser at War*, 7.

83  A. Abdel-Malek, *Egypte Societe Militaire*, Paris: Editions du Seuil, 1962, 100; Gordon, *Nasser's Blessed Movement*, 183; Stephens, *Nasser*, 136; R. Mitchell, *Society of the Muslim Brothers*, New York: Oxford University Press, 1993, 151, 162; L. Wright, *The Looming Tower*, New York: Vintage, 2006, 33.

84  Telegram from Caffery (Cairo), 'Transmitting Memorandum of Conversation Concerning Moslem Brotherhood.'

85  Mitchell, *Society*, 156n134.

86  Ibid., 156.

87  Telegram from Caffery (Cairo), 'Transmitting Memorandum of Conversation Concerning Moslem Brotherhood.'

88  Telegram from Jones (Cairo) to DOS, 'Nasser Reportedly Believes Re-Emergence of Brotherhood Inevitable,' 25 January 1955, no. 1448, NARA, 774.00/1–2555.

89  Airgram from Byroade (Cairo), 'Stability of the Military Regime in Egypt – An Evaluation.'

90  Lucas, *Divided We Stand*, 64.

91  Lacouture, *Nasser*, 266–267.

92  Department of State, Office of Intelligence Research, Intelligence Report, 'The Israeli Spy Trial in Egypt,' 10 January 1955, no. 6790, NARA.

93  Telegram from Caffery (Cairo) to DOS, 'Report of Geographic Attaché for Period April 25 – May 31 1954,' 1 June 1954.

94  I. Black and B. Morris, *Israel's Secret Wars*, New York: Grove Weidenfeld, 1991, 108; Golan, *Operation Susannah*, 16, 27, 33; M. Bar-Zohar, *Spies in the Promised Land*, trans. by Monroe Stearns, Boston: Houghton Mifflin, 1972, 135.

95  Bar-Zohar, *Spies*, 138.

96  Bar-Zohar, *Spies*, 133–134, 140; Golan, *Operation Susannah*, 61–72; Black and Morris, *Israel's Secret Wars*, 112; D. Raviv and Y. Melman, *Every Spy a Prince*, Boston: Houghton Mifflin, 1990, 59.

97  Golan, *Operation Susannah*, 109–111, 118.

98  Caroz, *Arab Secret Services*, 49–50.

99  Telegram from Caffery (Cairo) to DOS, 'Incendiary Fires at USIS Libraries, Cairo and Alexandria, Egypt,' 5 November 1954, no. 860, NARA, 774.00/11–554.

100 Telegram from Lamprecht (Alexandria) to DOS, 'Local Jewish Protest against Allegations of Radio Israel,' 22 December 1954, no. 81, NARA, 674.84A/12–2254.

101 Golan, *Operation Susannah*, 183.

102 Ibid., 188.

103 W. Lotz, *The Champagne Spy*, New York: St Martin's, 1972, 17–18.

104 James, *Nasser at War*, 8–10; Correspondence from Dulles, Director, CIA to Brigadier General Chester V. Clifton, Military Aide to the President, 8 February 1961, Declassified Documents Reference System (hereafter DDRS), Eisenhower Presidential Library; Aburish claims Susannah forced the United States to cancel a visit to Washington by Egyptian intelligence officers. Nasser interpreted this as a sign the United States would not sign a pending intelligence deal with Egypt: S. Aburish, *Nasser: The Last Arab*, New York: Thomas Dunne, 2004, 67, 71, 74–75.

105 Michael Oren, 'Secret Egypt–Israel Peace Initiatives Prior to the Suez Campaign,' *MES*, 27, 1990, 361; Kyle, *Suez*, 81.

106 Ophera McDoom, 'Israeli Spy Ring Spawned Feared Egyptian Intelligence,' Reuters, 15 April 2003.

107 The saboteurs alleged El Ad betrayed them: Golan, *Operation Susannah*, 80–84, 285; Raviv and Melman, *Every Spy a Prince*, 60.

108 El Ad, *Decline*, 168.

## 4 General intelligence

1  A. Hewedy, 'Nasser and the Crisis of 1956,' in W. Louis and R. Owen, *Suez 1956*, Oxford: Clarendon Press, 1989, 163–164.
2  'Abd al-Fattāḥ Abū al-Faḍl, *Kuntu nā'iban li-ra'īs al-mukhābarāt*, Cairo: Dār al-Ḥurrīyah, 1986, 105.
3  W. Scott Lucas, *Divided We Stand*, London: Hodder and Stoughton, 1996, 64.
4  Ibid., 113.
5  Correspondence from the Governor-General (Khartoum) to African Department, FO, no. GG/5-2-13, 7 October 1953, BNA, FO 371/102869; Abu āl-Faḍl, *Kuntu nā'iban*, 147–149; 164–165; 169.
6  J. Lacouture, *Nasser*, trans. by David Hofstadter, New York: Knopf, 1973, 202; A. Nutting, *Nasser*, New York: E.P. Dutton, 1972, 112–113.
7  Abu āl-Faḍl, *Kuntu nā'iban*, 169–170.
8  A. Hewedy, 'Nasser and the Crisis of 1956,' 163–164; K. Kyle, *Suez*, New York: St Martin's, 1991, 48
9  Quoted in K. Wheelock, *Nasser's New Egypt*, New York: Praeger, 1960, 213–214.
10  Abū al-Faḍl, *Kuntu nā'iban*, 117.
11  Ibid., 113–115.
12  J. Gordon, *Nasser's Blessed Movement*, New York: Oxford University Press, 1992, 169, 226n3; 'Egyptian Soldiers Learn the German Way,' *Daily Telegraph*, 17 July 1953; Intelligence Summary, General Staff Intelligence (hereafter GSI), Headquarters British Troops in Egypt, 'Subject: PARA-MIL Organizations,' no. EA/36 G(Int), May 1953, BNA, FO 371/102869; Abu āl-Faḍl, *Kuntu nā'iban*, 115–116; 313–314.
13  Abu āl-Faḍl, *Kuntu nā'iban*, 124–125; 127–135.
14  A. Abdel-Malek, *Egypte Societe Militaire*, Paris: Editions du Sueil, 1962, 102; Kyle, *Suez*, 52; M. Copeland, *Game of Nations*, New York: Simon & Schuster, 1969, 104–141; Lucas, *Divided We Stand*, 30–31.
15  M. Fathi al-Dib, *'Abd al-Nasir wa-haraka al-Tahrir al-Yemeni*, Cairo: Dar al-Mustaqbal al-Arabi, 1990, 15.
16  Ibid., 15–18.
17  Ibid., 18.
18  J. Baud, *Encyclopedie du Renseignement*, Paris: Editions Lavauzelle, 1997, 184.
19  Y. Caroz, *Arab Secret Services*, London: Corgi, 1978, 55.
20  S. Nasr and 'Abd Allah Imam, *Al-Thawrah, Al-Naksah, Al-Mukhabarat*, Cairo: Dar al-Khayyal, 1999, 57.
21  Abū al-Faḍl, *Kuntu nā'iban*, 216.
22  Copeland, *Game of Nations*, 97–98.
23  Nasr and Imam, *Al-Thawrah*, 59, 79; Baud, *Encyclopedie du Renseignement*,183; Copeland, *Game of Nations*, 97–98; Caroz, *Arab Secret Services*, 54.
24  Abū al-Faḍl, *Kuntu nā'iban*, 251–252.
25  Nasr and Imam, *Al-Thawrah*, 63, 79.
26  Ibid., 23, 57, 59.
27  W. Eveland, *Ropes of Sand*, New York: W.W. Norton, 1980, 103; Gary Rawnsley, 'Overt and Covert: The Voice of Britain and Black Radio Broadcasting in the Suez Crisis, 1956,' *INS*, 11, 1996, 504.
28  Eveland, *Ropes of Sand*, 103; P. Linebarger, *Psychological Warfare*, Washington, DC: Infantry Journal Press, 1948, 113.
29  Memorandum from the Chief of Station (Munich) to Chief, Near East Division, CIA, 19 March 1958, '[Redacted] Near Eastern Connections,' NSA. Online, available at: www.gwu.edu?~nsarchiv/nsaebb/nsaebb150/box14_do_file_vol. 1/doc41/pdf.
30  Memorandum from the Chief of Station (Munich), 19 March 1958; also see Airgram from Dunnigan (Bonn) to DOS, 'Nazi War Criminals in the UAR,' 16 March 1965, no. A-1573, NARA, Box 2764, POL 15-1 UAR.

31  L. James, *Whose Voice? Nasser, the Arabs, and 'Sawt al-Arab' Radio*. Online, available at: www.tbsjournal.com/jamespf.html, accessed 1 April 2007.
32  Weathersby, United States Information Service (hereafter USIS) (Cairo) to DOS, 'Voice of the Arabs,' 2 October 1954, no. 589, NARA, 974.40/10–254; Airgram from McKee (Cairo) to DOS, 'Egyptian Broadcasting Operations,' 23 August 1957, no. 169, NARA, 974.40/8–2357.
33  Weathersby, USIS (Cairo) to DOS, 'Persian Language Broadcasts by Egyptian State Broadcasting,' 3 July 1954, no. 260, NARA, 974.40/7–354.
34  Nutting, *Nasser*, 76; Minute by JHA Watson, FO, 'Cairo Radio in British East Africa,' 23 February 1956, BNA, FO 371/119303.
35  P. Seale, *The Struggle for Syria*, London: Oxford University Press, 1965, 230n25.
36  Weathersby, USIS (Cairo) to United State Information Agency (hereafter USIA), 'Radio: Anti-Communist Material for Egyptian Broadcasting System,' 31 August 1954, no. TOUSI 45, NARA, 974.40/8–3154.
37  Gordon, *Nasser's Blessed Movement*, 186.
38  Weathersby, USIS (Cairo), 'Voice of the Arabs,' 2 October 1954.
39  Eveland, *Ropes of Sand*, 103; Lucas, *Divided We Stand*, 133.
40  Quoted in D. Boyd, 'Development of Egypt's Radio: "Voice of the Arabs" under Nasser,' *Journalism Quarterly*, 52, 1975, 646.
41  Abū al-Faḍl, *Kuntu nā'iban*, 253–258.
42  H. Jacquin, *La Guerre Secrete en Algerie*, Paris: Editions Olivier Orban, 1977, 70.
43  M. Fathi Al-Dib, *Abdel Nasser et la Revolution Algerienne*, Paris: L'Harmattan, 1985, 131.
44  Ibid.
45  Fathi al-Dib had authority to direct Voice of the Arabs attacks on France: Al-Dib, *Abdel Nasser et la Revolution Algerienne*, 51.
46  Ibid., 21.
47  Ibid.
48  Al-Dib, *Abdel Nasser et la Revolution Algerienne*, 27, 29; Nutting, *Nasser*, 312–313; Y. Courriere, *La Guerre d'Algerie (1954–1957)*, Paris: Robert Laffont, 1990, 323.
49  Al-Dib, *Nasser et la Revolution Algerienne*, 72.
50  Ibid., 38, 41–42, 71.
51  Ibid., 40–41. Also see Kyle, *Suez*, 112.
52  Kyle, *Suez*, 112; Jacquin, *Guerre Secrete en Algerie*, 71; al-Dib, *Nasser et la Revolution Algerienne*, 67, 69.
53  Al-Dib, *Nasser et la Revolution Algerienne*, 40–41, 43, 58–59, 142, 144.
54  Ibid., 170.
55  The FLN cadre in Cairo resented al-Dib's role as 'filter' for the senior Egyptian leadership: Y. Courriere, *La Guerre d'Algerie (1958–1962*, Paris: Robert Laffont, 1990, 227.
56  Courriere, *La Guerre d'Algerie (1958–1962)*, 226–227; D. Neff, *Warriors at Suez*, New York: Linden Press, 1981, 162; Courriere, *La Guerre d'Algerie (1954–1957)*, 459–460.
57  Al-Dib, *Nasser et la Revolution Algerienne*, 6–7, 433.
58  Courriere, *La Guerre d'Algerie (1954–1957)*, 323.
59  R. Faligot and P. Krop, *La Piscine*, Paris: Editions du Sueil, 1985, 151.
60  A. Ibrahim, 'Obituary: Master of Strategy,' *Al-Ahram Weekly*, no. 642, 12–18 June 2003, 180; B. Morris, *Israel's Border Wars, 1949–1956*, Oxford: Clarendon Press, 1997, 86–87.
61  A. Hart, *Arafat*, Bloomington: Indiana University Press, 1984, 102–103.
62  United Nations Security Council (hereafter UNSC), 'Report of the Chief of Staff of the Truce Supervision Organization Concerning the Incident of 28 February 1955 Near Gaza,' 17 March 1955, S/3373. Online, available at: http://domino.un.org/unispal.nsf, accessed 26 March 2007; Caroz, *Arab Secret Services*, 51–52; Memorandum

of Conversation, 'Violence on the Israel–Egyptian Frontier,' 25 March 1955, NARA, 674.84A/3–2555; Kyle, *Suez*, 64.

63 Caroz, *Arab Secret Services*, 51–52; UNSC, 'Report of the Chief of Staff of the Truce Supervision Organization Concerning the Incident of 28 February 1955 Near Gaza.'

64 Telegram from Heath (Beirut) to SecState, 8 December 1956, no. 1477, NARA, 674.83A/12–856 HBS; Telegram from Heath (Beirut) to SecState, 12 December 1956, no. 1503, NARA, 674.83A/12–1256 HBS.

65 Kyle, *Suez*, 107.

66 S. Steven, *The Spymasters of Israel*, New York: Ballantine Books, 1980, 108.

67 E-mail correspondence with Nonie Darwish, 24 May 2007. Ms. Darwish is Mustafa Hafez's daughter.

68 Caroz, *Arab Secret Services*, 51.

69 Memorandum of Conversation, 'Violence on the Israel–Egyptian Frontier'; Kyle, *Suez*, 64.

70 M. Oren, 'Escalation to Suez: The Egypt–Israel Border War, 1949–56,' *Journal of Contemporary History*, 24, 1989, 357; Morris, *Israel's Border Wars*, 338.

71 UNSC, 'Report of the Chief of Staff of the Truce Supervision Organization Concerning the Incident of 28 February 1955 near Gaza.'

72 Morris, *Israel's Border Wars*, 350. Both Egypt and Israel had been conducting a tentative dialogue on a future peace deal: W.S. Lucas, *Divided We Stand*, 34.

73 M. Heikal, *Cutting the Lion's Tail*, New York: Arbor House, 1987, 67.

74 Quoted in Black and Morris, *Israel's Secret Wars*, 93, 119; Kyle, *Suez*, 107.

75 Caroz, *Arab Secret Services*, 51–52; E-mail correspondence with N. Darwish, 24 May 2007; Morris, *Israel's Border Wars*, 332.

76 Y. Sayigh, 'Reconstructing the Paradox: The Arab Nationalist Movement, Armed Struggle, and Palestine, 1951–1966,' *MEJ*, 45, 1991, 609–610; N. Livingstone and D. Halevy, *Inside the PLO*, New York: William Morrow, 1990, 201; Kyle, *Suez*, 65.

77 Morris, *Israel's Border Wars*, 354, 359–360.

78 Airgram from Hamilton (Tel Aviv) to DOS, 'Report on Fedayeen Personnel, Materiel, and Activities by IDF Intelligence,' 12 April 1956, no. 634, NARA, 674.84A/4–1256.

79 Morris, *Israel's Border Wars*, 356, 356n88, 357; Telegram from Hamilton (Tel Aviv) to DOS, 'Government of Israel Statements Regarding Egyptian Guerilla Activities,' 14 October 1955, no. 270, NARA, 674.84A/10–1455.

80 Morris, *Israel's Border Wars*, 357.

81 Seale, *Struggle for Syria*, 238.

82 Airgram from Byroade (Cairo) to DOS, 'Radio Free Egypt Follows Moderate Anti-Regime Line that Appeals to Egyptian Nationalism and the Muslim Brotherhood,' 30 April 1955, no. 2049, NARA, 974.40/4–3055; Airgram from Moose (Damascus) to DOS, 'Moslem Brethren Paper Reports Clandestine Egyptian Radio Heard Here,' 11 April 1955, no. 400, NARA, 974.40/4–1155.

83 Telegram from Byroade (Cairo) to DOS, 18 May 1955, no. 1733, NARA, 674.87/5–1855; Telegram from Gallman (Baghdad) to DOS, 16 May 1955, no. 929, NARA, 674.87/5–1655.

84 Boyd, 'Development of Egypt's Radio,' 649–650.

85 Quoted in W. Ellis, 'Nasser's Other Voice,' *Harper's Magazine*, 222, June 1961, 56–57. It became the Baghdad Pact with Britain's April 1955 accession.

86 Nutting, *Nasser*, 121; Telegram from Cole (Jerusalem) to DOS, 22 November 1955, no. 165, NARA, 674.84A/11–2255; H. Trevelyan, *The Middle East in Revolution*, London: Macmillan, 1970, 57.

87 King Hussein of Jordan, *Uneasy Lies the Head*, London: Heinemann, 1962, 91.

88 Telegram from Byroade (Cairo) to DOS, 'Conversation with Nasser, August 8, 1955,' 11 August 1955, no. 164, NARA, 611/74/8–1155; Telegram from Schnee (Cairo) to DOS, 'Regime Attempts to Limit Contacts Between Foreign Officials and Egyptian Civil Servants,' 30 September 1955, no. 360, NARA, 774.00/9–3055.

212   *Notes*

Telegram from Byroade (Cairo), 'Conversation with Nasser, August 8, 1955'; Telegram from Schnee (Cairo), 'Regime Attempts to Limit Contacts between Foreign Officials and Egyptian Civil Servants.'
90 Telegram from Byroade (Cairo), 'Conversation with Nasser, August 8, 1955.'
91 Telegram from Schnee (Cairo) to DOS, 'Regime Controls Army But Dissatisfied Elements Still Exist,' 22 September 1955, no. 333, NARA, 774.5/9–2255.
92 M. Heikal, *Cutting the Lion's Tail*, 76.
93 Telegram from Finch (Cairo) to DOS, 'Egyptian Government Actions Regarding Social Affairs Investigations,' 15 October 1955, no. 420, NARA, 874.00/10–1555; Telegram from Schnee (Cairo), 'Regime Attempts to Limit Contacts Between Foreign Officials and Egyptian Civil Servants.'
94 Airgram from Edgar (Alexandria) to DOS, 'Biographic Intelligence: Ahmed Ayad,' 29 June 1955, no. 219, NARA, 774.521/6–2955.
95 Caroz, *Arab Secret Services*, 63–64.
96 Ibid.
97 Ibid.
98 Office Memorandum from Stevens, (NEA/DOS) to Mr. Allen (NEA/DOS), 18 June 1956, NARA, 774.5811/6–1856.

## 5 Egyptian intelligence and the Suez Crisis

1 D. Little, 'Mission Impossible: The CIA and the Cult of Covert Action in the Middle East,' *Diplomatic History*, 28, 2004, 679–681; T. Bower, *The Perfect English Spy*, New York: St Martin's Press, 1995, 194.
2 Airgram from Washburn (Alexandria) to DOS, 'US Navy Plane Makes Forced Landing At Alexandria,' 14 June 1956, no. 155, NARA, 774.5411/6–1456; Telegram from Byroade (Cairo) to SecState, 13 June 1956, no. 2482, NARA, 774.5411/6–1356.
3 Airgram from Washburn (Alexandria) to DOS, 'United States Naval Aircraft Departs from Alexandria,' 28 June 1956, no. 160, NARA, 774.5411/6–2856.
4 M. Bar-On, *The Gates of Gaza*, New York: St Martin's Press, 1994, 16–18.
5 I. Black and B. Morris, *Israel's Secret Wars*, New York: Grove, 1991, 124.
6 Airgram from Hamilton (Tel Aviv), 'Report on Fedayeen Personnel, Materiel, and Activities by IDF Intelligence,' 12 April 1956; Telegram from Lawson (Tel Aviv) to DOS, 15 April 1956, no. 1098, NARA, 674.84A/4–1556.
7 Y. Caroz, *Arab Secret Services*, London: Corgi, 1978, 69–70.
8 J. Alterman, 'American Aid to Egypt in the 1950s: From Hope to Hostility,' *MEJ*, 52, 1998, 67–68.
9 Y. Sheffy, 'Unconcern at Dawn, Surprise at Sunset: Egyptian Intelligence Appreciation Before the Sinai Campaign, 1956,' *INS*, 5, 1990, 45.
10 R. Stephens, *Nasser*, New York: Simon & Schuster, 1971, 198; Sheffy, 'Unconcern at Dawn,' 10.
11 M. Heikal, *Cairo Documents*, New York: Doubleday, 1973, 88.
12 M. Heikal, *Cutting the Lion's Tail*, New York: Arbor House, 1987, 120; M. Heikal, *The Sphinx and the Commissar*, New York: Harper & Row, 1978, 67–68; K. Love, *Suez: The Twice-Fought War*, New York: McGraw-Hill, 1969, 334–335.
13 'Abd al-Fattāḥ Abū al-Faḍl, *Kuntu nā'iban li-ra'īs al-mukhābarāt*, Cairo: Dār al-Ḥurrīyah, 1986, 182–184.
14 H. Jacquin, *Guerre Secrete en Algerie*, Paris: Editions, Olivier Orban, 1977, 139–140n2.
15 R. Faligot and P. Krop, *La Piscine*, Paris: Editions du Seuil, 1985, 152; Black and Morris, *Israel's Secret Wars*, 173; Bar-On, *Gates of Gaza*, 167; Y. Courriere, *Guerre d'Algerie (1954–1957)*, Paris: Robert Laffont, 1990, 749.
16 Jacquin, *La Guerre Secrete*, 139–140; F. Al-Dib, *Nasser et la Revolution Algerienne*, Paris: L'Harmattan, 1985, 171.

17 Courriere, *Guerre d'Algerie (1954–1957)*, 748–749; J. Lacouture, *Nasser*, trans. by D. Hofstadter, New York: Knopf, 1973, 483. French Foreign Minister Christian Pineau told his British counterpart that 'One Successful Battle in Egypt would be Worth Ten in North Africa': S.W. Lucas, *Divided We Stand*, London: Hodder & Stoughton, 1996, 149.

18 Al-Dib, *Nasser et la Revolution Algerienne*, 269–271.

19 L. James, *Nasser at War*, London: Palgrave Macmillan, 2006, 19; A. Hewedy, 'Nasser and the Crisis of 1956' in W. Louis and R. Owen, eds., *Suez 1956*, Oxford: Clarendon Press, 1989, 168–169; Abū al-Faḍl, *Kuntu nā'iban*, 218.

20 James, *Nasser at War*, 19; Sheffy, 'Unconcern at Dawn,' 53n75.

21 K. Muhi al-Din, *Memories of a Revolution*, Cairo: AUC Press, 1995, 255.

22 K. Kyle, *Suez*, New York: St Martin's Press, 1991, 350; Hewedy, 'Nasser and the Crisis of 1956' in Louis and Owen, eds., *Suez 1956*, 169.

23 Love, *Suez*, 466–467.

24 Sheffy, 'Unconcern at Dawn,'31, 54n92.

25 Caroz, *Arab Secret Services*, 75–76.

26 W. Eveland, *Ropes of Sand*, New York: W.W. Norton, 1980, 226; S. Nasr and 'Abd Allah Imam, *Al-Thawrah, Al-Naksah, Al-Mukhabarat*, Cairo: Dar al-Khayyal, 1999, 239; Sheffy, 'Unconcern at Dawn,' 30.

27 Nasr and Imam, *Al-Thawrah*, 236–237, 240, 257.

28 S. Dorril, *MI6*, New York: Free Press, 2000, 610.

29 Dorril, *MI6*, 610; Heikal, *Cairo Documents*, 97–98.

30 Nasr and Imam, *Al-Thawrah*, 240.

31 Heikal, *Cutting the Lion's Tail*, 140.

32 Sheffy, 'Unconcern at Dawn,'17, 19; Heikal, *Cutting the Lion's Tail*, 122, 189.

33 Sheffy, 'Unconcern at Dawn,'21.

34 Heikal, *Cairo Documents*, 86, 105; P. Wright, *Spycatcher*, New York: Viking, 1987, 156–157; Telegram from Battle (Cairo) to DOS, no. 3652, 18 April 1965, *Foreign Relations of the United States* (hereafter *FRUS*), 1964–1968, vol. XVIII, no. 208.

35 Love, *Suez*, 483.

36 Heikal, *Cairo Documents*, 105–106.

37 Sheffy, 'Unconcern at Dawn,' 40.

38 Ibid., 8, 15, 18.

39 Ibid., 19.

40 Telegram from Army Attaché (Cairo) to SecState, 17 April 1956, no. CX 103–56, NARA, 774.5/4–1756.

41 Sheffy, 'Unconcern at Dawn,' 19.

42 Telegram from Trevelyan (Cairo) to FO, 29 August 1956, no. 1766, BNA, FO 371/119304; Caroz, *Arab Secret Services*, 26.

43 Lucas, *Divided We Stand*, 101, 193.

44 Bower, *Perfect English Spy*, 197; Dorril, *MI6*, 633.

45 Bower, *Perfect English Spy*, 198; V. Marchetti and J. Marks, *The CIA and the Cult of Intelligence*, New York: Knopf, 1974, 200; C. Andrew, *For the President's Eyes Only*, New York: HarperPerennial,1995, 235.

46 Sheffy, 'Unconcern at Dawn,'33–34, 37; Black and Morris, *Israel's Secret Wars*, 131.

47 Lucas, *Divided We Stand*, 233.

48 Heikal, *Cairo Documents*, 105–106.

49 L. Nordeen and D. Nicolle, *Phoenix over the Nile*, Washington, DC: Smithsonian, 1996, 159.

50 Sheffy, 'Unconcern at Dawn,'7.

51 Heikal, *Cutting the Lion's Tail*, 179.

52 Nutting, *Nasser*, 169.

53 Heikal, *Cairo Documents*, 114.

54 Lucas, *Divided We Stand*, 273.
55 Caroz, *Arab Secret Services*, 94.
56 Love, *Suez*, 598; 'Leading Personalities in Arab Republic of Egypt 1972,' FCO 39/1205; Kyle, *Suez*, 455; Abū al-Faḍl, *Kuntu nā'iban*, 184–186, 204.
57 Heikal, *Cutting the Lion's Tail*, 188; S. Blackwell, 'Saving the King: Anglo-American Strategy and British Counter-subversion Operations in Libya, 1953–59,' *MES*, 39, 2003, 5; Caroz, *Arab Secret Services*, 81–82. SIS apparently had some foreknowledge of Egypt's subversive plan for Libya: Lucas, *Divided We Stand*, 183.
58 Airgram from Heath (Beirut) to DOS, 'Wave of Bomb Incidents in Lebanon,' 4 December 1956, no. 237, NARA, 783A.00/12–456 HBS; Telegram from Heath (Beirut) to SecState, 23 November 1956, no. 1315, NARA, 783A.00/11–2356.
59 Quoted in Lucas, *Divided We Stand*, 219.
60 Little, 'Mission Impossible,' 682.
61 Eveland, *Ropes of Sand*, 244–248; Little, 'Mission Impossible,' 682; R. Parker, *The Politics of Miscalculation in the Middle East*, Bloomington: Indiana University Press, 1993, 02, 253n1.
62 S. Aburish, *Nasser*, New York: Thomas Dunne, 2004, 127; Nutting, *Nasser*, 202.
63 Telegram from Hare (Cairo) to SecState, 29 May 1957, no. 3627, NARA, 774.11/5–2957.
64 Telegram from Hare (Cairo) to SecState, 2 July 1957, no. 22, NARA, 774.11/7–257.
65 Dorril, *MI6*, 659; Airgram from Ross (Cairo) to DOS, 'Monarchy Conspiracy Case,' 10 May 1958, no. 1108, NARA, 774.00/5–1058; 'S/Ldr. Khalil had a choice of 6 plots,' *Egyptian Gazette*, 16 November 1958, BNA, FO 371/134004.
66 Telegram from Washburn (Alexandria) to SecState, 20 December 1956, no. 312, NARA, 874.411/12–2056.
67 Telegram from Cuomo (Port Said) to SecState, 15 January 1957, no. 112, NARA, 774.00/1–1557, HBS; Telegram from Cuomo (Port Said) to SecState, 16 January 1957, no. 113, NARA, 774.00/1–1657; Telegram from Dulles to (DOS) to various American Embassies, 15 January 1957, no. 605, NARA, 774.551/1–1557 CS/F; R. Stephens, *Nasser*, New York: Simon & Schuster, 1971, 245; Telegram from Washburn (Alexandria), 20 December 1956, no. 312; Shields, 'Jewish Refugees from Arab Countries,'3.
68 Airgram from Schnee (Cairo) to DOS, 'Public Security Sections of GOE Penal Code Amended,' 19 June 1957, no. 1000, NARA, 774.34/6–1957.
69 Ibid.
70 Nasr and Imam, *Al-Thawrah*, 44–45, 47.
71 S. Nasr, *Muddakirat: al-Juz' al-Awwal*, Cairo: Dar al-Khayyal, 1999, 421–422.
72 Among 'Ali Sabri's tasks was to serve as Nasser's Suez crisis liaison to the CIA: Lucas, *Divided We Stand*, 217.
73 Nasr and Imam, *Al-Thawrah*, 57, 59. Nasser told Salah Nasr: 'I need you to revive (*taruh*) the General Intelligence': Salah Nasr, *Muddakirat, al-juz' al-awwal*, 422.
74 Nasr, *Muddakirat, al-juz' al-awwal*, 422.
75 Nasr and Imam, *Al-Thawrah*, 59.
76 Ibid., 57–59.
77 Among Nasr's output: *Tarikh al-Mukhabarat*, Cairo: Dar al-Khayyal, 2002 and *Muddakirat*.
78 Nasr and Imam, *Al-Thawrah*, 70.
79 Nasr and Imam, *Al-Thawrah*, 65–66.
80 Airgram from Battle (Cairo) to DOS, 'Salah Nasr Writes a Book,' 2 March 1967, no. A-729, NARA, Box 2553, POL 6 UAR.
81 Ibid.
82 Nasr and Imam, *Al-Thawrah*, 63.
83 Nutting, *Nasser*, 224–225.
84 Nasr and Imam, *Al-Thawrah*, 64.

85 Nasr, *Muddakirat: al-Juz' al-Awwal*, 33.
86 Nasr and Imam, *Al-Thawrah*, 111.


6 Unity, subversion and secession

1 Quoted in K. Kyle, *Suez*, New York: St Martin's Press, 1991, 106.
2 H. Trevelyan, *Middle East in Revolution*, London: Macmillan, 1970, 87; D. Neff, *Warriors at Suez*, New York: Linden Press, 1981, 82–83; K. Muhi al-Din, *Memories of a Revolution*, Cairo: AUC Press, 1995, 45.
3 A. Nutting, *Nasser*, New York: E.P. Dutton, 1972, 304; M. Copeland, *Game of Nations*, New York: Simon & Schuster, 1969, 172–173.
4 Muhi al-Din, *Memories*, 240.
5 Trevelyan, *Middle East in Revolution*, 88–89.
6 Muhi al-Din, *Memories*, 240.
7 Ibid., 241.
8 F. Abdel-Khaliq, 'Memories of High Tide,' *Al-Ahram Weekly*, 15–21 January 2004. Online, available at: http://weekly.ahram.org.eg/print/2004/673/bo1.htm, accessed 1 October 2006.
9 M. Heikal, *Autumn of Fury*, London: Corgi, 1978, 46–47.
10 J. Barron, *KGB: The Secret Work of Soviet Secret Agents*, New York: Bantam, 1981, 69–71.
11 J. Badeau, *The Middle East Remembered*, Washington, DC: Middle East Institute, 1983, 229.
12 C. Andrew and O. Gordievsky, *KGB: The Inside Story*, New York: HarperCollins, 1990, 496–497; Y. Caroz, *Arab Secret Services*, London: Corgi, 1978, 66; Barron, *KGB*, 69–71; Airgram from Parker (Cairo) to Amcongen Marseille, 'Biographic Data: Abdel Kader Khalil – New UAR Consul General at Marseille,' no. A-125, 11 August 1965, NARA, Box 2766, POL 17 UAR-FR.
13 Quoted in C. Andrew and V. Mitrokhin, *The World Was Going Our Way*, New York: Basic Books, 2005, 146.
14 L. James, *Nasser at War*, London: Palgrave Macmillan, 2006, 2.
15 Andrew and Mitrokhin, *World*, 148–149.
16 S. Nasr, *Muddakirat Al-Juz' al-Thani*, Cairo: Dar al-Khayyal, 1999, 107. Serov gave Nasr an antique Caucasian sword adding that he hoped Egypt would use it defeat the 'imperialists.'
17 Andrew and Mitrokhin, *World*, 148–149; Barron, *KGB*, 69–71.
18 Caroz, *Arab Secret Services*, 66; Barron, *KGB*, 69–71; Airgram from Bruce (London) to DOS, '*Sunday Telegraph* on Egypt's Spy Network,' 6 December 1966, A-1328, NARA, Box 2765, POL 23–6 UAR.
19 Quoted in H. Womack, ed., *Undercover Lives: Soviet Spies in the Cities of the World*, London: Weidenfeld and Nicolson, 1998, 55.
20 Ibid., 57, 60–63, 69–73.
21 P. Seale, *Struggle for Syria*, New York: Oxford University Press, 1965, 281.
22 Nasr, *Muddakirat al-Juz' al-Thani*, 146.
23 Caroz, *Arab Secret Services*, 113, 269.
24 Nasr, *Muddakirat al-Juz' al-Thani*, 146.
25 Nutting, *Nasser*, 193–194.
26 Airgram from Thacher (Baghdad) to DOS, 'Publication of Nasser's Speech Revealing Egyptian Tactics,' 10 July 1957, no. 42, NARA, 774.11/7–1057. Questions remain about the authenticity of this speech: Caroz, *Arab Secret Services*, 426n29. Still, the speech rings true to the mood and method of Egyptian covert action at this time.
27 J. Tusan, 'Propagande et Orientation Nationale en Egypte,' *Orient*, 1, 1957, 132.
28 Quoted in Tusan, 142.
29 King Hussein, *Uneasy Lies the Head*, London: Heinemann, 1962, 195.

30  S. Shpiro, 'Intelligence Services and Political Transformation in the Middle East,' *IJIC*, 17, 2004–2005, 579.
31  King Hussein, *Uneasy Lies the Head*, 174–175.
32  Ellis, 'Nasser's Other Voice,' *Harper's Magazine*, 22, 1961, 54.
33  Copeland, *Game of Nations*, 232–233.
34  Nutting, *Nasser*, 232; A. Rathmell, 'Brotherly Enemies: The Rise and Fall of the Syrian–Egyptian Intelligence Axis, 1954–1967,' *INS*, 13, 1998, 237.
35  'A List of Reports Received by the US Government Bearing on UAR Intervention in Lebanon, May–June 1958,' Paper submitted by Under Secretary of State Christian Herter to the Senate Foreign Relations Committee, DDRS, 78–210, Eisenhower Library, James Hagerty Papers, Box 7, Middle East (Lebanon) 1958; M. Fry, 'The Uses of Intelligence: The United Nations Confronts the United States in the Lebanon Crisis, 1958,' *INS*, 10, 1995, 64; Y. Sayigh, 'Reconstructing the Paradox,' *MEJ*, 45, 1991, 613; Airgram from McClintock (Beirut) to DOS, 'Lebanon-United Arab Republic Relations,' 4 June 1958, no. 696, NARA, 683A.86/6–458; Nasr, *Muddakirat Al-Juz' al-Thani*, 111–113.
36  Quoted in Fry, 'The Uses of Intelligence,' 73.
37  Nutting, *Nasser*, 242.
38  Salah Nasr asserts that while Nasser knew a revolution was being planned in Iraq he was not aware of the role Qasim would play in it: *Muddakirat Al-Juz' al-Thani*, 113.
39  M. Heikal, *Cairo Documents*, New York: Doubleday, 1973, 96, 129.
40  Quoted in Ellis, 'Nasser's Other Voice,' 56.
41  Nasr, *Muddakirat al-Juz' al-Thani*, 118, 122.
42  Nutting, *Nasser*, 255; M. Kerr, *The Arab Cold War*, New York: Oxford University Press, 1971, 17–18.
43  Nutting, *Nasser*, 260–261.
44  Caroz, *Arab Secret Services*, 94–95.
45  Nutting, *Nasser*, 257, 260–261; Caroz, *Arab Secret Services*, 97–99; M. Heikal, *The Sphinx and The Commissar*, New York: Harper & Row, 1978, 106–107.
46  A. Rathmell, *Secret War in the Middle East: The Covert Struggle for Syria, 1949–1961*, London: I.B. Tauris, 1995, 156.
47  Caroz, *Arab Secret Services*, 101; Y. Aboul-Enein, 'Spymaster: Former Egyptian Intelligence Chief Discusses Psychological Warfare,' *Infantry*, 2006.
48  Telegram from Caffery (Cairo) to DOS, 'Egyptian View on Potential Results of Saudi–Egyptian Military Cooperation,' 30 June 1954, no. 2997, NARA, 674.86A/6–3054.
49  Airgram from Jenkins (Jidda) to DOS, 'Growth of Egyptian Influence in Saudi Arabia,' 5 September 1956, no. 59, NARA, 674.86A/9–556.
50  Quoted in D. Boyd, 'Development of Egypt's Radio: 'Voice of the Arabs' under Nasser,' *Journalism Quarterly*, 52, 1975, 652.
51  Ibid.
52  Airgram from Houghton (Jidda) to DOS, 'Further Information on Recent Riyadh Incident,' 12 June 1957, no. 291, NARA, 674.86A/6–1257; K. Wheelock, *Nasser's New Egypt*, New York: Praeger, 1960, 255–256; Airgram from Houghton (Jidda) to DOS, 'Discovery of Arms Cache in Riyadh and its Implications to Saudi–Egyptian Relations,' 23 May 1957, no. 273, NARA, 674.86A/5–2357.
53  Caroz, *Arab Secret Services*, 251,252; D. Little, 'Mission Impossible: The CIA and the Cult of Covert Action in the Middle East,' *Diplomatic History*, 28, 2004, 682–683.
54  C. Jones, *Britain and the Yemen Civil War, 1962–1965*, Portland, OR: Sussex Academic Press, 2004, 33.
55  D. Raviv and Y. Melman, *Every Spy A Prince*, Boston: Houghton-Mifflin, 1990, 151–152; Caroz, *Arab Secret Services*, 125, 128.
56  M. Bar-Zohar, *Spies in the Promised Land*, trans. by M. Stearns, Boston: Houghton-Mifflin, 1972, 158–163.

57 Airgram from Clark (Alexandria) to DOS, '1) Treatment of Dr Fritz Katz and Mr. Rashid Rizk, who are charged with complicity in Israeli spy case; 2) Criticism of General Investigations Department (GID) Director Mamduh Salem,' 11 May 1960, no. 246, NARA, 786B.5284A/5–1160; Airgram from Close (Alexandria) to DOS, 'Progress in the Trial of Suspects Allegedly Implicated in Israeli Espionage,' 26 August 1960, no. 28, NARA, 786B.00/8–260; Correspondence from UK Diplomatic Mission in Cairo to FO, 25 April 1960, BNA, FO 371/165349.
58 Airgram from Clark (Alexandria) to DOS, 11 May 1960.
59 Airgram from Clark (Alexandria) to DOS, 'Views of U.A.R. High Court Judge Mohamed Issawi on Trial of Suspects Allegedly Implicated in Israeli Espionage,' 23 May 1960, no. 257, NARA, 786B.5284A/5–2360.
60 Bar-Zohar, *Spies*, 218,220; I. Black and B. Morris, *Israel's Secret Wars*, New York: Grove, 1991, 206–207; Caroz, *Arab Secret Services*, 120; Correspondence from British Embassy (Cairo) to North and East African Department, FO, 29 April 1961, BNA, FO 371/165349.
61 Bar-Zohar, *Spies*, 218–220; Raviv and Melman, *Every Spy A Prince*, 139.
62 Bar-Zohar, *Spies*, 222; Raviv and Melman, *Every Spy A Prince*, 139.
63 Airgram from American Embassy (Cairo) to DOS, 'Joint Weeka no. 18,' 4 May 1961, no. 888, NARA, 786B.00(W)/5–461.
64 Telegram from Jones (Port Said) to DOS, 'Biographic Directory, Port Said Consular District,' 7 January 1955, no. 35, NARA, 774.521/1–755,.
65 Copeland, *Game of Nations*, 96–98.
66 W. Lotz, *Champagne Spy*, New York: St Martin's, 1972, 21.
67 Airgram from Clark (Alexandria) to DOS, 'Arrests in Alexandria of Greeks and Other Foreigners; a British Subject and a Cypriot also Involved,' 6 September 1961, no. 46, NARA, 786B.00/9–661.
68 Ibid.
69 Nasr, *Muddakirat al-Juz' al-Thani*, 107.
70 'Retired Officer Recounts Experience in Fighting Communism,' *Akhbar al-Yawm*, 29 March 1980, Joint Publications Research Service (hereafter JPRS), no. 2130, 29 March 1980.
71 'Retired Officer Recounts Experience in Fighting Communism'; A. Abdel-Malek, *Egypte Societe Militaire*, Paris: Editions du Seuil, 1962, 130; J. Beinin, 'The Communist Movement and Nationalist Political Discourse in Nasirist Egypt,' *MEJ*, 41, 1987, 582.
72 Quoted in G. Perrault, *A Man Apart*, trans. by Bob Cumming, London: Zed Books, 1994, 201.
73 'Retired Officer Recounts Experience in Fighting Communism,' Musaylihi: 'If you study the Communists profoundly, you will find in them complexes, deformities and family reasons that make them ready to accept Communism. They are either agents or social malcontents.'
74 Quoted in Wheelock, *Nasser's New Egypt*, 275.
75 Nasr, *Muddakirat al-Juz' al-Thani*, 146.
76 Ibid., 171–173.
77 Ibid., 172.
78 Telegram from American Consulate General (Damascus) to SecState, 28 September 1961, NARA, 786B.00/9–2861; Telegram from Badeau (Cairo) to SecState, 28 September 1961, no. 587, NARA, 786B.00/9–2861.
79 Airgram from American Embassy (Cairo) to DOS, 'Joint Weeka no. 40,' 5 October 1961, no. 176, NARA, 786B.00(W)/10–561; Circular Telegram from the Department of State to Certain Near Eastern Posts, no. 636, 3 October 1961, *FRUS*, 1961–1963, vol. XVII, Document 118.

## 7 Intelligence and the Yemen Wars

1 F. Al-Dib, *'Abd al-Nasir wa-haraka al-Tahrir al-Yemeni*, Cairo: Dar al-Mustaqbal al-Arabi, 1990, 20–24.
2 J. Walker, *Aden Insurgency*, Staplehurst: Spellmount, 2005, 11.
3 Al-Dib, *'Abd al-Nasir wa-haraka al-Tahrir al-Yemeni*, 22.
4 C. Jones, *Britain and the Yemen Civil War*, Portland: Sussex Academic Press, 2004, 33.
5 S. Dorril, *MI6*, New York: Free Press, 2001, 678.
6 Airgram from Kidder (Paris) to DOS, 'French Analysis of Nasser's Attempts at Subversion in Other Arab States,' 14 August 1962, no. A-361, NARA, 786B.5286/8–1462.
7 Memorandum from Director of the Bureau of Intelligence and Research (Hilsman) to SecState Rusk, 'Intelligence Note: Pro-Nasser Army Coup Plot in the Yemen,' *FRUS*, 1961–1963, vol. X III, Doc. 38.
8 L. James, *Whose Voice? Nasser, the Arabs, and 'Sawt al-Arab' Radio*. Online, available at: www.tbsjournal.com/jamespf.html, accessed 1 April 2007; D.A. Schmidt, *Yemen: The Unknown War*, New York: Holt, Rinehart and Winston, 1968, 71; Memorandum from Director of the Bureau of Intelligence and Research (Hilsman) 'Intelligence Note: Pro-Nasser Army Coup Plot in the Yemen.'
9 Stephens, *Nasser*, 380; M. Fawzi, 'The Three-Year War,' *Al-Ahram Weekly Online*, 5–11 June 1997. Online, available at: http://weekly.ahram.org.eg/archives/67–97/sup8.htm, accessed 8 September 2007; Aboul-Enein, 'The Egyptian–Yemen War'; D. Witty, 'A Regular Army in Counterinsurgency Operations: Egypt in North Yemen, 1962–1967,' *Journal of Military History*, 65, 2001, 412.
10 Telegram from Battle (Cairo) to SecState, 18 March 1966, no. 2368, NARA, Box 2764, POL 15–1 UAR; Stephens, *Nasser*, 424.
11 Y. Aboul-Enein, 'The Egyptian–Yemen War (1962–67): Egyptian Perspectives on Guerrilla Warfare,' *Infantry*, 2004; M. Kerr, *The Arab Cold War*, New York: Oxford University Press, 1971, 107.
12 Aboul-Enein, 'The Egyptian–Yemen War (1962–67)'; R. Stephens, *Nasser*, New York: Simon & Schuster, 1971, 390.
13 Aboul-Enein, 'The Egyptian–Yemen War'; A. Nutting *Nasser*, New York: E.P. Dutton, 1972, 318–319.
14 Aboul-Enein, 'The Egyptian–Yemen War.'
15 J. Badeau, *The Middle East Remembered*, Washington, DC: Middle East Institute, 1983, 199; Nutting, *Nasser*, 321.
16 Stephens, *Nasser*, 424; Telegram from Battle (Cairo), 18 March 1966.
17 M. Heikal, *Autumn of Fury*, London: Corgi, 1986, 41; Aboul-Enein, 'The Egyptian–Yemen War.'
18 Aboul-Enein, 'The Egyptian–Yemen War'; Schmidt, *Yemen*, 186.
19 K. Pollack, *Arabs at War*, Lincoln: University of Nebraska Press, 2002, 49; Rahmy, *Egyptian Policy in the Arab World*, 157; Witty, 'A Regular Army,'401, 408.
20 Witty, 'A Regular Army,'408.
21 Quoted in Witty, 'A Regular Army,'419n9.
22 Ali Abdel Rahman Rahmy, *The Egyptian Policy in the Arab World: Intervention in Yemen*, Washington, DC: University Press of America, 1983, 156–157; A. McGregor, *A Military History of Modern Egypt*, Westport: Praeger, 2006, 261; Aboul-Enein, 'The Egyptian–Yemen War'; Witty, 'A Regular Army,'410.
23 Witty, 'A Regular Army,' 409; Aboul-Enein, 'The Egyptian–Yemen War'; Telegram from Battle (Cairo) to DOS, no. 1311, 24 November 1965, *FRUS*, 1964–1968, vol. XVIII; Heikal, *Autumn*, 41.
24 Schmidt, *Yemen*, 115–116; Telegram from Badeau (Cairo) to SecState, 3 May 1964, no. 2585, NARA, DDRS, Lyndon Baines Johnson Library; Pollack, *Arabs at War*, 54.

25  Schmidt, *Yemen*, 281–282; Airgram from Slackiston (Jidda) to DOS, 'Yemen Royalist Treatment of Egyptian Prisoners,' 9 February 1965, no. A-220, NARA, Box 2766, POL 29 UAR; Witty, 'A Regular Army,'412; McGregor, *A Military History*, 263.
26  CIA, Special Report, 'Nasir's Arab Policy – The Latest Phase,' 28 August 1964, no. 00634/64A, DDRS.
27  Telegram from Badeau (Cairo) to DOS, no. 121, 11 July 1963, *FRUS*, 1961–1963, vol. XVIII, Document 294; Telegram from Badeau (Cairo) to DOS, no. 904, 21 October 1963, *FRUS*, 1961–1963, vol. XVIII, Document 348; Airgram from Bergus (Cairo) to DOS, 'Haikal Boasts of UAR's Intelligence Capabilities,' 26 January 1963, no. A-581, NARA, 786B.52/1–2663. Most royalist communications were by runner due to a lack of communications equipment. Couriers limited the ability of the Egyptians to intercept royalist communications: D. Smiley, *Arabian Assignment*, London: Leo Cooper, 1975, 132.
28  Schmidt, *Yemen*, 58–59; Memorandum from the Executive Secretary of the DOS (Read) to the President's Special Assistant for National Security Affairs (Bundy), 'Rising Tensions Among Officials in Aden and Latest Report on European Mercenaries Fighting with Yemeni 'Royalists,'' 8 May 1964, *FRUS*, 1964–1968, vol. XXI, Document 58; Smiley, *Arabian Assignment*, 216–217.
29  Witty, 'A Regular Army,'412; Schmidt, *Yemen*, 208.
30  Smiley, *Arabian Assignment*, 132, 144.
31  Rahmy, *Egyptian Policy*, 156–157.
32  Jones, *Britain and the Yemen Civil War*, 119.
33  T. Bower, *The Perfect English Spy*, New York: St Martin's, 1995, 251; Walker, *Aden Insurgency*, 50–51; Dorril, *MI6*, 689.
34  Dorril, *MI6*, 689.
35  Airgram from Battle (Cairo) to DOS, 'Biographic Data on Col. Mohammed Shawqat – Designated UAR Military Attaché, Baghdad,' 3 August 1966, no. A-78, NARA, Box 2766, POL 6 UAR.
36  Jones, *Britain and the Yemen Civil War*, 116; Walker, *Aden Insurgency*, 126–127.
37  Walker, *Aden Insurgency*, 126–127; Bower, *Perfect English Spy*, 246; Jones, *Britain and the Yemen Civil War*, 116.
38  Dorril, *MI6*, 698.
39  D. Boyd, 'Development of Egypt's Radio: 'Voice of the Arabs' under Nasser,' *Journalism Quarterly*, 52, 1975, 652.
40  Clive Jones, *Britain and the Yemen Civil War*, 61.
41  Abdel Magid Farid, *Nasser: The Final Years*, Reading: Ithaca Press, 1994, 157–158. Farid notes that Nasser later transferred the Saudi portfolio to EGIS.
42  S. Badeeb, *The Saudi–Egyptian Conflict over North Yemen, 1962–1970*, Boulder: Westview Press, 1986, 39–40.
43  Ibid., 39.
44  Airgram from Eilts (Jidda) to DOS, 'Statement on Bombings by Saudi Ministry of Interior,' 17 January 1967, no. A-231, NARA; CIA, 'Egyptian–Saudi Tensions,' no date. Online, available at: www.foia.cia.gov, accessed 27 September 2006.
45  Walker, *Aden Insurgency*, 60.
46  Memorandum from William J. Handley (State/NEA) to Acting SecState, 'Arrests of UAR Army Officers,' 19 April 1966, NARA, Box 2766, POL 29 UAR.
47  Ibid.
48  Memorandum from Handley (State/NEA), 'Arrests of UAR Army Officers'; Airgram from Battle (Cairo) to DOS, 'Another Plot against Nasser,' 10 May 1966, no. A-940, NARA, Box 2765, POL 15–1 UAR.
49  Quoted in Airgram from Battle (Cairo) to DOS, 'Nasser's Threat to Saudi Arabia,' 7 May 1966, no. A-927, NARA, Box 2765, POL 15–1 UAR.
50  Memorandum from Handley (State/NEA), 'Arrests of UAR Army Officers.'
51  Witty, 'A Regular Army,'315.

52  Nutting, *Nasser*, 373; Airgram from Battle (Cairo), 'Salah Nasr Writes a Book,' 2 March 1967.
53  S. Nasr and 'Abd Allah Imam, *Al-Thawrah, Al-Naksah, Al-Mukhabarat*, Cairo: Dar al-Khayyal, 1999, 198; Telegram from Bruce (London) to SecState, 7 October 1964, no. 1619, NARA, Box 2765, POL 23–7 UAR; Walker, *Aden Insurgency*, 72.
54  Airgram from Bruce (London), '*Sunday Telegraph* on Egypt's Spy Network,' 6 December 1966.
55  CIA, Special Memorandum, 'Outlook for Aden and the Federation of South Arabia,' 5 November 1965, no. 26–65, *FRUS*, 1964–1968, vol. XXI, Document 67; Clive Jones, 'Among Ministers, Mavericks and Mandarins: Britain, Covert Action and the Yemen Civil War, 1962–64,' *MES*, 40, 2004, 100; Walker, *Aden Insurgency*, 73, 77; S. Mawby, 'The Clandestine Defence of Empire: British Special Operations in Yemen 1951–1964,' *INS* 17, 2002, 121.
56  Mawby, 'The Clandestine Defence of Empire,' 122–123; Jones, 'Among Ministers, Mavericks and Mandarins,' 106.
57  Smiley, *Arabian Assignment*, 114; Mawby, 'The Clandestine Defence of Empire,' 108.
58  Jones, 'Among Ministers, Mavericks and Mandarins,' 110; Walker, *Aden Insurgency*, 141, 143; Airgram from Bruce (London), '*Sunday Telegraph* on Egypt's Spy Network'; CIA, Intelligence Memorandum, 'The Security Situation in Aden,' 9 June 1965, OCI no. 1812/65, *FRUS*, 1964–1968, vol. XXI, Document 61.
59  CIA, Intelligence Memorandum, 'The Security Situation in Aden'; CIA, Special Memorandum, 'Outlook for Aden and the Federation of South Arabia.' The quotation is found in Walker, *Aden Insurgency*, 141–142.
60  Correspondence from A.W. Cowper, Chief of Intelligence, Intelligence Centre, Aden, to R.M. Blaikley, Colonial Office, 5 July 1965, BNA, FO 371/183963, 183964, 183965.
61  Ibid.
62  Witty, 'A Regular Army,' 415; Nutting, *Nasser*, 373.
63  OLOS was created in 1965 with Egyptian intelligence aid as the fighting wing of the Popular Socialist Party: H. Lackner, *P.D.R. Yemen: Outpost of Socialist Development in Arabia*, London: Ithaca Press, 1985, 31, 43; Walker, *Aden Insurgency*, 176; H. Trevelyan, *The Middle East in Revolution*, London: Macmillan, 1970, 218.
64  Walker, *Aden Insurgency*, 59, 210; Airgram from Rusk (DOS) to Amembassy Lome, 'UAR Charge d'Affaires in Lome 'Attiya Mahmud 'Attiya,' 3 November 1967, no. CA-3359, NARA, POL-17 UAR-TOGO; Paper Prepared in the Department of State, 'Future of South Arabia,' no date, *FRUS*, 1964–1968, vol. XXI, Document 97; CIA, Intelligence Memorandum, 'South Arabian Dissident and Federal Armed Forces,' 9 March 1967, no. 0797/67, *FRUS*, 1964–1968, vol. XXI, Document 86; Memorandum from W. Howard Wriggins of the National Security Council Staff to the President's Special Assistant (Rostow), 'Arabian Peninsula,' 6 March 1967, *FRUS*, 1964–1968, vol. XXI, Document 85.
65  Circular Telegram from Rusk (DOS) to Certain Posts, no. 184507, 28 April 1967, *FRUS*, 1964–1968, vol. XXI, Document 441; Memorandum for Walt. W. Rostow, the White House, from B. Read, Executive Secretary, DOS, 4 May 1967, NARA, Box 2554, POL 15–1 UAR; Heikal, *The Cairo Documents*, 240.
66  Telegram from Rusk (DOS) to Amembassy Cairo, no. 187506, 4 May 1967, *FRUS*, 1964–1968, vol. XXI, Document 444.
67  Memorandum from the President's Special Assistant (Rostow) to President Johnson, 'Our Latest Brush with Nasser,' 10 May 1967, *FRUS*, 1964–1968, vol. XVIII, Document no. 417.
68  Ibid.
69  M. Wolf and A. McElvoy, *Man without a Face*, New York: Times Books, 1997, 264–265.

## 8 The Intelligence State

1 Annual Report by the British Air Attaché (Cairo), 14 January 1964, BNA, FO 371/179863.
2 Memorandum of Conversation, 'U.A.R. Activities in Iran (Two of two),' 12 March 1962, NARA, 686B.88/3–1262; Telegram from Badeau (Cairo) to SecState, 12 March 1962, no. 1329, NARA, 686B.88/3–1262; R. Stephens, *Nasser*, New York: Simon & Schuster, 1971, 241; S. Dorril, *MI6*, New York: Free Press, 2001, 690–691.
3 CIA, Intelligence Memorandum, 'The Arab Threat to Iran,' 21 May 1966, no. 1355/66, *FRUS*, 1964–1968, vol. XXII, Document 139.
4 Memorandum of Conversation, 'U.A.R. Activities in Iran (Two of two)'; Telegram from Schwartz (Cairo) to DOS, 'UAR–Iranian Propaganda Exchange and the Clandestine Radio *Free Voice of Iran*,' 31 March 1962, no. 442, NARA, 686B.88/3–3162; Telegram from Badeau (Cairo) to SecState, 12 March 1962.
5 Memorandum of Conversation, 'U.A.R. Activities in Iran (Two of two)'; Telegram from Badeau (Cairo) to SecState, 15 March 1962, no. 1342, NARA, 686B.88/3–1562; Telegram from Badeau (Cairo) to SecState, 17 March 1962, no. 1347, NARA, 686B.88/3–1762; Telegram from Badeau (Cairo) to SecState, 13 July 1962, no. 87, NARA, 686B.88/7–1362; Correspondence from A. Rumbold (Paris) to FO, 28 November 1961, BNA, FO 371/158864; Memorandum from V.H. Krulak of the Office of the Special Assistant for Counterinsurgency and Special Activities of the Joint Chiefs of Staff to the Chairman of the Joint Chiefs of Staff (Taylor), 'Subversive Insurgency in Iran,' SACSA-M 349–63, 13 June 1963, *FRUS*, 1961–1963, vol. XVIII, Document 271, 583–586; CIA, Intelligence Memorandum, 'The Shah of Iran and His Policies,' 5 June 1967, no. 1117/67, *FRUS*, 1964–1968, vol. XXII, Document 206; Telegram from American Embassy (Karachi) to SecState, 10 October 1964, no. 744, NARA, Box 2763, POL 9 UAR.
6 G.A. Nasser, *Egypt's Liberation: the Philosophy of the Revolution*, Washington, DC: Public Affairs Press, 1956, 110.
7 CIA, Special Memorandum, 'Nasser's Policy and Prospects in Black Africa,' no. 1–64, 9 January 1964. Online, available at: www.cia.gov, accessed 29 January 2006; S. Nasr and 'Abd Allah Imam, *Al-Thawrah, Al-Naksah, Al-Mukhabarat*, Cairo: Dar al-Khayyal, 1999, 125–126; A. Nutting, *Nasser*, New York: E.P. Dutton, 1972, 290; D. Raviv and Y. Melman, *Every Spy a Prince*, Boston: Houghton Mifflin, 1990, 153; I. Black and B. Morris, *Israel's Secret Wars*, New York: Grove, 1991, 186; Z. Levey, 'Israel's Strategy in Africa, 1961–67,' *International Journal of Middle East Studies*, 36, 2004, 78.
8 CIA, Special Memorandum, 'Nasser's Policy and Prospects in Black Africa'; K. Wheelock, *Nasser's New Egypt*, New York: Praeger, 1960, 254.
9 M. Copeland, *Game of Nations*, New York: Simon & Schuster, 1969, 190; D. Neff, *Warriors for Jerusalem*, New York: Simon & Schuster, 1984, 192; Airgram from Nes (Cairo) to DOS, 'The New UAR Cabinet,' 17 September 1966, no. A-206, NARA, Box 2764, POL 15–1 UAR; Airgram from Battle (Cairo) to DOS, 'New Minister of National Guidance Remains Nasser's Afro-Asian Minister,' 26 October 1966, no. A-373, NARA, Box 2764, POL 15–1 UAR; Airgram from Mautner (Khartoum) to DOS, 'Conversations with Tunisian Charge d'Affaires regarding Egyptian–Communist Activities in the Sudan,' 9 December 1964, no. A-226, NARA, Box 2763, POL 12 UAR.
10 J. Lefebvre, 'The United States and Egypt: Confrontation and Accommodation in Northeast Africa, 1956–60,' *MES*, 29, 1993, 323–324; Levey, 'Israel's Strategy in Africa,' 73; Raviv and Melman, *Every Spy a Prince*, 85.
11 D. Pool, *From Guerrillas to Government*, Athens, OH: Ohio University Press, 2001, 49–51.
12 Those grievances centered in part on the disputed Ogaden desert.

13 H. Bigart, 'Selassie Charges Egyptians Try Subversion in Ethiopia,' *NYT*, 16 February 1957, 1; Y. Caroz, *The Arab Secret Services*, London: Corgi, 1978, 82; Airgram from Korry (Addis Ababa) to DOS, 'Ministry of Foreign Affairs Tightens Controls on Assignment of Foreign Military Attachés to Ethiopia,' 31 March 1967, no. A-737, NARA; Airgram from Bruce (London) to DOS, '*Sunday Telegraph* on Egypt's Spy Network,' 6 December 1966.

14 Telegram from Timberlake (Leopoldville) to DOS, no. 1006, 19 October 1960, *FRUS*, 1958–1960, vol. XIV, Document 245; Airgram from American Embassy (Cairo) to DOS, 'Joint Weeka no. 32,' 12 August 1960, no. 109, NARA, 786B.00(W)/8–1260; Airgram from American Embassy (Cairo) to DOS, 'Joint Weeka no. 34,' 26 August 1960, no. 134, NARA, 786B.00(W)/8–2660.

15 Nutting, *Nasser*, 288–292; CIA, Intelligence Memorandum, 'Situation in the Congo,' 9 February 1962, DDRS, LBJ Library; L. Nordeen and D. Nicolle, *Phoenix Over the Nile*, Washington, DC: Smithsonian Press, 1996, 187; CIA, Weekly Report, 'The Situation in the Congo,' 24 February 1965, no. 00778/65, DDRS, LBJ Library; CIA, Weekly Report, 'The Situation in the Congo,' 7 April 1965, no. 00784/65, DDRS, LBJ Library.

16 Editorial Note, *FRUS*, 1964–1968, vol. XXVIII, Document 1.

17 Memorandum of Conversation, '1) US–UAR Relations, etc.,' 31 December 1964, *FRUS*, 1964–1968, vol. XVIII, Document 117; Telegram from Rusk (DOS) to Amembassy Cairo, no. 4008, 12 January 1965, *FRUS*, 1964–1968, vol. XVIII, Document 120; Telegram from Battle (Cairo) to DOS, no. 2671, 1 February 1965, *FRUS*, 1964–1968, vol. XVIII, Document 132.

18 Telegram from Rusk (DOS) to Amembassy Cairo, no. 6049, 2 April 1965, *FRUS*, 1964–1968, vol. XVIII, Document 200; CIA, Weekly Report, 'The Situation in the Congo,' 21 April 1965, no. 00786/65, DDRS, LBJ Library.

19 CIA, Intelligence Report, 'Soviet Military Aid to the United Arab Republic, 1955–66,' March 1967, no. RR IR 67–9. Online, available at: www.foia.cia.gov, accessed 29 January 2006.

20 CIA, Intelligence Memorandum, 'Situation in the Congo,' 27 January 1965, DDRS, LBJ Library; Telegram from Battle (Cairo) to SecState, 1 October 1966, no. 1702, NARA, Box 2762, POL 7 UAR; Telegram from Battle (Cairo) to SecState, 18 October 1966, no number, NARA, Box 2762, POL 8 UAR.

21 Telegram from Battle (Cairo) to SecState, 15 February 1966, no. 2077, NARA, Box 2766, POL 17 UAR-MALAWI; Telegram from Battle (Cairo) to SecState, 17 February 1966, no. 2110, NARA, Box 2766, POL MALAWI-UAR.

22 Levey, 'Israel's Strategy in Africa,' 73–74.

23 Ibid., 72, 83.

24 Ghana and Guinea believed Egyptian 'cultural centers' in their countries served as intelligence fronts and shut them down: Airgram from Bruce (London) to DOS, '*Sunday Telegraph* on Egypt's Spy Network.'

25 Y. Sayigh, 'Reconstructing the Paradox: The Arab Nationalist Movement, Armed Struggle, and Palestine, 1951–1966,' *MEJ*, 45, 1991, 623.

26 Caroz, *Arab Secret Services*, 165–172.

27 'The Spy Who Came In from the Trunk,' *Time*, 27 November 1964. Online, available at: www.time.com/printout/0,8816,871392,00.html, accessed 22 March 2007.

28 Airgram from Moline (Cairo) to DOS, 'UAR Diplomatic Trunks,' 19 December 1964, no. A-410, NARA, Box 2765, POL 23–6 UAR.

29 Caroz, *Arab Secret Services*, 147–155; 'The Spy Who Came in from the Trunk,' *Time*; Airgram from Moline (Cairo), 'UAR Diplomatic Trunks'; Raviv and Melman, *Every Spy a Prince*, 140–141.

30 W. Lotz, *The Champagne Spy*, New York: St Martin's, 1972, 24–25.

31 Ibid., 25–26, 59–61.

32 E. Volkman, *Spies: The Secret Agents who Changed the Course of History*, New

York: John Wiley, 1994, 148; Raviv and Melman, *Every Spy a Prince*, 145; S. Steven, *The Spymasters of Israel*, New York: Ballantine, 1980, 200; Telegram from Battle (Cairo) to SecState, 24 September 1964, no. 1009, NARA, Box 2765, POL 23–8 UAR; Airgram from Bergus (Cairo) to DOS, 'Bomb Sent German Scientist,' 24 October 1964, no. A-285, NARA, Box 2765, POL 23–8 UAR.

33 Airgram from Badeau (Cairo) to SecState, 'The UAR in March 1962,' 3 March 1962, no. A-304, NARA, 786B.00/3–362.

34 Correspondence from L.D. Battle, DOS to McGeorge Bundy, The White House, 27 October 1961, NARA; Airgram from Clark (Alexandria) to DOS, 'Sequestrations and G.I.D. Activity Deepen Fear and Anxiety Among Alexandria Residents,' 30 October 1961, no. 75, NARA, 786B.00/10–3061; Telegram from Badeau (Cairo) to SecState, 29 November 1961, no. 904, NARA, 601.5186B/11–2961; Airgram from Clark (Alexandria) to DOS, 'British Consul General Decides Grounds are Insufficient for Protest Against Sequestration of Property of British Head of Alexandria Israelite Community,' 6 November 1961, no. 80, NARA, 786B.00/11–661.

35 K. Beattie, *Egypt during the Nasser Years*, Boulder: Westview Press, 1994, 26.

36 Ibid., 161; S. Aburish, *Nasser: the Last Arab*, New York: Thomas Dunne, 2004, 245–246.

37 J. Lacouture, *Nasser*, trans. by D. Hofstadter, New York: Knopf, 1973, 354–355; A. Nutting, *Nasser*, New York: E.P. Dutton, 1972, 306; Airgram from Bruce (London) to DOS, '*Sunday Telegraph* on Egypt's Spy Network'; T. Plate and A. Darvi, *Secret Police*, Garden City, NY: Doubleday, 1981, 108.

38 Quoted in Beattie, *Egypt during the Nasser Years*, 161.

39 Caroz, *Arab Secret Services*, 182–183; Airgram from Battle (Cairo) to DOS, 'The Arab Socialist Union Displays Continuing Vitality,' 8 July 1966, no. A-10, NARA, Box 2765, POL 15–1 UAR; Airgram from Battle (Cairo) to DOS, 'Nasser as Head of the ASU,' 25 November 1966, no. A-467, NARA, Box 2764, POL 15–1 UAR; Correspondence from Tesh, British Interests Section, Cairo, to Unwin, North and East African Department, FO, 8 December 1966, BNA, FO 371/186303.

40 Beattie, *Egypt during the Nasser Years*, 126.

41 Ibid., 195; M. Oren, *Six Days of War*, New York: Oxford University Press, 2002, 41.

42 G. Kepel, *Muslim Extremism in Egypt*, trans. by J. Rothschild, Berkeley, CA: University of California Press, 1993, 27–29.

43 Ibid., 41–42.

44 Ibid., 20; Airgram from Parker (Cairo) to DOS, 'Qutb Moslem Brotherhood Plot,' 15 March 1966, no. A-761, NARA, Box 2765, POL 23–9 UAR.

45 Airgram from Parker (Cairo), 'Qutb Moslem Brotherhood Plot'; Airgram from Quinlan (Cairo) to DOS, 'Moslem Brotherhood Plot – Cairo Group,' 8 April 1966, no. A-833, NARA, Box 2765, POL 23–9 UAR; L. Wright, *The Looming Tower*, New York: Vintage, 2006, 36.

46 Airgram from Springer (Port Said) to DOS, 'Port Said Governor to Visit Algeria,' 28 February 1967, no. A-51, NARA, POL 7 UAR.

47 Telegram from Battle (Cairo) to SecState, 9 September 1965, no. 690, NARA, Box 2765, POL 23–9 UAR; Airgram from Parker (Cairo), 'Qutb Moslem Brotherhood Plot'; Telegram from Nes (Cairo) to SecState, 17 September 1965, no. 779, NARA, Box 2765, POL 23–9 UAR; Airgram from Springer (Port Said) to DOS, 'Discontent Rising in Canal Zone,' 1 September 1965, no. A-23, NARA, Box 2763, POL 18 UAR.

48 R. Hrair Dekmejian, *Egypt under Nasir*, Albany: SUNY Press, 1971, 232–233.

49 Correspondence from Fletcher, British Interests Section, Cairo, to Unwin, North and East African Department, FO, 30 June 1966, BNA, FO 371/186301; Correspondence from Daniell, British Interests Section, Cairo, to Speares, North and East African Department, FO, 30 June 1966, BNA, FO 371/186301.

50 Correspondence from W.H.G. Fletcher, British Special Interests Section, Canadian Embassy (Cairo) to P.W. Unwin (Foreign Office), no. 1016/660, 25 August 1966, BNA, FO 371/190250.

51 Memorandum of Conversation, '1) US–UAR Relations, etc.,' 31 December 1964; Memorandum of Conversation, 'US Policy Toward UAR,' 21 December 1962, *FRUS*, 1961–1963, vol. XVIII, 269–271; Memorandum from Nicholas G. Thacher to Lewis Jones, 'Call on you by UAR Counselor,' 21 March 1961, NARA, 786B.5211/3–2161; Memorandum from William D. Brewer, (State/NE) to Files, 'UAR Counselor Bagdadi's Efforts to Establish High-Level US–UAR Contact,' 22 March 1961, NARA, 786B.5211/3–2261.

52 J. Badeau, *The Middle East Remembered*, Washington, DC: Middle East Institute, 1983, 220–221.

53 Ibid., 180, 190.

54 Beattie, *Egypt during the Nasser Years*, 58; S. Nasr and 'Abd Allah Imam, *Al-Thawrah, Al-Naksah, Al-Mukhabarat*, Cairo: Dar al-Khayyal, 1999, 221.

55 Caroz, *Arab Secret Services*, 175–176; Airgram from Nes (Cairo) to DOS, 'Amin Case,' 22 August 1966, no. A-130, NARA, Box 2766, POL 29 UAR.

56 See part iv of Nasr and Imam, *Al-Thawrah*.

57 Memorandum of Conversation, 'US Intelligence Activities in the U.A.R. (2 of 3),' 7 January 1962, NARA, 786B.5211/1–762.

58 Telegram from Battle (Cairo) to SecState, 'US–UAR Relations: Alternatives to Present Policy,' 9 December 1964, no. 2016, DDRS; Telegram from Battle (Cairo) to SecState, 3 December 1964, no. 1945, NARA, Box 2765, POL 23–8 UAR.

59 Memorandum of Conversation, 'Luncheon Discussions on UAR–US Relations,' 3 and 10 August 1965, *FRUS*, 1964–1968, vol. XVIII, Document 232; Telegram from Rusk (DOS) to Amembassy Cairo, no. 88396, 21 November 1966, *FRUS*, 1964–1968, vol. XVIII, Document 341.

60 Telegram from Rusk (DOS), no. 88396, 21 November 1966.

61 Ibid.

62 Ibid., Document 341n3.

63 Oren, *Six Days of War*, 42.

64 Memorandum, NEA/CIA Weekly Meetings, 1967–1969, *FRUS*, 1964–1968, vol. XVIII, Document 396, 776n3.

65 Telegram from Battle (Cairo) to SecState, no. 5036, 5 March 1967, NARA, Box 2556, POL UAR–US.

66 H. Eilts, 'Reflections on the Suez Crisis: Security in the Middle East,' in W. Louis and R. Owen, eds., *Suez 1956*, Oxford: Clarendon Press, 1989, 360.

67 Memorandum of Conversation, 'Luncheon Discussions on UAR–US Relations.'

68 Ibid.

69 Memorandum, NEA/CIA Weekly Meetings, 1967–1969, Document 396.

70 Ibid.

71 Ibid.

72 V. Sakharov, *High Treason*, New York: Ballantine, 1980, 203; J. Barron, *KGB: The Secret Work of Soviet Secret Agents*, New York: Bantam, 1981, 69–71; Airgram from Bruce (London) to DOS, '*Sunday Telegraph* on Egypt's Spy Network.'

73 C. Andrew and V. Mitrokhin, *The World Was Going Our Way*, New York: Basic Books, 2005, 147.

74 Barron, *KGB*, 69–71.

75 Memorandum of Conversation, 'Luncheon Discussions on UAR–US Relations.'

## 9 The 1967 War

1 Quoted in Airgram from Bergus (Cairo), 'The Conspiracy Trial,' 16 April 1968.

2 In 1966 and early 1967, the Soviets informed Egypt that the IDF was mobilizing for a

large raid into Syria: M. Oren, *Six Days of War*, New York: Oxford University Press, 2002, 43.

3 'Leading Personalities in Arab Republic of Egypt 1972'; M. Jawadi, *Muddakirat Qada al-'Askariya al-Misriya 67–72 Fi 'Aqab al-Naksa*, Cairo: Dar al-Khayyal, 2001, 266–267, 352.

4 S. El-Shazly, *The Crossing of the Suez*, San Francisco: American Mideast Research, 1980, 96.

5 Y. Aboul-Enein, 'Book Review: Learning and Rebuilding a Shattered Force – Memoirs of Pre-Yom Kippur War Egyptian Generals, 1969–1972,' *Strategic Insights*, IV, 2005. Online, available at: www.ccc.nps.navy.mil/si/2005/mar/aboul-eneinmar05.pdf, accessed 11 August 2007.

6 M. El-Gamasy, *The October War*, Cairo: AUC Press, 1993, 46–47.

7 'A Lesson We Should Have Learned,' *Al-Ahram Weekly On-Line*, 5–11 June 1997. Online, available at: http://weekly.ahram.org.eg/archives/67–97/sup10.htm, accessed 3 October 2006; J. Bowen, *Six Days*, New York: St Martin's Press, 2003, 91.

8 Jawadi, *Muddakirat*, 279.

9 'Refaat Elgamal,' online, available at: http://en.wikipeida.org/wiki/Refaat_ElGamal, accessed 31 August 2006.

10 'Who was Jack Bitton? Part One: In Love and War,' *Cairo Times*. Online, available at: www.geocities.com/galianoboy/bitton1.html?20068, accessed 8 September 2006.

11 Ibid.

12 'Refaat Elgamal,' online, available at: http://en.wikipeida.org/wiki/Refaat_ElGamal; I. Black and B. Morris, *Israel's Secret Wars*, New York: Grove, 1991, 146; 'L'intelligence Politique Avant L'Information,' *Al-Ahram Hebdo*. Online, available at: http://hebdo.ahram.org.eg/arab/ahram/2003/8/13/doss2.htm, accessed 10 November 2006.

13 'Refaat Elgamal,' online, available at: http://en.wikipeida.org/wiki/Refaat_ElGamal.

14 S. El-Gammal, 'Son Loses Court Battle Over Gripping Egyptian Spy Drama,' *Reuters*, 10 April 1990.

15 Ibid.

16 S. Musri, *Rif'at al-Hagan*, Cairo, 1988.

17 Ibid.

18 Y. Caroz, *The Arab Secret Services*, London: Corgi, 1978, 159–160.

19 Bowen, *Six Days*, 90, 109.

20 Jawadi, *Muddakirat*, 279; Bowen, *Six Days*, 123; Youssef Aboul-Enein, 'Book Review.'

21 Jawadi, *Muddakirat*, 280.

22 Oren, *Six Days*, 66.

23 One lesson learned from the 1967 war was to improve the MID's Hebrew capabilities.

24 Abdel-Magid Farid, *Nasser: the Final Years*, Reading: Ithaca Press, 1994, 121.

25 Caroz, *Arab Secret Services*, 183–184; I. Ginor and G. Remez, *Foxbats Over Dimona*, New Haven: Yale University Press, 2007, 56, 98; J. Barron, *KGB: The Secret Work of Soviet Secret Agents*, New York: Bantam, 1981, 11.

26 Barron, *KGB*, 11.

27 Bowen, *Six Days*, 91, 126.

28 Bowen, *Six Days*, 91, 126; Jawadi, *Muddakirat*, 276.

29 K. Pollack, *Arabs at War*, Lincoln: University of Nebraska Press, 2002, 61–62; Y. Sayigh, 'Escalation or Containment? Egypt and the Palestine Liberation Army, 1964–67,' *International Journal of Middle East Studies*, 30, 1998, 103; Bowen, *Six Days*, 80.

30 Bowen, *Six Days*, 80; L. James, 'Nasser and His Enemies: Foreign Policy Decision Making in Egypt on The Eve of The Six Day War,' *Middle East Review of International Affairs*. Online, available at: http://meria.idc.ac.il/journal/2005/issue2/jv9no2a2.html, accessed 22 March 2007.

31 Ben Dan, *The Secret War*, New York: Sabra Books, 1970, 161–165.
32 Black and Morris, *Israel's Secret Wars*, 232; 'Radioelectronic Warfare in Israeli-Arab Wars,' *Voyenno-Istoricheskiy Zhurnal*, 7 (25 June 1980), JPRS, no. 2229, 5 December 1980; P. Seale, *Asad of Syria: The Struggle for the Middle East*, London: I.B. Tauris, 1988, 136.
33 Jawadi, *Muddakirat*, 286.
34 Ibid., 277.
35 Bowen, *Six Days*, 90; El-Gamasy, *October War*, 44, 46; Oren, *Six Days*, 160; Black and Morris, *Israel's Secret Wars*, 232–233; Pollack, *Arabs at War*, 61–62.
36 Jawadi, *Mudakkirat*, 284–285.
37 Ibid.
38 Parker, *Politics of Miscalculation*, 42–43; Heikal, *The Sphinx and the Commissar*, New York: Harper & Row, 1978, 174–175; Ginor and Remez, *Foxbats*, 90.
39 Parker, *Politics of Miscalculation*, 42–43; Oren, *Six Days*, 47, 57, 65.
40 Seale, *Asad*, 136; Bowen, *Six Days*, 85, 101.
41 Oren, *Six Days*, 63.
42 Heikal, *Sphinx*, 175.
43 Oren, *Six Days*, 64; Parker, *Politics of Miscalculation*, 8–9; Jawadi, *Muddakirat*, 284.
44 Jawadi, *Muddakirat*, 284–285.
45 Parker, *Politics of Miscalculation*, 14. Parker was a US diplomat in Egypt during the 1967 war.
46 Oren, *Six Days*, 62–63.
47 The MID assured the military leaders that original warnings of Israeli mobilization were now 'confirmed': Parker, *Politics of Miscalculation*, 248n25. Sadiq argues the MID repeatedly warned that intelligence of the IDF concentrations on Syria was false, but the leadership proceeded with the Sinai deployments anyway: Jawadi, *Muddakirat*, 285, 296.
48 Quoted in D. Hofstadter, *Egypt and Nasser*, vol. 3, New York: Facts on File, 1973, 19.
49 A. Cohen, 'Cairo, Dimona, and the June 1967 War,' *MEJ*, 50, 1996, 205–206; Bowen, *Six Days*, 59.
50 Quoted in D. Neff, *Warriors for Jerusalem*, New York: Simon & Schuster, 1984, 138–139. Emphasis is mine.
51 Hofstadter, *Egypt and Nasser*, vol. 3, 20.
52 Jawadi, *Muddakirat*, 277.
53 A. Rubinstein, *Red Star on the Nile*, Princeton: Princeton University Press, 1977, 16n19; Oren, *Six Days*, 118; Ginor and Remez, *Foxbats*, 115–116; L. James, *Whose Voice? Nasser, the Arabs, and 'Sawt al-Arab' Radio*. Online, available at: www.tbsjournal.com/jamespf.html, accessed 1 April 2007
54 Oren, *Six Days*, 120.
55 Jawadi, *Muddakirat*, 278, 281–283.
56 Oren, *Six Days*, 158; Jawadi, *Muddakirat*, 281; Bowen, *Six Days*, 82; El-Gamasy, *October War*, 44; M. Heikal, *The Cairo Documents*, New York: Doubleday, 1973, 28.
57 Airgram from Bergus (Cairo), 'The Conspiracy Trial,' 23 August 1971.
58 'A Lesson We Should Have Learned,' *Al-Ahram Weekly On-Line*, 5–11 June 1997.
59 I. Black and B. Morris, *Israel's Secret Wars*, New York: Grove, 1991, 223, 225; El-Gamasy, *October War*, 55–56; Bowen, *Six Days*, 105; S. Steven, *The Spymasters of Israel*, New York: Ballantine, 1980, 230.
60 According to Sadiq it was 'Amr who gave the order to retreat: Jawadi, *Mudakkirat*, 295.
61 Quoted in Oren, *Six Days*, 311.
62 Bowen, *Six Days*, 110, 121.
63 Ibid., 119.

64 Nutting, *Nasser*, 441.
65 Black and Morris, *Israel's Secret Wars*, 233; Hofstadter, *Egypt and Nasser*, vol. 3, 21.
66 'Abd al-Fattāḥ Abū al-Faḍl, *Kuntu nā'iban li-ra'īs al-mukhābarāt*, Cairo, Dār al-Ḥurrīyah, 1986, 7–8, 283–301.
67 R. Parker, *The Politics of Miscalculation in the Middle East*, Bloomington: Indiana University Press, 1993, 90.
68 Telegram from Wellman (Lisbon) to DOS, no. 1517, 2 June 1967, *FRUS*, 1964–1968, vol. XIX, Document 129.
69 Quoted in R. Stephens, *Nasser*, New York: Simon & Schuster, 1973, 482.
70 Jawadi, *Muddakirat*, 275–276.
71 Ibid., 274.
72 Barron, *KGB*, 11; MID Director Sadiq believed Soviet intelligence planted this disinformation to escalate tensions between Syria and Israel and set the stage for a communist take-over of the Syrian government: Aboul-Enein, Youssef, 'Book Review.'
73 Bowen, *Six Days*, 34–35.
74 Seale, *Asad*, 128–129; Nutting, *Nasser*, 398; Parker, *Politics of Miscalculation*, 19.
75 J. Lacouture, *Nasser*, trans. by D. Hofstadter, New York: Knopf, 1973, 362–363.

## 10  Nasser's twilight

1 S. Nasr and' Abd Allah Imam, *Al-Thawrah, Al-Naksah, Al-Mukhabarat*, Cairo: Dar al-Khayyal, 1999, 162, 174.
2 Ibid., 162.
3 Telegram from Nolte (Cairo) to SecState, 8 June 1967, no. 8697, DDRS, LBJ Library.
4 Ibid.
5 M. Oren, *Six Days of War*, New York: Oxford University Press, 2002, 286.
6 Telegram from Nolte (Cairo) to DOS, 9 June 1967, no. 8711, *FRUS*, 1964–1968, vol. XXI, Document 228; Memorandum from the Director of the Bureau of INR (Hughes) to SecState Rusk, 'The Current Situation in the UAR and its Bearing on UAR Approaches to the US and France,' *FRUS*, 1964–1968, vol. XIX, Document 339.
7 Nasr and Imam, *Al-Thawrah*, 181–182.
8 Ibid.
9 Memorandum from the Director of the Bureau of INR (Hughes), 'The Current Situation in the UAR.'
10 Ibid.
11 Ibid.
12 Oren, *Six Days*, 320.
13 'Leading Personalities in Arab Republic of Egypt 1972,' FCO 39/1205: Sadiq entry. Sadiq did not detail his role in the post-1967 war power struggle between Nasser and 'Amr: M. Jawadi, *Muddakirat Qada al-'Askariya al-Misriya 67–72: Fi 'Aqab Al-Naksa*, Cairo: Dar al-Khayyal, 2001, 354.
14 K. Beattie, *Egypt during the Nasser Years*, Boulder: Westview, 1994, 212, 231n18.
15 J. Bowen, *Six Days*, New York: St Martin's, 2003, 320–322.
16 Ibid.
17 Nasr and Imam, *Al-Thawrah*, 153, 189,
18 Y. Caroz, *The Arab Secret Services*, London: Corgi, 1978, 186.
19 R. Stephens, *Nasser*, New York: Knopf, 1971, 533; Caroz, *Arab Secret Services*, 184.
20 K. Beattie, *Egypt during the Sadat Years*, New York: Palgrave, 2000, 7.
21 Stephens, *Nasser*, 571.
22 M. Kerr, *The Arab Cold War*, New York: Oxford University Press, 1971, 139.
23 D. Livingstone and D. Halevy, *Inside the PLO*, New York: William Morrow, 1990, 65.

24 A. Hart, *Arafat*, Bloomington: Indiana University Press, 1984, 190–191.
25 Hart, *Arafat*, 186; Y. Sayigh, 'Turning Defeat into Opportunity: the Palestinian Guerrillas after the June 1967 War,' *MEJ*, 46, 1992, 252n42.
26 Hart, *Arafat*, 172.
27 Abu Iyad (Salah Khalaf) and E. Rouleau, *My Home, My Land*, trans. by Linda Butler Koseoglu, New York: Times Books, 1981, 47–48.
28 Quoted in Sayigh, 'Turning Defeat into Opportunity,' 258.
29 M. Heikal, *The Road to Ramadan*, New York: Ballantine, 1976, 57–58.
30 Quoted in Iyad and Rouleau, *My Home*, 45.
31 Sayigh, 'Turning Defeat into Opportunity,' 258.
32 Caroz, *Arab Secret Services*, 413–414. Abu Iyad also notes training of FATAH counterintelligence cadres in Egypt: Iyad and Rouleau, *My Home*, 56.
33 Sayigh, 'Turning Defeat into Opportunity,' 258.
34 'Foray into Jordan,' *Time*, 29 March 1968. Online, available at: www.time.com/time/magazine/article/0,9171,838079–1,00.html, accessed 11 July 2007; Farid, *Nasser*, 126.
35 Caroz, *Arab Secret Services*, 196–198.
36 A. Rubinstein, *Red Star on the Nile*, Princeton: Princeton University Press, 1977, 29; the 20,000 figure comes from C. Andrew and O. Gordievsky, 'More 'Instructions from the Centre': Top Secret Files on KGB Global Operations, 1975–1985,' *INS* 7 1992, 82; L. Nordeen and D. Nicolle, *Phoenix Over the Nile*, Washington, DC: Smithsonian Press, 1996, 225.
37 Jawadi, *Muddakirat*, 273–274.
38 J. Barron, *KGB: The Secret Work of Soviet Secret Agents*, New York: Bantam, 1981, 63; V. Sakharov, *High Treason*, New York: Ballantine, 1980, 189.
39 Beattie, *Egypt during the Sadat Years*, 46.
40 M. Wolf and A. McElvoy, *Man without a Face*, New York: Times Books, 1997, 257–258; Memorandum of Conversation, DOS, 'Herman Nickel's Interest in Bergus–Riad Meeting,' 20 May 1971, NARA, Box 2642, POL UAR–US.
41 'Egyptian General Intelligence Directorate,' Wikipedia entry. Onlune, available at: http://en.wikipedia.org/wiki/egyptian_general_intelligence_directorate, accessed 22 March 2007. These activities were linked to Nasser's suspicions that CIA was recruiting assets in the Egyptian military: Farid Abdel Magid, *Nasser: the Final Years*, Reading: Ithaca Press, 1994, 136.
42 Correspondence from Joseph J. Sisco, DOS, NEA to Under Secretary, DOS, 'Letter from Ambassador Middendorf, The Hague – Action Memorandum,' 3 April 1970, NARA, Box 2642, POL 17 UAR.
43 Ibid.
44 Amin Howeidi, 'Waiting for the Fish to Bite,' *Al-Ahram Weekly On-Line*, 6–12 August 1998. Online, available at: http://weekly.ahram.org.eg/1998/289/op2.htm, accessed 2 October 2006.
45 A. Hewedy, 'Nasser and the Crisis of 1956' in W. Louis and R. Owen, *Suez 1956*, Oxford: The Clarendon Press, 1989, x–xi; Abdel-Khaliq Farouk, 'Memories of High Tide,' *Al-Ahram Weekly*, 15–21 January 2004. Online, available at: http://weekly.ahram.org.eg/print/2004/673/bo1.htm, accessed on 1 October 2006; A. Howeidy, 'Picking up the Pieces,' *Al-Ahram Weekly On-Line*, 5–11 June 1997. Online, available at: http://weekly.ahram.org.eg/archives/69–97/sup5.htm, accessed 22 September 2006.
46 Howeidi, 'Picking up the Pieces.'
47 M. El-Gamasy, *The October War*, Cairo: AUC Press, 1993, 92.
48 K. Pollack, *Arabs at War*, Lincoln: University of Nebraska Press, 2002, 99–100.
49 Ibid.
50 Caroz, *Arab Secret Services*, 187–193.
51 Ibid., 188.

52 Nordeen and Nicolle, *Phoenix*, 221.
53 Ibid., 222.
54 S. El-Shazly, *The Crossing of the Suez*, San Francisco: American Mideast Research, 116.
55 Rubinstein, *Red Star*, 46; Nordeen and Nicolle, *Phoenix*, 262; Y. Aboul-Enein, 'Book Review: Learning and Rebuilding a Shattered Force – Memoirs of Pre-Yom Kippur War Egyptian Generals, 1969–1972,' *Strategic Insights*, IV, 2005. Online, available at:www.ccc.nps.navy.mil/si/2005/mar/aboul-eneinmar05.pdf, accessed 11 August 2007.
56 'Electronic Warfare Accomplishments Reviewed,' *Al-Musawwar*, 2 January 1981, JPRS, no. 2322, 4 May 1981.
57 'Electronic Warfare Accomplishments Reviewed,' *Al-Musawwar*.
58 Israeli commandos attacked the Egyptian Red Sea base at Ras Ghaleb and used a helicopter to carry off a P-12 Spoon Rest early warning radar. See J. Richelson, *Foreign Intelligence Organizations*, Cambridge: Ballinger, 1988, 202; D. Raviv and Y. Melman, *Friends in Deed: Inside the US–Israel Alliance*, New York: Hyperion, 1994, 153.
59 Pollack, *Arabs at War*, 100–101; D. Hofstadter, *Egypt and Nasser vol. 3*, New York: Facts on File, 1973, 168.
60 Pollack, *Arabs at War*, 99–100; M. Heikal, *The Road to Ramadan*, New York: Ballantine, 1976, 247–248.
61 Heikal, *Road to Ramadan*, 247.
62 Pollack, *Arabs at War*, 99–100.
63 Jawadi, *Muddakirat*, 317.
64 Bureau of Intelligence and Research, 'The Israel-UAR Front: "*Danse Macabre*,"' Research Memorandum, 6 March 1970, INRM-28, NARA, Box 2051, POL 27 ARAB-ISR.
65 'Leading Personalities in Arab Republic of Egypt 1972,' FCO 39/1205; R. Parker, *The Politics of Miscalculation in the Middle East*, Bloomington: Indiana University Press, 1993, 137. When he became Chief of Staff, Sadiq retained his responsibility for liaison with FATAH: see Heikal, *Road to Ramadan*, 119.
66 Parker, *Politics of Miscalculation*, 141; Rubinstein, *Red Star*, 108.
67 Stephens, *Nasser*, 533–534.
68 G. Abdo, *No God but God*, New York: Oxford University Press, 2000, 116.
69 A. Roussillon, 'Republican Egypt Interpreted: Revolution and Beyond,' *The Cambridge History of Egypt*, Volume II, ed. M.W. Daly, Cambridge: Cambridge University Press, 1998, 358; Bureau of Intelligence and Research, 'UAR: Student Riots Symptomatic of Deepening Malaise,' Research Memorandum, 29 November 1968, RNA-37, NARA, Box 2555, POL 23–8 UAR.
70 Telegram from Bergus (Cairo) to SecState, 3 December 1968, no. 4037, NARA, Box 2554, POL 12 UAR; Telegram from Bergus (Cairo) to SecState, 4 December 1968, no. 4052, NARA, Box 2554, POL 12 UAR.
71 INR, 'UAR: And Quiet Flows the Nile – The Internal Scene,' Research Memorandum, 20 October 1969, RNA-52, NARA, Box 2554, POL 15 UAR.

## 11 Power struggles

1 Shortly before his death, Nasser reportedly intended to make 'Abd al-Latif al-Boghdadi his new vice president: M. Jawadi, *Muddakirat Qada al-'Askariya al-Misriya 67–72: Fi 'Aqab Al-Naksa*, Cairo: Dar al-Khayyal, 2001, 297.
2 Ibid., 333.
3 A. Sadat, *In Search of Identity*, New York: Harper & Row, 1979, 206.
4 M. Heikal, *Autumn of Fury*, London: Corgi, 1978, 47.
5 Ibid.

6 CIA, Intelligence Memorandum, 'Nasir's Death: The Immediate Aftermath,' 29 September 1970, no. CIA/OCI/IM-1467/70, DDRS; Telegram from Rogers (Department of State) to various embassies, 'Internal Political Situation in UAR,' 14 October 1970, no. 169785, NARA, RG 59, Box 2641, POL 15–1 UAR; Jawadi, *Muddakirat*, 303.

7 Jawadi, *Muddakirat*, 300–301.

8 A. Kamel, *Aḥmad Kāmil yatadhakkar: min awrāq Ra'īs al-Mukhābarāt al-Miṣrīyah al-asbaq*, Cairo: Dar al-Hilal, 1990, 13.

9 Kamel later argued that he repeatedly tried to warn the president about the conspiracy but Sadat would not see him. Kamel also believed Sharaf did not pass his warning reports to Sadat: Kamel, *Aḥmad Kāmil yatadhakkar*, 14–16; Y. Caroz, *The Arab Secret Services*, London: Corgi, 1978, 212–213.

10 Kamel, *Aḥmad Kāmil yatadhakkar*, 29.

11 Quoted in K. Beattie, *Egypt during the Sadat Years*, New York: Palgrave, 2000, 75.

12 M. Heikal, *The Road to Ramadan*, New York: Ballantine, 1976, 122; Beattie, *Egypt during the Sadat Years*, 40; Heikal *Road to Ramadan*, 122.

13 Caroz, *Arab Secret Services*, 66; Telegram from Wiley (Cairo) to SecState, 17 October 1970, no. 2368, NARA, Box 2641, POL 15–1 UAR; Heikal, *Road to Ramadan*, 123; 'Leading Personalities in Arab Republic of Egypt 1972,' FCO 39/1205; Airgram from Horgan (Cairo) to Department of State, 'UAR Representatives on Joint UAR-Iraqi Presidency Council,' 3 July 1964, no. A-20, NARA, POL 6 UAR.

14 Heikal, *Road to Ramadan*, 134. Also see Jawadi, *Muddakirat*, 309.

15 Beattie, *Egypt during the Sadat Years*, 41.

16 Heikal, *Autumn of Fury*, 181; Heikal, *Road to Ramadan*, 133. Sadiq warned the Republican Guard commander against siding with Sharaf: Jawadi, *Muddakirat*, 310, 318–319.

17 Beattie, *Egypt during the Sadat Years*, 46, 48, 68; Jawadi, *Muddakirat*, 267, 302–304.

18 Caroz, *Arab Secret Services*, 211.

19 Beattie, *Egypt during the Sadat Years*, 74, 291n126; Jawadi, *Muddakirat*, 316; Caroz, *Arab Secret Services*, 210–211.

20 General Fawzi and Sharaf believed Sadat would let them run Egypt with the president as a figurehead: Jawadi, *Muddakirat*, 301–302.

21 Beattie, *Egypt during the Sadat Years*, 56, 60–61.

22 Beattie, *Egypt during the Sadat Years*, 59–60; Sadat, *In Search of Identity*, 223; Jawadi, *Muddakirat*, 309–310.

23 Jawadi, *Muddakirat*, 312–314.

24 Guma'a and Sharaf may have known of Sadat's plans against Sabri from EGIS phone taps: Caroz, *Arab Secret Services*, 209.

25 Caroz, *Arab Secret Services*, 210; Telegram from Bergus (Cairo) to SecState, 'Sadat Speech May 14: Revelation of "Gomaa Plot,"' 15 May 1971, no. 1177, NARA, Box 2641, POL 15 UAR; Hirst and Beeson, *Sadat*, 115–116; Jawadi, *Muddakirat*, 337.

26 M. Perry, *Eclipse: The Last Days of the CIA*, New York: William Morrow, 1992, 52–53.

27 Beattie, *Egypt during the Sadat Years*, 67; Telegram from Bergus (Cairo) to SecState, 'Arab Issues in UAR Press,' 18 May 1971, no. 1203, NARA, Box 2641, POL 15 UAR.

28 Jawadi, *Muddakirat*, 327.

29 Kamel, *Aḥmad Kāmil yatadhakkar*, 23; Caroz, *Arab Secret Services*, 213–214. The GID director and his deputy were arrested while attempting to destroy wire tap tapes: Telegram from Bergus (Cairo), 'Sadat Speech May 14: Revelation of "Gomaa Plot,"' 15 May 1971 and Telegram from Bergus (Cairo) to SecState, 'Egypt: End of the Interregnum,' 17 May 1971, no. 1190, NARA, Box 2642, POL 23–9 UAR; Jawadi, *Muddakirat*, 337.

30 Caroz, *Arab Secret Services*, 211; Telegram from Bergus (Cairo) to SecState, 'UAR Conspiracy Trials Announced,' 23 August 1971, no. 2112, NARA, Box 2642, POL 29 UAR.

31 Caroz, *Arab Secret Services*, 211.
32 Telegram from Bergus (Cairo), 'Egypt: End of the Interregnum,' 17 May 1971; R. Baker, *Egypt's Uncertain Revolution under Nasser and Sadat*, Cambridge: Harvard University Press, 1978, 151–152.
33 Airgram from Bergus (Cairo) to DOS, 'Abolition of University Police,' 30 August 1971, no. A-69, NARA, Box 2641, EDU 9–3 UAR. The US Interests Section correctly predicted the government would never abolish the university police. It was reintroduced in September 1979: Beattie, *Egypt during the Sadat Years*, 98.
34 Telegram from Bergus (Cairo) to SecState, 'Sadat Speech to Military, August 12,' 13 August 1971,' no. 2024, NARA, Box 2641, POL 15–1 UAR.
35 Telegram from Bergus (Cairo) to SecState, 'Arab Issues in UAR Press,' 18 May 1971; Human Rights Watch, *Behind Closed Doors: Torture and Detention in Egypt*, New York: HRW, 1992, 3.
36 R. Springborg, *Mubarak's Egypt: Fragmentation of the Political Order*, Boulder: Westview, 1989, 129n43.
37 'Leading Personalities in Arab Republic of Egypt 1972,' FCO 39/1205; Perry, *Eclipse*, 52–53.
38 'Leading Personalities in Arab Republic of Egypt 1972,' FCO 39/1205.
39 Ibid.
40 Beattie, *Egypt during the Sadat Years*, 53; Heikal, *Autumn*, 72.
41 EGIS was introduced to the channel after Sadat placed Ahmed Isma'il in the EGIS director slot: M. Heikal, *The Sphinx and the Commissar*, New York: Harper & Row, 1978, 239.
42 Beattie, *Egypt during the Sadat Years*, 56; Heikal, *Autumn of Fury*, 54.
43 Heikal, *Road to Ramadan*, 148; S. El-Shazly, *The Crossing of the Suez*, San Francisco: American Mideast Research, 1980, 111.
44 Heikal, *Road to Ramadan*, 149–150; Caroz, *Arab Secret Services*, 218.
45 Heikal, *Road to Ramadan*, 150–151. There is no declassified material at the US National Archives to confirm Heikal's version of events.
46 Heikal, *Road to Ramadan*, 152; El-Shazly, *Crossing*, 112.
47 Caroz, *Arab Secret Services*, 219.
48 Telegram from Greene (Cairo) to Secretary of State, 'Retired Egyptian General Muhib Abdel Ghafar Sentenced,' 27 November 1972, no. 3167, NARA, RG 59, Box 2251, POL 29 EGY. Ghafar reportedly provided the Americans with data on Egyptian public opinion. The United States in turn provided Ghafar with pamphlets and newspapers to distribute.
49 Telegram from Greene (Cairo) to Secretary of State, 'Egyptian–American Relations,' 19 June 1972, no. 1795, NARA, RG 59, Box 2251, POL 17 US–EGY. Other reports highlight Egyptian concerns with US espionage. In August 1972 Egyptian intelligence was convinced the CIA had helped spark a new round of Muslim–Copt violence: Telegram from Greene (Cairo) to Secretary of State, 'Sectarian Trouble in Egypt,' 16 August 1972, no. 2256, NARA, Box 2251, POL EGY–US.
50 D. Smiley, *Arabian Assignment*, London: Leo Cooper, 1975, 181–182; also see R. Bronson, *Thicker Than Oil*, New York: Oxford University Press, 2006, 113.
51 Heikal, *Autumn*, 39–40.
52 D. Hirst and I. Beeson, *Sadat*, London: Faber & Faber, 1981, 97; Heikal, *Autumn*, 39–40.
53 Quoted in Hirst and Beeson, *Sadat*, 97.
54 Bronson, *Thicker Than Oil*, 113–114.
55 Beattie, *Egypt during the Sadat Years*, 52; Heikal, *Sphinx*, 226.
56 Bronson, *Thicker Than Oil*, 114.
57 A 'very knowledgeable Free Officer' told Beattie that Sadat had contacted CIA with Nasser's permission in the 1960s: Beattie, *Egypt during the Sadat Years*, 51–52.
58 Quoted in Heikal, *Sphinx*, 216.

59 C. Andrew and V. Mitrokhin, *The World Was Going Our Way*, New York: Basic Books, 2005, 154; Heikal, *Sphinx*, 227.
60 Andrew and Mitrokhin, *World*, 155.
61 C. Andrew and O. Gordievsky, *KGB: The Inside Story*, New York: HarperCollins, 1990, 496–497.
62 V. Sakharov, *High Treason*, New York: Ballantine, 1980, 210–213.
63 Ibid., 213–214.
64 Andrew and Mitrokhin, *World*, 158; C. Andrew and O. Gordievsky, 'More "Instructions from the Centre": Top Secret Files on KGB Global Operations, 1975–1985,' *INS* 7, 1992, 82.
65 Andrew and Gordievsky, 'More Instructions from the Centre,' 82.
66 Caroz, *Arab Secret Services*, 222–223.
67 A. Rubinstein, *Red Star on the Nile*, Princeton: Princeton University Press, 1977, 190; 'Leading Personalities in Arab Republic of Egypt 1972,' FCO 39/1205; Bronson, *Thicker Than Oil*, 114.

## 12 Grand deception in the 1973 War

1 D. Hirst and I. Beeson, *Sadat*, London: Faber and Faber, 1981, 143–144; Telegram from Greene (Cairo) to SecState, 31 October 1972, no. 2920, NARA, Box 2250, POL 23–9 EGY; Telegram from Greene (Cairo) to SecState, 'Strange Events on October 12,' 20 October 1972, no. 2834, NARA, Box 2250, POL 23–9 EGY; S. El-Shazly, *The Crossing of the Suez*, San Francisco: American Mideast Research, 1980, 170–172.
2 Shazly, *Crossing*, 193–194; Information Memorandum, DOS, Joseph J. Sisco to SecState Rogers, 'Shift of Egyptian War Ministers,' 31 October 1972, NARA, Box 2250, POL 15–1 EGY; M. Jawadi, *Muddakirat Qada al-'Askariya al-Misriya 67–72: Fi 'Aqab Al-Naksa*, Cairo: Dar al-Khayyal, 2001, 353.
3 Jawadi, *Muddakirat*, 340–341, 351.
4 E. Kahana, 'Early Warning versus Concept: The Case of the Yom Kippur War 1973,' *INS*, 17, 2002, 84; Y. Caroz, *The Arab Secret Services*, London: Corgi, 1978, 222; Telegram from Greene (Cairo) to SecState, 'Beni Suef Affair,' 16 November 1972, no. 3078, NARA, Box 2250, POL 23–9 EGY.
5 Telegram from Greene (Cairo) to SecState, 'Beni Suef Affair – Apparent Act of Insubordination,' 20 November 1972, no. 3107, NARA, Box 2250, POL 23–9 EGY; Telegram from Greene (Cairo), 'Beni Suef Affair,' 16 November 1972.
6 El-Shazly, *Crossing*, 192–193.
7 A. Sadat, *In Search of Identity*, New York: Harper & Row, 1979, 215.
8 M. El-Gamasy, *The October War*, Cairo: AUC Press, 1993, 186–187.
9 K. Pollack, *Arabs at War*, Lincoln: University of Nebraska Press, 2002, 103–104.
10 El-Gamasy, *October War*, 193–194; Pollack, *Arabs at War*, 103–104.
11 'Egyptian General Intelligence Directorate,' Wikipedia entry. Online, available at: http://en.wikipedia.org/wiki/egyptian_general_intelligence_directorate, accessed 22 March 2007.
12 C. Herzog, *The Arab–Israeli Wars*, New York: Vintage, 1984, 228; A. Rabinovich, *The Yom Kippur War*, New York: Schocken Books, 2004, 44; Pollack, *Arabs at War*, 103–104.
13 A. Rabinovich, 'Intelligence Follies,' *Jerusalem Post*, 21 December 2001, 8.
14 S. Steven, *The Spymasters of Israel*, New York: Ballantine, 1980, 361–362. 'Like any good lie, a deception contains as much truth as possible. The deceiver uses what the enemy "knows" to be true against him. In a certain sense, the target *wants* to be fooled.' P. Gerard, *Secret Soldiers*, New York: Plume, 2002, 93.
15 Pollack, *Arabs at War*, 103–104.
16 Ibid.
17 Caroz, *Arab Secret Services*, 231.

18 I. Black and B. Morris, *Israel's Secret Wars*, New York: Grove, 1991, 296–297; M. Heikal, *The Road to Ramadan*, New York: Ballantine, 1976, 7.
19 Caroz, *Arab Secret Services*, 229.
20 El-Gamasy, *October War*, 180.
21 Egypt claims Jack Bitton passed intelligence on the Bar-Lev line: 'L'intelligence Politique Avant L'Information,' *Al-Ahram Hebdo*. Online, available at: http://hebdo. ahram.org.eg/arab/ahram/2003/8/13/doss2.htm, accessed 10 November 2006.
22 Caroz, *Arab Secret Services*, 227.
23 Rabinovich, *Yom Kippur War*, 80–81.
24 Rabinovich, *Yom Kippur War*, 29; A. McDermott, *Egypt from Nasser to Mubarak*, London: Croom Helm, 1988, 169–170; H. Blum, *The Eve of Destruction*, New York: HarperCollins, 2003, 127.
25 McDermott, *Egypt from Nasser to Mubarak*, 169–170.
26 J. Hughes-Wilson, *Military Intelligence Blunders and Cover-Ups*, New York: Carroll and Graf, 2004, 257–258.
27 Caroz, *Arab Secret Services*, 120; McDermott, *Egypt from Nasser to Mubarak*, 169–170. Egypt's Electronic Warfare Directorate reportedly created its own ELINT collection devices after reverse engineering Soviet models: 'Electronic Warfare Accomplishments Reviewed,' *Al-Musawwar*.
28 El-Shazly, *Crossing*, 116; R. Hotz, 'Battlefield Equation Changes Seen,' *AWST*, 14 July 1975, 14–15.
29 Hotz, 'Battlefield Equation Changes Seen,' 14.
30 El-Shazly, *Crossing*, 115, 273–274; others claim Moscow did not provide access to imagery until after the Deversoir crossing: Hotz, 'Battlefield Equation Changes Seen,' 15; Heikal, *Road to Ramadan*, 258.
31 Caroz, *Arab Secret Services*, 228.
32 Herzog, *Arab–Israeli Wars*, 228.
33 Herzog, *Arab–Israeli Wars*, 228; Kahana, 'Early Warning versus Concept,' 83.
34 El-Shazly, *Crossing*, 31–33. During a 3 September 1973 meeting Fuad Nasser assessed that the IDF would have sufficient warning to mobilize 18 brigades to meet the Egyptian canal crossing. He also warned that the IDF counteroffensive could come within hours of the Egyptian canal crossing attempt. The MID estimated total Egyptian casualties could be as high as 10,000 killed and 20,000 wounded in the initial assault: Heikal, *Road to Ramadan*, 5; El-Shazly, *Crossing*, 31–33.
35 El-Shazly, *Crossing*, 33; Heikal, *Road to Ramadan*, 5.
36 El-Shazly, *Crossing*, 118–121.
37 Blum, *Eve of Destruction*, 32–38, 330; H. Blum, 'Who Killed Ashraf Marwan? Death of a Spy,' *International Herald Tribune*, 14 July 2007, 1; Kahana, 'Early Warning versus Concept,' 99–100n13.
38 Blum, 'Who Killed Ashraf Marwan?'; Kahana, 'Early Warning versus Concept,' 99–100n13; Blum, *Eve of Destruction*, 36–38.
39 Blum, 'Who Killed Ashraf Marwan?'; Black and Morris, *Israel's Secret Wars*, 300; Blum, *Eve of Destruction*, 39.
40 Kahana, 'Early Warning versus Concept,' 87.
41 That code word was 'Radish.'
42 Rabinovich, *Yom Kippur War*, 72–73; Blum, 'Who Killed Ashraf Marwan?' Other sources indicate that Top Source warned of impending attack on 1 October, a date which coincided with the start of a large Egyptian military exercise: Kahana, 'Early Warning versus Concept,' 92; Rabinovich, 'Intelligence Follies.'
43 Blum, 'Who Killed Ashraf Marwan?'; Kahana, 'Early Warning versus Concept,' 95, 102n92. In 1975 the US House of Representatives Select Committee on Intelligence revealed that US intelligence was monitoring Egyptian communications in the lead-up to the 1973 war: C. Andrew, *For the President's Eyes Only*, New York: HarperPerennial, 1995, 391, 413–414.

44 Rabinovich, *Yom Kippur War*, 504; C. Andrew and V. Mitrokhin, *The World Was Going Our Way*, New York: Basic Books, 2005, 530n68.
45 The first warning came in December 1972, the second in April 1973: Rabinovich, *Yom Kippur War*, 72–73.
46 Kahana, 'Early Warning versus Concept,'84.
47 Blum, 'Who Killed Ashraf Marwan?'
48 There are several examples of Egyptian double agent operations. See 'Egyptian Intelligence Officials Disclose 8-Year Espionage Operation,' *NYT*, 25 December 1976, 14.
49 Others argue that Top Source's 6 October warning was not that risky since the Soviet evacuation of personnel and dependants had already prompted the Israelis to begin war preparations: Blum, *Eve of Destruction*, 154.
50 King Hussein warned Israel on 25 September that Egypt and Syria were about to launch an attack: Rabinovich, 'Intelligence Follies'; Rabinovich, *Yom Kippur War*, 49–50; Blum, *Eve of Destruction*, 95.
51 El-Shazly, *Crossing*, 212–213. During the war the MID briefed the Soviet liaison officer, General Samakhodsky on wartime developments; however the MID resisted Soviet requests for samples of US and Israeli weapons captured on the battlefield: El-Shazly, *Crossing*, 273–274; V. Israelyan, *Inside the Kremlin during the Yom Kippur War*, University Park, PA: Penn State Press, 1995, 74–75.
52 Israelyan, *Inside the Kremlin*, 248; Pollack, *Arabs at War*, 120; Hotz, 'Battlefield Equations Seen.'
53 D. Raviv and Y. Melman, *Friends in Deed*, New York: Hyperion, 1994, 153; The Center 10 taps were considered the 'Crown Jewels' of Unit 848: Blum, *Eve of Destruction*, 120; Black and Morris, *Israel's Secret Wars*, 298.
54 Kahana 'Early Warning versus Concept,' 99–100n13.
55 Kahana, 'Early Warning versus Concept,' 101n43; Black and Morris, *Israel's Secret Wars*, 288.
56 Black and Morris, *Israel's Secret Wars*, 282; R. Hotz, 'Changing Egypt,' *AWST*, 102, 30 June 1975, 7.
57 Black and Morris, *Israel's Secret Wars*, 231.
58 Heikal, *Road to Ramadan*, 2; Black and Morris, *Israel's Secret Wars*, 298.
59 Rabinovich, *Yom Kippur War*, 69; M. Smith, *The Secret Wars Volume II: Intelligence, Propaganda and Psychological Warfare, Covert Operations, 1945–1980*, Santa Barbara, CA: ABC-Clio, 1981, lxix; Black and Morris, *Israel's Secret Wars*, 298.
60 Blum, *Eve of Destruction*, 281–282; Black and Morris, *Israel's Secret Wars*, 314; Andrew, *For the President's Eyes Only*, 392.
61 'Minister of Defense Discusses October War, Al-Sadat's Assassination,' *Al-Ahram*, 6 October 1982, JPRS, no. 2672, 7 December 1982.
62 'Minister of Defense Discusses October War,' *Al-Ahram*, 6 October 1982; the Palestinian intelligence boss Abu Iyad wrote that Egyptian intelligence officers disguised as Bedouin alerted headquarters that bridging equipment was being routed through al-Arish: Abu Iyad and E. Rouleau, *My Home, My Land*, trans. by Linda Butler Koseoglu, New York: Times Books, 1981, 127.
63 Abu Iyad, *My Home*, 127. Egypt did fly MiG-21 aerial reconnaissance sorties early in the war: L. Nordeen and D. Nicolle, *Phoenix over the Nile*, Washington, DC: Smithsonian Press, 1996, 280, 290.
64 V. Israelyan, 'The October 1973 War: Kissinger in Moscow,' *MEJ*, 49, 1995, 248; Heikal, *Road to Ramadan*, 252. Al-Shazly reveals that Soviet imagery was 'our main source of information about enemy activity' after the ceasefire: El-Shazly, *Crossing*, 273–274.
65 Pollack, *Arabs at War*, 116, 126, 129.
66 One author claims that Israel had 11 specific warnings immediately prior to the attack: Rabinovich, 'Intelligence Follies.' Also see Heikal, *Road to Ramadan*, 8.

67 According to a US intelligence assessment dated 6 October, 'We can find no hard evidence of a major, coordinated Egyptian/Syrian offensive across the Canal and in the Golan Heights area': quoted in H. Kissinger, *Years of Upheaval*, Boston: Little, Brown and Co., 1982, 458.
68 S. Abu Shneif, 'Nothing More Could Be Said,' *Al-Ahram Weekly Online*, 5–11 June 1997. Online, available at: http://weekly.ahram.org.eg/archives/67–97/sup4.htm, accessed 8 September 2007.
69 Kissinger, *Years of Upheaval*, 459, 465.
70 One of the Egyptian negotiators at the Morocco talks was the early Nasser-era intelligence official Hasan al-Tohamy: 'Abd al-Fattāḥ Abū al-Faḍl, *Kuntu nā'iban li-ra'īs al-mukhābarāt*, Cairo: Dār al-Ḥurrīyah, 1986, 210.
71 Under the deal Egypt and Israel could maintain one SIGINT site near Giddi Pass. Both accepted a US proposal to build 3 early warning facilities manned by US personnel. See Raviv and Melman, *Friends in Deed*, 169; El-Gamasy, *October War*, 378.
72 Steven, *Spymasters*, xxi, xxii, xxiv.

## 13  Rejectionists

1 R. Dudney, 'Egypt's Growing Importance for US,' *US News and World Report*, 12 May 1980. Online, available at: www.lexisnexis.com, accessed 18 July 2007.
2 B. Woodward, *Veil: The Secret Wars of the CIA 1981–1987*, New York: Simon & Schuster, 1987, 312–313; M. Heikal, *Autumn of Fury*, London: Corgi, 1978, 77; J. Persico, *Casey*, New York: Viking, 1990, 317.
3 Heikal, *Autumn*, 185.
4 S. El-Saadany, *Egypt and Libya From Inside, 1969–1976*, Jefferson, NC: McFarland, 1994, 170–173.
5 'Intelligence Forces Training,' KUNA, JPRS, 15 April 1980; M. Kaiser and R. Stokes, *Odyssey of an Eavesdropper*, New York: Carroll & Graf, 2005, 96–98.
6 Kaiser and Stokes, *Odyssey*, 103.
7 Woodward, *Veil*, 87.
8 M. Hasanein Heikal, *Iran: The Untold Story*, New York: Pantheon, 1981, 113; J. Richelson, *Foreign Intelligence Organizations*, Cambridge, MA: Ballinger, 179.
9 Heikal, *Iran*, 113; Richelson, *Foreign Intelligence Organizations*, 179.
10 Heikal, *Iran*, 114.
11 Heikal, *Iran*, 114; Saudi–US Relations Information Service, 'Perspectives on Conflicts, Cooperation, and Crises: A Conversation with Saudi Arabia's New Ambassador to the United States,' Part 2. Online, available at: www.saudi-us-relations.org/articles/2006/interviews/060314-turki-interview-2.html, accessed 29 April 2007.
12 Heikal, *Iran*, 114–115. The Safari Club offered the Somalis arms if they would expel the Soviets. Given Soviet inroads in Ethiopia – a Somali adversary – the Somalis did not need much persuading: Richelson, *Foreign Intelligence Organizations*, 179; B. Boutros-Ghali, *Egypt's Road to Jerusalem*, New York: Random House, 1997, 63, 321, 327; Saudi–US Relations Information Service, 'Perspectives on Conflicts, Cooperation, and Crises'; R. Bronson, *Thicker Than Oil*, New York: Oxford University Press, 2006, 178.
13 Richelson, *Foreign Intelligence Organizations*, 179; R. Faligot and P. Krop, *Piscine*, Paris: Editions du Seuil, 1985, 325.
14 Heikal's knowledge of the Safari Club was gleaned from documents he read in Iran after the fall of the Shah: Heikal, *Iran*, 116.
15 J. Cooley, *Unholy Wars*, Sterling, VA: Pluto Press, 1999, 25, 27; Y. Trofimov, *The Siege of Mecca*, New York: Doubleday, 2007, 192.
16 C. Andrew and V. Mitrokhin, *The World Was Going Our Way*, New York: Basic Books, 2005, 162.
17 Ibid., 163.

18  '*October* Editorial Comments on Soviet Espionage,' MENA, FBIS, 19 January 1981.
19  'SNA: Egypt Expels Assistant Soviet Military Attaché,' Riyadh SNA, FBIS, 2 April 1979.
20  'Interior Minister Discusses Bulgarian Plan to Harm Egypt,' Cairo Domestic Service, FBIS, 25 May 1979.
21  'Cabinet Expels Soviet Diplomats, Others 15 Sep,' Cairo Domestic Service, FBIS, 16 September 1981; 'Television Links Sectarian Suspects with Soviets,' MENA, FBIS, 15 September 1981; 'Interior Minister Discusses Soviet Expulsion,' MENA, FBIS, 17 September 1981.
22  'Cabinet Expels Soviet Diplomats, Others 15 Sep'; 'Moscow "Retaliation" Scoffed,' MENA, FBIS, 18 September 1981.
23  'Soviet Role in Stirring Up Strife Detailed,' *Al-Akhbar*, JPRS, 24 November 1981; D. Ottaway, 'Top Soviets Expelled by Egypt,' *Washington Post*, 16 September 1981, A1.
24  K. Pollack, *Arabs at War*, Lincoln: University of Nebraska Press, 2002, 132; Caroz, *Arab Secret Services*, 241, 403.
25  Pollack, *Arabs at War*, 132; ''Ali Denies Charge of Interference in Chad,' *Al-Sharq Al-Awsat*, FBIS, 8 December 1980.
26  Pollack, *Arabs at War*, 132; ''Ali Denies Charge of Interference in Chad,' 3 December 1980; Faligot and Krop, *Piscine*, 347.
27  Pollack, *Arabs at War*, 132; El-Saadany, *Egypt and Libya*, 175.
28  Heikal, *Autumn*, 102–103; S. Steven, *The Spymasters of Israel*, New York: Ballantine, 1980, xxii–xxiii.
29  'Israel's Secret Contacts,' *Time*, 14 August 1978. Online, available at: www.time.com/time/magazine/article/0,9171,946966–1,00.html, accessed 11 July 2007; K. Beattie, *Egypt during the Sadat Years*, New York: Palgrave, 2000, 227; J. Anderson, 'The Most Dangerous Game in the Middle East,' *Washington Post*, 29 October 1980, B16; 'Maxi Plots behind a Strange Mini-War,' *Time*.
30  'Israel's Secret Contacts,' *Time*.
31  Faligot and Krop, *Piscine*, 347.
32  'Anti-Egyptian Group Supported by Libya Reported,' MENA, FBIS, 1 June 1978.
33  '*Al-Ahram* Reports Abortive Libyan Invasion Attempt,' MENA, FBIS, 9 May 1979; '*October*: Al-Qadhdhafi Forms "Suicide Squad" Against Cairo,' MENA, FBIS, 9 May 1979; 'Trial of Libyan Agents to Resume 4 June,' Cairo *Middle East News Agency*, FBIS, 17 May 1979.
34  'Libyan Intelligence Agent Receives Prison Sentence,' Cairo Middle East News Agency, FBIS, 10 July 1979.
35  S. Bakhash, *The Reign of the Ayatollahs*, New York: Basic Books, 1984, 232–236.
36  'Iranian Terrorist Captured; Sabotage Plan Disclosed,' MENA, FBIS, 7 January 1980; 'Iranian Terrorist Confesses, Asks Forgiveness,' *Al-Akhbar*, JPRS, 19 March 1980.
37  R. Baker, *Egypt's Uncertain Revolution under Nasser and Sadat*, Cambridge: Harvard University Press, 1978, 152; Caroz, *Arab Secret Services*, 186.
38  Quoted in Baker, *Egypt's Uncertain Revolution*, 152–153; Beattie, *Egypt during the Sadat Years*, 182–183.
39  Beattie, *Egypt during the Sadat Years*, 182–183; H. Tanner, 'Greatest Box-Office Hit in Cairo Now is *Karnak*,' *NYT*, 29 February 1976, 2. Salah Nasr took umbrage at the apparent portrayal of him as the intelligence boss in *Karnak*: S. Nasr and 'Abd Allah Imam, *Al-Thawrah, Al-Naksah, Al-Mukhabarat*, Cairo: Dar al-Khayyal, 1999, 136–140.
40  J. Burke, *Al-Qaeda*, London: I.B. Tauris, 2003, 63.
41  Boutros-Ghali, *Egypt's Road to Jerusalem*, 321.
42  My source for Egyptian covert action in Afghanistan is Engineer Mohamed Eshaq, a close associate of the deceased Afghan resistance leader, Ahmed Shah Masood: E-Mail Correspondence with Engineer Mohammed Eshaq, Panjshir Afghanistan, 23

July 2007. I am grateful to Engineer Eshaq for his help in obtaining this information from Afghan intelligence experts.

43 O. Roy, *Afghanistan: From Holy War to Civil War*, Princeton: Darwin Press, 1995, 70.

44 C. Murphy, *Passion for Islam*, New York: Scribner, 2002, 72; M. Bearden and J. Risen, *The Main Enemy*, New York: Random House, 2003, 218–219; 'Volunteers for Afghanistan,' MENA, FBIS, 7 January 1980.

45 Telegram from Atherton (Cairo) to Secretary of State, 'Egypt Takes Strong Measures in Response to Soviet Invasion of Afghanistan' 7 January 1980, no. 00364, National Security Archive, Afghanistan file; 'As-Sadat on Afghanistan, Offer of "Facilities,"' AFP, FBIS, 7 January 1980.

46 Bearden and Risen, *Main Enemy*, 217–218; D. Cordovez and S. Harrison, *Out of Afghanistan*, New York: Oxford University Press, 1995, 68–69; Intelligence Report from USDAO Kabul to Defense Intelligence Agency, 'Anti-Aircraft Missiles Reported Provided to Afghan National Islamic Insurgents,' 24 July 1980, no. IR 6 800 0053 80, dtg 241202Z Jul 80. National Security Archive; J. Fullerton, *The Soviet Occupation of Afghanistan*, Hong Kong, *South China Morning Post*, no date; B. Amstutz, *Afghanistan: The First Five Years of Soviet Occupation*, Washington, DC: NDU, 1986, 206–207.

47 Telegram from Atherton (Cairo) to Secretary of State, 'Cairo Press Review: Minister of Interior Says Extremists Fail to Stir up Sectarian Strife,' 16 January 1980, no. 01155, National Security Archive, Afghanistan file.

48 ''Ali: Camps Ordered to Train Afghan Rebels,' MENA, FBIS, 25 January 1980. It is not known if any Afghan mujahedin actually trained in Egypt.

49 Amstutz, *Afghanistan*, 206–207; Telegram from Atherton (Cairo) to Secretary of State, 'Egypt Intensifies Support for Afghan Rebels,' 7 January 1981, no. 00396, National Security Archive, Afghanistan file.

50 Beattie, *Egypt during the Sadat Years*, 102–103, 118.

51 Ibid., 117–118.

52 Caroz, *Arab Secret Services*, 238; El-Saadany, *Egypt and Libya*, 133.

53 Baker, *Egypt's Uncertain Revolution*, 166; Hirst and Beeson, *Sadat*, 249.

54 Beattie, *Egypt during the Sadat Years*, 222–223.

55 Andrew and Mitrokhin, *World*, 164.

56 G. Kepel, *Muslim Extremism in Egypt*, trans. by Jon Rothschild, Berkeley, CA: University of California Press, 1993, 95.

57 Murphy, *Passion for Islam*, 61; 'President Mubarak Interviewed by US Papers,' MENA, FBIS, 21 October 1981.

58 L. Wright, *The Looming Tower*, New York: Vintage, 2006, 57.

59 Kepel, *Muslim Extremism in Egypt*, 212.

60 'Two-Part Series on Confessions of Al-Sadat's Killers,' *Al-Musawwar*, nos. 298, 2979, JPRS, 24 December 1981; Wright, 'The Man behind Bin Laden,' 13.

61 F. Ajami, 'The Sorrows of Egypt,' *Foreign Affairs*, 74, 1995, 72–74.

62 '*Al-Ahram*: Mubarak on Details of As-Sadat Plot,' MENA, FBIS, 27 October 1981; 'Details of Plot Leading to Assassination of al-Sadat Discussed,' *Al-Ahram*, JPRS, 28 December 1981.

63 '*Al-Ahram*: Mubarak on Details of As-Sadat Plot,' MENA; 'Details of Plot Leading to Assassination of al-Sadat Discussed,' *Al-Ahram*.

64 '*Al-Ahram*: Mubarak on Details of As-Sadat Plot,' MENA; 'Details of Plot Leading to Assassination of al-Sadat Discussed,' *Al-Ahram*.

65 '*Al-Ahram* on Secrets of Terrorist Organization,' MENA, FBIS, 22 October 1981; 'Details of Plot Leading to Assassination of al-Sadat Discussed,' *Al-Ahram*.

66 Heikal, *Autumn*, 267.

67 Ibid., 261.

68 'Official Statements on As-Sadat Assassination,' MENA, FBIS, 13 October 1981.

69  Heikal, *Autumn*, 263.
70  Heikal, *Autumn*, 279; Y. Aboul-Enein, 'Islamic Militant Cells and Sadat's Assassination,' *Military Review*, 84, 2004.

### 14  Troubles at home and abroad

1  R. Springborg, *Mubarak's Egypt: Fragmentation of the Political Order*, Boulder: Westview Press, 1989, 24.
2  Airgram from Greene (Cairo) to DOS, 'Biographic: Air Marshal Husni Mubarak,' 28 April 1972, no. A-49, NARA, Box 2250, POL 15–1 EGY; '"*Gazette*" Details Mubarak's Background,' *Egyptian Gazette*, JPRS, 27 October 1981; 'Biographic Information on Muhammad Husni Mubarak,' *Al-Akhbar*, JPRS, 1 November 1981.
3  E. Dowek, *Israeli–Egyptian Relations 1980–2001*, London: Frank Cass, 2001, 52; A. McDermott, *Egypt from Nasser to Mubarak*, London: Croom Helm, 1988, 72.
4  Springborg, *Mubarak's Egypt*, 31.
5  Springborg, *Mubarak's Egypt*, 20–21; K. Ezzelarab, 'Safwat al-Sharif, Pillar of Egypt's Old Guard, is Honorably Retired,' *Daily Star*, 28 June 2004. Online, available at: www.factiva.com, accessed 18 July 2007.
6  'Comment Eviter La Pente Algerienne,' *Le Monde*, 1 April 1993. Online, available at: www.lexisnexis.com, accessed 28 July 2007; Dowek, *Israeli–Egyptian Relations*, 47, 70.
7  Y. Aboul-Enein, 'Islamic Militant Cells and Sadat's Assassination,' *Military Review* 84, 2004; 'Minister of Defense Discusses October War, Al-Sadat's Assassination,' *Al-Ahram*, JPRS, 7 December 1982.
8  Aboul-Enein, 'Islamic Militant Cells and Sadat's Assassination'; F. Prial, 'Egypt Discharges 18 Army Officers It Calls Fanatics,' *NYT*, 13 October 1981, 1.
9  '*Al-Akhbar* on Confessions of As-Sadat's Killers,' MENA, FBIS, 19 November 1981.
10  M. Heikal, *Autumn of Fury*, London: Corgi, 1986, 272; G. Kepel, *Muslim Extremism*, trans. by Jon Rothschild, Berkeley, CA: University of California Press, 1993, 214; Prial, 'Egypt Discharges 18 Army Officers.'
11  'Husni Mubarak Interviewed on US Relations,' MENA, FBIS, 9 October 1981.
12  Prial, 'Egypt Discharges 18 Army Officers.'
13  Ibid.
14  'Question of Guards' Role in Assassination Pondered,' *Al-Majallah* 90, JPRS, 30 December 1981.
15  '*Al-Hawadith* Interviews Defense Minister, *Al-Hawadith*,' FBIS, 20 November 1981.
16  Aboul-Enein, 'Islamic Militant Cells and Sadat's Assassination'; '"Source" Denies Officers Sacked in As-Sadat Case,' FBIS, 29 October 1981.
17  '*Al-Ahram*: Mubarak on Details of As-Sadat Plot,' MENA, FBIS, 27 October 1981; L. Wright, 'The Man Behind Bin Laden,' *New Yorker*, 9 September 2002. Online, available at: www.newyorker.com/printables/fact/020916fa_fact2, accessed 5 September 2006; L. Wright, *The Looming Tower*, New York: Vintage Press, 2006, 60.
18  '*Al-Hawadith* Interviews Defense Minister, *Al-Hawadith*.'
19  'Reportage on As-Sadat's Assassination, Aftermath,' MENA, FBIS, 7 October 1981; Heikal, *Autumn*, 256; '*Al-Hawadith* Interviews Defense Minister, *Al-Hawadith*.'
20  'State Security Investigations Chief,' *October*, no. 261, JPRS, 20 December 1981.
21  Wright, *Looming Tower*, 60; 'Arrested "Terrorist" is As-Sadat Murder Suspect,' AFP, FBIS, 19 October 1981; Al-Zayyat, *Road to al-Qaeda*, 38–39; 'Two-Part Series on Confessions of Al-Sadat's Killers,' *Al-Musawwar*, nos. 298, 2979, JPRS, 24 December 1981; 'Details of Plot Leading to Assassination of al-Sadat Discussed,' *Al-Ahram*, JPRS, 28 December 1981; '*Al-Ahram*: Mubarak on Details of As-Sadat Plot,' MENA, 27 October 1981.
22  'Security Men Exchange Fire with Asyut Fighters,' Cairo Domestic Service, FBIS, 13 October 1981; Aboul-Enein, 'Islamic Militant Cells and Sadat's Assassination.'

23 'AFP Reports Crackdown on Fundamentalists,' AFP, FBIS, 19 October 1981.

24 Quoted in S. Grey, *Ghost Plane*, New York: St Martin's Press, 2006, 259.

25 B. Woodward, *Veil*, New York: Simon & Schuster, 1987, 168–169.

26 Mubarak denied any CIA role in the Sadat investigation: 'President Mubarak Interviewed by *Washington Post*,' MENA, FBIS, 3 November 1982.

27 Woodward, *Veil*, 269.

28 'Egypt Sentences American to 5-Year Term for Spying,' *Global and Mail*, 21 July 1989. Online, available at: www.lexisnexis.com, accessed 29 June 07; 'Survey of Recent Spying Cases,' London: *Al-Tadamun*, JPRS-NEA-89–068, 23 October 1989; 'With My Little Eye,' *The Economist*, 29 July 1989, 37; 'Defence Lawyers Seek to Arrange Swap for "CIA Spy,"' *Independent*, 25 July 1989, 11. According to one uncorroborated account the CIA recruited Cairo-based businessmen to spy on companies operating in Egypt. These businessmen reportedly obtained information on Egypt's role in the Condor II ballistic missile and chemical warfare programs: M. Perry, *Eclipse*, New York: William Morrow, 1992, 197, 199, 201–202.

29 'Defence Lawyers Seek to Arrange Swap for "CIA Spy,"'; 'American Returns Home After Being Held As Spy,' *NYT*, 1 November 1993, A14.

30 J. Walcot, 'You Can Run But You Can't Hide,' *Newsweek*, 21 October 1985, 22; T. Naftali, *Blind Spot*, New York: Basic Books, 2005, 172–173.

31 Walcot, 'You Can Run'; Woodward, *Veil*, 414–415. Naftali attributes some of the SIGINT on this operation to the Israelis: Naftali *Blind Spot*, 173.

32 Woodward, *Veil*, 416.

33 L. Nordeen and D. Nicolle, *Phoenix Over the Nile*, Washington, DC: Smithsonian, 1996, 330.

34 M. Dornheim, 'Egypt Begins Using Unmanned Aircraft for Reconnaissance,' *AWST* 130, 23 January 1989, 56.

35 Nordeen and Nicolle, *Phoenix*, 330.

36 B. Amstutz, *Afghanistan: The First Five Years of Soviet Occupation*, Washington, DC: National Defense University, 1986, 212.

37 J. Persico, *Casey*, New York: Viking, 1990, 311.

38 M. Bearden and J. Risen, *Main Enemy*, New York: Random House, 2003, 218–219.

39 M. Al-Zayyat, *Road to al-Qaeda*, trans. by Ahmed Fekry, London: Pluto Press, 2004, 52; Wright, 'The Man.'

40 Wright, 'The Man.'

41 P. Bergen, *The Osama bin Laden I Know*, New York: Free Press, 2006, 74; J. Burke, *Al-Qaeda*, London: I.B. Tauris, 2003, 8. Wright dates the birth of al-Qa'ida to 10 September 1988: Wright, *Looming Tower*, 152.

42 Wright, 'The Man'; Bergen, *Osama*, 83. Saif al-'Adl reportedly was a colonel in Egyptian special forces: Wright, *Looming Tower*, 148.

43 Wright, 'The Man,' 21.

44 Burke, *Al-Qaeda*, 79.

45 Bergen, *Osama*, 120–121.

46 B. Gwertzman, 'Schultz Asserts Libyan Threat Has "Receded,"' *NYT*, 21 February 1983, 1; L. Cannon and G. Wilson, 'US Says Libya Eyed Sudan Coup,' *Washington Post*, 19 February 1983, A1.

47 D. Ottaway, 'Sudan, Egypt Minimize Report of Coup Plot,' *Washington Post*, 20 February 1983, A1.

48 Perry, *Eclipse*, 165.

49 P. Tyler, 'US Aborted 1983 Trap Set for Libyan Forces; Leaks Halted Scheme Against Ghadafi,' *Washington Post*, 12 July 1987, A1.

50 '*Akhbar Al-Yawm* Reports Libyan Agents' Arrest,' MENA, FBIS, 2 May 1983; 'MENA reports on Libyan Intelligence Organization,' MENA, FBIS, 13 September 1983; 'Nine Persons Detained on Spying Charges,' MENA, FBIS, 14 September 1983.

51 'Egypt on Alert for Libyan Terrorist Acts,' *Los Angeles Times*, 19 November 1984, A4; D. Ottaway, 'Egyptians Revel in Duping of Libya,' *Washington Post*, 18 November 1984, A14.

52 'Cairo Fakes Pictures And Foils Libyan Death Plot,' *NYT*, 18 November 1984, 1; 'Egypt on Alert for Libyan Terrorist Acts,' *Los Angeles Times*, 19 November 1984, A4; 'Egypt Foils Khadafy Plot Fakes Killing of Ex-Prime Minister,' Associated Press, 18 November 1984; 'Mubarak Reveals Other Plots,' MENA, FBIS, 19 November 1984.

53 Naftali, *Blind Spot*, 167–168.

54 The operation against the American embassy in Cairo was planned jointly by Libyan intelligence and the Abu Nidal Organization. Egyptian success reportedly was due to Egyptian monitoring of communications between Libyan intelligence and Abu Nidal operatives. '*Akhbar Al-Yawm* Cited,' MENA, FBIS, 28 May 1985; D. Shipler, 'Terror: Americans As Targets,' *NYT*, 26 November 1985, 9; 'Reported Libyan Plot to Destabilise Egypt,' BBC, 3 April 1985; 'Cairo Reports Khadafy Plot Against Egypt – 5 Arrested,' *San Francisco Chronicle*, 2 April 1985, 19; 'Returnees Searched to Guard Against Libyan Terrorism,' Abu Dhabi WAM, FBIS, 22 August 1985; 'Possible Military Action Seen,' *Al-Ra'y Al-'Amm*, FBIS, 23 August 1985; 'Security Foils Libyan Assassination Attempt,' MENA, FBIS, 12 November 1985; 'Names of Accused Reported,' MENA, FBIS, 12 November 1985.

55 'Alert on Border with Libya,' Muscat Domestic Service, FBIS, 25 November 1985; J. Adams, *Secret Armies*, New York: Atlantic Monthly Press, 1987, 92–93;

56 R. Gates, *From the Shadows*, New York: Touchstone, 1996, 352; Woodward, *Veil*, 414; Perry, *Eclipse*, 165; Naftali, *Blind Spot*, 169.

57 Woodward claims the CIA worked closely with Egyptian intelligence but his book lacks specifics: Woodward, *Veil*, 411.

58 Ibid.

59 'Libya Claims Egypt Helped Guide US Bombers in Raids,' *Houston Chronicle*, 17 May 1986, 22; 'Alleged Involvement of Egyptian Spy Ring in Libya in Guiding US Raid,' BBC, 17 May 1986.

60 'Libyan Soldiers Asked to Act Against Al-Qadhdhafi,' Voice of the Arabs, FBIS, October 1986.

61 The Egyptian assessment was drawn from B. Slavin, 'Ghadafi's Military Failings in Chad Weigh Heavily on His Future,' *St Petersburg Times*, 12 April 1987, 23A and B. Slavin, 'Pariah in the Desert: The Increasing Isolation of Qadaffi,' *Business Week*, 30 November 1987, 57.

62 'Libya Announces Troop Pullback from Border with Egypt,' *Los Angeles Times*, 29 March 198, A13; S. El-Saadany, *Egypt and Libya from Inside, 1969–1976*, Jefferson, NC: McFarland, 1994, 178; B. Slavin, 'Opposition Drive Against Gadhafi Gaining Strength,' *St Petersburg Times*, 21 February 1989, 11A.

## 15 State security

1 E. Dowek, *Israeli–Egyptian Relations*, London: Frank Cass, 2001, 34.

2 Ibid., 35–36, 38, 60, 76–77, 116.

3 Ibid. 103–104.

4 *The 9/11 Commission Report*, New York: W.W. Norton, nd, 240–241.

5 M. Acoca, 'US Sale of Weapons to Iran Reportedly Part of Coup Plan,' *Houston Chronicle*, 25 October 1987, 4; 'Operation of Foreign Radio Sites Denied,' MENA, FBIS, 17 March 1987.

6 P. Tyler, 'Egypt Says US Arms Fill Iran's Needs,' *Washington Post*, 28 December 1986, A15.

7 'Security Receives Report on Iranian Subversion,' *Al-Wafd*, FBIS, 9 June 1987.

8 'Members of Khomeyni-Linked Group Arrested,' *Al-Majallah*, JPRS-NEA-88–055, 3 August 1988.

9 'More Details on Underground Group Uncovered,' MENA, FBIS-NES-88-116, 16 June 1988; 'Iraqi Embassy Target of Underground Group,' Kuwait *Al-Ra'y Al-'Amm*, FBIS-NES-88-121, 23 June 1988.

10 D. Pugh and L. Hilsum, 'Sudanese Junta Calls Peace Talks,' *Guardian*, 6 July 1989. Online, available at: www.lexisnexis.com, accessed 30 June 2007.

11 M. Boyle Mahle, *Denial and Deception*, New York: Nation Books, 2004, 98–99; L. Wright, 'The Man Behind Bin Laden,' *New Yorker*, 9 September 2002. Online, available at: www.newyorker.com/printables/fact/020916fa_fact2, accessed 5 September 2006; J. Burke, *Al-Qaeda*, London: I.B. Tauris, 2003, 130.

12 'Sudanese-Iranian Military Cooperation Detailed,' *Al-Wafd*, FBIS-NES-91-250, 30 December 1991; R. Dowden, 'Government Steps up War on Rebels with Iran's Help,' *Independent*, 12 March 1992, 15; T. Walker, 'Sudanese Political Trends Alarm Cairo,' *Financial Times*, 13 February 1992, 4.

13 Dowden, 'Government Steps up War'; T. Walker, 'Sudanese Political Trends'; 'Sudanese-Iranian Military Cooperation Detailed'; Wright, 'The Man'; B. Gertz, *Breakdown*, Washington, DC: Regnery, 2002; *9/11 Commission Report*, 61.

14 Mahle, *Denial*, 100; Wright, 'The Man,' 24.

15 'Military Leaders Puzzled by Failures of Their Intelligence Service,' *Independent*, 4 October 1990, 14.

16 K. Pollack, *Arabs at War*, Lincoln: University of Nebraska Press, 2002, 139; K. Bin Sultan and P. Seale, *Desert Warrior*, London: HarperCollins, 1995, 222.

17 T. Naftali, *Blind Spot*, New York: Basic Books, 2005, 218.

18 K. Donovan, 'At The Front,' *Toronto Star*, 9 February 1991, A1.

19 'Americans are "Restrictees" for Now, Official in Iraq Says,' *St Louis Post-Dispatch*, 15 August 1990, 11A; P. Ford and G. Moffett III, 'Confidence Weighs Against Caution in Gulf,' *Christian Science Monitor*, 17 January 1991, 3.

20 'Security Services Arrest Five More "Saboteurs,"' MENA, FBIS-NES-90-197, 11 October 1990; Bin Sultan and Seale, *Desert Warrior*, 242, 395–396.

21 'Government Closes Iraqi Military Attaché's Office,' MENA, FBIS-NES-90-186, 25 September 1990.

22 Human Rights Watch, *Behind Closed Doors: Torture and Detention in Egypt*, New York: 1992, 56; 'Arrested "Terrorists" Said to Have Iraqi Backing,' *Al-Wafd*, FBIS-NES-90-193, 4 October 1990; 'Paper Cites Interior Minister on Terrorist Cases,' Voice of Lebanon, FBIS-NES-90-193, 4 October 1990; 'Terrorists Held in Cairo Admit Ba'th Link,' *Al-Wafd*, FBIS-NES-90-196, 10 October 1990; 'Security Services Arrest Five More "Saboteurs,"' MENA.

23 'Canal Security Stepped Up Against Possible Iraqi Sabotage,' Associated Press, 21 December 1990.

24 'US, Egypt Vow Support for Iraqi Opposition,' *Al-Wafd*, FBIS-NES-91-059, 27 March 1991.

25 E. Walsh, 'The Prince,' *New Yorker*, 24 March 2003. Online, available at: www.newyorker.com, accessed 15 February 2009.

26 C. Andrew, *For the President's Eyes Only*, New York: HarperPerennial, 1995, 536.

27 'Source Denies Involvement in Gates Mission,' MENA, FBIS-NES-92-027, 10 February 1992.

28 'Interior Minister Discusses Security Situation,' *Al-Musawwar*, FBIS-NES-87-242, 17 December 1987.

29 'Interior Minister Sees No Internal Threats to Egypt,' *Akhbar Al-Yawm*, JPRS-NEA-86–034, 20 March 1986.

30 C. Murphy, 'Kuwait Reported Moving to Curb Rights Abuses,' *Washington Post*, 2 October 1991, A20.

31 Human Rights Watch, *Behind Closed Doors*, 31.

32 Ibid., 31n10.

33 R. Springborg, *Mubarak's Egypt: Fragmentation of the Political Order*, Boulder:

Westview Press, 1989, 149. Also see 'Weekly Raps State Security Investigation Service,' *Akhbar Al-Yawm*, FBIS, 25 March 1986.

34 Springborg, *Mubarak's Egypt*, 150.

35 R. Matthews and L. Fares, 'Mubarak Dismisses Minister After Riots,' *Financial Times*, 1 March 1986, 3; Springborg, *Mubarak's Egypt*, 150.

36 M. Weaver, *A Portrait of Egypt*, New York: Farrar, Straus & Giroux, 1999, 88–89.

37 Geneive Abdo, *No God but God*, New York: Oxford University Press, 2000, 21.

38 Weaver, *Portrait*, 88, 89, 147; Abdo, *No God but God*, 147.

39 C. Murphy, *Passion for Islam*, New York: Scribner, 2002, 74–75; Weaver, *Portrait*, 147.

40 Murphy, *Passion*, 65.

41 Wright, 'The Man,' 24.

42 R. Al-Faris, 'Interview with Fouad Allam, Former Head of the State Security Apparatus,' *Watani* 342, 2 September 2007. Online, available at: www.wataninet.com, accessed 9/7/07; Human Rights Watch, *Behind Closed Doors*, 29.

43 Former SSIS Director Fuad Allam told one journalist that there are no Copt SSIS officers because of an unspecified event in the 1970s: al-Faris, 'Interview with Fouad Allam.'

44 O. McDoom, 'Israeli Spy Ring Spawned Feared Egyptian Intelligence,' Reuters, 15 April 2003.

45 Human Rights Watch, *Behind Closed Doors*, 33.

46 Human Rights Watch, *Behind Closed Doors*, 31–32; Al-Ibrashi, Wa'il, 'Writer Views Police Use of Telephone Taps,' *Rose al-Yusuf*, FBIS-NES-95-088, 8 May 1995.

47 Human Rights Watch, *Behind Closed Doors*, 12; T. Plate and A. Darvi, *Secret Police*, Garden City, Doubleday, 1981, 73.

48 Amnesty International, *Egypt: Ten Years of Torture*, New York: 1991, 1, 3, 6.

49 Human Rights Watch, *Behind Closed Doors*, 9–10.

50 Human Rights Watch, *Behind Closed Doors*, 73.

51 Amnesty International, *Egypt: Ten Years of Torture*, 8.

52 Human Rights Watch, *Behind Closed Doors*, 73, 76–77.

53 Ibid., 195; Amnesty International, *Report on Torture*, New York: 1975, 226–227.

54 Wright, 'The Man,' 18.

55 Wright, 'The Man,' 15; M. al-Zayyat, *Road to al-Qaeda*, trans. by Ahmed Fekry, London: Pluto Press, 2004, 31; Zawahiri once said that 'The toughest thing about captivity is forcing the mujahid, under the force of torture, to confess about his colleagues, to destroy his movement with his own hands, and offer his and his colleagues' secrets to the enemy': L. Wright, *The Looming Tower*, New York: Vintage, 2006, 62, 69–70.

56 Human Rights Watch, *Behind Closed Doors*, 44.

57 Ibid., 44, 50, 112.

58 Murphy, *Passion for Islam*, 77.

59 Ibid., 66–67.

60 'Ministry Plants "Undercover" Agents in "Extremist" Cells,' FBIS-NES-95-068, 10 April 1995.

61 'Counterterrorism Squad Sent to Algeria,' *Al-Sha'b*, FBIS-NES-92-023, 4 February 1992.

62 'Jihad Members leave Afghanistan for Sudan'; C. Berger, 'Egypt Arrests Afghan-War Vets in Crackdown on Radicals,' *Christian Science Monitor*, 15 October 1992, 1.

63 E-Mail correspondence with Eshaq, Panjshir Afghanistan, 23 July 2007.

64 A. Rashid and C. Berger, 'Pakistan Cracks Down on Its Legacy of Terror,' *Sunday Times*, 9 May 1993, 3; C. Berger, 'Egypt Arrests Afghan-War Vets in Crackdown on Radicals'; 'Pakistan: Le Boomerang "Afghan,"' *Le Monde*, 29 April 1993. Online, available at: http://lexisnexis.com, accessed 28 July 2007; S. Reeve, *The New Jackals*, Boston: Northeastern Press, 1999, 55–56.

65 'Egypt Seeks Repatriation of 1,500 "Afghan Veterans" from Pakistan,' *Agence France-Presse*, 2 May 1993; Rashid and Berger, 'Pakistan Cracks Down on its Legacy.'
66 Murphy, *Passion*, 79.
67 'Further on Investigation,' MENA, FBIS-NES-90-199, 15 October 1990; 'Abu-Nidal Link Suggested,' *Al-Wafd* (13 October 1990), FBIS-NES-90-201, 17 October 1990; Human Rights Watch, *Behind Closed Doors*, 190; Murphy, *Passion*, 79.
68 'Counterterrorism Squad Sent to Algeria.'
69 Murphy, *Passion*, 81; '1992 Security Incidents Reviewed,' *Al-Wafd*, JPRS-NEA-93–021, 10 February 1993.
70 W. Al-Ibrashi, 'Writer Views Police Use of Telephone Taps,' *Rose al-Yusuf*, FBIS-NES-95-088, 8 May 1995.
71 K. Sharaf al-Din, 'Investigations Solve Mystery of Some Violent Incidents, Assassinations, and Explosions in Egypt Over 12 Years,' *Al-Sharq Al-Awsat* (9 March 1999), FBIS, MM1003112499.
72 Ibid.
73 'Detained "Terrorist" Abd-al-Ghani Interviewed,' Cairo ESC Television, FBIS-NES-95-160, 18 August 1995.
74 Human Rights Watch, *World Report 1994*, New York: 1993, 280.
75 Sharaf al-Din, 'Investigations Solve Mystery of Some Violent Incidents'; 'Egyptian Militants Score Key Blow by Killing Deputy Security Chief,' *Guardian* (11 April 1994): 8; Murphy, *Passion*, 90–91.
76 Murphy, *Passion*, 92.
77 Ibid., 95, 294n57.
78 Ibid., 93.
79 Wright, 'The Man,' 25; Wright, *Looming Tower*, 209–210.
80 'Ministry Plants "Undercover" Agents in 'Extremist' Cells,' AFP, FBIS-NES-95-068, 10 April 1995.
81 'Security Chief on "Terrorism," Muslim Brotherhood,' *Al-Ahali*, FBIS-NES-95-061, 30 March 1995.
82 Human Rights Watch, *World Report 1997*, New York: 1996, 278; Human Rights Watch, *World Report 1995*, New York: 1994, 267; Murphy, *Passion*, 298n17; S. Grey, 'America's Gulag,' *New Statesman*, 17 May 2004, 1.
83 Weaver, *Portrait*, 150–152; Murphy, *Passion*, 108–112.

## 16 General intelligence wars

1 According to one account, Soleiman entered the public domain in 2000: No'am Amit 'The Puppet Master,' *Ma'ariv*, 2 May 2003, FBIS. Online, available at: www.fas.org/irp/world/egypt/sulayman.html, accessed 5/9/2003; also see Mohamed Bazzi, 'He Keeps Everyone Talking,' *Newsday*, published in *Chicago Tribune*, 2 July 2006. Online, available at: www.chicagotribune.com/ny-woegypt024804658 jul02,0,3784914, accessed 23 March 2007.
2 M. Weaver, 'Pharaohs-in-Waiting,' *Atlantic Monthly* 292, 2003, 86–87; Bazzi, 'He Keeps Everyone Talking.'
3 Amit, 'The Puppet Master.'
4 George Tenet and Bill Harlow, *At the Center of the Storm*, New York: Harper-Collins, 2007, 80.
5 Quoted in Amit, 'The Puppet Master.'
6 Ibid.
7 Quoted in Weaver, 'Pharaohs-in-Waiting,' 91–92.
8 Amit, 'The Puppet Master'; 'Egyptian Intelligence Official Discusses Hamas with Italian Paper,' BBC, 2 February 2006.
9 L. Wright, 'The Man Behind Bin Laden,' *New Yorker*, 9 September 2002. Online,

available at: www.newyorker.com/printables/fact/020916fa_fact2, accessed 5 September 2006; L. Wright, *Looming Tower*, New York: Vintage, 2006, 242.

10 Wright, *Looming Tower*, 243; S. Coll, *Ghost Wars*, New York: Penguin, 2004, 275–276.

11 Weaver, 'Pharaohs-in-Waiting,' 87; Bazzi, 'He Keeps Everyone Talking.'

12 M. Mahle, *Denial and Deception*, New York: Nation Books, 2004, 190; Weaver, 'Pharaohs-in-Waiting,' 87; 'Ethiopian TV Provides Details of Attack on Mubarak,' Addis Ababa ETV Television Network, FBIS-NES-95-123, 27 June 1995; 'Armed Forces Renews Allegiance to Mubarak,' Cairo ESC Television, FBIS-NES-95-124, 28 June 1995; 'Mubarak Speeches Address Assassination Attempt,' Arab Republic of Egypt Radio Network, FBIS-NES-95-125, 29 June 1995; 'Mubarak Decorates Officers, Bodyguards,' Arab Republic of Egypt Radio, FBIS-NES-95-126, 30 June 1995; 'Detained "Terrorist" Abd-al-Ghani Interviewed,' Cairo ESC Television, FBIS-NES-95-160, 18 August 1995; 'Weekly Gives Details of Attempt,' MENA, FBIS-NES-95-173, 7 September 1995.

13 'Mubarak Accuses Sudan's al-Turabi,' ESC Television, FBIS-NES-95-123, 27 June 1995; 'MENA Cites Eyewitnesses, Sources,' MENA, FBIS-NES-95-123, 27 June 1995; 'Mubarak on Sudanese, Ethiopian, European Terrorism Role,' Arab Republic of Egypt Radio Network, FBIS-NES-95-126, 30 June 1995; ' "Vital Clues" Said Found on Mubarak Attack,' MENA, FBIS-NES-95-130, 7 July 1995; 'Sudanese "Terrorist" Connection Revealed,' *Al-Musawwar*, FBIS-NES-95-131, 10 July 1995; 'Detained Islamists Interrogated on Mubarak Attack,' *Al-Sha'b*, FBIS-NES-95-156, 14 August 1995; 'Evidence Said to Implicate Sudan in Mubarak Attack,' MENA, FBIS-NES-95-156, 14 August 1995; 'Shaykh's Conviction Shows Country's Security Skills,' *Al-Ahram*, FBIS-NES-95-196, 11 October 1995.

14 'Military Strike Against Sudan Urged,' AFP, FBIS, FBIS-NES-95-129, 6 July 1995; S. Sackur and M. Huband, 'Egyptian Hardliners Call for Attack over Sudan Hit Squad,' *Observer*, 2 July 1995, 14.

15 M. Weaver, *Portrait of Egypt*, New York: Farrar, Straus & Giroux, 1999, 177.

16 'Sudanese Diplomats Reportedly "Attacked" in Cairo,' AFP, FBIS-NES-95-136, 17 July 1995; 'Mubarak Envoy Visits Injured Diplomats,' MENA, FBIS-NES-95-136, 17 July 1995.

17 'Intelligence Seizes Sudanese Arms, "Terrorist," ' MENA, FBIS-NES-95-218, 13 November 1995.

18 Wright, 'The Man,' 26–27; Wright, *Looming Tower*, 244–246.

19 Muhammad Salah, 'According to the Egyptian Interrogation of Defendants in the Case, al-Zawahiri Ordered the Blowing Up of the Embassy in Pakistan in Retaliation for the Attempt to Assassinate Him in Sudan,' *Al-Hayah*, FBIS, MM2212115798; 'Delegation Leaves for Islamabad to Investigate Bombing,' MENA, FBIS, FBIS-NES-95-223, 20 November 1995; 'Paper Details Embassy Blast Investigation Progress,' MENA, FBIS-NES-95-224, 21 November 1995.

20 'Embassy Attackers Identified; Arabs Under Arrest,' MENA, FBIS-NES-95-228, 28 November 1995.

21 'Arrest of Embassy Bombers Said Delayed Due to "Leak," ' *Al-Ahram*, FBIS-NES-95-233, 5 December 1995.

22 'Egypt: Security Agreement Signed with Pakistan,' MENA, FBIS-NES-048, 11 March 1996; 'Egypt: Perpetrators of Egyptian Embassy Blast in Pakistan Arrested,' *Al-'Arabi*, FBIS-NES-96-151, 5 August 1996.

23 'Plan to Increase Security, Retrieve "Terrorists" Viewed,' MENA, FBIS-NES-95-227, 27 November 1995.

24 Ibid., 27; also see Wright, *Looming Tower*, 252, 282, 284.

25 B. Gertz, *Breakdown*, Washington, DC: Regnery, 2002, 56.

26 Fawaz A. Gerges, 'The End of the Islamist Insurgency in Egypt?' *MEJ*, 54, 2000, 595; Human Rights Watch, *World Report 2000*, New York: 1999, 345.

27 Human Rights Watch, *World Report 2000*, 345.
28 'Intelligence Service Law Modifications Approved,' MENA, JPRS-NEA-89–002, 5 January 1989.
29 A. Higgins and A. Cullison, 'The Unmasking of a Traitor to Jihad,' *Wall Street Journal Europe*, 20 December 2002, A1. For more on the al-Qa'ida sympathies of PSO officers, see Wright, *Looming Tower*, 373.
30 Human Rights Watch, *Black Hole: The Fate of Islamists Rendered to Egypt* 17, 2005.
31 R. Henderson, *Brassey's International Intelligence Yearbook 2003*, Dulles, VA, Brassey's, 2003, 251.
32 Khalid Sharaf al-Din 'Egypt: The Death Sentences Against Jihad Leaders Will be Dropped When They are Arrested and Tried in Person,' *Al-Sharq Al-Awsat*, FBIS, MM2304144099.
33 Mahmud Sadiq, untitled article in *Al-Watan al-'Arabi*, FBIS, JN0306071099.
34 Wright, *Looming Tower*, 222; S. Reeve, *The New Jackals*, Boston: Northeastern University Press, 1999, 182.
35 'Security Delegation Travels to Europe,' *Al-'Arabi*, FBIS-NES-95-017, 26 January 1995.
36 'Egypt: Cairo Says Britain 'Sheltering' Egyptian Militants,' Paris AFP, FBIS-NES-96-039, 27 February 1996.
37 Richard Owen and Daniel McGrory, 'The Man to Really Fear,' *The Times*, 11 October 2001, 1.
38 M. Rudner, 'Hunters and Gatherers: The Intelligence Coalition Against Islamic Terrorism,' *IJIC* 17, 2004, 214; Adel Darwish, 'America's War on Terrorism,' 15 February 2002. Online, available at: www.mideastnews.com/zawahiri.html, accessed 5/8/2006.
39 'Egypte: Hassan al-Alfi Impose Ses Hommes,' *Le Monde*, 17 June 1993. Online, available at: www.lexisnexis.com, accessed 28 July 2007.
40 Shyam Bhatia, 'Drugged Carlos Seized "During Liposuction Operation,"' *Observer*, 21 August 1994, 1; Wright, *Looming Tower*, 249; for a different account of Carlos's apprehension see B. Waugh and T. Keown, *Hunting the Jackal*, New York: Morrow, 2004.
41 'Embassy Rejects Newspaper Report on Hit-Squads,' *Independent*, 7 December 1995, 12; R. Fisk, 'Cairo's Dirty War Spills Across Europe,' *Independent*, 6 December 1995, 13.
42 Fisk, 'Cairo's Dirty War Spills Across Europe.'
43 Coll, *Ghost Wars*, 259–260.
44 Paul Eedle, 'FBI Team Collects Bomb Suspect from Egypt,' Associated Press, 24 March 1993; T. Naftali, *Blind Spot*, New York: Basic Books, 2005, 237–238.
45 Reeve, *New Jackals*, 55. 183.
46 'Pakistan: Le Boomerang Afghan,' *Le Monde*, 29 April 1993, 1.
47 L. McQuillan, 'Clinton, Mubarak Optimistic on Mideast Talks,' Reuters, 6 April 1993.
48 'Clinton: US Won't Fight Serbs Alone; Vows Probe of NYC Blast; Could US Have Foiled It?' *Salt Lake Tribune*, 7 April 1993, A1.
49 'Egyptian Says Confession Links Iran to WTC Bombing,' Associated Press, 15 July 1993.
50 Mahle, *Denial*, 192.
51 Naftali, *Blind Spot*, 244–245.
52 S. Grey, *Ghost Plane*, New York: St Martin's, 2006, 141–142; Coll, *Ghost Wars*, 268, 271, 323, 376–377; interview with Michael Scheuer, 23 February 2009.
53 Grey, *Ghost Plane*, 141–142.
54 Ibid., 139–141; J. Mayer, 'Outsourcing Torture,' *New Yorker*, 14 February 2005. Online, available at: www.newyorker.com/printables/fact/050214fa_fact6, accessed 5 February 2006.

55  Mayer, 'Outsourcing Torture,' 5; Human Rights Watch, *Black Hole*, 17.
56  Mayer, 'Outsourcing Torture,' 4–5; Grey, *Ghost Plane*, 142; Mahle, *Denial*, 203–204.
57  Mayer, 'Outsourcing Torture,' 5; Human Rights Watch, *Black Hole*, 21; 'La Structure des 'Albanais' Egyptiens,' *Le Monde*, 26 November 1998. Online, available at: www.lexisnexis.com, accessed 28 July 2007; Wright, 'The Man,' 29; S. Sachs, 'An Investigation in Egypt Illustrates Al Qaeda's Web,' *New York Times*, 21 November 2001, 1.
58  Grey, 'America's Gulag,' *New Statesman*, 17 May 2004, 1; Grey, *Ghost Plane*, 143; Mayer, 'Outsourcing Torture,' 5; K. Sharaf Al-Din, 'Egypt: The Death Sentences Against Jihad Leaders Will be Dropped,' *Al-Sharq Al-Awsat*, 23 April 1999, FBIS, MM2304144099.
59  M. Al-Shafi'i, 'Investigations into Detained Egyptian Fundamentalists Reveal They Planned to use Gliders in Armed Attacks,' *Al-Sharq Al-Awsat*, FBIS, MM16014134599.
60  Ibid.
61  Quoted in Grey, *Ghost Plane*, 144.
62  Tenet and Harlow, *At the Center*, 116; *9/11 Commission Report*, New York: Norton, 116–118; Vernon Loeb, 'US Wasn't Sure Plant Had Nerve Gas Role; Before Sudan Strike, CIA Urged More Tests,' *Washington Post*, 21 August 1999, A1. Former CIA case officer Milt Bearden believed the agent who collected the samples was either Egyptian or Tunisian: Wright, *Looming Tower*, 479. Also see Coll, *Ghost Wars*, 411.
63  Human Rights Watch, *Black Hole*, 24, 27–28; Wright, *Looming Tower*, 140.
64  Ibid., 4, 25–26; Grey, *Ghost Plane*, 144; Wright, 'The Man,' 31.
65  R. Kessler, *The CIA At War*, New York: 2003, 143; Tenet and Harlow, *At the Center*, 155.

**17  September 2001 and beyond**

1  G. Tenet and B. Harlow, *At the Center*, New York: Harper-Collins, 2007, 121; M. Rudner, 'Hunters and Gatherers: The Intelligence Coalition Against Islamic Terrorism,' *IJIC*, 17, 2004, 194.
2  'Mubarak Says Egypt Warned US of al-Qaeda Plot One Week Ahead of 9/11,' Agence France-Presse, 4 June 2002; 'Interview with Egyptian President Husni Mubarak,' *American Morning with Paula Zahn*, 7 June 2002; J. Risen, 'Traces of Terror,' *NYT*, 4 June 2002, 1.
3  P. Tyler and D. Priest, 'We Gave US A Week's Warning of September 11, Claims Mubarak.' Online, available at: www.smh.com.au/2002/06/05/12229827018901, accessed 22 March 2007; 'No Specific Warning of Attack from Egypt – US,' Reuters (4 June 2002); 'Mubarak Says Egypt Warned US of al-Qaeda Plot One Week Ahead of 9/11.'
4  *9/11 Commission Report*, New York: Norton, 128–129.
5  Ibid., 259.
6  Ibid., 258; D. Sanger, '2 Leaders Tell of Plot to Kill Bush in Genoa,' *NYT*, 26 September 2001, 1.
7  'L'alerte des Services Egyptiens a Washington,' *Le Monde*, 5 July 2001. Online, available at: www.lexisnexis.com, accessed 28 July 2007.
8  L. Wright, 'The Man Behind Bin Laden,' *New Yorker*, 9 September 2002. Online, available at: www.newyorker.com/printables/fact/020916fa_fact2, accessed 5 September 2006.
9  'US Pleased With Egyptian Intelligence Sharing,' *Fox News*, 20 January 2002. Online, available at: www.foxnews.com/0,3566,43500,00.html, accessed 22 March 2007.
10  *9/11 Commission Report*, 494n64.
11  'Saudi, Egyptian Intelligence Officers Questioning Arab al-Qaeda Captives in

Pakistan,' *Al-Bawaba News*, 31 December 2001, 1; Kessler, *CIA at War*, New York: St Martin's, 234.

12 Human Rights Watch, *Black Hole* 17, 2003, 34; C. Whitlock, 'A Secret Deportation of Terror Suspects,' *Washington Post*, 25 July 2004, A1; S. Grey, *Ghost Plane*, New York: St Martin's, 24–36.

13 Grey, *Ghost Plane*, 24–36; Whitlock, 'A Secret Deportation of Terror Suspects.'

14 Grey, *Ghost Plane*, 36.

15 C. Bonini and G. D'Avanzo, *Collusion*, trans. by James Marcus, Hoboken, NJ, Melville House, 2007, 166–167; Grey, *Ghost Plane*, 188–211.

16 Grey, *Ghost Plane*, 189–191; Bonini and D'Avanzo, *Collusion*, 167.

17 J. Mayer, 'Outsourcing Torture,' *New Yorker*, 14 February 2005. Online, available at: www.newyorker.com/printables/fact/050214fa_fact6, accessed 5 February 2006; Grey, *Ghost Plane*, 241; Tenet and Harlow, *At the Center*, 269.

18 Mayer, 'Outsourcing Torture.'

19 'Azerbaijan Hands over Egyptian Terror Suspect,' Agence France-Presse, 12 October 2001.

20 'Egyptian Intelligence Accused of Detaining Yemeni Official,' Agence France-Presse, 30 October 2002; Human Rights Watch, *Black Hole*, 37.

21 Human Rights Watch, *Black Hole*, 37; A. Higgins and A. Cullison, 'The Unmasking of a Traitor to Jihad,' *Wall Street Journal Europe*, 20 December 2002, A1.

22 Human Rights Watch, *Black Hole*, 39–40, 46.

23 The United Nations Special Rapporteur on Torture has said that torture in Egypt is 'habitual, widespread and deliberate…': quoted in Human Rights Watch, *World Report 2002*, New York: 2002, 421.

24 D. Remnick, 'Going Nowhere,' *New Yorker*, 12–19 July 2004. Online, available at: www.newyorker.com, accessed 5 April 2006.

25 S. Shapiro, 'The Telegenic Face of Conservative Islam,' *NYT*, 29 April 2006.

26 Human Rights Watch, *World Report 2006*, New York: 2005, 435; Human Rights Watch, *Black Hole*, 6.

27 'L'intelligence Politique Avant L'Information,' *Al-Ahram Hebdo*. Online, available at: http://hebdo.ahram.org.eg/arab/ahram/2003/8/13/doss2.htm, accessed 10 November 2006.

28 E. Silverman, 'Starving Gaza,' *Al-Ahram Weekly On-Line*, 23–29 March 2006. Online, available at: http://weekly.ahram.org.eg/print/2006/787/re3.htm, accessed 2 October 2006.

29 S. Shpiro, 'Intelligence Services and Political Transformation in the Middle East,' *IJIC* 17, 2004–2005, 593; R. Epstein, 'Intelligence Organisations Play Direct Role in Israeli–Palestinian Peace Process,' Australian Broadcasting Corporation, 12 June 2003.

30 Tenet and Harlow, *At the Center*, 80–81.

31 Shphiro, 'Intelligence Services,' 593–594.

32 Amit, 'The Puppet Master'; Shphiro, 'Intelligence Services,' 595; 'PFLP Wary About Truce After Meeting with Egyptian Intelligence Officials,' Agence France-Presse, 16 December 2003.

33 Shpiro, 'Intelligence Services,' 594–595.

34 A. Cordesman, *Peace and War*, Westport, CT, Praeger, 2002, 237. Cordesman details some of these agencies and their respective personnel strength as of 2002: Preventive Security (3,000); General Intelligence (3,000); Presidential Security (3,000); Military Intelligence (500); 'Retrait de Gaza: des Officiers Palestiniens Seront Entraines en Egypte,' Agence France Presse, 24 June 2004. Online, available at: www.lexisnexis.com, accessed 28 July 2007.

35 A. La Guardia, 'Egyptian Agents Aid Pullout From Gaza,' *Calgary Herald*, 15 June 2005, A18; 'L'Egypte Arme le Fatah en Palestine,' *Le Figaro*, 29 December 2006. Online, available at: www.lexisnexis.com, accessed 29 July 2007.

36 Silverman, 'Starving Gaza.'
37 'L'Egypte Arme le Fatah en Palestine'; 'Egyptian Security Delegation in Gaza Heading Home,' Xinhua News Agency, 15 June 2007.
38 'Egypt, Sudan Pursue Normalization Efforts,' AFP, 29 December 1997.
39 'Sudanese Delegation, Opposition Team Achieve Positive Results in Cairo,' BBC, 29 August 2004, derived from Voice of Sudan, 29 August 2004.

## Conclusion

1 A. Bozeman, 'Political Intelligence in Non-Western Societies: Suggestions for Comparative Research' in R. Godson, ed. *Comparing Foreign Intelligence* (Washington, DC: Pergamon-Brassey's, 1988, 149.
2 C. Andrew and V. Mitrokhin, *The World Was Going Our Way*, New York: Basic Books, 21.
3 H. Bradford Westerfield, 'America and the World of Intelligence Liaison,' *INS* 11, 1996, 539.
4 Y. Caroz, *Arab Secret Services*, London: Corgi, 1978, 13.
5 Caroz believes counterintelligence is the most efficient part of the Egyptian security apparatus: Caroz, *Arab Secret Services*, 420.
6 Quoted in Westerfield, 'America and the World of Intelligence Liaison,' 540.
7 'L'intelligence Politique Avant l'Information,' *Al-Ahram Hebdo*, August 2003, 1.
8 Christopher Andrew, 'Intelligence, International Relations and "Under-theorisation,"' *INS* 19, 2004, 177.
9 T. Plate and A. Darvi, *Secret Police*, Garden City, NY: Doubleday & Company, 1981, 291.
10 H. Mustafa, 'Ending the Silent War in Egypt,' *Washington Post*, 24 December 2005, A17.

# Bibliography

Abd al-Wahhab Bakr Muhammad, *al-Būlīs al-Miṣrī, 1922–1952*, al-Qāhirah: Maktabat Madbūlī, 1988.

Abdel-Malek, A., *Egypte Societe Militaire*, Paris: Editions du Seuil, 1962.

Abdo, G., *No God but God*, New York: Oxford University Press, 2000.

Aboul-Enein, Y., 'The Egyptian–Yemen War (1962–67): Egyptian Perspectives on Guerrilla Warfare,' *Infantry*, January–February 2004.

——, 'Islamic Militant Cells and Sadat's Assassination,' *Military Review*, 84, 4, 1 July 2004.

——, 'Spymaster: Former Egyptian Intelligence Chief Discusses Psychological Warfare,' *Infantry*, July-August 2006.

——, 'Book Review: Learning and Rebuilding a Shattered Force – Memoirs of Pre-Yom Kippur War Egyptian Generals, 1969–1972,' *Strategic Insights*, IV, 3, March 2005. Online, available at: www.ccc.nps.navy.mil/si/2005/mar/aboul-eneinmar05.pdf, accessed 11 August 2007.

Abū al-Faḍl, 'Abd al-Fattāḥ, *Kuntu nā'iban li-ra'īs al-mukhābarāt*, Cairo: Dār al-Ḥurrīyah, 1986.

Abu Iyad (Salah Khalaf) and Eric Rouleau, *My Home, My Land*, translated by Linda Butler Koseoglu, New York: Times Books, 1981.

Aburish, S.K., *Nasser: The Last Arab*, New York: Thomas Dunne Books, 2004.

El-Ad, A., *Decline of Honor*, Chicago: Henry Regnery Company, 1976.

Adams, J., *Secret Armies*, New York: Atlantic Monthly Press, 1987.

Almany, A., 'Government Control of the Press in the United Arab Republic, 1952–70,' *Journalism Quarterly*, 49, 2, 1972, 340–348.

Alterman, J.B., 'American Aid to Egypt in the 1950s: From Hope to Hostility,' *MEJ*, 52, 1, 1998, 51–69.

Amnesty International, *Report on Torture*, New York: Farrar, Straus and Giroux, 1975.

——, *Egypt: Ten Years of Torture*, New York: Amnesty International, 1991.

——, *Report 1999*, New York: Amnesty International USA, 1999.

——, *Torture Worldwide: An Affront to Human Dignity*, New York: Amnesty International USA, 2000.

Amstutz, J.B., *Afghanistan: The First Five Years of Soviet Occupation*, Washington, DC: National Defense University Press, 1986.

Andrew, C., *For the President's Eyes Only*, New York: HarperPerennial, 1995.

——, 'Intelligence, International Relations and "Under-theorisation,"' *Intelligence and National Security*, 19, 2, 2004, 170–184.

Andrew, C. and D. Dilks, *The Missing Dimension*, Urbana: University of Illinois Press, 1984.

Andrew, C. and O. Gordievsky, *KGB: The Inside Story*, New York: HarperCollins Publishers, 1990.

——, eds. 'More "Instructions from the Centre": Top Secret Files on KGB Global Operations, 1975–1985,' *Intelligence and National Security*, 7, 1, January, 1992.

Andrew, C. and V. Mitrokhin, *The World Was Going Our Way*, New York: Basic Books, 2005.

Aussaresses, P., *The Battle of the Casbah*, translated by Robert L. Miller, New York: Enigma Books, 2002.

Badeau, J.S., *The Middle East Remembered*, Washington, DC: Middle East Institute, 1983.

Badeeb, S.M., *The Saudi–Egyptian Conflict over North Yemen, 1962–1970*, Boulder, CO: Westview Press, 1986.

Badrawi, M., *Political Violence in Egypt 1910–1924: Secret Societies, Plots and Assassinations*, London: Curzon, 2000.

*Baedeker's Egypt 1929*, London: George Allen & Unwin, 1974.

Baker, R.W., *Egypt's Uncertain Revolution under Nasser and Sadat*, Cambridge, MA: Harvard University Press, 1978.

Bakhash, S., *The Reign of the Ayatollahs*, New York: Basic Books, 1984.

Bar-Joseph, U., 'Israel Caught Unaware: Egypt's Sinai Surprise of 1960,' *International Journal of Intelligence and Counterintelligence*, 8, 2, 1995, 203–219.

——, 'Intelligence Failure and the Need for Cognitive Closure: The Case of Yom Kippur,' *Paradoxes of Strategic Intelligence*, eds. Richard K. Betts and Thomas G. Mahnken, London: Frank Cass, 2003.

Bar-On, M., *The Gates of Gaza*, New York: St Martin's Press, 1994.

Barron, J., *KGB: The Secret Work of Soviet Secret Agents*, New York: Bantam Books, 1981.

Bar-Zohar, M., *Spies in the Promised Land*, translated by Monroe Stearns, Boston: Houghton Mifflin Company, 1972.

Baud, J., *Encyclopedie du Renseignement et des Services Secrets*, Paris: Editions Lavauzelle, 1997.

Bearden, M. and J. Risen, *The Main Enemy*, New York: Random House, 2003.

Beattie, K.J., *Egypt during the Nasser Years*, Boulder: CO: Westview Press, 1994.

——, *Egypt during the Sadat Years*, New York: Palgrave, 2000.

Beinin, J., 'The Communist Movement and Nationalist Political Discourse in Nasirist Egypt,' *Middle East Journal*, 41, 4, autumn, 1987, 568–584.

Ben Dan, *The Secret War*, New York: Sabra Books, 1970.

Bergen, P., *The Osama bin Laden I Know*, New York: Free Press, 2006.

Bin Sultan, K. and P. Seale, *Desert Warrior*, London: HarperCollins, 1995.

Black, I. and B. Morris, *Israel's Secret Wars*, New York: Grove Weidenfeld, 1991.

Blackwell, S., 'Saving the King: Anglo-American Strategy and British Counter-subversion Operations in Libya, 1953–59,' *Middle Eastern Studies*, 391, January, 2003, 1–18.

Blum, H., *The Eve of Destruction*, New York: HarperCollins, 2003.

Bonini, C. and G. d'Avanzo, *Collusion*, translated by James Marcus, Hoboken, NJ: Melville House Publishing, 2007.

Bonthous, Jean-Marie, 'Understanding Intelligence Across Cultures,' *International Journal of Intelligence and Counterintelligence*, 7, 3, 1994, 275–311.

Botman, S., 'Egyptian Communists and the Free Officers: 1950–54,' *Middle Eastern Studies*, 22, 3, July, 1986.

——, *The Rise of Egyptian Communism, 1939–70*, Syracuse, NY: Syracuse University Press, 1988.

Boutros-Ghali, B., *Egypt's Road to Jerusalem*, New York: Random House, 1997.

Bowen, J., *Six Days*, New York: St Martin's Press, 2003.

Bower, T., *The Perfect English Spy*, New York: St Martin's Press, 1995.

Boyd, D., 'Development of Egypt's Radio: "Voice of the Arabs" under Nasser,' *Journalism Quarterly*, 52, 4, 1975: 645–653.

Boyle, C., *Boyle of Cairo*, London: Titus Wilson and Son, 1965.

Breitman, R. and N.J.W. Goda, T. Naftali, and R. Wolfe, *US Intelligence and the Nazis*, New York: Cambridge University Press, 2005.

Bronson, R., *Thicker Than Oil*, Oxford: Oxford University Press, 2006.

Burdett, A., ed., *The Arab League, British Documentary Sources, 1943–1963*, 2, 3, and 7, Oxford: Archive International Group, 1995.

Burke, J., *Al-Qaeda*, London: I.B. Tauris, 2003.

Carman, B. and J. McPherson, eds., *Bimbashi McPherson: A Life in Egypt*, London: British Broadcasting Corporation, 1983.

Caroz, Y., *The Arab Secret Services*, London: Corgi Books, 1978.

Cassandra, 'The Impending Crisis in Egypt,' *Middle East Journal*, 49, 1, 1995, 9–27.

Clayton, G.F., *An Arabian Diary*, ed. Robert O. Collins, Berkeley: University of California Press, 1969.

Cohen, A., 'Cairo, Dimona, and the June 1967 War,' *MEJ*, 50, 2, spring, 1996, 190–210.

Coll, S., *Ghost Wars*, New York: Penguin Press, 2004.

Collins, L. and D. Lapierre, *O Jerusalem!*, New York: Simon and Schuster, 1972.

Cookridge, E.H., *Gehlen: Spy of the Century*, New York: Random House, 1971.

Copeland, M., *The Game of Nations*, New York: Simon and Schuster, 1969.

——, *Beyond Cloak and Dagger: Inside the CIA*, New York: Pinnacle Books, 1975.

——, *Game Player*, London: Aurum Press, 1989.

Cordesman, A., *Peace and War*, Westport, CT: Praeger, 2002.

Cordovez, D. and S.S. Harrison, *Out of Afghanistan*, New York: Oxford University Press, 1995.

Courriere, Y., *La Guerre d'Algerie (1954–1957)*, Paris: Robert Laffont, 1990.

——, *La Guerre d'Algerie (1958–1962)*, Paris: Robert Laffont, 1990.

Crile, G., *Charlie Wilson's War*, New York: Grove Press, 2003.

Dawisha, A.I., 'Intervention in the Yemen: An Analysis of Egyptian Perceptions and Policies,' *MEJ*, 29, 1, 1975, 46–64.

Dayan, M., 'Israel's Border and Security Problems,' *Foreign Affairs*, 33, 1955, in Lustick, ed. *From War to War*, New York: Garland Publishing, 1994.

Dekmejian, R.H., *Egypt under Nasir*, Albany: State University of New York Press, 1971.

Al-Dib, Mohamed Fathi, *Abdel Nasser et la Revolution Algerienne*, Paris: L'Harmattan, 1985.

——, *'Abd al-Nasir wa-haraka al-Tahrir al-Yemeni*, Cairo: Dar al-Mustaqbal al-Arabi, 1990.

——, *'Abd al-Nāṣir wa-taḥrīr al-Mashriq al-'Arabī*, Cairo: Markaz al-Dirāsār al-Siyāsīyah wa-al-Istirātījīyah, 2000.

Dorril, S., *MI6*, New York: The Free Press, 2000.

Dovey, H.O., 'Operation Condor,' *Intelligence and National Security*, 4, 2, April, 1989, 357–373.

Dowek, E., *Israeli–Egyptian Relations, 1980–2000*, London: Frank Cass, 2001.

Egyptian Organization for Human Rights, *Torture in Egypt: Police Excesses and the*

*Difficulty of Obtaining Evidence*, Cairo: EOHR, February, 1999. Online, available at: www.derechos.org/human-rights/mena/eohr/tort.html, accessed 3 May 2006.

Ellis, W.S., 'Nasser's Other Voice,' *Harper's Magazine*, 222, 1333, June, 1961, 54–59.

Eveland, W.C., *Ropes of Sand*, New York: W.W. Norton and Company, 1980.

Faligot, R. and P. Krop, *La Piscine*, Paris: Editions du Seuil, 1985.

Farid, Abdel Magid, *Nasser: The Final Years*, Reading: Ithaca Press, 1994.

Fisk, R., *Pity the Nation*, New York: Nation Books, 2002.

Fry, M.G., 'The Uses of Intelligence: The United Nations Confronts the United States in the Lebanon Crisis, 1958,' *Intelligence and National Security*, 10, 1, January, 1995, 59–91.

Fullerton, J., *The Soviet Occupation of Afghanistan*, Hong Kong: South China Morning Post Publications, no date.

El-Gamasy, M. Abdel Ghani, *The October War*, Cairo: American University in Cairo Press, 1993.

Gates, R.M., *From the Shadows*, New York: Touchstone, 1996.

Gehlen, R., *The Service*, translated by D. Irving, New York: World Publishing Company, 1972.

Gerard, P., *Secret Soldiers*, New York: Plume, 2002.

Gerges, F.A., 'The End of the Islamist Insurgency in Egypt?: Costs and Prospects,' *MEJ*, 54, 4, 2000, 592–612.

Gertz, B., *Breakdown*, Washington, DC: Regnery Publishing, 2002.

Ginor, I. and G. Remez, *Foxbats Over Dimona*, New Haven: Yale University Press, 2007.

Godson, R., ed., *Comparing Foreign Intelligence*, Washington, DC: Pergamon-Brassey's, 1988.

Golan, A., *Operation Susannah*, trans. by P. Kidron, New York: Harper & Row, Publishers, 1978.

Gordon, J., *Nasser's Blessed Movement*, New York: Oxford University Press, 1992.

Grafftey-Smith, L., *Bright Levant*, London: John Murray, 1970.

Grey, S., *Ghost Plane*, New York: St Martin's Press, 2006.

Grose, P., *Gentleman Spy: The Life of Allen Dulles*, Boston: Houghton Mifflin Company, 1994.

Harb, I., 'The Egyptian Military in Politics: Disengagement or Accommodation?' *Middle East Journal*, 57, 2, spring, 2003, 269–290.

Harkabi, Y., 'Basic Factors in the Arab Collapse during the Six-Day War,' *Orbis*, 11, 1967, 677–691.

Hart, A., *Arafat*, fourth edition, Bloomington: Indiana University Press, 1984.

Heikal, M.H., *The Cairo Documents*, New York: Doubleday & Company, 1973.

——, *The Road to Ramadan*, New York: Ballantine Books, 1976.

——, *The Sphinx and the Commissar*, New York: Harper & Row, Publishers, 1978.

——, *Iran: The Untold Story*, New York: Pantheon Books, 1981.

——, *Autumn of Fury*, London: Corgi Books, 1986.

——, *Cutting the Lion's Tail*, New York: Arbor House, 1987.

Henderson, R. D'A., *Brassey's International Intelligence Yearbook 2003*, Dulles, VA: Brassey's, 2003.

Hersh, B., *The Old Boys*, St Petersburg, FL: Tree Farm Books, 2002.

Herzog, C., *The Arab–Israeli Wars*, New York: Vintage Books, 1984.

Heyworth-Dunne, J., *Religious and Political Trends in Modern Egypt*, Washington, DC: Self-published by Author, 1950.

Hinsley, F.H. and C.A.G. Simkins, eds., *British Intelligence in the Second World War: volume IV*, New York: Cambridge University Press, 1990.

Hirst, D. and I. Beeson, *Sadat*, London: Faber and Faber, 1981.

Hofstadter, D., *Egypt and Nasser*, volumes 1–3, New York: Facts on File, 1973.

Hohne, H. and H. Zolling, *The General Was a Spy*, New York: Coward, McCann and Geoghegan, 1971.

Hughes-Wilson, J., *Military Intelligence Blunders and Cover-Ups*, New York: Carroll & Graf Publishers, 2004.

Human Rights Watch, *World Report 1992*, New York: Human Rights Watch, 1991.

——, *Behind Closed Doors: Torture and Detention in Egypt*, New York: Human Rights Watch, 1992.

——, *World Report 1994*, New York: Human Rights Watch, 1993.

——, *World Report 1995*, New York: Human Rights Watch, 1994.

——, *World Report 1997*, New York: Human Rights Watch, 1996.

——, *World Report 1999*, New York: Human Rights Watch, 1998.

——, *World Report 2000*, New York: Human Rights Watch, 1999.

——, *World Report 2001*, New York: Human Rights Watch, 2000.

——, *World Report 2002*, New York: Human Rights Watch, 2002.

——, *World Report 2005*, New York: Human Rights Watch, 2004.

——, *Black Hole: The Fate of Islamists Rendered to Egypt*, 17, 5, (E), May, 2005.

——, *World Report 2006*, New York: Human Rights Watch, 2005.

Intelligence Community Staff (US), *Glossary of Intelligence Terms and Definitions*, Washington, DC: ICS (US), June 1989.

Ismael, T.Y., 'The United Arab Republic and the Sudan,' *MEJ*, 23, 1, 1969, 14–28.

Israelyan, V., *Inside the Kremlin during the Yom Kippur War*, University Park, PA: Pennsylvania State University Press, 1995.

——, 'The October 1973 War: Kissinger in Moscow,' *MEJ*, 49, 2, spring, 1995, 248–268.

Jacquin, H., *La Guerre Secrete en Algerie*, Paris: Editions Olivier Orban, 1977.

James, L., *Nasser at War: Arab Images of the Enemy*, London: Palgrave Macmillan, 2006.

——, 'Nasser And His Enemies: Foreign Policy Decision Making in Egypt on The Eve of The Six Day War,' *Middle East Review of International Affairs*. Online, available at: http://meria.idc.ac.il/journal/2005/issue2/jv9no2a2.html, accessed 22 March 2007.

——, *Whose Voice? Nasser, the Arabs, and 'Sawt al-Arab' Radio*. Online, available at: www.tbsjournal.com/jamespf.html, accessed 1 April 2007.

Jawadi, M., *Muddakirat Qada al-'Askariya al-Misriya 67–72: Fi 'Aqab Al-Naksa*, Cairo: Dar al-Khayyal, 2001.

Jones, C., 'Among Ministers, Mavericks and Mandarins: Britain, Covert Action and the Yemen Civil War, 1962–64,' *Middle Eastern Studies*, 40, 1, January 2004, 99–126.

——, *Britain and the Yemen Civil War, 1962–1965*, Portland, OR: Sussex Academic Press, 2004.

Jones, M., 'The "Preferred Plan": The Anglo-American Working Group Report on Covert Action in Syria, 1957,' *Intelligence and National Security*, 19, 3, autumn, 2004, 401–415.

Kahana, E., 'Early Warning versus Concept: The Case of the Yom Kippur War 1973,' *Intelligence and National Security*, 17, 2, 2002, 81–104.

——, 'Analyzing Israel's Intelligence Failures,' *International Journal of Intelligence and Counterintelligence*, 18, 2, 2005, 262–279.

Kaiser, M. and R.S. Stokes, *Odyssey of an Eavesdropper*, New York: Carroll & Graf, 2005.

Kamel, A., *Aḥmad Kāmil yatadhakkar: min awrāq Ra'īs al-Mukhābarāt al-Miṣrīyah al-asbaq*, Cairo: Dār al-Hilāl, 1990.

Kechichian, J. and J. Nazimek, 'Challenges to the Military in Egypt,' *Middle East Policy*, V, 3, September, 1997, 125–139.

Kepel, G., *Muslim Extremism in Egypt*, translated by J. Rothschild, Berkeley, CA: University of California Press, 1993.

Kerr, M.H., *The Arab Cold War*, third edition, London: Oxford University Press, 1971.

Kessler, R., *The CIA at War*, New York: St Martin's Press, 2003.

King Hussein of Jordan, *Uneasy Lies the Head*, London: Heinemann, 1962.

Kinzer, S., *All the Shah's Men*, Hoboken, NJ: John Wiley & Sons, 2003.

Kissinger, H., *Years of Upheaval*, Boston: Little, Brown and Company, 1982.

Kyle, K., *Suez*, New York: St Martin's Press, 1991.

Lackner, H., *P.D.R. Yemen: Outpost of Socialist Development in Arabia*, London: Ithaca Press, 1985.

Lacouture, J., *Nasser*, translated by D. Hofstadter, New York: Alfred A. Knopf, 1973.

Lacouture, J. and S. Lacouture, *Egypt in Transition*, translated by F. Scarfe, New York: Criterion Books, 1958.

Laskier, M., 'Egyptian Jewry under the Nasser Regime, 1956–70,' *Middle Eastern Studies*, 31, 3, July, 1995, 573–619.

Lefebvre, J.A., 'The United States and Egypt: Confrontation and Accommodation in Northeast Africa, 1956–60,' *Middle Eastern Studies*, 29, 2, April, 1993, 321–338.

Levey, Z., 'Israel's Strategy in Africa, 1961–67,' *International Journal of Middle East Studies*, 36, 1, February, 2004, 71–87.

Linebarger, P., *Psychological Warfare*, Washington, DC: Infantry Journal Press, 1948.

Little, D., 'Mission Impossible: The CIA and the Cult of Covert Action in the Middle East,' *Diplomatic History*, 28, 5, November, 2004, 663–701.

Livingstone, N.C. and D. Halevy, *Inside the PLO*, New York: William Morrow and Company, 1990.

Lotz, W., *The Champagne Spy*, New York: St Martin's Press, 1972.

Love, K., *Suez: The Twice-Fought War*, New York: McGraw-Hill, 1969.

Loya, A. 'Radio Propaganda of the United Arab Republic – An Analysis,' *Middle Eastern Affairs*, XIII, 4, April, 1962, 98–109.

Lucas, W. Scott, *Divided We Stand: Britain, the US and the Suez Crisis*, London: Hodder & Stoughton, 1996.

McBride, B. St Clair, *Farouk of Egypt*, London: Robert Hale, 1967.

McDermott, A., *Egypt from Nasser to Mubarak*, London: Croom Helm, 1988.

McGregor, A., *A Military History of Modern Egypt*, Westport, CT: Praeger Security International, 2006.

Mader, J., *Who's Who in CIA*, Berlin: Julius Mader, 1968.

Mahle, M. Boyle, *Denial and Deception*, New York: Nation Books, 2004.

Mansfield, P., *The British in Egypt*, New York: Holt, Rinehart and Winston, 1972.

Marchetti, V. and J.D. Marks, *The CIA and the Cult of Intelligence*, New York: Alfred A. Knopf, 1974.

Mawby, S., 'The Clandestine Defence of Empire: British Special Operations in Yemen 1951–1964,' *Intelligence and National Security*, 17, 3, autumn 2002, 105–130.

Mayer, J., 'Outsourcing Torture,' *New Yorker*, 14 February 2005. Online, available at: www.newyorker.com/printables/fact/050214fa_fact6, accessed 2 May 2006.

Ministry of the Interior (Egypt), *Annual Report of the Cairo City Police for the Year 1945*, Cairo: Government Press, 1946.

Mitchell, R.P., *The Society of the Muslim Brothers*, New York: Oxford University Press, 1993.

Mohi El Din, K., *Memories of a Revolution*, Cairo: American University in Cairo Press, 1995.

Morris, B., *Israel's Border Wars, 1949–1956*, Oxford: Clarendon Press, 1997.

Mosley, L., *The Cat and the Mice*, New York: Harper & Brothers Publishers, 1958.

Murphy, C., *Passion for Islam*, New York: Scribner, 2002.

Musri, S., *Rif'at al-Hagan*, Cairo, 1988.

Naftali, T., *Blind Spot*, New York: Basic Books, 2005.

Naguib, M., *Egypt's Destiny*, New York: Doubleday & Company, 1955.

Nasr, S., *Muddakirat*, Cairo: Dar al-Khayyal, 1999.

Nasr, S. and 'Abd Allah Imam, *Al-Thawrah, Al-Naksah, Al-Mukhabarat*, Cairo: Dar al-Khayyal, 1999.

Nasser, G.A., *Egypt's Liberation: the Philosophy of the Revolution*, Washington, DC: Public Affairs Press, 1956.

Nasser, G.A. and W. Khalidi, 'Nasser's Memoirs of the First Palestine War,' *Journal of Palestine Studies*, 2, 2, 1973, 3–32.

National Commission on terrorist Attacks, *The 9/11 Commission Report*, New York: W.W. Norton & Company.

Neff, D., *Warriors at Suez*, New York: The Linden Press, 1981.

——, *Warriors for Jerusalem*, New York: Simon & Schuster, 1984.

Nordeen, L. and D. Nicolle, *Phoenix over the Nile*, Washington, DC: Smithsonian Institution Press, 1996.

Nutting, A., *Nasser*, New York: E.P. Dutton & Company, Inc., 1972.

Oren, M.B., 'Escalation to Suez: The Egypt–Israel Border War, 1949–56,' *Journal of Contemporary History*, 24, 1989, 347–373.

——, 'Secret Egypt–Israel Peace Initiatives Prior to the Suez Campaign,' *Middle Eastern Studies*, 27, 3, July, 1990, 351–370.

——, *Six Days of War*, New York: Oxford University Press, 2002.

Parker, R.B., 'The June 1967 War: Some Mysteries Explored,' *MEJ*, 46, 2, spring 1992, 177–197.

——, *The Politics of Miscalculation in the Middle East*, Bloomington: Indiana University Press, 1993.

Perrault, G., *A Man Apart: The Life of Henri Curiel*, translated by B. Cumming, London: Zed Books, 1994.

Perry, M., *Eclipse: The Last Days of the CIA*, New York: William Morrow, 1992.

Persico, J.E., *Casey*, New York: Viking, 1990.

Piekalkiewicz, J., *World History of Espionage: Agents, Systems, Operations*, translated by W.M. Henhoeffer and G.L. Liebenau, Washington, DC: National Intelligence Book Center, 1988.

Plate, T. and A. Darvi, *Secret Police*, Garden City, NY: Doubleday & Company, 1981.

Pollack, K.M., *Arabs at War*, Lincoln: University of Nebraska Press, 2002.

Pool, D., *From Guerrillas to Government*, Athens, OH: Ohio University Press, 2001.

Popp, R., 'Stumbling Decidedly into the Six-Day War,' *Middle East Journal*, 60, 2, spring, 2006, 281–309.

Quinlivan, J.T., 'Coup-proofing: Its Practice and Consequences in the Middle East,' *International Security*, 24, 2, 1999, 131–165.

Rabinovich, A., *The Yom Kippur War*, New York: Schocken Books, 2004.

'Radioelectronic Warfare in Israeli-Arab Wars,' *Voyenno-Istoricheskiy Zhurnal*, 7, 25 June, 1980, 65–71, JPRS, no. 2229, 5 December 1980.

Rahmy, Ali Abdel Rahman, *The Egyptian Policy in the Arab World: Intervention in Yemen*, Washington, DC: University Press of America, 1983.

Rathmell, A., *Secret War in the Middle East: The Covert Struggle for Syria, 1949–1961*, London: I.B. Tauris, 1995.

——, 'Syria's Intelligence Services: Origins and Development,' *Journal of Conflict Studies*, XVI, 2, 1996. Online, available at: www.lib.unb.ca/texts/jcs/j97/articles/Rathmellwp1.htm, accessed 2 January 2006

——, 'Brotherly Enemies: The Rise and Fall of the Syrian–Egyptian Intelligence Axis, 1954–1967,' *Intelligence and National Security*, 13, 1, spring, 1998, 230–253.

Raviv, D. and Y. Melman, *Every Spy a Prince*, Boston: Houghton Mifflin, 1990.

——, *Friends in Deed: Inside the US–Israel Alliance*, New York: Hyperion, 1994.

Rawnsley, G.D. 'Overt and Covert: The Voice of Britain and Black Radio Broadcasting in the Suez Crisis, 1956,' *Intelligence and National Security*, 11, 3, July, 1996, 497–522.

Reeve, S., *The New Jackals*, Boston: Northeastern University Press, 1999.

Reid, D.M., 'Political Assassination in Egypt, 1910–1954,' *International Journal of African Historical Studies*, 15, 4, 1982, 625–651.

Remnick, D., 'Going Nowhere,' *New Yorker*, 12–19 July 2004. Online, available at: www.newyorker.com, accessed 4 May 2006.

Reporters without Borders, *Egypt – Annual Report 2004*. Online, available at: www.rsf.org, accessed 2 May 2006

Richelson, J.T., *Foreign Intelligence Organizations*, Cambridge, MA: Ballinger Publishing Company, 1988.

Rubin, B. and J. Colp Rubin, *Yasir Arafat: A Political Biography*, Oxford: Oxford University Press, 2003.

Rubinstein, A.Z., *Red Star on the Nile*, Princeton: Princeton University Press, 1977.

Rudner, M., 'Hunters and Gatherers: The Intelligence Coalition against Islamic Terrorism,' *International Journal of Intelligence and Counterintelligence*, 17, 2, 2004, 193–230.

Russell, T., *Egyptian Service*, London: John Murray, 1949.

El-Saadany, S., *Egypt and Libya From Inside, 1969–1976*, Jefferson, NC: McFarland & Co., 1994.

Sabit, A.M., *A King Betrayed*, London: Quartet Books, 1989.

Sadat, A., *Revolt on the Nile*, New York: The John Day Company, 1957.

——, *In Search of Identity*, New York: Harper & Row, Publishers, 1979.

Sadat, J., *A Woman of Egypt*, New York: Pocket Books, 1987.

Sakharov, V., *High Treason*, New York: Ballantine Books, 1980.

Salim, J., *al-Būlīs al-siyāsī yaḥkum Miṣr, 1910–1952*, Cairo: al-Qāhirah lil-Thaqāfah al-'Arabīyah, 1975.

Sansom, A.W., *I Spied Spies*, London: George G. Harrap and Company, 1965.

Sayigh, Y., 'Reconstructing the Paradox: The Arab Nationalist Movement, Armed Struggle, and Palestine, 1951–1966,' *MEJ*, 45, 4, autumn, 1991, 608–629.

——, 'Turning Defeat into Opportunity: the Palestinian Guerrillas After the June 1967 War,' *MEJ*, 46, 2, spring, 1992, 244–265.

——, 'Escalation or Containment? Egypt and the Palestine Liberation Army, 1964–67,' *International Journal of Middle East Studies*, 30, 1, February, 1998, 97–116.

Schmidt, D.A., *Yemen: The Unknown War*, New York: Holt, Rinehart and Winston, 1968.

Scott, L. and P. Jackson, 'The Study of Intelligence in Theory and Practice,' *Intelligence and National Security*, 19, 2, 2004, 139–169.

Seale, P., *The Struggle for Syria*, London: Oxford University Press, 1965.

——, *Abu Nidal: A Gun for Hire*, New York: Random House, 1992.

——, *Asad of Syria: The Struggle for the Middle East*, London: I.B. Tauris & Company, 1988.

Seth, R., *Russell Pasha*, London: William Kimber, 1966.

El-Shazly, S., *The Crossing of the Suez*, San Francisco: American Mideast Research, 1980.

Sheffy, Y., 'Unconcern at Dawn, Surprise at Sunset: Egyptian Intelligence Appreciation before the Sinai Campaign, 1956,' *Intelligence and National Security*, 5, 3, July, 1990, 7–56.

Shpiro, S., 'Intelligence Services and Political Transformation in the Middle East,' *International Journal of Intelligence and Counterintelligence*, 17, 4, 2004–2005.

Simpson, C., *Blowback*, New York: Collier/Macmillan, 1988.

Smiley, D., *Arabian Assignment*, London: Leo Cooper, 1975.

Smith, M.J., Jr, *The Secret Wars Volume II: Intelligence, Propaganda and Psychological Warfare, Covert Operations, 1945–1980*, Santa Barbara, CA: ABC-Clio, Inc., 1981.

Springborg, R., *Mubarak's Egypt: Fragmentation of the Political Order*, Boulder, CO: Westview Press, 1989.

Stephens, R., *Nasser*, New York: Simon and Schuster, 1971.

Steven, S., *The Spymasters of Israel*, New York: Ballantine Books, 1980.

*Suez 1956*, edited by W.M. Roger Louis and Roger Owen, Oxford: Clarendon Press, 1989.

Tauber, E., 'Egyptian Secret Societies, 1911,' *Middle Eastern Studies*, 42, 4, July, 2006, 603–623.

Tenet, G. and B. Harlow, *At the Center of the Storm*, New York: Harper-Collins, 2007.

Thomas, E., *The Very Best Men*, New York: Simon & Schuster, 1995.

Thomas, M., *Empires of Intelligence*, Berkeley: University of California Press, 2008.

Tollefson, H., *Policing Islam*, London: Greenwood Press, 1999.

Trevelyan, H., *The Middle East in Revolution*, London: Macmillan, 1970.

Trofimov, Y., *The Siege of Mecca*, New York: Doubleday, 2007.

Tusan, J., 'Propagande et Orientation Nationale en Egypte,' *Orient*, 1, 4, 1957, 121–143.

*Undercover Lives: Soviet Spies in the Cities of the World*, ed. Helen Womack, London: Weidenfeld and Nicolson, 1998.

United Arab Republic, Maṣlaḥat al-Ist'lama't, *The French Spy-ring in the UAR: A Conspiracy Confirmed By Confessions*, Cairo: Information Department, 1962.

Vatikiotis, P.J., *The Egyptian Army in Politics*, Bloomington, IN: Indiana University Press, 1961.

——, *The History of Modern Egypt*, fourth edition, Baltimore: Johns Hopkins University Press, 1992.

Volkman, E., *Spies: The Secret Agents who Changed the Course of History*, New York: John Wiley & Sons, Inc., 1994.

Walker, J., *Aden Insurgency*, Staplehurst: Spellmount Ltd, 2005.

Waugh, B. and T. Keown, *Hunting the Jackal*, New York: Morrow, 2004.

Weaver, M.A., *A Portrait of Egypt*, New York: Farrar, Straus & Giroux, 1999.

——, 'Pharaohs-in-Waiting,' *Atlantic Monthly*, 292, 3, October, 2003, 79–92.

Weiner, T., *Legacy of Ashes*, New York: Doubleday, 2007.

Westerfield, H.B., 'America and the World of Intelligence Liaison,' *Intelligence and National Security*, 11, 3, July, 1996, 523–560.

Wheelock, K., *Nasser's New Egypt*, New York: Frederick A. Praeger, 1960.

Witty, D.M., 'A Regular Army in Counterinsurgency Operations: Egypt in North Yemen, 1962–1967,' *Journal of Military History*, 65, 2, April, 2001.

Wolf, M. and A. McElvoy, *Man without a Face*, New York: Times Books, 1997.

Woodward, B., *Veil: The Secret Wars of the CIA 1981–1987*, New York: Simon & Schuster, 1987.

——, *Bush at War*, New York: Simon & Schuster, 2002.

Wright, L., 'The Man behind Bin Laden,' *New Yorker*, 9 September 2002. Online, available at: www.newyorker.com/printables/fact/020916fa_fact2, accessed 9 May 2006.

——, *The Looming Tower*, New York: Vintage Books, 2006.

Wright, P., *Spycatcher*, New York: Viking, 1987.

Al-Zayyat, M., *The Road to Al-Qaeda*, translated by A. Fekry, London: Pluto Press, 2004.

# Index